AGENCY & PARTNERSHIP

By

LEONARD GROSS

Professor of Law
Southern Illinois School of Law

THE PROFESSOR SERIES

Published by

 **emanuel**®

Agency & Partnership, 5th Edition (1998)
Emanuel Publishing Corp. • 1865 Palmer Avenue • Larchmont, NY 10538

ISBN 1-56542-106-X

DEDICATION

To my family

Abbreviations Used in Text

R&G — Reuschlein and Gregory, *Handbook on the Law of Agency & Partnership* (2d ed. 1990)

Hamilton — Hamilton, *Cases and Materials on Corporations* (5th ed. 1994).

Hynes — Hynes, *Agency & Partnership: Cases, Materials, Problems* (4th ed. 1994)

Rest. (2d) — Restatement (Second) of Agency

UPA — Uniform Partnership Act

RUPA — Revised Uniform Partnership Act

RULPA — Revised Uniform Limited Partership Act

Ribstein — Larry E. Ribstein, *Ribstein and Keating on Limited Liability Companies* (1992)

Posner — Posner, Economic Analysis of Law (3d ed. 1986).

TABLE OF CONTENTS

Chapter 1
THE AGENCY RELATIONSHIP

Chapter 2
RIGHTS AND DUTIES BETWEEN
PRINCIPAL AND AGENT

CHAPTER 3

NOTIFICATION AND IMPUTED KNOWLEDGE

CHAPTER 4

AGENT'S AUTHORITY TO BIND PRINCIPAL TO CONTRACT

CHAPTER 5

RELATIONSHIPS BETWEEN AGENT AND THIRD PARTY: CONTRACTS

CHAPTER 6

RATIFICATION

CHAPTER 7

RIGHTS AND LIABILITIES OF PARTIALLY DISCLOSED AND UNDISCLOSED PRINCIPALS

CHAPTER 8

PRINCIPAL'S LIABILITY FOR TORTS OF AN AGENT

CHAPTER 9

RIGHTS AND LIABILITIES OF AGENTS IN TORT

CHAPTER 10

CRIMINAL RESPONSIBILITY OF PRINCIPAL AND AGENT

CHAPTER 11

TERMINATION OF THE AGENCY RELATIONSHIP

CHAPTER 12

ANALYSIS OF PARTNERSHIP

CHAPTER 13

NATURE OF A PARTNERSHIP

CHAPTER 14

PARTNERSHIP PROPERTY

CHAPTER 15

PROPERTY RIGHTS OF A PARTNER

CHAPTER 16

RELATIONS OF PARTNERS TO PERSONS DEALING WITH THE PARTNERSHIP

CHAPTER 17

RELATIONSHIPS BETWEEN PARTNERS

Chapter 18

DISSOLUTION AND WINDING UP

Chapter 19

PARTNERSHIP BANKRUPTCY

Chapter 20

LIMITED PARTNERSHIPS

CHAPTER 21

REGISTERED LIMITED LIABILITY
PARTNERSHIPS (LLPs)

CHAPTER 22

LIMITED LIABILITY COMPANIES (LLCs)

CHAPTER 1

THE AGENCY RELATIONSHIP

ChapterScope

In parsing a complex set of facts controlling a set of legal relationships and consequences, it is often important to know whether an agency relationship exists. Legal consequences attach by virtue of this relationship. The agency relationship creates **duties** which the agent owes to the principal and the principal to the agent. (See *infra,* p. 30). Under some circumstances, **notice** to the agent may bind the principal; under others, the agent's **knowledge** may be imputed to the principal. (See *infra,* p. 37). A principal will be liable for authorized **contracts** his agent makes, and he will be able to enforce those contracts against the person with whom the agent contracts. (See *infra*, p. 3). Further, the **negligence** of a servant is often imputed to the master under the doctrine of **respondeat superior**. (See *infra*, p. 89). The tentacles of agency law extend into every other field of law, including contracts, property, sales, torts, trusts and criminal law.

Definitions: (See Restatement (Second) of Agency § 1)[1]

- **Agency:** The fiduciary relation which results from the manifestation of consent by one person to another that the other shall act on his behalf and subject to his control, and consent by the other so to act.

- **Principal:** The person for whom action is to be taken.

- **Agent:** The person who acts or is to act on behalf of the principal.

- **Servant:** A type of agent who is subject to the detailed control of his principal (his "master"). Most employees fall into this category.

- **Master:** A type of principal who controls the details of her agent's acts. Most employers fall into this category as they relate to their employees.

In this book, the principal will often be designated as **"P;"** the agent will be called **"A;"** and any third person will often be called **"T."**

I. CREATION OF THE AGENCY RELATIONSHIP

  A. **Consensual:** Subject to certain exceptions, an agency relationship is typically consensual.

   1. **Consent of both required:** The agency relationship requires the **consent of both the principal and agent**. The agent must agree to act **on behalf of**, and **subject to control** by, the principal. In order to determine if the "on behalf of" test has been met, courts

---

1. The Restatement will be referred to throughout this book as Rest. (2d).

look to whether the agent intended to act for the principal or for himself.

2. **No consideration required:** *Consideration* between principal and agent to establish the agency relationship is not required. Mere consent by both is sufficient.

3. **Express or implied:** Consent can be *express or implied*. The course of prior dealings between the parties can imply consent to create an agency. For example, if A has driven P's car on a dozen previous occasions with P's consent, the implication of consent will arise when A moves the car again on another occasion and P does not object. *Biedenbach v. Teague,* 166 A.2d 320 (Pa. Super. 1960).

B. Operation of law: An agency by operation of law is usually created by statute and may not require the consent of the parties.

Example: A statute in State X provides that any non-resident who drives his car on X's highways shall constitute X's Superintendent of Motor Vehicles as his agent to receive service of process in any case arising out of the non-resident's use of X's highways. The Superintendent is required to forward the summons and complaint to the non-resident by registered mail. P, a non-resident, enters X with his car and negligently injures T. T sues P and complies with the statute. P appears specially and objects to the court's jurisdiction.

Held, T may bring suit in State X by serving P's statutory agent, the Superintendent. Under its police power, a state may pass statutes for the safety and protection of the public. This statute is intended to prevent the unreasonable hardship on the injured residents of X of compelling them to follow the wrongdoer into another state for purpose of suit. It compels the wrongdoer to submit to the jurisdiction of the courts in the state where the wrong is committed. Under the statute, the Superintendent became the agent of non-resident P when P entered the state and used its highways. *Hess v. Pawloski,* 274 U.S. 352 (1927); *Mann v. Humphrey's Adm'x,* 79 S.W.2d 17 (Ky. Ct. App. 1935).

C. Estoppel: This is not a true agency because the alleged agent has no real authority. However, the "principal" is held liable as though there were an agency. The underlying theory is that his conduct has been such that it would now be unjust to permit him to deny the agency. Liability is limited to the *reliance damages* suffered by the third party.

Example: T goes into P's furniture store and is waited on by A. T pays A for some furniture and arranges to have the furniture delivered to her. When the furniture is not delivered, T sues P. P claims that A was an imposter and not his servant or agent.

Held, even a nonemployee may be P's agent by estoppel. T's evidence is based solely on the actions of A, the apparent salesman. That evidence is insufficient to establish a true agency relationship between P and A. However, P had a duty to exercise reasonable care and vigilance to protect customers against losses occasioned by persons impersonating salesmen. If circumstances led T, as a person of ordinary prudence, to believe that A was P's salesman, P will be liable for T's loss under the theory of agency by estoppel. However, in estoppel, P would not be liable for T's lost profits.

To establish agency by estoppel, it is necessary to show that P allowed A to hold himself out as P's agent. Because the case was not tried on the theory of agency by estoppel, a new trial will be required on that issue. *Hoddeson v. Koos Bros.*, 135 A.2d 702 (N.J. Super. Ct. App. Div. 1957).

1. **Proof:** Agency by estoppel is created and proven by establishing all of the following elements:

   a. **Apparent authority:** P allows, or is negligent in allowing, A to hold himself out to T as P's agent;

   b. **Reasonable reliance:** T reasonably relies on the holding out; and

   c. **Change of position:** T changes his position to his detriment. *See* Authority by Estoppel, *infra,* p. 56. *Compare* Agent with Apparent Authority, *infra*, p. 51.

D. **Formalities:** No particular formality is required to create an agency relationship. It may arise by an oral or written agreement or by the conduct of the parties.

1. **Equal Dignities Rule:** When the purpose of the agency is to permit the ***agent to perform any act which is required to be in writing*** to satisfy the Statute of Frauds, the general rule (called the "equal dignities rule") ***requires that the agent's authority also be in writing*** with the same formalities as required for the act itself.

   Example: P executes a deed and gives it to A. P orally instructs A to fill in the name of X as grantee. However, A fills in the name of Z instead. In a suit by P the court held that the deed was invalid. The court reasoned that since the deed had to be under seal, the authority of A to complete the deed also had to be in a sealed instrument. *Bretta v. Meltzer*, 182 N.E. 827 (Mass. 1932).

   a. **Statute of Frauds:** In many states which observe the equal dignities rule, the agent's authority must be in writing in order for him to bind the principal to:

- *contracts for the sale or conveyance of land*;

- *contracts which cannot be performed within one year*; and

- *contracts for the sale of goods exceeding $500* (this provision is not always included).

b. Sale of land by broker: Where land is listed for sale with a real estate broker, most courts hold that the power of the broker is limited to finding a purchaser ready, willing and able to purchase the property, not to execute a contract. *Authority to execute a contract of sale on behalf of the seller must be specifically given in writing*. *Landskroener v. Henning,* 191 N.W. 943 (Mich. 1923).

c. Exceptions to equal dignities rule: There are exceptions to the equal dignities rule.

    i. When P is present: If the agent acts in the *presence of the principal and at his direction, then no writing is required* to establish the agent's authority. *Gardner v. Gardner,* 59 Mass. (5 Cush.) 483 (1850).

    Note: If an instrument has been made and signed by the agent and the *principal thereafter delivers it to the third party*, it is valid either on the theory of *acknowledgment* or on the theory of *adoption* by the principal. No writing is necessary to establish the authority of the agent in such a case.

    ii. A is a partner: If the agent is acting in his capacity *as a partner, then no written authority is required.* *Fincher & Womble v. Hanson,* 77 S.E. 1068 (Ga. Ct. App. 1913).

    iii. High corporate officer: Many states hold that a corporate *executive officer may bind the corporation without written authority.* *Jeppi v. Brockman Holding Co.,* 206 P.2d 847 (Cal. 1949); see also *Rosenblum v. New York Central R.R. Co.,* 57 A.2d 690 (Pa. Super. Ct. 1948).

    iv. Non-officers: Some states hold that persons who are not corporate officers may nevertheless bind the corporation if they are given *specific authority* to do so.

      (1) Facts: P Corporation, a landlord, granted its managing agent A (who was neither an officer nor a director) a six-year written extension of employment. A's duties, some of which were unwritten, included collection of rents, negotiation of leases and lease extensions, and arrangement of

bids for contracts concerning painting, plumbing and electrical work. A granted T a three-year lease extension, in
writing as required by the Statute of Frauds. P Corporation gave its building to New Landlord, which then tried
to sell the building. When New Landlord learned of T's
lease extension, it brought an action seeking to declare
the extension invalid. New Landlord claimed that A
lacked the written authority to grant a lease extension
under the doctrine of equal dignities. T argued that since
P was a corporation, and since corporations can only act
through agents, A's authorization did not need to be in
writing. T also argued that A's authorization was con-
firmed by the writing extending his term of employment.

(2) Held: A managing agent is not the equivalent of a corporate officer or director. The title "managing agent" is often
honorific and sometimes refers to a janitor with incidental authority to negotiate leases. ***Authority to manage
does not imply any authority to execute leases or
renewals.*** Second, a managing agent's ***authority to execute lease extensions must be specific***. In this case, A
was given no specific authority to do so. *Commission on
Ecumenical Mission & Relations of United Presbyterian
Church v. Roger Gray, Ltd.*, 267 N.E.2d 467 (N.Y. 1971).

v. **Corporations excepted:** Some states except corporations
from the application of the equal dignities rule on the ground
that ***corporations must always act through their corporate agents.*** These states apply the rule only to natural persons. *Whiteway Neon-Ad, Inc. v. Opporunities
Industrialization Center of Atlanta, Inc.*, 252 S.E.2d 604 (Ga.
1979). See also *Travel Centre, Ltd. v. Starr-Mathews Agency,
Inc.*, 346 S.E.2d 840 (Ga. Ct. App. 1986).

d. **Effect of non-compliance:** If there is noncompliance with the
equal dignities rule, the contract is ***voidable at the option of
the principal.*** The principal may ratify the contract later in
writing, thereby making it enforceable by both parties; otherwise, the contract is unenforceable against the principal.

II. CAPACITY OF THE PARTIES

A. **Capacity of agent:** Any person may act as an agent so long as he is
able to perform the task of the agency as that task is defined by the
principal. In some cases, the agent may be capable of performing the
task required by the principal even when he lacks the capacity to per-

form it for himself. The *fact that the agent may not have sufficient capacity to perform the act for himself is not controlling,* because the agent does not act for himself, but for his principal.

1. **Agent's incapacity may affect principal's remedies against agent:** A minor (or mentally incompetent person) may act as an agent. However, if the agent breaches his duty to the principal, the *agent's lack of capacity may leave the principal without the usual remedies for the agent's breach of fiduciary duty.* In most cases of disability, the principal will nevertheless have the remedy of restitution to prevent the unjust enrichment of the agent.

B. Capacity of principal: A person who is not under any legal disability may act as a principal or master and do anything through an agent or servant which he is competent to do if personally present and acting, unless the principal, either by operation of law or by virtue of a specific agreement, is required to perform the service personally. (For example, a baseball player may not designate another player to bat for him; and the lead actor may not authorize his stand-in to act for him.)

1. **Minors:** A person who has not reached the legal age (usually 18) is competent to act as a principal, but special rules apply to him in certain situations.

   a. **Minor as principal:** Any *contracts* made by an agent for the minor are *voidable at the minor's election* during her minority or within a reasonable time after she reaches majority. *Goldfinger v. Doherty,* 276 N.Y.S. 289 (N.Y. App. Term 1934).

      i. **Voidable:** In most jurisdictions, when the principal is a minor, the *agency relationship is voidable at the minor's option*. But the minor must act to void the agency.

      Example: P, a minor, borrows his father's car. P allows A, another minor, to drive the car. While driving the car, A negligently injures T, who sues P for damages. P argues that he is not liable because he lacked the capacity to appoint A as his agent. *Held,* the agency created by a minor is voidable, not void. Because P elected to continue the agency relationship with A, P is liable to T. *Scott v. Schisler,* 153 A. 395 (N.J. 1931).

      ii. **Exception:** A few jurisdictions hold that a minor's attempt to create an agency is void.

   b. **Minor as master (employer):** A minor may also act as a master (See definition of "master." p. 1, *supra*). In that event, the minor is liable for the torts of his servants under the theory of *respondeat superior* if the servant's tortious act or omission is within the scope of his employment and in furtherance of his master's business. *See* Relation Between Principal and Third Person in Tort, p. 8, *infra*, for a detailed analysis of a master's liability in tort.

2. **Insane persons:** When a mentally incompetent person purports to act as a principal, the legal effect of his act depends on whether or not the person has been adjudicated insane.

   a. **Adjudication of insanity:** If the principal has been adjudicated insane, his purported appointment of an agent will be *void,* as will contracts made on his behalf by the purported agent.

   b. **No adjudication:** If the principal has not been adjudicated insane, but is in fact incompetent, contracts made on his behalf by his agent are *voidable* by the principal. Until the contract is legally avoided or disaffirmed, it remains in effect.

   Note: Generally, A does not warrant the capacity of P to contract. A may, however, be liable for breach of warranty of authority if P is completely incompetent and T is unaware of that fact, or if P is partially incompetent, and A knows this, but T does not. Rest. (2d) § 332.

III. PROOF OF THE AGENCY RELATIONSHIP

A. **Burden of proof:** The burden of proof as to the existence of an agency relationship falls *on the person who claims that it exists*.

B. **Type of evidence:** The fact of agency may be proved by any of the following:

   1. **Oral testimony:** Any person, including the alleged agent, can testify as to *what was said or done in the creation of the agency*.

   2. **Writing not always persuasive:** Whether the parties have stated in a writing that they have or have not created an agency relationship is an important, though not conclusive, factor in determining whether an agency relationship was created.

   Example: An agreement between an insurance company and an insurance broker termed the broker an *"independent contractor."* At issue in the case was whether the insurance broker was an agent of the insurance company; if it was, the company's payment to the broker would not satisfy its obligation to another broker who had reimbursed a customer for an unearned premium.

Held, in construing the writings between the company and the broker, the court found that although one writing specifically termed the broker an independent contractor, other writings described the broker as the company's "legal representative and true and lawful attorney to act in the Company's behalf." The mere fact that the parties called the broker an "independent contractor" did not prevent him from acting also as agent. *Palmer & Cay/Carswell, Inc. v. Condominium/Apartment Insurance Services, Inc.,* 409 S.E.2d 806 (S.C. Ct. App. 1991).

3. **Significance of *Palmer* case: *Because an independent contractor can also be an agent*,** the parties will wish to make their intentions clear by using simple and unambiguous language. If they want to make it difficult for a court to find an agency relationship, they should state in so many words that no agency relationship is created or intended. Though a court will not necessarily abide by what the parties have called their relationship, it will be more likely to find an agency relationship if the parties call it one, or to reject it if the parties say they don't mean to create one.

4. **Other significant factors:** Two other factors may help to prove or disprove an agency relationship: ***the conduct of the parties***, and ***other surrounding circumstances.***

   Example: A real estate broker was held to be the agent of the sellers rather than the buyers. The court observed that the sellers, not the buyers, had the right to control the agent's conduct. The sellers paid the agent's commissions. In addition, the buyers did not believe the broker to be their agent. *Allen v. Lindstrom,* 379 S.E.2d 450 (Va. 1989).

C. **Presumption of authority for lawyers:** An attorney who appears in court on behalf of a client need not prove he is authorized. A ***presumption of authority exists because the attorney is an officer of the court and subject to its rules***.

IV. AGENCY DISTINGUISHED FROM OTHER RELATIONSHIPS

It is important to know whether a relationship is an agency relationship, or some other type of legal relationship, because the legal consequences to the parties, or between the parties and third persons, may differ depending upon how the relationship is characterized.

Example 1: A customer tells his broker that he wants to purchase a particular unlisted security at a designated price. The broker is not paid a commission, but derives his profit from the difference between the price he pays for the designated stock and the price fixed by the customer. In other words, the broker is really acting for himself because his income derives from his ability to get a lower price than the price designated by the customer. The transaction between the broker and his customer is a sales transaction, not a principal-agent relationship, and is subject to the Statute of Frauds. *F.C. Adams, Inc. v. Elmer F. Thayer Estate,* 155 A. 687 (N.H. 1931), *aff'd on rehearing,* 156 A. 697 (N.H. 1931).

Example 2: The stock transaction described in Example 1. above is not the typical transaction. More often, the relationship between a stockbroker and his customer is one of principal-agent. The customer instructs the broker to buy or sell stock at specified prices and the broker charges a commission for each transaction. Because the broker is not selling shares to the customer, or buying shares from him, he is acting as the customer's agent and the Statute of Frauds does not apply. *Stott v. Greengos,* 230 A.2d 154 (N.J. Super. Ct. App. Div. 1967).

A. Buyer and seller: Whether a principal-agent relationship exists is often critical in sales transactions.

1. **Tests used:** Key factors to consider in determining whether the transaction is a buyer-seller transaction or a transaction between principal and agent include:

    - *whether the buyer fixes his resale price:* if so, he is likely to be considered a purchaser rather than an agent;

    - *whether title passes* from seller to buyer: if so, it is more likely to be deemed a purchase;

    - *whether the buyer is acting primarily for the benefit of the seller* or for his own benefit: the latter favors a buyer-seller relationship. Rest. (2d), § 14J;

    - *how the parties have labeled the relationship* (relevant but not determinative);

    - *the amount of control reserved to the seller* (the greater the control, the more likely it is that the transaction will be characterized as an agency relationship); and

    - *whether the buyer has an independent business* in buying and selling similar property (if so, we would be more inclined to view him, as a purchaser and not an agent). Rest. (2d) § 14K.

2. **Manufacturer-Distributor transaction:** The issue whether an agency exists often arises when a plaintiff attempts to hold a *product manufacturer liable for the acts of its distributor.* Key fac-

tors are whether the distributor obtains title to the product and the extent to which the manufacturer retains control over the distributor.

Example 1: An automobile dealer sued Chrysler, a manufacturer, under the Automobile Dealer's Day in Court Act (15 U.S.C. §§ 1221-25). The dealer argued that Chrysler's distributor, from whom the dealer had procured the autos, was Chrysler's agent, thereby subjecting Chrysler to possible liability under the act. Chrysler argued that the distributor was merely a buyer of its autos, not its agent, and that Chrysler had no manufacturer-dealer relationship with the plaintiff-dealer and could not be liable under the Act.

Held, the relationship between the distributor and Chrysler was not an agency relationship, but that of buyer-seller. The fact that the distributor obtained title to the cars was important to the decision. Although Chrysler had reserved substantial control over the distributor, the control was the kind normally reserved by manufacturers over distributors and did not create an agency relationship. Because the distributor was not Chrysler's agent, the dealer could not maintain an action against Chrysler. *Stansifer v. Chrysler Motors Corp.,* 487 F.2d 59 (9th Cir. 1973).

Example 2: G.E. required its 21,000 dealers to sell G.E. lamps at prices fixed by G.E. Under existing anti-trust laws, if the distributors were G.E.'s agents, G.E. could set their resale rates; but if they were G.E.'s purchasers, G.E. was prohibited from setting the resale rate. The government argued the dealers were really purchasers. G.E. argued that the dealers were G.E.'s agents who merely held possession of its lamps on consignment.

Held, the dealers are G.E.'s agents, not its purchasers. The Supreme Court focused on the following facts: the dealers did not get title; they had no control over their own purchase prices; unused lamps were to be returned to G.E.; and once each month the dealers were required to turn over all sales proceeds to G.E., less only their commissions. It was not inconsistent with the finding of agency that the dealers had to account to G.E. for damage to the lamps in their possession; this was simply a reasonable way to ensure that the dealers took good care of the lamps. *United States v. General Electric Co.,* 272 U.S. 476 (1926).

Example 3: Hunter hired Hubco to install computer software at its business. Hubco breached the agreement. Hunter sought to hold MAI, the software manufacturer, liable, claiming that Hubco was MAI's agent. MAI and Hubco had a dealership agreement which required Hubco to maintain "appropriate" premises, to inform MAI of changes in Hubco management and to submit monthly reports on the number of prepackaged software units it installed. MAI had the right to monitor the advertisement of certain of Hubco's products. MAI also had the right to discontinue sales to Hubco if Hubco did not maintain certain credit standards.

Held, the controls reserved by MAI were not the type of controls determinative of an agency relationship. MAI had no right to control the day-to-day of operations of Hubco. In addition, Hubco had a right to purchase MAI software at a stated price and to resell it at a higher price without having to account to MAI for its profits. MAI lacked the power to control Hubco's business expenses, to fix its prices, or to demand a share of its profits. *Hunter Mining Laboratories, Inc. v. Management Assistance, Inc.*, 763 P.2d 350 (Nev. 1988).

3. **Key questions:** Typically, a seller's agent must account to the principal for his profits on the sale of goods. An agent does not typically acquire title to the goods; instead, title passes directly from the seller to the seller's customer. In a dealership arrangement, the manufacturer will typically reserve some controls in order to protect his reputation and goodwill. The key question is ***whether the manufacturer has retained such detailed controls over the operations of the dealership as to create an agency relationship***.

4. **Restatement factors:** The Restatement lists several factors for determining whether a consignee of goods is a purchaser or an agent. "The following factors indicate a sale, although no one factor is determinative." Rest. (2d) § 14J, comment b:

- That the consignee gets legal title and possession of the goods.

- That the consignee becomes responsible for an agreed price, either at once or when the goods are sold.

- That the consignee can fix the price at which he sells without accounting to the transferor for the difference between what he obtains and the price he pays.

- That the goods are incomplete or unfinished and it is understood that the transferee is to make additions to them or to complete the process of manufacture.

- That the risk of loss by accident is upon the transferee.

- That the transferee deals, or has a right to deal, with the goods of persons other than the transferor.

- That the transferee deals in his own name and does not disclose that the goods are those of another.

B. Escrow holder: An escrow holder is not initially the agent of either party to the escrow agreement. Instead, an escrow holder has an obligation to hold designated property entrusted to her until the happening or non-happening of a defined event. If the event happens or fails to happen as designated in the escrow agreement, the property is to be delivered to a third person; otherwise the escrow holder is to return the property to the depositor. The ***escrow holder becomes an agent of one of the parties to the agreement only upon the happening or non-happening of the event specified*** in the escrow agreement which terminates the escrow relation. Rest. (2d) § 14D.

1. **Agreement among all three parties required:** A valid escrow agreement is a three-party agreement among the intermediary (the escrowee or escrow holder), the depositor, and a third party. If the third party does not join in the agreement, the intermediary is merely the depositor's agent. Rest. (2d) § 14D, comment a.

   Example: The Olsons agreed to sell property to the Kings. They executed a deed of trust and deposited it with the Bank's escrow department. The Olsons and the Bank (but not the Kings) signed a set of "Collection Instructions" which required the Bank to accept the Kings' payments on their note, to transmit some of the proceeds to the state in satisfaction of the Olsons' obligations under the purchase contract and to remit the balance to the Olsons. Olson went to the Bank and unilaterally altered the collection instructions, providing that all of the payments would go to the Olsons' account. After paying in full, the Kings could not get title to the property because the Olsons had not paid the state. Kings sued the Bank for breach of the "escrow agreement" in failing to remit payment to the state.

   Held, the Bank was not liable as an escrow holder because the Kings were not parties to the document creating the collection instructions. The court denied the Bank's summary judgment motion, however, on the theory that the Bank, as the Olsons' agent, could be liable as a third party beneficiary. *King v. First National Bank of Fairbanks,* 647 P.2d 596 (Alaska 1982).

   a. **Criticism of third-party beneficiary theory:** Loose application of the third party beneficiary theory can leave an escrow agent, like the Bank, in a severe quandary. If it follows the instructions of its customer-principal scrupulously, it may become liable to the third party on the third-party beneficiary theory. On the other hand, if it fails to follow the instructions, it will be liable to its principal. The Restatement solves this dilemma by providing that the agency relationship with the principal terminates when the agent is confronted with conflicting responsibilities. Rest. (2d) § 14L, comment e. *See* Hynes, p. 34.

Example: Seller retains Broker to sell his trucking business. Broker finds a buyer and drafts a sales contract signed by both Seller and Buyer. The contract requires Buyer to deposit the purchase price with Broker until the state approves the transfer of the public utility license. Broker absconds with the money. Seller argues that the contract created an escrow agreement with Broker as Buyer's escrow agent. The loss should fall on Buyer, who deposited the money in escrow.

Held, Broker is not an escrow agent, but the agent of Seller. Consequently, the loss falls on Seller, rather than Buyer. The court was probably influenced by the fact that Seller was in the better position to avoid the loss. Also, Seller had hired Broker, had paid his commission, and had overseen the drafting of the agreement. *Paul v. Kennedy,* 102 A.2d 158 (Pa. 1954).

C. **Bailments:** A bailment involves the transfer of possession of a chattel from the bailor to the bailee. Title to the chattel remains in the bailor. The ***usual bailment does not result in an agency because the bailor does not delegate any authority to the bailee and does not exercise any control*** over the bailee.

Example: P sells cars. P delivers a car to T to enable T to test-drive it. T drives the car negligently and injures X. X sues P for damages.

Held, X cannot recover from P. The arrangement between P and T created a bailment and not a master-servant relationship, a type of principal-agent relationship. X can recover from P only if T was acting as a servant of P. P's duty was complete when he delivered the car to T. The delivery created a bailment between T and P in which P was the bailor and T was the bailee. In the absence of a statute to the contrary, or of knowledge by P that T was a negligent driver, the bailment relationship places no liability on the bailor (P) for the bailee's (T's) negligent driving. T was not an agent or servant of P because the parties did not contemplate that T was acting for P. Also, T had complete control over where, when and how he would drive the car.

☞ **Exam tip:** A bailment may be converted into an agency if the parties manifest their intention to do so by their words or their conduct. You should be careful to analyze the facts on exam questions to determine the precise relationship(s) among the parties. Remember that one or more relationships can exist at the same time.

D. **Trust relationship:** "A trust is a fiduciary relationship with respect to property, subjecting the person by whom title is held to equitable duties to deal with the property for the benefit of another person, which arises as a result of a manifestation of an intention to create it." Restatement (Second) of Trusts § 2. ***A person can be both an agent and a trustee.***

Example 1: R appoints T to act as trustee to hold property for the benefit of B's children. If nothing more is said, T will act as trustee, not as agent of R. Even if R retains the power to revoke the trust, the relationship will probably remain a trust relationship, not an agency relationship. But if R retains the power to control trust investments and to direct distributions of principal and interest, T will probably be deemed both the agent of R and trustee for the children.

Example 2: Plaintiffs transferred title to certain securities to their daughter. Title to the securities was to revert to plaintiffs if their daughter predeceased them. Plaintiffs reserved the right to direct the sale of the securities, and to receive the proceeds from any sale. Plaintiffs also received the dividends from the securities. The issue was whether plaintiffs could revoke the original title transfer. The plaintiffs claimed they could, arguing both that the trust was revocable and that the daughter was their agent. Defendants argued that the title transfer was an irrevocable gift or an irrevocable trust.

Held, the relationship created was one of agency. Daughter was subject to the direction and control of her parents with respect to the sale of the securities and the payment of proceeds to them. Even if the plaintiffs viewed it as a trust, they had reserved the right to revoke it. *Dierksen v. Albert*, 254 A.2d 809 (N.J. Super. Ct. App. Div. 1969).

E. **Marriage:** Marriage by itself ***does not create an agency relationship*** between the parties. Although marriage is a consensual relationship containing the elements of trust and confidence, it does not by itself give one spouse the authority to act on behalf of the other.

CHAPTER 2

RIGHTS AND DUTIES BETWEEN PRINCIPAL AND AGENT

ChapterScope

The relationship between *principal* and *agent* imposes a number of *unique rights and duties on both parties*. The chapter covers the *principal duties owed by the agent to his principal* and the *remedies available to the principal for the agent's breach* of those duties. An employee (servant) is one special type of agent and the rules applicable to agents also apply to employees or servants.

I. INTRODUCTION

A. **Fiduciary relationship:** The agency relationship carries with it a number of reciprocal duties and responsibilities which can be characterized as *fiduciary* (a relationship founded on trust and reliance) in nature. Page 16 shows a chart which summarizes the duties owed by an agent to his principal; the remedies available to the principal for the agent's breach of duty; the duties of a principal to his agent; and the remedies available to the agent for the principal's breach.

II. AGENT'S DUTIES TO PRINCIPAL

A. **Specific obligations:** A confidential or fiduciary relationship exists between an agent and her principal. The fiduciary duties and other obligations required of an agent include:

1. **Duty of care:** An agent owes her principal a duty of care commensurate with the *ordinary skill of other agents performing similar tasks in the locality*. Rest. (2d) § 379. However, an agent holding herself out as an *expert is held to a higher standard*. *Walker v. Bangs,* 601 P.2d 1279, 1283 (Wash. 1979). In that case, a lawyer who held himself out as a specialist was held to the higher standard of care of those holding themselves out as specialists in the area.

   a. **Must expend reasonable efforts:** An agent who fails to *expend reasonable efforts* on behalf of her principal will be held liable for the damages caused to the principal.

   Example: Plaintiff (P) hired a travel agent (A) to book a package tour offered by a tour company called Total Hawaii. A suggested that P not use Total Hawaii but did not explain why. P

Figure 2-1
Duties and Remedies of the Principal and Agent

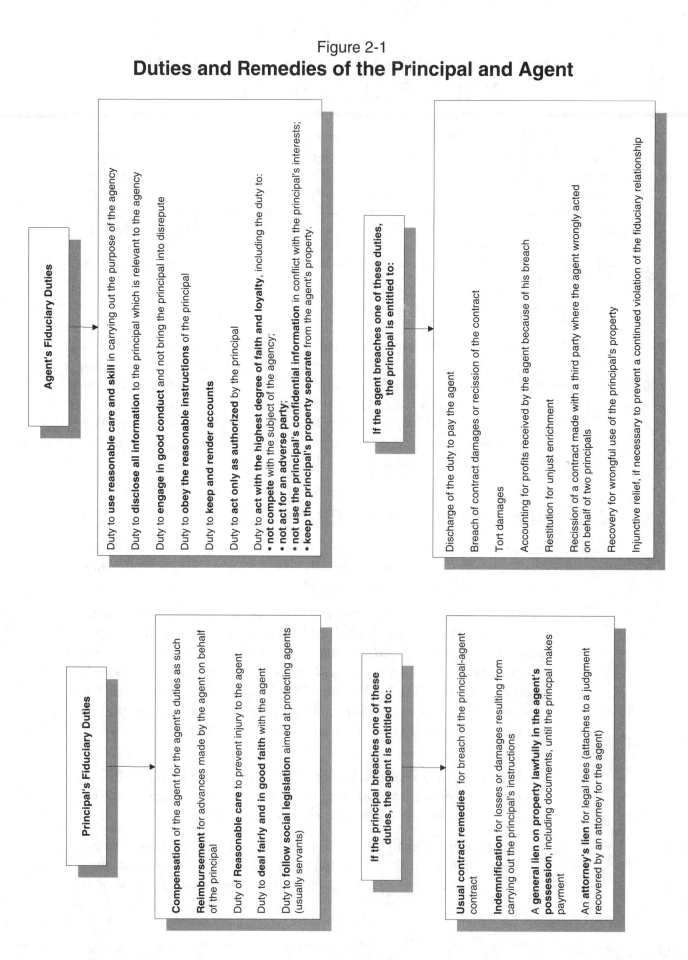

Agent's Fiduciary Duties

Duty to **use reasonable care and skill** in carrying out the purpose of the agency

Duty to **disclose all information** to the principal which is relevant to the agency

Duty to **engage in good conduct** and not bring the principal into disrepute

Duty to **obey the reasonable instructions** of the principal

Duty to **keep and render accounts**

Duty to **act only as authorized** by the principal

Duty to **act with the highest degree of faith and loyalty**, including the duty to:
• **not compete** with the subject of the agency;
• **not act for an adverse party**;
• **not use the principal's confidential information** in conflict with the principal's interests;
• **keep the principal's property separate** from the agent's property.

If the agent breaches one of these duties, the principal is entitled to:

Discharge of the duty to pay the agent

Breach of contract damages or recission of the contract

Tort damages

Accounting for profits received by the agent because of his breach

Restitution for unjust enrichment

Recission of a contract made with a third party where the agent wrongly acted on behalf of two principals

Recovery for wrongful use of the principal's property

Injunctive relief, if necessary to prevent a continued violation of the fiduciary relationship

Principal's Fiduciary Duties

Compensation of the agent for the agent's duties as such

Reimbursement for advances made by the agent on behalf of the principal

Duty of **Reasonable care** to prevent injury to the agent

Duty to **deal fairly and in good faith** with the agent

Duty to **follow social legislation** aimed at protecting agents (usually servants)

If the principal breaches one of these duties, the agent is entitled to:

Usual contract remedies for breach of the principal-agent contract

Indemnification for losses or damages resulting from carrying out the principal's instructions

A **general lien on property lawfully in the agent's possession**, including documents, until the principal makes payment

An **attorney's lien** for legal fees (attaches to a judgment recovered by an attorney for the agent)

decided to use Total Hawaii anyway and paid it for airline tickets and hotel accommodations. Total Hawaii went bankrupt, and P did not obtain his air tickets or hotel accommodations.

Held, A was liable for the damages caused to P because of her failure to make a reasonable inquiry to determine if Total Hawaii was solvent. A was apparently on notice that something was amiss when she suggested that P use a different tour company. A failed to inquire further when P failed to obtain his tickets or an immediate response from Total Hawaii. *Douglas v. Steele,* 816 P.2d 586 (Okla. Ct. App. 1991).

2. **Duty of full disclosure:** An agent must fully disclose to the principal all information related to the agency.

   Example: A was given the responsibility for finding a financially responsible buyer for P's business. A recommended B as Buyer, despite his failure to investigate Buyer's financial condition and lack of funds. A failed to learn and to disclose that a person not known to Seller was in the Buyer group and was a source of financing. After the sale was completed, Buyer defaulted on the purchase money note and mortgage.

   Held, P had the burden of proving the lack of full disclosure by A. If P had clearly alleged A's failure to disclose a conflict of interest or a dual agency, A would have borne the burden of proving that he had made full disclosure of his conflicting interest. *Lindland v. United Business Investments, Inc.,* 693 P.2d 20 (Or. 1984).

3. **Duty of good conduct:** An agent owes his principal a duty of *good conduct*, and *a duty not to bring his principal into disrepute.* For example, a bank teller breaches his duty to his principal by gambling while off duty. See *Gregory v. Anderson,* 109 N.W.2d 675, 679 (Wis. 1961), which found that a truck driver (A) was properly denied unemployment compensation benefits for violating an off-duty non-drinking rule. The violation might have harmed P's business interests.

4. **Duty of obedience:** An agent must *obey the reasonable instructions of his principal.* An example of this principle as it applies in a particular context is Rule 5.2(b) of the ABA Model Rules of Professional Conduct, which provides that "[a] subordinate lawyer does not violate the rules of professional conduct if that lawyer acts in accordance with a supervisory lawyer's reasonable resolution of an arguable question of professional duty." On the other hand, an agent has no duty to obey unreasonable instructions. Even an at-will employee who violates the instructions of his principal may not be fired if the instructions violate public policy. *Ford v. Wis-*

consin Real Estate Examining Board, 179 N.W.2d 786, 792 (Wis. 1970), *cert. denied,* 401 U.S. 993 (1971). In *Ford,* the court held that a real estate broker (A) had no duty to obey seller's (P's) instruction to engage in racial discrimination in showing P's property.

5. **Duty of loyalty:** The agent owes a duty of loyalty to the principal. The duty of loyalty encompasses the following elements:

   a. **Competing interests:** Within the scope of the agency, the agent must act ***solely*** for the benefit of his principal, with ***no adverse or competing interest.*** Rest. § 389.

      i. **If the agent has a competing interest:** If the agent has a personal interest adverse to that of his principal, the agent must either ***make no contract at all, or disclose all the facts to his principal and obtain the principal's consent.***

         Example 1: P instructs his agent, A, to buy stock in X corporation at $40 per share. A, a broker, personally owns stock in X, and sells his own stock to P at a price less than $40 per share, without disclosing that the shares sold were his own.

         Held, P may rescind this transaction. A has violated his duty to act solely for the benefit of P. That is true even though P has benefited from the transaction.

         Example 2: A is president of P corporation, which operates a large number of retail stores selling candy, ice cream and soft drinks. A and other officers of P corporation are unhappy with the price they pay for Coca-Cola products, and they consider either acquiring Pepsi-Cola or changing to Pepsi-Cola products, which they can buy at substantial savings. Subsequently, M informs A that Pepsi-Cola has gone into bankruptcy, and that M is in a position to acquire its assets. A does not inform other P corporation officers of this, but instead makes an agreement with M. Under this agreement M buys the Pepsi-Cola formula and trademark, and the two men form a new corporation. A uses P corporation personnel and facilities to enable the new corporation to conduct its business. Pepsi products are marketed in P corporation outlets. P corporation sues A.

         Held, A must give all his Pepsi-Cola stock to P corporation, without compensation. The opportunity was closely associated with P's existing business. A and M formed their agreement at a time when P corporation officers were interested in reducing their cost of Coca-Cola products. P corporation had the financial resources and facilities to acquire the

Pepsi-Cola formula and produce it. A decided to adopt Pepsi as the cola to be sold by P corporation and he supplied it to the company, but he deprived P corporation of the opportunity of acquiring the principal assets of the bankrupt Pepsi firm. A is estopped to deny that he acted for himself and not for P corporation when he acquired the Pepsi formula and trademark. P is entitled to relief also because A used the resources of P corporation to further his own business. As an officer and director of P corporation, A could not use P corporation assets or resources to finance his own business. *Guth v. Loft, Inc.,* 5 A.2d 503 (Del. 1939).

ii. **Partner's duty to partnership:** A partner or joint venturer must not take advantage of an opportunity that is presented to him as a partner in the business.

Example: S obtains a twenty year lease of a hotel from O, the owner. S agrees to convert the hotel to use as shops and offices. S forms a joint venture with M to complete the conversion. M supplies half the money, but S retains sole power to manage and operate the building. The venture is very profitable. Before the lease expires, S is offered a new long-term lease by O. Under this lease, the building is to be razed and another, larger building constructed. O does not know that M is the business partner of S. Neither O nor S notifies M of the new lease. M sues to impress a trust on the new lease as an asset of the joint venture. S contends that the new lease is not a renewal of the old lease, but a new venture in which M has no interest.

Held, M is entitled to his share of the new opportunity so long as he assumes his proportionate share of the obligations. "Joint adventurers, like copartners, owe to one another, while the enterprise continues, the duty of the finest loyalty." *Meinhard v. Salmon,* 164 N.E. 545 (N.Y. 1928). S used his position as manager to obtain the new business opportunity, and thereby breached his fiduciary duty to M. S had the duty to notify M of this opportunity. Note that if O presented S with an opportunity to invest in a venture in Australia, S probably would not need to notify M of this opportunity, because it does not relate to the subject of their joint venture.

b. **Dual agency:** An agent owes to his principal a *duty not to act for an adverse party* in any transaction within the scope of the agency. An agent may act for both parties to a transaction, even though their interests are adverse, but *only if both parties are* *fully informed* of all the pertinent facts, including the fact that the agent is representing both, *and both parties consent.*

Example 1: P lists land for sale with A, a real estate broker. A visits T to offer the land. Before A can say anything to T, T authorizes A to act as agent for T to purchase P's land. A arranges for the sale and purchase of the land, but does not advise either party that he has been authorized by, and is acting as agent for, both. A collects commissions from both P and T. When P learns that A acted for both parties, P seeks to rescind the sale.

Held, P may rescind the sale. A may not act as agent for both P and T with fidelity when as agent for P it is his duty to obtain the maximum price for the land, and as agent for T it is his duty to pay the minimum price. A transaction conducted wholly or in part by an agent of one of the parties, who acts at the same time for the opposite party, may be rescinded by the party who is ignorant of the double employment *without the need to show any injury* or intent to deceive. In this case, both principals were ignorant of A's double agency. Each has the right to rescind the sale and recover the commission paid to A. *Olson v. Pettibone,* 210 N.W. 149 (Minn. 1926), Rest. (2d) § 391.

Example 2: P engages A to purchase a house for him. T also engages A to sell a house for him. A calls P and T to his office, introduces them, and informs them that he is acting for both parties. A tells them that he will act as intermediary for both if they so desire, but that in so doing he will be absolutely impartial and give them all the facts concerning the property. Both P and T agree that A may act for both. A tells them that it appears T's house is what P desires, and that it seems to be worth the price which T is asking. T's house is sold to P.

Held, Neither P nor T may rescind the sale. An agent may act for adverse parties with their consent as long as they are fully advised of all the facts. In that case, A is entitled to a commission from each if he is impartial and fair in his dealing with each. Rest. (2d) § 392.

c. **Competition with employer:** An employee may compete in business with his former employer after the employment is terminated, unless he has agreed otherwise. If he has agreed not to compete at the end of his employment, and the agreement is *reasonable,* the courts will enforce it.

Example: D signs a partnership agreement with other doctors at a clinic. The agreement provides that if a doctor withdraws from the partnership, his interest shall be purchased at a certain percentage of its value. It also provides that the doctor will not practice medicine within 25 miles of the clinic for five years after leaving the partnership. Any unpaid portion of the purchase price of the partnership interest will be forfeited as liquidated damages for violation of the covenant not to compete. D withdraws from the partnership and sets up practice in violation of the agreement. He forfeits the balance of the money due for his interest. When the other partners sue to enjoin his new practice, D contends that the restriction is void as an unreasonable restraint of trade and contrary to public policy, and that the provision for forfeiture of the balance constitutes liquidated damages barring other relief.

Held, D is enjoined from the practice of medicine within the area, in accordance with the agreement. The limitation as to territory is reasonable and there is consideration for the restraint. The elimination of one doctor in the community will not cause substantial injury to the public. Thus, there is no unreasonable restraint of trade. There is no special hardship to D by granting the injunction, and the provision for liquidated damages is an additional remedy, not an exclusive remedy, for the other partners. *Bauer v. Sawyer,* 134 N.E.2d 329 (Ill. 1956). See also, *Karpinski v. Ingrasci,* 268 N.E.2d 751 (N.Y. 1971).

i. **Criteria for reasonableness in agreement:** If the employee makes an agreement with his employer not to compete after leaving his employment, in determining whether the agreement is enforceable, courts will consider whether the employee's services were ***unique*** and whether to require protection for the former employer's ***trade secrets, formulae,*** or ***confidential information,*** such as customer lists. The court may find the non-compete agreement unenforceable if:

(1) **Time:** It runs for an unreasonable length of time;

(2) **Geographical area:** It includes an area beyond which the employer does business, or which unduly restricts the employee from practicing his trade or profession or from earning a reasonable livelihood; or

(3) **Benefit-detriment to parties:** Its enforcement would cause serious injuries to the employee without affording substantial protection to the employer.

Example 1: A agrees to work as a clerk for P for three years and not to enter any business competing with P for three years after A leaves P's employment. P promises nothing in exchange for A's promise not to compete. Three years later A and X open a store within three blocks of P's store. P seeks to enjoin A's breach of his contract not to compete, but makes no showing that A is using any of P's trade secrets (such as a list of customers) or that A is a unique person, or that P is incurring irreparable injury.

Held, P's suit is dismissed. Unless the former employee is a ***unique person,*** or is ***using trade secrets*** obtained while working for the employer, or there is ***irreparable injury*** to the employer, an injunction will not issue. To grant it would do more harm than good. A is an ordinary person whose sole means of support is his right to work. His right to offer his services for wages is a vital and necessary property right which should not be limited by an injunction in the absence of irreparable injury to P. *Menter Co. v. Brock,* 180 N.W. 553 (Minn. 1920); *Bonney v. Northern Ariz. Amusement Co.,* 277 P.2d 248 (Ariz. 1954). In *Bonney,* the court enforced a non-compete clause in conjunction with the sale of his stock by the corporate president/general manager, on the ground that he was provided consideration for his covenant, including forgiven loans, a market for the sale of his stock, and the employer's agreement not to compete with him.

☞ **Exam Tip:** In analyzing problems in this area, the student should weigh the following factors: (a) What is the interest that the employer wants to protect? Is it a trade secret, a restricted formula, a list of customers, or a unique company service or product which may be harmed irreparably? (b) Is the restraint reasonable when measured by time limits and the area covered? (c) Is there an identifiable public interest or public policy, such as that which favors a person's ability to follow his chosen profession without restrictions?

Example 2: P employed A to sell hearing aids. A signed a contract which declared a list of P's customers and prospects to be trade secrets. A agreed to pay P $5,000 as liquidated damages if he used the list to P's detriment. He also agreed not to compete with P for one year in the state of Utah. He agreed to pay $3,000 in damages if he breached that covenant. A breached his agreement by selling a competitor's products to prospects on P's list without compensating P. He also competed with P in

Utah during the one year period prohibited by the non-competition clause.

Held, A was subject to liability for using the customer list in violation of his agreement. However, the non-competition clause was held unenforceable. It was not necessary to protect P's list of customers; the trade secret agreement adequately did that. Furthermore, there was no indication that A was uniquely or specially responsible for P's goodwill; nor was there any proof that competition from A had any greater effect on P than the competition of any other salesman. A's job required little training and the company's investment in him was small. Balancing the hardship to A arising from enforcement of the non-compete clause against the hardship to P from nonenforcement, the court determined that the covenant was unreasonable and therefore unenforceable. *Robbins v. Finlay,* 645 P.2d 623 (Utah 1982).

d. Use of confidential information: An agent may not use confidential information obtained during the course of his agency to compete with his principal.

Example: A had worked as a tax collector and as a conveyancer. A became employed as P's agent in drawing up certain deeds. As a result, he learned that P's title to certain property was doubtful, and he informed P of this. During the course of his service to P, A also learned that P was attempting to convey property that A knew P really did not own. A used that information to P's detriment by going to a commissioners' sale and buying land that P did own but mistakenly believed he had validly conveyed to others.

Held, A breached his obligation not to use confidential information which he learned during his employment to the detriment of P. The fact that A was employed to draw up deeds and not to search titles was irrelevant to his breach of duty. He nevertheless used information acquired in the course of his employment to his principal's detriment. A was not relieved of his fiduciary obligation by the fact that he warned P that his title was doubtful. "It would defeat the very purpose of the rule to permit defendant [A], having learned during his service to plaintiff [P] of a defect in plaintiff's title, to give plaintiff full warning that he was going to take advantage of the defect." *Chalupiak v. Stahlman,* 81 A.2d 577 (Pa. 1951).

i. Use of information after employment: Even after an employee has left his employment, he has no right to use trade secrets, lists of names, or other confidential information which he has acquired from his former employer, in competition with him.

Example 1: P is engaged in cleaning homes, and employs several crews to do the work. A, B, and C, while employed by P in various supervisory positions, agree to form a company on their own to compete with P. They resign their positions at the same time, form a new company, and solicit P's customers for their new business. P sues to enjoin them, and for an accounting and damages. The court held that the conduct of A, B, and C, while employed by P, in resigning *en masse,* forming a competing business and soliciting P's customers, violated their obligations as P's employees. P's petition for relief was granted. *Town & Country House & Home Service v. Newberry,* 147 N.E.2d 724 (N.Y. 1958); see also *Arnold's Ice Cream Co. v. Carlson,* 330 F. Supp. 1185 (E.D.N.Y. 1971).

Example 2: Four salaried associates broke off from their law firm and formed their own firm. One of the associates, while still at his old offices but after he had announced he was leaving, sought to solicit old clients, both in person and through telephone calls. He pursued contacts derived from cases on which he had worked and mailed form letters to former clients by which the clients would discharge the former firm and name him as new counsel.

Held, The right of the associates to pursue their own business interests was not absolute. They breached their continuing fiduciary duty to their former firm by taking advantage of the "still subsisting confidential relation created during the prior agency relation." If the associates had waited until they were no longer physically within the offices of the old firm and had then simply mailed announcement cards advising former clients of the formation of the new firm and the opening of their new offices, their actions would have been construed as reasonable notice of their availability as practitioners and would have been permissible. *Adler, Barish, Daniels, Levin, & Creskoff v. Epstein,* 393 A.2d 1175 (Pa. 1978), cert. denied and appeal dismissed, 442 U.S. 907 (1979). See also Gross, *Ethical Problems of Law Firm Associates,* 26 WM. & MARY L. REV. 259, 281-86 (1985).

ii. **Trade secrets:** A trade secret is a **secret** compound, process, formula, device, list, or fact, used in business, and communicated in confidence to employees. **Wrongful use** of a trade secret, such as the act of making it known to a competitor, can be enjoined. *Henry Hope X-Ray Prods., Inc. v. Marron Carrel, Inc.,* 674 F.2d 1336 (9th Cir. 1982).

Example: The internal configuration of operating parts of a machine when novel in design and unique in its field, may constitute a trade secret even if the ideas used were generally known. This may occur when substantial research improves known ideas and the improvements are kept secret by the employer. These secret improvements constitute a trade secret which may not be used or disclosed by an employee. *General Aniline & Film Corp. v. Frantz,* 272 N.Y.S.2d 600 (N.Y. Sup. Ct. 1966).

Note: For more information on trade secrets and their protection, see *The Professor Series* on *Intellectual Property,* Ch. 2-V to VI.

Note: An invention or trade secret created by an employee ***belongs to the employer if the employee was hired to do research of the type which lead to the invention;*** otherwise, it belongs to the employee. However, if the employee uses the employer's time and facilities to develop his invention, the employer is entitled to ***shop rights*** to the invention. A shop right is an irrevocable, non-exclusive, non-assignable right or license to use the invention or trade secret in the employer's business, royalty-free.

iii. **Publicly available information:** If the information used by the agent is based on general public information or general business experience, the agent will not have breached his fiduciary duty.

Example: Agent used information that was confidential and had not been disclosed by his former principal to his successor principal, as part of the negotiation for the purchase of stock of the former principal.

Held, Agent breached his fiduciary duty by using confidential information. The court noted that an agent is precluded from using confidential information to compete with his former principal, even though the information is readily available (but not publicly available) from third parties or by other means. *ABKCO Music Inc. v. Harrisongs Music, Ltd.,* 722 F.2d 988 (2d Cir. 1983).

6. **Segregation of principal's property:** It is the duty of an agent to keep separate and apart from his own property or funds, all prop-

erty and funds which are placed in his possession by his principal. *Hibberd v. Furlong*, 257 N.W. 737 (Mich. 1934); Rest. (2d) § 398.

a. **Duty of attorney:** An attorney who receives funds as agent for a client ***may not place those funds into his or her own personal account*** even though the funds in that account are sufficient to pay all his obligations. *Black v. State Bar of Cal.*, 368 P.2d 118 (Cal. 1962). Most states have adopted strict rules for the segregation by lawyers of client funds into special accounts and for the distribution of client funds. See ABA Model Rules of Professional Conduct, Rule 1.15, *Safekeeping Property;* also, ABA Model Code of Professional Responsibility, Canon 9, DR 9-102.

B. **Principal's remedies:** If the agent breaches a duty, one or more of the following remedies may be available to the principal.

1. **Denial of compensation:** Some, but not all, courts will deny the agent compensation for his services.

Example: In *Hartford Elevator v. Lauer,* 289 N.W.2d 280 (Wis. 1980), the court rejected a rule which would require that the agent forfeit his compensation in every case. Instead, the court said that it was appropriate to look at how much damage the agent had caused to the principal and at the value of the agent's services. The agent has the burden of proving that the value of his services exceeded the harm that he caused by his breach.

Compare British American & Eastern Co. v. Wirth Ltd., 592 F.2d 75 (2d Cir. 1979). In *British,* the court held that the agent was properly denied compensation even though there was no proof that his bribe-taking had caused the principal any harm. The court reasoned that the strong public policy against bribe-taking requires that injury to the employer be presumed. Harm can occur both to the principal-agency relationship and to the principal's relations with its customers.

2. **Contract remedies:** The principal may seek remedies at law for breach of the agency contract. However, ***specific performance is not usually a remedy*** because the agent's services are considered personal.

3. **Tort remedies:** If the agent is negligent or intentionally wrongs the principal, and her actions cause the principal to suffer a loss, the principal may sue the agent in tort. See *infra*, p. 27. Tort remedies can include both ***compensatory damages***, and, in those states which permit them when the tort is wilful and/or in violation of the agent's fiduciary duty, ***punitive damages***.

a. **Establishing a tort:** If the principal seeks tort damages for the agent's failure to use reasonable care and skill, the principal must establish:

- A *duty* by the agent;

- *Breach* of the agent's duty;

- *Injury* or loss to the principal; and that the

- *Breach was the proximate cause* of the injury.

4. **Accounting for and restitution of improper profits:** If an agent acts for himself or for another principal in disregard of the duties of the agency, the principal may recover the profits realized improperly by the agent.

Example: A broker (A) falsely represented himself to a land buyer (X) as the seller's agent. A made a secret profit by first acquiring the land for himself and then reselling it at a profit to X.

Held, Although A was not X's agent, A should not profit by his wrongdoing. The court imposed a constructive trust for X's benefit on the secret profits and also awarded punitive damages for A's dishonest conduct. *Ward v. Taggart,* 336 P.2d 534 (Cal. 1959).

5. **Secret commission from a third party:** If an agent accepts a secret commission from a third party, the principal may be able to secure the commission for himself.

Example: The Gussins (P) hired Shockey (A) to assist them in buying, maintaining, breeding, and selling horses. A's commission was to be 5% of the profit on the sale of each horse. A assisted P in purchasing six or seven horses. A did not reveal to P that he was able to buy horses at prices lower than those he declared to P. A had a secret arrangement with his sources which enabled him to keep the difference between the true price and the price he quoted to P. Under this arrangement, when he acted for P to purchase a horse for $650,000 on a base price of $525,000, he pocketed $125,000 for himself. A never told P of this arrangement.

Held, P was entitled to recover all the secret commissions paid by his sources to A. A's counterclaim for his share of the profits on the sales of P's horses was denied because A was not entitled to compensation for conduct which constituted a deliberate breach of A's duties. *Gussin v. Shockey,* 933 F.2d 1001 (4th Cir. 1991).

a. **Intercession by courts:** In order to deter fiduciary breaches of this kind, courts will usually intercede and require all secret commissions or bribes to be paid over to the principal.

6. Rescission of third party contract: The principal may even be able to rescind a transaction with a third party if the agent is also an agent of the third party.

Example: Real estate broker (A) was the agent for both Buyer and Seller. He told Seller that he would sell the Seller's house on a non-exclusive basis and that the Buyer would take care of his compensation. A's agreement with the Buyer provided that the Buyer would execute a secured note payable to A in the amount of $5,000. Buyer also agreed to pay A 50% of the profits resulting from sale of the house within the next year. Neither A nor Buyer told Seller about this arrangement. The Seller refused to close and the Buyer sued for specific performance to compel the sale.

Held, the trial court erred in granting specific performance to Buyer. A failed to make full disclosure of the terms of his agency. Because A was also working for Buyer, Buyer should not be allowed to profit from the agent's breach of his fiduciary duty to Sellers. *Velten v. Robertson,* 671 P.2d 1011 (Colo. Ct. App. 1983). Although Seller was not paying A directly, A's failure to reveal the terms of his payment directly affected Seller. A had an incentive to induce the sale at a low price because he stood to profit on resale. Seller was not limited to recourse against A because A was also employed by Buyer. Buyer should not be permitted to profit from the agent's misbehavior.

a. Agent liable for fees and expenses: Even though an agent's fiduciary breach may enable the principal to rescind a transaction with a third party, the ***agent may still be liable for the expenses*** which the principal incurred in the transaction. *Tarnowski v. Resop,* 51 N.W.2d 801 (Minn. 1952). These may include court costs and attorneys' fees.

7. Wrongful use of principal's property: The agent is liable to his principal for wrongful use of the principal's property which is in the agent's possession. Rest. (2d) § 404.

Example: P leaves his automobile with his employee, A, while P is on a business trip. During that time A rents P's car to T and collects $50, but does not disclose that fact to P. A is liable to P not only for the money received in rent, but also for any damage which has been caused by T's wrongful use.

a. Injunctive relief: The court may order the agent to stop acting for the principal or from misusing the principal's property, if necessary, to prevent continued violation of the terms of the agency.

III. EMPLOYEE'S RIGHT TO INVENTIONS

Introductory note: The rules set forth in this section govern rights of employers and employees at common law. They may be altered by express agreement between the parties or by statute.

A. **Ownership of invention:** An invention perfected by an employee *belongs to the employee* and not to the employer, *unless the employment was for the purpose of experimentation and invention.* The employee owns the invention even if the employee wrongfully uses the time, tools and facilities of the employer. *Manton-Gaulin Mfg. Co. v. Colony,* 151 N.E. 71 (Mass. 1926).

1. **Employer's shop right:** If the employee was not hired for experimentation and invention, but nevertheless uses his employer's time and materials to conceive and perfect an invention for which the employee obtains a patent, the employer is entitled to an *irrevocable, nonexclusive, nonassignable right to manufacture, use and sell* the invention without paying a royalty. This is known as a *"shop right."* It is based upon equitable principles, because the employee used the employer's time and facilities when he was hired to do other work. However, the employee is still entitled to ownership of the patent. *Gemco Engineering & Mfg. Co. v. Henderson,* 84 N.E.2d 596 (Ohio Ct. App. 1949). *See,* Barrett, The Professor Series on *Intellectual Property,* Chapter 2, The Law of Trade Secrets.

2. **Constructive trust:** If an employee hired for the purpose of creating inventions wrongfully patents in his own name an invention which belongs to his employer, the employee holds the patent in *constructive trust* for his employer. A constructive trust is a wrong-rectifying remedy by means of which anyone who has wrongfully acquired title to property is made to hold title in trust for the person who should own it.

   Example: P employs A for the purpose of developing inventions which will improve specific farm machinery. A perfects an invention which improves the lifting of gang plows out of the soil. A procures a patent for that invention in his own name. P sues A.

   Held, A holds the patent in constructive trust for P and will be ordered to transfer it to P. A acquired title to the invention by breaching his contract of employment. *Standard Parts Co. v. Peck,* 264 U.S. 52 (1924); Rest. (2d) § 397.

IV. DUTIES OWED BY PRINCIPAL TO AGENT

A. Specific duties: Just as the agent owes various duties to the principal, so the principal owes collateral duties to the agent. These duties include:

1. **Compensation:** An agent's right to compensation for services rendered for the principal is usually a matter of contract between them. If no consideration is agreed upon, the courts permit the agent to recover in *quantum meruit* for the reasonable value of the services performed.

    a. **Consideration for services contrasted with consideration at creation of agency:** The rule relating to consideration for services rendered should be contrasted with the basic rule that no consideration is necessary to *create* the agency relationship.

      Example 1: P asks a business or professional person to act as his agent. It is presumed that payment is to be made for the services rendered, unless the parties are close relatives or the circumstances show that the services were intended to be gratuitous.

      Example 2: P asked A to find buyers for property on which P was foreclosing. A did so. The court allowed A to recover the reasonable value of his services from P. *McCollum v. Clothier,* 241 P.2d 468 (Utah 1972).

      Example 3: A real estate broker paid by commission is normally expected to bear his own travel expenses. See Hynes, p. 210 (citing Seavey, *Law of Agency,* p. 266 (1964)). An attorney paid on a contingency basis, however, does not usually bear the costs of experts and court filing fees. In the absence of a specific agreement between the parties, we look to **what is normal and expected in the industry** to determine whether there is an obligation to pay.

      Example 4: Defendant (P) employed A as its exclusive manufacturer's representative to sell certain auto parts to specified automobile manufacturers. The agreement further provided that A would be paid a commission on any items A might sell to the manufacturers. A sold the parts, and P paid A at first. Then P felt that A was being paid too much for the amount of work he was doing, so P informed A that he would be paid no more than $2,000 per month. Subsequently P fired A. A sued P, claiming (a) that it was entitled to continuing commissions on all subsequent sales for all accounts it had initially procured; and (b) because it was P's exclusive agent, it was entitled to continuing commissions on all sales to accounts over which it had been granted exclusive representation.

Held, A was entitled to commissions only on the sales that it directly procured. The court rejected A's claim that it was entitled to post-termination commissions based on its having been P's exclusive agent. The court observed that there were two types of exclusive representation agreements. These were: (a) an *exclusive right to sell*, which confers on the agent the sole right to sell in a certain geographic area (under this arrangement, the agent gets commissions on all sales in its territory, whether or not he was the procuring cause of the sale); and (b) *an exclusive agency*, which is the more common arrangement. Under an exclusive agency, the principal is prohibited only from employing other agents to sell the goods or property. He is free to sell the goods or property himself and is not liable to the agent for commissions on the sales he (the employer) makes. The court interpreted the agreement as an exclusive agency rather than as an exclusive right to sell. The court pointed to the specific contractual language which gave A commissions only on the items that A might sell. This suggested that A was not to be paid commissions on sales made by P. The court also noted that in the absence of specific language in the contract terming a relationship an exclusive right to sell, it would characterize the relationship as simply an exclusive agency. *Roberts Associates, Inc. v. Blazer Int'l Corp.,* 741 F. Supp. 650 (E.D. Mich. 1990).

b. **Compensation based on agent's reasonable belief:** If a principal leads an agent to believe that he has been chosen as the principal's agent, the agent's compensation will be the amount which the principal causes the agent to believe he will be paid. See *Moran Travel Bureau, Inc. v. Clair,* 421 N.E.2d 103 (Mass. App. Ct. 1981).

c. **Duty to subagents:** *A subagent* is an agent's agent. A subagency is created whenever A1 delegates to A2 a performance that P has authorized A1 to delegate. Rest. (2d) § 5. A principal is *not required to pay the subagent in the absence of an agreement* to the contrary. An agreement permitting the agent to delegate his duties to others does not, by itself, render the principal responsible for payment of the subagents. *McKnight v. Peoples-Pittsburgh Trust Co.,* 61 A.2d 820 (Pa. 1948).

d. **Breach by principal in wrongful discharge:** Because of the confidential relationship which exists between principal and agent, the principal *always has the power to discharge the*

agent. However, the principal will be liable for damages if he breaches his contract with the agent by discharging him.

2. **Attorney's contingent fee contract:** The nature of the attorney-client relation dictates that a client must have confidence in the integrity and ability of his attorney; absolute fairness and candor must characterize all dealings between them. For this reason, a client has the right to terminate the services of his attorney at any time. When the client discharges a lawyer, the lawyer is entitled to payment in ***quantum meruit*** for the reasonable value of his services. If there is a contingent fee agreement between them, that agreement will control the amount of compensation, as well as the time of payment. *Plaza Shoe Store, Inc. v. Hermel, Inc.*, 636 S.W.2d 53 (Mo. 1982).

3. **Reimbursement for advances:** The principal is required to reimburse the agent for any advances the agent makes for the principal.

4. **Reasonable care to prevent injury:** The law imposes a duty on the principal to provide a suitable workplace for the agent, as well as a duty to use reasonable care to prevent injury to the agent during his work.

5. **Cooperation:** The principal must provide reasonable assistance to the agent in the performance of his duties, and must not act to prevent the agent's performance.

   Example 1: A real estate broker is entitled to recover a commission from a seller whose conduct prevents the sale from being consummated. *Brady v. East Portland Sheet Metal Works*, 352 P.2d 144 (Or. 1960).

   Example 2: When the seller agrees to pay the broker his commission "if and when title closes," the broker has no cause of action either against the purchaser who defaults on the contract or against the seller. *Caryl v. Greenwald*, 196 N.Y.S.2d 427 (N.Y. Sup. Ct. 1960).

   Example 3: If the purchaser employs a broker and agrees to pay him when he finds satisfactory land—and the broker performs—the purchaser is liable to the broker for a commission even though the broker was to look to the seller for the commission. *Tanner Assocs., Inc. v. Ciraldo*, 161 A.2d 725 (N.J. 1960).

6. **Duty to deal fairly and in good faith.** The principal has an obligation to treat his agent fairly and not to libel or demean him. The principal also owes her agent an obligation to warn him of circumstances which might subject the agent to physical or pecuniary loss in dealing with the principal's product. The understanding is that

the principal will use care to prevent harm or injury to the agent. This requires that the principal not only warn the agent of physical dangers, but, also, that he disclose facts which, if unknown, would be likely to subject the agent to a pecuniary loss. Rest. (2d) § 435, comment a.

Example: A, a salesman for P company, alleged that P had failed to supply it with timely notice of consumer complaints regarding some of P's pacemakers, thereby injuring A's professional reputation.

Held, P exercised reasonable diligence in notifying its sales force when it learned of the consumer complaints indicating that the pacemakers posed a threat to consumers. It was not obligated to notify its sales force when the first consumer complaints came in; it was reasonable to wait until it knew the nature, seriousness, or extent of the problem.

7. **Social legislation:** An employer also must comply with state and federal legislation protecting workers. This legislation is extensive and includes:

- worker's compensation — *infra,* p. 129;

- unemployment compensation laws;

- laws requiring rehiring of veterans;

- the 1964 Civil Rights statute and comparable state statutes precluding discrimination in employment on the basis of race, color, religion, sex, or national origin (the federal statute applies to employers with 15 or more employees);

- the Age Discrimination in Employment Act, preventing discrimination on the basis of age (applies to employers with 20 or more employees);

- minimum wage laws;

- management-labor legislation affecting bargaining between employers and unions (such as the National Labor Relations Act);

- employee safety statutes such as OSHA;

- the Worker Adjustment and Retraining Notification Act, requiring 60-days notice before plant closings or massive layoffs (applies to employers with 100 or more employees);

- the Americans with Disabilities Act of 1990; and

- the Family and Medical Leave Act of 1993 (applies to employers with 50 or more employees).

See Hynes, p. 222.

B. Agent's remedies: In the event the principal breaches a duty to the agent, one or another of the following remedies may be available to the agent.

1. **Contract remedies.** Generally, the usual contract remedies are available to an agent if the principal breaches the agency agreement.

2. **Indemnification:** The agent may sue to enforce indemnification by the employer. The principal must indemnify the agent *for losses or damages resulting from carrying out the principal's instructions.* However, there is no right to indemnification for losses resulting from unauthorized or illegal acts.

    Example 1: A agrees to manage and operate a ship under a contract with P. A employs a subagent, S, to outfit the vessel for a voyage. The outfitting is done, but the vessel is lost at sea in a typhoon. The owners of the cargo which was lost sue S for their losses. S defends the suit and it is dismissed. S sues A for S's legal expenses. A brings P into the action, and contends that P is responsible for S's expenses.

    Held, S is entitled to be reimbursed for the costs of defending the suit. An agent may recover any expenditures necessarily incurred in the transaction of his principal's affairs. Thus, an agent compelled to defend a baseless suit grounded upon acts performed in the principal's business, may recover the expenses of his defense. The reason for this rule is that since the venture is that of the principal, and the principal receives the profits, he should also bear the expenses. S is entitled to reimbursement from A, and A is entitled to exoneration from P for this claim. *Admiral Oriental Line v. United States,* 86 F.2d 201 (2d Cir. 1936); Rest. (2d) § 439(d).

    Example 2: Gulf Oil Corporation (P) handled Holiday Inn's (A's) credit card transactions. Plaintiff checked into a Holiday Inn. A's clerk woke plaintiff at 5:00am, told him that his credit card had made an indistinct impression and that another one was needed. Plaintiff turned over his credit card. A's clerk then took possession of the card and informed plaintiff that his credit had been revoked and that he had authority from Gulf Oil (P) to pick up Plaintiff's card and terminate his credit. Although Gulf Oil (P) had authorized Holiday Inn (A) to revoke credit and secure possession of certain cards, there was no evidence that Gulf Oil (P) authorized rudeness or false pretenses in securing the credit cards. Plaintiff sued Holiday Inn (A), and A wanted Gulf Oil (P) to indemnify it.

    Held, Gulf Oil (P) had no duty to indemnify Holiday Inn (A). There was no indication that the clerk was an agent of Gulf Oil (P).

Even if he had been an agent for the purpose of revoking the credit card, Gulf Oil (P) had no duty to indemnify Holiday Inn (A) because the damage was caused by the clerk's own tortious conduct, even though the conduct was committed within the clerk's scope of employment. [One could view this case as an ***ambiguous principal problem.*** See *infra,* p. 81. Viewed in that way, Holiday Inn was clearly in a better position to prevent the clerk's misconduct than Gulf. Therefore, the loss should fall on Holiday Inn.] *Wood v. Holiday Inns, Inc.,* 508 F.2d 167 (5th Cir. 1975).

3. **Liens:** An agent has a general lien on documents or other property of the principal lawfully in his possession, until the principal pays any money due to the agent.

   a. **General lien:** This lien is sometimes called a ***retaining lien.*** It applies only when the agent possesses the principal's property, and it may be asserted for the entire amount due on an account. The lien continues until the debt is paid or the property is surrendered. Surrender of the property terminates the lien whether or not or payment was made.

   b. **Charging lien of attorney:** This lien is called a charging lien or, sometimes, a ***special lien.*** It is not based on possession, but occurs instead when a judgment is recovered through the attorney's efforts and there is an agreement, express or implied, that the attorney is to be paid out of the judgment.

   c. **Distinction:** An attorney's charging lien attaches only to the proceeds recovered by the attorney through his professional services. An attorney's general lien attaches to any property belonging to the client which the attorney receives in his professional capacity.

      Example 1: A is employed as an attorney for P at a salary payable semi-annually. P discharges A, but P allows A to prosecute a suit for P which is pending at the time of discharge. A then obtains a judgment for P and asserts a lien on the judgment for the value of his services in obtaining the judgment and for his unpaid salary. P is bankrupt.

      Held, A has a charging lien on the judgment for the value of his services in obtaining it, but no lien for his unpaid salary. A charging lien may not be used to recover the general balance of an account, but only for services rendered in a specific action. *Matter of Heinsheimer,* 108 N.E. 636 (N.Y. 1915).

      Example 2: A1 and A2, both attorneys, represent P in a lawsuit. A1 withdraws from the case before trial and claims a retaining lien on documents in his possession until he is paid for his legal services.

Held, A1 may be ordered to release the documents so that the litigation can proceed. However, since A1's attorney-client relationship was terminated for reasons other than improper conduct, A1 must be given adequate security. A lien on the judgment to be obtained in the case is not adequate security because it is not yet in existence and may never be obtained. *Upgrade Corp. v. Michigan Carton Co.,* 410 N.E.2d 159 (Ill. App. Ct. 1980).

CHAPTER 3

NOTIFICATION AND IMPUTED KNOWLEDGE

ChapterScope

Because the agency relationship enables the agent to bind the principal, it's important to identify and analyze the ***kind of notice or knowledge*** which must be manifested to all the parties involved in order to establish the existence of an enforceable transaction. In this chapter, we examine when ***notice by a third party to an agent constitutes notice to the principal***; when ***knowledge of the agent is imputed to the principal***; the agent's ***obligation to inform the principal***; special rules relating to ***corporate officers and*** directors; the circumstances under which knowledge of an agent is ***not imputed to the principal***; and whether knowledge of the principal is imputed to the agent.

I. NOTIFICATION

A. Definition: *Notification* is the act of informing someone of a relevant fact by adequate or specified means, or the consequence of a person's being informed of facts or circumstances from which that person has reason to know, or should know, a relevant fact. See Rest. (2d) § 9.

1. **Failure to inform:** When a third party ***notifies*** (gives information to) an agent who has actual or apparent authority to receive the notice, that notice binds the principal ***even if*** the agent ***never actually*** gives that information to his principal. The principal is deemed to have notice of a fact if his agent has knowledge of the fact, has reason to know it or should know it, or has been given notification of it within the rules of agency. Rest. (2d) § 9(3).

   Example: Customer (T) comes into bank (P) at lunch hour and asks teller (A) to stop payment on a check. T does not realize that A is off duty. A fails to stop payment.

   Held, the notification by T to A binds the bank (P). A had ***apparent authority*** to receive T's request (notice) to P. Rest. (2d) § 268. (See *infra,* p. 43.)

2. **Casual notice:** If an agent receives notice casually, that notice may not be enough to bind his principal.

   a. **Facts:** Bridge Company's president (T) met casually and informally with Electric Company's (P's) new local manager (A), at a local restaurant. T advised A that for safety reasons, the Electric Company (P) should have a representative present during repairs on a bridge on which Bridge Company was working. Electric Company (P) failed to put a representative in place, and a worker was injured. Electric Company (P) argued that T's notice to A was not sufficient notice from Bridge Company of the need to have a representative in place.

b. Notice not sufficient: The court ruled that Electric Company (P) was not liable because T's notice to A was insufficient. The notice to A was given *casually* when he was *not in his official or representative capacity.* Under these facts, when T told A of the bridge repairs, there was *no reasonable expectation* that A would do anything with the information. *St. Louis & St. Charles Bridge Co. v. Union Elec. Light & Power Co.,* 268 S.W. 404 (Mo. Ct. App. 1925).

c. Reasonable expectation is basis of rule: As in the law of contracts, the doctrine of notification in agency law is based on fulfilling the *reasonable expectations* of the parties.

B. Adverse actions: The doctrine of notification states that even if the agent is *acting adversely* to the principal, the principal will still be bound by notification from a third party to the agent, unless the third person *realizes that A is acting adversely* to the principal. Rest. (2d) § 271.

Example: T serves notice of a motion on P's attorney (A). A does not tell P and does not oppose the motion, because he intends to injure P (or his interests). P is nevertheless bound because T reasonably believed A had authority as attorney to receive the notice, and *T did not know* that A intended to act adversely to P. See Rest. (2d) § 271, Illustration 3; Hynes, p. 486.

Caveat: *If A told T* that he hated P and would do anything he could to injure him, P *would probably not be* bound by A's actions. If T was himself an attorney, he might have a special duty to advise the court of A's misconduct. A third party should not be permitted to profit from, or take advantage of, the acts of an agent who is acting adversely to his principal, if he has knowledge of the agent's adverse interest.

II.   IMPUTED KNOWLEDGE

A. Based on principal's right to control agent: As we have seen, the doctrine of notification is premised on the reasonable expectations of the parties. In contrast, the doctrine of imputed knowledge is based upon the principle that the principal should be deemed to have the same knowledge as his agent, because he has **control** over the agent and **profits** from his labor. In this, the doctrine of imputed knowledge is similar to the theory underlying the doctrine of ***respondeat superior.*** (See *infra,* pp. 89, 91.)

Even if the principal does not ***actually*** know the facts which the agent has learned, he is said to have ***constructive knowledge*** of the facts. In the absence of this fundamental doctrine, a principal would be able to shield himself from adverse consequences merely by claiming he did not know the requisite facts when he allowed an agent to act for him. *First Ala. Bank v. First State Ins. Co.,* 899 F.2d 1045, 1061 (11th Cir. 1990).

1. **Failure to inform principal:** An agent's knowledge can be imputed to her principal, ***even if the agent fails to do her job adequately*** and does not report the information to her principal.

   Example: P hires A to research the title to land to find out if it is free from encumbrances. A discovers that T has an easement across the land that does not appear either of record or on inspection of the property. A negligently fails to report the encumbrance to P, who buys the land assuming it is clear of encumbrances.

   Held, A's ***knowledge will be imputed*** to P. P cannot rescind the sale on the ground that T has an easement. Even though A ***did not actually tell*** P of the easement, A's knowledge will be imputed to P, who will be said to have bought the property with knowledge of the easement. The Restatement says that "P is affected by A's knowledge." Rest. (2d) § 272, Illustration 4.

   Example: P authorizes his agent, A, to sell P's 2-year old heifer to T for breeding purposes. A knows that the heifer is sterile. P does not know that fact, and A does not tell him. A sells the heifer to T as a breeder. When T learns that the heifer is sterile, he sues to rescind the contract and recover the purchase price.

   Held, T may rescind the contract. A's knowledge that the heifer is sterile is imputed to P. P is deemed to know the fact because ***the law assumes that A has done his duty and informed*** P. Rest. (2d) § 272, Illustration 2.

B. **Agent's duty to inform principal:** An agent's knowledge can be imputed to the principal ***only if*** the agent has a ***duty*** to transmit that knowledge to the principal.

   Example: P's janitor (A) overhears a conversation in which T says he plans to sue P for breach of contract. P does not have imputed knowledge of T's claim of breach because the janitor ***had no duty*** to convey that information to his principal; a janitor's duties do not include receiving and conveying notice of tenants' claims. The fact that the janitor acquired the knowledge casually is not the critical fact. What is critical is that A did not have a duty to receive and convey the information to his principal. Rest. (2d) § 275, comment c, § 276.

C. Principal-agent relationship necessary: In imputed knowledge cases, the issue often turns on the answer to the question: **for *whom is the the agent working*?** A principal cannot be liable on the basis of imputed knowledge unless the knowledge attributed to him is that of a person who can reasonably be identified as **his agent.**

Example: School hired Architect to supervise roof construction. School also hired Chalkraft as project representative and paid his salary. Architect prepared a standard agreement between Architect and School. The agreement contained language suggesting that the project representative was working at the direction of Architect in overseeing the work. Architect also supplied a document entitled "Suggested Instructions to Full-Time Project Representative." Architect notified Chalkraft of a construction defect. Chalkraft did not tell School about this defect. When the completed roof began to leak, School sued Architect. The issue at trial was whether School had been effectively notified of the construction problem when Architect told Chalkraft about it. School argued that Chalkraft's knowledge of the defect should not be imputed to it because Chalkraft was Architect's agent, not School's agent. Architect argued that Chalkraft was School's agent and Chalkraft's knowledge should be imputed to School.

Held, Architect failed to show as a matter of law that Chalkraft was an agent of School rather than his agent. Even if Chalkraft were the agent of the School, his knowledge **would not be imputed to School** because it could be inferred that Chalkraft **had no duty** to report information relating to the roof to School. Chalkraft knew that the matter was being handled directly by Architect. *Board of Education v. Sargent,* 539 N.Y.S.2d 814 (App. Div. 1989).

D. Knowledge imputed to corporations: Corporate officers and employees are **agents of the corporation.** Any information they get will be imputed to the corporation if their duties are such as to enable them to appreciate the significance of the information to the **corporation**. Rest. (2d) § 283. Illustration 4).

Example: P Bus Co. hires A and assigns him the duty of keeping the bus terminal clean and free from dangerous objects. A banana peel lies on the lobby floor for over 24 hours with A's knowledge. T slips on the peel and is injured. T sues P. P argues that some third person unknown to P dropped the peel, and that P did not have sufficient notice of the condition.

Held, A's knowledge is imputed to P. ***A's duty*** was to deal with ***such conditions.*** Because A knew of the peel on the floor, his knowledge is imputed to P.

Caveat: If the agent reasonably fails to appreciate the significance of the information (for example, if the information becomes relevant and significant only when it is combined with information from other agents or sources), the principal is not charged with knowledge. *Colby v. Riggs Nat'l Bank,* 92 F.2d 183, 195 (D.C. Cir. 1937); *See* Rest. (2d) § 272, comment b.

1. **Rule for corporate directors:** Knowledge acquired casually by corporate directors is ***not imputed*** to the corporation. Unlike corporate officers, directors ***are not deemed employees*** of the corporation. As a result, information they acquire casually will generally not be imputed to the corporation, since they have no duty to inform the corporation.

   Example: Robinson, a real estate broker and an outside member of the board (not a corporate officer) of P Corporation, had been T's personal friend for years. Robinson may have known that T was attempting to defraud some of her creditors. Robinson introduced T to P Corporation and then withdrew from the transaction between them. P Corporation loaned T $750,000 in exchange for a mortgage on T's property. T used this transaction to further her fraud. A bankruptcy trustee sought to set the mortgage aside as a fraudulent transfer. To succeed, the trustee had to show that P Corporation knew of T's fraudulent intentions. P Corporation argued that it did not know of the fraud and that Robinson did not know of the fraud. Furthermore, even if Robinson did know, his knowledge could not be imputed to P corporation; any knowledge Robinson had was acquired casually and not in his capacity as a director of the corporation.

   Held, P Corporation was not bound. Knowledge of ***facts acquired casually by individual directors*** will not be imputed to the corporation. *In re Ocean Devs. of Am. Inc.,* 22 B.R. 834 (Bankr. S.D. Fla. 1982).

2. **Notification & imputed knowledge distinguished:** Because notification requires some affirmative act to bring a matter to a principal's attention, casual notice to his agent ordinarily will not suffice to bind a principal on the basis of notice. For example, if a statute or rule requires that a person (T) notify P of some information in order to have or enforce some right against P, P will not be bound by her Agent's casual receipt of the information or notice. T must affirmatively notify P or her agent in order to bind P. On the

other hand, if affirmative or formal notice to P is not required, P can be bound on the theory of imputed knowledge if his Agent learns the information, even casually, and has a duty to report it to P. Knowledge through notification lasts indefinitely, but imputed knowledge can be terminated by the passage of time.

E. Prior to agency relationship: A principal can be charged with the knowledge of his agent even if the agent acquired the knowledge before the agency relationship began. This retroactive attribution of knowledge to the principal can occur if there is clear proof that the agent *had the information in his mind* at the time he entered into the relevant transaction. The court relied on this theory in *Constant v. University of Rochester*, 19 N.E. 631 (N.Y. 1889).

    1. Facts: P, the University of Rochester, acquired property at a sale. T had an unrecorded mortgage affecting the property. Constant, P's attorney (A), had previously represented T's decedent several years earlier in acquiring the mortgage lien. Constant (A) did not tell P about the existence of the unrecorded mortgage. P denied having actual or imputed knowledge of the prior mortgage.

    2. P was bona fide purchaser without notice: The court found that P was a bona fide purchaser which acquired the property without knowledge of the prior mortgage. A had not acquired the knowledge while representing P and it could not be established that A had present knowledge of the prior transaction. His knowledge, if any, would not be imputed to P *unless Agent clearly recalled the information* at the time he represented P. The court ruled that a principal *cannot automatically avoid* the imputation to him of his agent's knowledge by claiming that he learned of the information before the agent did. However, in this case, because A acquired the knowledge several years earlier *and* there was no proof that he had *retained the knowledge in his head* at the time of the transaction, his knowledge could not be imputed to P. *Constant v. University of Rochester,* 19 N.E. 631 (N.Y. 1889).

F. Principal's knowledge not imputed to agent: Although an agent's knowledge may be imputed to her principal, the *principal's knowledge is not imputed to her agent. Rosenbaum v. Texas Energies, Inc.,* 736 P.2d 888, 892 (Kan. 1987). A principal may be liable for negligence if he *fails to tell the agent* information which is necessary under the circumstances.

Example: If P puts A in charge of a piece of dangerous machinery but fails to give A the information she needs to operate the machinery safely, P may be liable for any resulting injuries to A. R&G, p. 121.

G. Exceptions to imputed knowledge: There are several exceptions to the general rule that an agent's knowledge is imputed to his principal.

1. **Knowledge acquired outside of apparent authority.** When an agent is given apparent, but not actual, authority by his principal, only the ***knowledge acquired by him as a result of his apparent authority*** will be imputed to his principal. Knowledge acquired by the agent by means ***outside his apparent authority*** will not be imputed to the principal. Rest. (2d) § 273, comment a, Illustration 1.

2. **Knowledge from a confidential source:** When an agent gets information from a source which requires the duty or obligation of confidentiality, that knowledge will not be imputed to his principal. Otherwise, ***the agent would be deemed to violate his legal duty*** to the person from whom he received the information.

   Example: B mortgages his land to M for $5,000. The transaction is finalized in the office of attorney A, who acts for both parties. A knows that M's mortgage has not been recorded. Subsequently, P asks A to act for him in buying that same land from B for its full value of $10,000. A does so. B executes a deed to P, which is recorded. P has no knowledge of M's mortgage.

   Held, P is not charged with A's knowledge of M's unrecorded mortgage. A learned of M's mortgage while acting as attorney for M and B. This knowledge is confidential and privileged, and A must not reveal it. Therefore, A's knowledge is not imputed to P, who is a bona fide purchaser who takes title free of M's unrecorded mortgage lien. Rest. (2d) §§ 281, 381.

   Example: C owed T money. T arranged to get an attachment bond against C's real property from P, through P's agent, A. T told A not to tell P of the pending attachment bond. C then went to another division of P to get a loan against the same property. P, unaware of T's application for an attachment bond, gave the loan to C, securing it with a mortgage on C's property. P recorded its mortgage. Then T perfected its attachment on C's property. However, P's lien was superior to T's because it was created first. T claimed that P should be charged with knowledge of T's interest at the time P made its mortgage, because A knew about T's interest in the property.

   Held, A's knowledge was not imputed to P; P's mortgage has priority over T's attachment bond on the property. T's request that A keep the information confidential destroyed any argument that A's knowledge should be imputed to P. The agent's knowledge will not be imputed "when the third party knows that the agent will not advise the principal." *Imperial Fin. Corp. v. Finance Factors, Ltd.,* 490 P.2d 662 (Haw. 1971).

3. **Deception by third party:** Knowledge may not be imputed to the principal if a third person **deceives the agent** into not telling the principal about certain facts.

Example: T wanted to sell a horse to P. T gave P's agent (A) a doctor's report stating the horse had a bad heart, but falsely told A that P was already aware of the report. P bought the horse and, upon learning of the horse's condition, sued T.

   Held, T was not entitled to summary judgment merely because he had notified A. Because T also deceived A into not conveying the information to P, a jury verdict for P was proper. *Fancher v. Benson,* 580 A.2d 51 (Vt. 1990).

4. **Adverse acts:** When the agent and a third person collude to cheat the principal, or the agent acts adversely to the interests of his principal **for his own purposes**, the agent's knowledge will not be imputed to the principal. The courts reason that when an agent is off **"on a frolic of his own"** (i.e., acting outside the scope of the agency), the principal cannot be charged because he lacks control over the agent. There is no reason, under these circumstances, to inflict the loss on the principal rather than on the third party who may have conspired to cause the loss. Rest. (2d) § 282.

Example: X applies for automobile insurance from P Insurance Company's agent, A, who submits the application to P. P refuses to insure X because of his poor driving record. At A's suggestion, X transfers title to his brother, B. B then gets insurance from P, although X uses the car exclusively. X has an accident. P refuses to pay, contending that the policy is void for fraud because X is the actual owner of the car, even though B holds title. X contends that A's knowledge of the reason for the title transfer should be imputed to P and should estop P from voiding the policy.

   Held, A's knowledge is not imputed to P, and P may void the policy. A knew of the false representations of ownership and colluded against P. A's knowledge is not imputed to P **because A acted adversely to P's interests.** *Southern Farm Bureau Casualty Ins. Co. v. Allen,* 388 F.2d 126 (5th Cir. 1967).

   a. **Adverse interest must be substantial:** The adverse interest doctrine applies only when the agent's interest is **substantially adverse** to that of his principal. Unless the principal will clearly suffer loss because of the agent's conduct, the fact that the agent may make additional profit will not necessarily cause him to be viewed as acting adversely to the principal.

Example: Salesman (A) of a company (P) that manufactured alcohol conspired with bootleggers to divert P's alcohol into drinking alcohol to increase A's commissions. However, P's sales also increased dramatically because of A's activities. A tax suit was instituted against P.

Held, P was properly charged with knowledge of A's activities, even though it had no actual knowledge. A's activities were not substantially adverse to P's interests merely because A received additional income. *In re Mifflin Chem. Corp.,* 123 F.2d 311, 315-16 (3d Cir. 1941).

Example: An insurance broker (A) got insurance for his principal (P). Through the device of hidden charges buried in the insurance, A charged P an additional administrative fee for his services in excess of the insurance company's administrative costs. P tried to recover these excessive fees from the insurance company. The company argued that A's knowledge of the surcharges should be imputed to P. P argued that A acted adversely to P and that, therefore, A's knowledge should not be imputed to P.

Held, whether an agent has acted adversely to his principal is an issue of fact for the jury and should not be decided as a matter of law. *LanChile Airlines v. Connecticut Gen. Life Ins.,* 759 F. Supp. 811 (S.D. Fla. 1991).

b. **"Sole actor" exception:** The ***sole actor*** or ***single agent*** rule is an exception to the general rule that an agent's knowledge is not imputed to her principal when the single agent acts adversely to the principal's interests. The agent's knowledge is imputed ***regardless of*** the agent's motive(s) ***if the principal accepts a benefit*** from its sole agent.

Example 1: Harriman (A), president of Bank (P), made fraudulent representations to T. These representations caused T to lend A securities that A later pledged as collateral for personal loans from Bank (P) to A. T sought to rescind his loan of securities to A. T also sought rescission against Bank (P). T claimed that Bank (P) was chargeable with knowledge of A's fraud. Bank (P) argued that A's knowledge should not be imputed to Bank (P) because A's interest in pursuing his own fraudulent scheme was adverse to Bank's interests.

Held, T could rescind against Bank (P) because A was the sole actor (or single agent) in the transaction. He dominated P's loan committee. He induced P to make the loan and accept the collateral. Under the sole actor doctrine, the principal cannot accept the benefits of the transaction from its agent while denying knowledge of the information known by that agent. *Munroe v. Harriman*, 85 F.2d 493 (2d Cir. 1936).

Example 2: P commissions A, P's sole agent, to acquire certain property for him. A acquires the land from T by fraud and transfers it to P.

Held, the **acceptance of the land** by P imputes knowledge of A's fraudulent act to P. T may recover the property from P by showing A's fraud. *Curtis, Collins & Holbrook Co. v. United States,* 262 U.S. 215 (1923).

CHAPTER 4

AGENT'S AUTHORITY TO BIND PRINCIPAL TO CONTRACT

ChapterScope ━━━━━━━━━━━━━━━━━━━━━━━━━━━

No person or entity can bind another unless she or it has **authority** to do so. But authority can take **many forms and shapes**. In this chapter, we discuss the various form of authority which are recognized by the law. We cover **express authority**, **implied authority** (including the implied authority of corporate officers and lawyers); **apparent authority**; authority by **estoppel**, including estoppel by silence, **inherent authority**; and the **delegation** of an agent's authority to her **subagents**.

━━

I. AGENT'S AUTHORITY

A. Authority defined: "[a]uthority is the power of the agent to affect the legal relation of the principal by acts done in accordance with the principal's manifestation of consent to him." Rest. (2d) § 7. As used in the Restatement, authority is the power of the agent to conduct a transaction on account of the principal because the principal has manifested his intent to have the agent act for him. In this sense, "authority" is the same as "actual authority," and is to be distinguished from apparent authority, from authority by estoppel, from inherent agency power (belonging to a general agent or of one entrusted with property), and from a power held by one in his own interest. Rest (2d) § 7, comment a.

   1. Express authority and implied authority: The principal's **manifestations** involve the expressions of his intent to the agent, in contrast to his undisclosed intentions. Actual authority is derived from a principal's **objective manifestation** of power to the agent. Actual authority takes two forms: **express authority** and **implied authority**.

   2. Express authority: Express authority exists when the principal tells the agent in detail what he is authorized to do and the agent acts within these directions.

      a. Power of attorney: One example of express authority is a power of attorney. By a power of attorney, the grantor (the principal) gives the holder of the power (the agent) the power to do those things specifically enumerated in the document. Powers of attorney are generally construed narrowly in order to protect the principal against an agent who may misconstrue or exceed his authority, give the principal's property away, or wrongfully act for his own benefit.

i. General and special powers: A *general power of attorney* is a power in which the agent is given authority to perform a variety of defined acts (for example, the power to act for the principal in all real estate transactions). If the principal also includes specific powers in a general power, the specific powers will be limited to those acts which are incidental to the general power and will not confer new or different powers. A *special power of attorney* is a limited power conferring the authority to perform only a limited act or function (for example, the authority to sell a specific building). Many states have legislated forms of power which define most transactions in detail. A principal can specify which transactions he wishes his agent to perform by placing his initials alongside the appropriate transactions and signing his name at the bottom of the form.

Example: W, an American citizen, and her husband (P), a German citizen, left for Europe in July, 1939. Because war was imminent, P left an agent (A) in charge of his affairs in the United States. P gave A a general power of attorney to do all acts which P could do, and A was permitted to do certain specific tasks which were not to detract from the fullness of his power. P was unable to return to the United States because of the war. A gave P's property to W. The property was seized by the United States government, which claimed that it was P's property. W brought suit, claiming that A had the authority under the power of attorney to give P's property to her.

Held, W may not recover the property. The general power of attorney did not authorize A to make a gift of P's property. A's general powers were defined by enumerated, specific powers. The specific powers were limited to running and maintaining P's property and business, not destroying it or giving it away.. There was nothing in the grant of ordinary business powers which permitted A to give P's property away. *Von Wedel v. McGrath,* 180 F.2d 716 (3d Cir. 1950), *cert. denied,* 340 U.S. 816 (1950).

3. Implied authority: An agent's implied authority is derived from the scope of his express authority. The agent has the implied authority to perform all acts which are reasonably necessary to carry out his express authority. The extent of the implied authority will be defined by the facts and circumstances surrounding the transaction, by the words used by the parties, by the customs of the trade and the area, and by the relations between the principal and agent.

Example 1: P gives A the authority to sell her car. A has the implied power to show the car to prospective purchasers, to negotiate a fair price with them, to transfer title and to receive payment.

Example 2: P employed A as a farm manager. A had complete charge of P's property. He was to collect the net proceeds of all grain sales from P's farming tenants, retaining a percentage of the proceeds for himself. A endorsed checks payable to P and deposited the full amount in his farm management account, which was not designated as a trust account. P sued A's bank for conversion of his funds. The trial court dismissed P's petition on the ground that A had the implied authority to endorse checks payable to P.

Held, decision affirmed. A did have implied authority to endorse P's checks, and P's suit was properly dismissed. The agreement between P and A specified that A was to collect the proceeds and remit the net sum to P. A was to retain a percentage for himself. This gave him the implied authority to cash the checks in order to pay himself a percentage. Although there was allegedly an oral agreement contrary to the express provisions of their written agreement, P *acquiesced* in A's practice over a number of years. Therefore, A's actions could be viewed as either *impliedly authorized* or as *ratified by P's acquiescence. Fort Dodge Creamery Co. v. Commercial State Bank,* 417 N.W.2d 245 (Iowa Ct. App. 1987).

Caveat: Under the ABA Model Rules and Model Code, and the rules of most states, an attorney who receives a check in which the client has any interest is required to deposit the check into a special trust account and not to commingle the funds with his own.

a. **Implied authority of corporate officer:** The express authority of a corporate officer often derives from the corporation's charter and bylaws. The implied authority of a corporate president or CEO will generally include the power to bind the corporation in most ordinary business transactions. The other corporate officers typically have much narrower implied authority. The delegation of special powers by the board of directors may create greater implied authority, as may the board's acquiescence in, or ratification of, specific acts or transactions.

b. **Emergency situations:** In an *emergency* situation, an agent may possess *expanded implied authority.* The agent may be able to do acts which are in excess of, or even contrary to, the principal's instructions, in order to protect the principal's interests.

i. Who may act: Most courts require the highest ranking officer or employee on the scene to exercise the necessary emergency authority. Under this theory, the principal is usually liable to any third person who renders medical care at the direction of the agent in control.

Example: B is a brakeman on P railroad. While B is acting within the scope of his employment many miles from home, he falls under the train and is severely injured. A, the train conductor and highest ranking employee present, directs T, a doctor, to give medical aid to B. A has no express authority to bind P for T's services to B. T sues P for the value of his services.

Held, T can recover the value of his services from P. In this emergency situation, A's implied authority to act is determined by *whether a reasonable person in A's position would conclude that P expected him to act.* The courts reasoned that when P creates an agency, he says to the agent as a matter of general policy: "Act for me as a reasonable person would act in any emergency." *Sheehan v. Elliott Mfg. Co.,* 145 A. 139 (N.H. 1929).

ii. Theories of liability in emergencies: Three theories have been advanced for imposing liability on a principal when the agent acts outside of her express authority in response to an emergency:

Legal duty: The principal or master owes a duty of care and protection to the ill or injured person or to the person threatened by the emergency.

Public policy: Treatment is necessary upon humanitarian grounds or as a matter of general public policy, such as our interest in minimizing injury or liability. The public policy theory is not applied in all cases. *Balinovic v. Evening Star Newspaper Co.,* 113 F.2d 505 (D.C. Cir.), *cert. denied,* 311 U.S. 675 (1940). In *Balinovic,* an employee truck driver was acting outside the scope of his employment when he chased a fleeing convict and negligently caused an accident, even though he was acting under the instructions of a policeman. The employer was absolved of liability.

Principal's wishes followed: The agent was only doing what the principal would have done if confronted with the same emergency. The agent's authority is expanded to encompass the unstated but understood wishes of the principal.

c. Implied authority of attorneys: Most courts hold that the implied authority of lawyers to conduct litigation *does not include the authority to settle cases*.

Example: P and T were in a property title dispute. P gave its attorney (A) the general authority to represent its interest and the specific authority to conduct settlement negotiations. P gave A the authority to settle the dispute by paying T $10,000. T refused the offer and sued P. Thereafter, P did not give A any specific authority to settle the matter for any sum. A nonetheless subsequently offered T $60,000 in settlement of the controversy. T accepted. P claimed that it was not bound by the settlement because A had neither the express nor the implied authority to settle the matter.

Held, P is not bound by A's unauthorized settlement. In order to preserve a client's ultimate control over his case, his attorney has no authority to settle or dismiss the case without the *express* permission of the client. *New Eng. Educ. Training Serv., Inc. v. Silver St. Partners,* 528 A.2d 1117 (Vt. 1987).

B. Apparent authority: A principal cloaks an agent with apparent authority when she *manifests to a third party* that the agent has authority to act for her in a transaction or transactions. The critical requirement is that the *principal's manifestations be given to the third party* and not, as in the case of express authority or implied authority, to the agent himself. Rest. (2d) § 8, comment a. An agent who acts with apparent authority binds the principal in the same way as an agent who acts with actual authority or implied authority.

1. Manifestations to third person regarding agent's authority ("indicia of authority"): Apparent authority exists when three factors converge: 1) the *principal manifests the authority to a third party either directly*, or *indirectly by means of words or acts* which should reasonably be understood by the principal as causing the third person to believe the agent has authority; 2) the manifestation would lead a *reasonable third person to believe* that the agent has the authority; and 3) the *third person believes* the principal's manifestations.

a. Objective theory in contracts law: Apparent authority is premised on the objective theory of contracts: a person is bound by what she says and does even when she intends something else. Under this theory, for example, a person who makes what appears to be a reasonable offer to sell an object, is bound by his offer even if he is only joking and has no real intention of completing the sale.

Example: P gives A a written power of attorney to sell Blackacre and Whiteacre. P does not know either B or C. A shows the power of attorney to B. A sells Blackacre to B. A then sells Whiteacre to C, without showing him the power of attorney.

Held, A had apparent authority to sell Blackacre to B but not to C. P has ***clothed A with the manifestation of authority*** to sell both Blackacre and Whiteacre. However, P is not bound by A's sale of Whiteacre to C because C was not aware of the manifestation of authority from P to A; he did not see the power of attorney and would have no way of knowing that A was acting for P. Rest. (2d) § 8, Illustration 5.

2. **Removal of apparent authority:** If a principal ***changes his mind*** and does not want third parties to believe that the agent has the authority to act for him, he must remove the ***indicia of authority.*** In the previous example, if P wanted to remove A's apparent authority to sell Blackacre and Whiteacre, he would demand the return and destruction of the power of attorney. Prudence would suggest that he also obtain from A a list of persons who have seen the power and advise each of them of the termination of authority.

3. **Knowledge of third person:** If the third person ***knows*** or ***should reasonably be held to know*** that the agent lacks authority, then apparent authority cannot exist.

Example 1: Photographer (P) entrusted agent (A) with copies of nude photos. P wanted A to sell the photos to a magazine. P gave A authority to negotiate the best deal available, but P retained the right of final approval. P held a press conference and announced A's appointment, but made no statement as to the scope of A's authority. During negotiations with Hustler magazine (T), A repeatedly told T that he lacked authority to conclude a binding contract, and that P retained the right of final approval. Sensing that he was in danger of losing the deal, A signed an agreement with T. However, A explained again that the agreement would not bind P unless P was willing to ratify it. P refused to ratify the agreement, but T printed the photos anyway. P sued T for copyright infringement. T claimed P was bound by the contract signed by A.

Held, P was not bound by the contract A signed, and T violated P's copyright when it printed the photos. A lacked apparent authority to sell the photos to the magazine. T ***should have known*** that the deal required P's final approval. P had done nothing to indicate that A had the final authority to negotiate the deal and *no testimony was presented that proved a contradictory industry custom.* The court observed that T had failed to sustain its *burden of proof* that A possessed apparent authority. *Blackman v. Hustler Magazine, Inc.,* 620 F. Supp. 1501 (D.D.C. 1984).

Example 2: T wanted to buy a division of Consolidated Foods (P). T needed money to buy the division and applied to its lenders for funds. Lenders asked for proof that P had approved the sale. At T's request, P's secretary and general counsel sent T a telegram advising that P's board had approved the sale, although the board had not actually done so. P then refused to sell to T. T sued P to enforce the sale, relying on the argument that P's secretary-counsel had sent the telegram as P's agent (A). T claimed A had apparent authority to make the deal on P's behalf. T argued that P had clothed A with the authority by giving A the title of corporate secretary and general counsel. T asked the judge to instruct the jury that "P is bound by A's acts if P's officers, including A, acted within the powers P gave them, or if T could reasonably have believed they acted within P's authority based upon the officers' and A's titles, positions, actions, and the actions or inactions of P."

Held, the court affirmed a jury verdict for P. T's proposed instruction was defective. It is necessary not only that T *reasonably believe* that A had authority but that T *actually believe* it. The facts suggested that T, an experienced investor, knew that the sale of an entire corporate division would require the approval of a company's board of directors. Moreover, T, not P, had asked A to provide the statement of board approval. See *Chase v. Consolidated Foods Corp.,* 744 F.2d 566 (7th Cir. 1984). See also *Jacobson v. Leonard,* 406 F. Supp. 515 (E.D. Pa. 1976). In *Jacobson,* which involved a professor who was seeking appointment, the court held that the professor had reason to know, based on oral and written communications to him, that his appointment required the approval of the appointment committee, not merely the department chairperson.

Example 3: T wanted to lease some real property to P. T negotiated with A, a real estate agent acting for P. A told T that any lease agreement needed the approval of P, but he also told T that P's approval was a mere formality. When A represented to T that "we have a deal," T incurred expenses in anticipation of the deal. P then refused to lease the property. T sued P for his expenses. T argued that P had given A apparent authority to commit the lease, because P had placed A in a position which entitled T to assume reasonably that A could deliver as promised. P argued that A lacked the apparent authority to close the deal because A told T that the lease was subject to review by P's office.

Held, T could reasonably believe that A had the authority to close the deal because of the position that P had given to A and because A had assured T that a lease would be forthcoming from P. *Mahoney v. Delaware McDonald's Corp.,* 770 F.2d 123 (8th Cir. 1985).

4. **Limits on apparent authority:** An agent's apparent authority may be limited or circumscribed by the principal's manifestations. For example, the agent may have the apparent authority to ***negotiate*** a sale or a lease, but ***not to execute it***. If the third party is aware of these limits, he cannot expect to hold the principal if the agent exceeds the limits. In *Mahoney,* although the agent said that the lease had to be approved, his subsequent statement that the execution of a lease was a mere formality was reasonably believable, given the nature of the deal. The *Mahoney* lease was not so large or consequential as the purchase of an entire corporate division in *Chase.* It was therefore more reasonable for a third party to believe that the agent could commit the deal himself.

5. **Apparent authority not dependent on third person's knowledge of industry custom:** An agent has the apparent authority to perform those acts which are customarily and usually performed by a person occupying the same or a similar position at that time and in that area, with respect to dealings with third parties who know what his position is, even if those third parties do not actually know what the agent's duties are. For example, if a customer believes an agent to be the manager of a business, the agent will have the apparent authority to do all the things managers ordinarily do, even if the customer himself does not know what those duties are. Rest. (2d) § 27, comment d. But see *Jacobson v. Leonard, supra,* in which a third party was found not bound by an agent's apparent authority because he did not have actual or constructive knowledge of the prevailing custom.

6. **Job title creating apparent authority:** Apparent authority can be created by a principal who gives an agent a title or office and then allows him to exercise certain powers in the performance of that office.

Example: Broker (T) assisted P Company in the sale of its business. P was a publicly held corporation with over 400 shareholders. A, who acted as P's vice president/treasurer-comptroller, provided information to T and solicited offers from T. In the name of P, A accepted an offer for the sale and leaseback of the company's entire business. T sought payment of his commission from P upon sale of the business.

Held, P was not bound to pay T's commissions by virtue of A's acceptance of the offer. A lacked actual or apparent authority to accept the offer. A's office did not give him the authority to accept an offer for such an extraordinary transaction as the sale of P's entire business. Although A had had several prior dealings with P, these were too dissimilar in scope and content to suggest apparent authority in A to accept an offer for the sale and leaseback of P's entire business. *Jennings v. Pittsburgh Mercantile Co.,* 202 A.2d 51 (Pa. 1964).

7. **Apparent authority of attorneys:** Attorneys who specialize in a particular area of the law possess the apparent authority to do those things which are routinely done in connection with that specialty. For example, a litigator has apparent authority to control procedural matters incident to litigation. *Reimer v. Davis,* 580 P.2d 81 (Kan. 1978). A lawyer who specializes in estates and wills has the apparent authority to obligate an estate to order and pay for a survey of property owned by the estate. *Bucher & Willis Consulting Eng'rs, Planners & Architects v. Smith,* 643 P.2d 1156, 1159 (Kan. Ct. App. 1982). A tax lawyer has the apparent authority to prepare and file forms and returns with the Internal Revenue Service.

   a. **No authority to settle cases:** On the other hand, most courts hold that attorneys do not have apparent authority to bind their clients to settlements without the client's consultation and approval. *Hopkins v. Holt,* 551 N.E.2d 400, 403 (Ill. App. Ct. 1990). *Compare Fennell v. TLB Kent Co.,* 865 F.2d 498 (2d Cir. 1989). In *Fennell,* the court concluded that a lawyer might be cloaked with apparent authority to settle a case under some circumstances, but that no such authority was given in this case. The client had never manifested to the other side that the attorney had authority to settle. (*See* p. 51, *supra.*)

C. **Liability by estoppel:** A person (P) who would not otherwise be liable or responsible for a transaction done by another for his account, becomes liable to third parties who ***change their position because they believe*** that the transaction was done ***by or for*** him (P). The term ***change of position*** means the payment of money, the expenditure of labor, the incurring of a loss, or the imposition of legal liability. Rest. (2d) § 8B. ***Liability by estoppel may be imposed*** when the principal ***intentionally or carelessly allows*** a third party to ***believe*** the agent is acting for him; or when, ***knowing that a third party believes*** the agent is acting for him and may change his position because of his belief, *fails to take reasonable steps* to notify the third party of the facts.

1. **Compare apparent authority:** Unlike apparent authority, which has its basis in contract (P overtly manifests A's authority), authority by estoppel is based in tort. It operates only to *compensate for losses incurred in reliance* upon the words or conduct of the principal. Damages are different for each: in estoppel cases, damages are based on the loss actually sustained by T; in apparent authority cases, damages are based "on the contract" (i.e., expectation damages). Moreover, in *estoppel cases, the purported principal has no right to enforce a contract entered into by his purported agent;* in cases of apparent authority, the principal is the real party in interest and is able to enforce the contract. It is possible in some cases to find both apparent authority and authority by estoppel.

    Example: P learns that A, who has no actual or apparent authority from P (P did not expressly appoint A or clothe A with the indicia of authority), is negotiating as P's agent with T for the sale of P's goods. P does nothing, although he has the opportunity to tell T that A is not his agent. T pays for the goods. P is not entitled to recover the goods, and he is also liable to T for breach of any customary warranty. Rest. (2d) § 8B, Illustration 1. P would not be able to recover an unpaid balance, if any, from T.

    Note: if T had not actually paid for the goods but had merely contracted with A to buy the goods, P would *not* be *liable by estoppel* because T did not change his position.

2. **Estoppel by silence:** Estoppel by silence may exist when P knows or has reason to know, that T is acting under a misapprehension and P fails to correct the misapprehension though he has a duty to do so.

3. **Estoppel by negligence:** P may be liable when he carelessly allows plaintiff to believe that A is his agent.

    Example: T enters a furniture store and a salesman (A) conducts her through the store. T picks out a number of pieces and pays for them by giving A the cash. The furniture is never delivered and T sues the store.

    Held, the store owner will be liable on the theory of estoppel. T may recover the amount she is out-of-pocket if she can show the company was negligent in allowing A to represent himself as its salesman. *Hoddeson v. Koos Bros., supra.* (Note: The *Hoddeson* case was cited earlier to illustrate the principle of apparent authority.)

4. **Government employees:** Most cases do not apply either apparent authority or authority by estoppel in *cases involving government employees.* The Restatement does not attempt to cover the application of agency principles to the government as principal. Rest. (2d) § 8B, comment f; *Blake Constr. Co. v. United States,* 296 F.2d 393, 396 (D.C. Cir. 1961).

D. **Inherent authority:** When a principal confers the powers of agency on her agent, the principal must expect to be bound not only by what the principal says and does or fails to say or do, but also by inherent powers of the agent which are implicit in the relationship itself. In other words, inherent authority is not derived from the words or manifestations defining the actual authority, or from apparent authority, or from estoppel. It is derived solely from the relation *qua* relation, and exists for the protection of third persons who deal with the agent. It consists of those peripheral powers which a third person would reasonably expect the agent to have under all the circumstances. Rest. (2d) § 8A.

A principal may be bound by the agent's acts under the principles of inherent authority, in the following circumstances:

1. **General agent activity:** In the case of a general agent, inherent authority extends to those acts which are usually performed by similar agents with the same general authority, i.e., acts which "usually accompany or are incidental to transactions which that type of agent is authorized to conduct." Rest. (2d) §§ 161, 161A.

   a. **General and special agents compared:** A general agent is defined as "an agent authorized to conduct a *series of transactions involving a continuity of service*." Rest. (2d) § 3(1). A general agent need not be a high ranking official. Frequency and continuity of service are the keys. On the other hand, A special agent is defined as "an agent authorized to conduct a single transaction or a series of transactions not involving continuity of service," such as a real estate agent. Rest. (2d) § 3(2).

   Example 1: P employs A to hire singers to perform tone test recitals (designed to show the accuracy of the reproductions of P's record). P instructs A to hire a singer only if A can get a dealer to book her recital and pay her. T agrees to sing, believing that she will be paid by P; A does not tell her that she must look to the dealer for payment. T seeks payment from P.

   Held, P is liable to T. The industry custom does not set limits on the authority of general agents to hire singers for pay. The very purpose of delegated authority is to allow third persons to rely on that authority as defined by the traditions of the industry, without constant resort to the principal for additional instructions. *Kidd v. Thomas A. Edison, Inc.,* 239 F. 405 (S.D.N.Y.), *aff'd,* 242 F. 923 (2d Cir. 1917).

Example 2: T employs P, an accounting firm, to advise her on tax matters and prepare her tax returns. These matters are handled by A, one of P's partners. When T sells her business, T asks A to perform additional services, including the collection and disbursement of funds. T pays P monthly for all of A's services. T's husband induces A to give some of T's business funds to him. A also draws a check payable to himself from T's business funds. T sues P for an accounting. P contends that A lacked authority to perform the additional services for T, so P is not liable to T in connection with those services.

Held, T may recover from P on the theory of A's inherent agency if she can show that she reasonably believed A's additional services were an inherent part of P's services. T's beliefs about A's authority are not measured by the profession's own description of normal accounting practices, but ***whether under the circumstances T's belief is reasonable***. *Croisant v. Watrud,* 432 P.2d 799, (Or. 1967).

Note: If, in fact, accountants frequently acted as trustees in the collection and disbursement of funds, there might be implied or apparent authority in A to hold P liable. However, since the fact is that accountants do not normally act as collection trustees, T may recover from P only by arguing and proving that A was exercising powers inherently possessed by accounting partners. ***Trade custom, industry usage or commonly held expectations are important factors in determining whether an agent possesses inherent authority***. *First Fidelity Bank v. Government of Antigua & Barbuda,* 877 F.2d 189 (2d Cir. 1989). In *First Fidelity,* an ambassador was found to lack inherent authority to borrow $250,000 from a commercial bank, purportedly to obtain goods and services for his country's diplomatic mission.

b. **Special agent's inherent authority:** Normally, a special agent has no authority to bind a principal to transactions in excess of his specific authority. Rest. (2d) §§ 161, 161A. However, there are a few *exceptions* to the general rule, and we will focus on the exceptions here. A special agent can bind his principal in the following circumstances:

i. **Agent violates instructions:** Agent names or discloses his principal's identity in violation of the principal's instructions.

ii. **Agent has improper motives:** The agent has *improper purposes or motives.* (This applies whether the agent is a general agent or specific agent.) If the *agent is authorized to perform an act but the agent acts for his own or for improper purposes,* a principal may nevertheless be bound under the doctrine of inherent authority. Rest. (2d) § 165, comment a.

Example: Wife (P) gives husband (A) a broad durable power of attorney. A signs P's name on notes and then pledges jointly owned stock as collateral for the notes. P sues the bank, arguing that A lacks the power to bind her on the notes. P argues that the express power given to A did not include the power to sign her name for the purpose of pursuing a fraudulent scheme for his own self-benefit.

Held, A has both the apparent and the inherent authority to execute the notes so as to bind P. As between the innocent third person and the principal, *the principal had a much better opportunity to police her agent's dishonesty* than did the third person (the bank). Consequently, it is not unfair to place the loss on P, who was in the better position to prevent the loss. *Kahn v. Royal Banks of Mo.,* 790 S.W.2d 503 (Mo. Ct. App. 1990).

iii. **Agent is negligent:** The agent is *negligent* in determining the facts upon which his authority is based.

iv. **Agent misrepresents to third party:** The agent makes *misrepresentations* to the third party.

v. **Undisclosed principal gives agent possession:** An undisclosed principal gives the special agent relevant *goods or documents*. If the special agent is given possession of goods or commercial documents, and authority to deal with them, but disposes of them in an *unauthorized manner*, the agent can nevertheless bind his principal.

Example: P delivers his used car to A, an automobile dealer. P authorizes A to sell the car for $600. A sells it for $300 in cash and $300 in ten monthly installments.

Held, P is bound by the transaction. A had the inherent authority to sell the car for cash and terms. Rest. (2d) § 201, Illustration 1.

c. **Inherent powers derived from apparent authority and estoppel:** The disclosed or partially disclosed principal also may be bound by his special agent's contracts if he has *given his* *agent apparent authority or is estopped to deny the agent's authority.* As we will learn (Chapter 5), a *disclosed principal* is a principal who *reveals both the existence of the agency relationship and his identity*; a *partially disclosed principal* is a principal who reveals the *existence of an agency relationship but not his identity*.

II.   DELEGATION TO SUBAGENTS

A. Delegation: In certain situations, an agent may use her own agents (called "subagents") to perform her duties to her principal. Generally, an agent may not delegate authority to a subagent unless there is *express or implied authorization by the principal.* Delegation from agent to subagent is permitted in the following cases:

1. **Authorization:** The principal *authorized the delegation*;

2. **No personal discretion:** The act is *mechanical or ministerial*;

3. **Custom and usage:** It is the *custom and usage* of the business to delegate a particular function or act; or

4. **Necessity:** Delegation is a *necessary or natural incident* to the work to be done.

5. **Applicable to employment relationships:** These rules relating to delegation may also be applicable in the master-servant relationship, *infra,* p. 89.

B. Chain of agency: When an agent properly authorizes a subagent to do an act, the subagent's actions have the same effect as those of the agent herself in binding the principal, i.e., in essence, a *"chain of agency"* exists from the subagent(s) back to the principal. *Stortroen v. Beneficial Finance Co. of Colorado,* 736 P.2d 391 (Colo. 1987). Because the facts in *Stortroen* involve a number of different parties, you may want to read the next paragraph a couple of times before moving on.

1. **Facts of *Stortroen*:** Beneficial, a real estate agency, gave Olthoff, a real estate broker, an exclusive listing contract to sell Q's house. The contract allowed Olthoff to list the property with any multiple listing service and to accept the assistance of other brokers. If another broker helped make the sale, the contract required Beneficial to pay that broker a commission. Stortroen, in the market for a house, went to Panio, another real estate broker, who had learned about Q's property through a real estate listing book. Stortroen offered to purchase Q's house for $105,000, and Panio communicated this offer to Beneficial. Beneficial made a written counteroffer of $110,000. The counteroffer stated that it could be accepted by the

purchaser's countersignature. Meanwhile, Carelli, another party in the market for a house, offered to purchase Q's house for a higher price than Stortroen. Beneficial left a message for Panio revoking its counteroffer to Stortroen. However, Stortroen had already signed the written counteroffer before Panio picked up the message. Beneficial refused to sell to Stortroen, and Stortroen sued Beneficial. Beneficial argued that Panio was the buyer's (Stortroen's) agent, and that its phone call to Panio should be imputed to Stortroen as principal.

2. **Colorado court disagrees:** The Colorado Supreme Court held instead that Panio was a *subagent* of the seller. The "chain of agency" ran from the seller to the listing agent (Orthoff) to the selling broker (Panio). The court reasoned that since Stortroen had not received independent notice of the revocation before Stortroen accepted the counteroffer, Beneficial's attempted revocation of the counteroffer (which would effectively revoke the subagency) was ineffective. Receipt of notice by Panio was irrelevant since Panio acted as a subagent of the seller rather than the buyer.

3. **Subagency relationship in real estate listing contracts:** A listing contract which authorizes a broker to list property with a multiple listing service creates a subagency with the other members of the multiple listing service. The listing of Q's property with the listing service for Beneficial created an *offer to the subagent* for a unilateral contract which required acceptance by return performance (the subagent's substantial performance in attempting to sell the property) as consideration. When Panio satisfied this requirement by making an offer on behalf of a willing buyer, she was a subagent of the *seller*, not an agent of the buyer.

   a. **Dual agency possible:** The court noted that though it was possible for the buyer and the seller's broker to establish an agency relationship between themselves, it would not find that agency in the absence of written disclosure and consent by all parties, in order to avoid conflicts of interest.

C. **Liability:** Misconduct of a subagent renders the agent, as well as the subagent, liable to the principal. The principal is bound by the acts of the subagent if they are within the limits of the authority delegated to the agent. Rest. (2d) § 428.

1. **Unauthorized delegation to subagent:** If the agent is not authorized to use a subagent, there is no agency between the subagent and the principal. In these cases, the principal is not responsible to third parties for the acts of the subagent. *White v. Consumers Finance Service, Inc.*, 15 A.2d 142 (Pa. 1940).

CHAPTER 5

RELATIONSHIPS BETWEEN AGENT AND THIRD PARTY: CONTRACTS

ChapterScope

The relationship between the agent and a third party in matters of contract will often depend on the extent to which the principal's identity *is disclosed to the third party*. A principal is *disclosed* if the agent reveals the *existence of the agency* relationship and the *identity of the principal*. A principal is *partially disclosed* if the third person knows of the agency relationship *but does not know the identity* of the principal. A principal is *undisclosed* if the other party has *no notice* that the agent is acting for a principal. This chapter covers the rules and exceptions in this area. It also covers the liability of corporations and promoters for pre-incorporation contracts entered into by promoters on behalf of corporations.

I. LIABILITY OF AGENT IN CONTRACT

  A. Disclosed principal: A disclosed principal is one who reveals both the existence of the agency relationship and his identity. An authorized agent who makes a contract with a third person on behalf of his disclosed principal is not liable on the contract unless the agent gives his personal promise to perform. The principal, not the agent, is the real party in interest and the proper party to the contract. *Resnick v. Abner B. Cohen Advertising, Inc.,* 104 A.2d 254 (D.C. Mun. Ct. App. 1954).

    1. Exception — agent's promise to perform: Although an agent for a disclosed principal is not generally liable on the contract to a third person, he will be liable:

      a. Express promise: if he expressly promises to perform; or

      b. By custom: in the custom of the trade or the relation between agent and principal, the third person would ordinarily look to the agent for performance, except when the agent disclaims responsibility to the third person.

      Example: Attorney (A), on his firm's stationery, asked court reporter (T) to "provide us" with the transcript of a hearing in a particular case. A's letter said "we shall be happy to remit the costs." A subsequently sent T the client's (P's) check as a down payment. T recognized P's name. When P refused to pay the balance, T sued A.

      Held, the attorney (A) was liable even though the identity of his client was disclosed to the court reporter (T). There was sufficient evidence from which the trial court could find that *A had agreed to be personally responsible.* The court focused particularly on A's statement, "we shall be happy to remit the costs." In addition, *local custom* entitled the court reporter to look to the attorney for payment. *Ingram v. Lupo,* 726 S.W.2d 791 (Mo. Ct. App. 1987).

Note: If A wanted to avoid liability for these costs, he should have specified that P, and not the law firm, would pay them.

2. **Exception — form of signature:** When the agent signs a contract, her signature *should clearly indicate that she is acting as agent* for the named principal [e.g., A, as agent (or attorney in fact) for P]. If the agent signs in her own name, she becomes a party to the contract and may be held personally liable in case of breach.

   a. **Rationale for signature rule:** This rule is derived from the parol evidence rule: when a writing is intended to be the final and complete understanding of the parties, extrinsic evidence is not admissible to change or modify the writing. Under the rule, the agent cannot later show that he was acting for a principal if he failed to sign as "agent"; that would alter the writing by switching one party to the contract (A) with another (P).

B. **Undisclosed and partially disclosed principals:** If the principal is undisclosed or only partially disclosed (i.e. the third party knows that A is acting as agent but does not know the identity of his principal), the *agent is personally liable* on the contract.

   1. **Third person's knowledge controls disclosure:** Whether a principal is fully or only partially disclosed depends upon the information which the third person knows at the time the contract is formed.

   Example: Arthur Jensen (A), an individual, agent for Arthur Jensen Builders, Inc. (P), a corporation, telephoned an appraisal company (T) and asked T to appraise some homes. A then sent building plans for T to use in making the appraisals. T appraised the homes and sent bills to "Arthur Jensen, Jensen Builders." A had not told T of the existence of the corporation. In past dealings with T, however, A had sent checks of the corporation to T's bookkeeper. The building plans revealed the existence of the corporation.

   Held, checks sent to T's bookkeeper were insufficient notice that a corporate principal of A existed. Also, disclosure of the corporate principal in the building plans was irrelevant. The critical issue was T's knowledge at the time the contract was formed. *Jensen v. Alaska Valuation Serv., Inc.,* 688 P.2d 161 (Alaska 1984).

2. **Undisclosed principal:** If the principal is undisclosed, the agent is ***personally liable on the contract.***

   Example: A manages a hotel for his mother, P, who owns it. A asks T to sell dairy products to the hotel. T does not know that P owns the hotel or that A is her agent. T's bills are paid by check signed "P by A, atty." Later, bills are not paid, and T sues A.

   Held, A is responsible because he was the agent for an undisclosed principal. A did not prove that the signature on the check was brought to the attention of T's officers or employees. Even if it was, the signature did not reveal P's involvement as principal in the transactions; as one example of a non-agency relationship, A may have merely been using funds borrowed from P. *Saco Dairy Co. v. Norton,* 35 A.2d 857 (Me. 1944).

   a. **Different results under different circumstances:** The result in *Saco* would not be tenable in other circumstances, i.e., in a retail store. Typically, a ***retail clerk is not expected to disclose*** to a customer that she is not the proprietor. The limitations of authority and responsibility placed upon retail sales clerks are recognized universally. A customer will be expected to know that he is dealing with a clerk who has only limited authority, and that the clerk will not be responsible personally for defects in merchandise or for other details of the transaction. *Hess v. Kennedy,* 171 N.Y.S. 51 (N.Y. App. Term 1918).

3. **Partially disclosed principal:** If the principal is partially disclosed (i.e., the third party knows that the agent is acting for someone else but does not know the identity of that someone), the ***agent may be held personally liable*** on the contract, unless the third person agrees otherwise. Disclosure by the agent that he is working for someone without full disclosure of the principal's identity, will not ordinarily suffice to cancel the agent's liability. It is ***up to the agent to disclose the identity of his principal;*** otherwise he risks full personal liability on the contract.

   Example: T asks A, an insurance broker, to obtain burglary insurance for a store. A gives T a "binder" (a provisional statement of coverage), and signs it for "London Lloyds." Lloyds itself does not write insurance policies, but its member insurance companies do write individual policies. At the moment the binder is signed, the identity of the member company which will underwrite that policy may be unknown. Before a particular insurance company accepts the coverage, T's store is burglarized. T sues A for the loss under the binder.

   Held, A is personally liable to T. When A signed the binder, T knew that A was acting as the agent for a principal (one of the

Lloyds' member companies) but the particular company had not been determined. Although T and A both contemplated that a principal would be identified at some future time, that fact does not relieve A of liability under the binder. *Ell Dee Clothing Co. v. Marsh,* 160 N.E. 651 (N.Y. 1928).

a. **Discovery of P's identity:** When the third party *learns the identity* of the partially disclosed principal *before contracting* with the agent, the *agent is not liable* on the contract. The principal becomes a disclosed principal even though the principal may not be named in the contract. Rest. (2d) § 149. However, a principal is not disclosed merely because the third person may be able to deduce who he is.

Example: A signed a contract for T to remodel a restaurant called "The Magic Moment." "The Magic Moment" was merely a trade name; the restaurant was owned by Seascape Restaurants, Inc. (P). A signed the contract as "A, The Magic Moment." A claimed that use of the trade name "The Magic Moment" should have put T on notice that Seascape Restaurants, Inc. (P) was the true owner of the restaurant.

Held, A was personally liable on the contract because A failed to give adequate information regarding the identity of P. The use of a trade name is not a sufficient disclosure of identity to bind the principal instead of the agent. *Van D. Costas, Inc. v. Rosenberg,* 432 So. 2d 656 (Fla. Dist. Ct. App. 1983).

b. **Public records:** If the principal's identity can be ascertained from public records, an agent may or may not be liable, depending on the jurisdiction.

   i. **Some courts hold agent liable:** Some courts hold that a principal is not fully disclosed even if the third person could ascertain his identity by resort to public records. See, e.g., *Lumer v. Marone,* 569 N.Y.S.2d 321 (N.Y. App. Term 1990). Although the third person could learn of the principal's identity by checking with the secretary of state and with the county clerk, the court considered that too great a burden. It was the agent's responsibility to disclose his principal's identity; his failure to do so renders him personally liable.

   ii. **Some courts absolve agent:** A few cases, however, take the position that if T can ascertain the principal's identity by resort to the public records, A will be absolved of liability. See, e.g., *Port Ship Serv. v. Norton, Lilly & Co.,* 883 F.2d 23, 24 (5th Cir. 1989), *cert. denied,* 495 U.S. 962 (1990). These cases seem to turn on the custom in a particular industry to require a check of public records in similar transactions. Hynes, p. 438.

C. Agent's warranty of authority: An agent may be personally liable to the third person with whom he contracts if (a) the *agent exceeds the authority given* to him by his principal; or (b) *there is, in fact, no principal* in existence. In either of these situations, the agent breaches his "warranty" to the third party that he has someone's authority to make the contract. Liability is often predicated on the agent's warranty of authority.

1. **Exception when T is on inquiry notice:** In some jurisdictions if T has knowledge which would reasonably instruct her to inquire as to A's authority and has a reasonable opportunity and the means to do so, then T is charged with the resulting knowledge, whether or not A was actually authorized. *Zugsmith v. Mullins,* 344 P.2d 739 (Ariz. 1959).

   Example 1: P's agent, A, leases a farm to T for 12 years. P refuses to accept the terms of the lease because P had not authorized A to execute a lease for that length of time. T sues P for specific performance of the lease. T's suit is dismissed because A lacked authority to enter into a lease with such a long term. T now sues A for damages.

   Held, T may recover damages from A. A induced T to contract with him by his assertion that A was authorized to act as P's agent. A is answerable to T for any damages which T sustained because A overstated his authority; his claim of authority to execute a long-term lease was untrue. T has been damaged even though A may have acted in good faith. *Collen v. Wright,* 8 E. & B. 647 (1857).

   Note: Although the court did not use the word *warranty*, the *Collen* decision was actually premised upon A's warranty of authority to act. This theory of recovery against an agent is accepted by courts *when the third party relies on the warranty* to his detriment.

   Example 2: A, President of P, Inc., negotiated a deal to sell P's charcoal plant and real estate to T. A represented himself as having the authority to enter into the transaction.

   Held, A was personally liable for acting in excess of his authority. Even if A acts in good faith, he will not be excused from liability for breaching his warranty of authority. *Husky Indus., Inc. v. Craig Indus., Inc.,* 618 S.W.2d 458 (Mo. Ct. App. 1981).

2. **How an agent may avoid incurring liability:** An agent may avoid personal liability when he contracts for his principal by the following steps:

a. **Express disclaimer and agreement:** An agent can avoid personal liability by disclaiming it and making sure that the third party understands and agrees to the disclaimer.

b. **Revealing facts and letting third party decide:** Alternatively, if the third party is doubtful whether the agent has authority, the agent can avoid personal liability by laying all the facts on the table concerning his authority and letting the third party decide whether the transaction will proceed without subjecting the agent to liability. *Cousins v. Taylor*, 239 P. 96 (Or. 1925).

3. **Damages:** The agent may be liable both on contract and in tort.

a. **Contract damages:** Contract damages are awarded when the agent breaches his implied warranty of authority even though he acts in good faith. Most courts hold that breach of warranty damages will be measured by the anticipated benefit of the bargain to the third party (expectation damages). Other courts have limited the third party's damage to the compensation necessary to return him to his original position (out-of-pocket damages). *Martha A. Gottfriend, Inc. v. Amster*, 511 So. 2d 595, 598 (Fla. Dist. Ct. App. 1987). In *Gottfriend*, the court suggested that benefit-of-the-bargain damages would be appropriate in cases of fraud or misrepresentation.

b. **Tort damages:** If the agent intentionally misrepresents his authority, she may be liable for the tort of misrepresentation or deceit.

D. **Compensation to agent by third party:** In some cases an agent may have a cause of action for compensation against the third person if agreed to by A and T.

Example: P authorizes A to sell certain land for $10,000, net to P; A is to receive any sum above the selling price as his commission. A agrees to sell the land to T for $10,500. T agrees that A may keep $500 as his commission. A written contract is executed covering the sale at a price of $10,500. Thereafter, T fails to complete the purchase. A sues T for the $500 commission.

Held, A may recover his commission from T because T agreed to pay it. The result is the same whether T made a separate agreement to pay A's commission, or T agreed that A's commission would be paid from the purchase price. A may recover his commission directly from T if T fails to perform the contract. See *Danciger Oil & Ref. Co. v. Wayman*, 37 P.2d 976 (Okla. 1934).

Note: If the contract in *Danciger* had not specified the amount of A's commission, then A would not have had a cause of action to recover it. Generally, an agent cannot maintain an action in his own name on a contract for his principal, because the agent lacks any special interest or property in the subject matter of the contract. The mere right to a portion of the proceeds as compensation is not a sufficient interest to permit the agent to maintain suit. *Scott v. Louisville & N.R. Co.*, 98 S.W.2d 90 (Tenn. 1936).

II.   STATUTORY LIABILITY

A. **Overview:** Statutes in many states impose liability by agents to third parties in certain situations:

1. **Extension of credit:** When credit is extended to the agent personally with the agent's consent;

2. **Lack of good faith:** When the agent executes a contract in his principal's name without believing in good faith that he has authority to do so;

3. **Wrongful act:** When the agent is guilty of some wrongful act (See, for example, Cal. Civ. Code § 2343); or

4. **Negotiable instruments:** In the case of a negotiable instrument, an agent who signs without authority, or without disclosing that he is acting for a principal, renders himself personally liable to anyone taking the instrument in good faith. Rest. (2d) § 324; UCC §§ 3-403, 3-404.

III.   PROMOTERS OF CORPORATIONS AND PRE-INCORPORATION AGREEMENTS

A. **Promoters:** A promoter is the person who causes a corporation to be formed, organized and financed.

1. **Agency:** A promoter is not strictly an agent. There can be no agency without a principal, and, by definition, no principal exists until the corporation is formed. However, agency-like problems can arise as a result of the promoter's activities. The promoter acts, in effect, as the agent for a corporation (principal) to be formed. In this capacity, the *promoter owes a fiduciary duty to:*

   • *the corporation in formation;*

   • *subscribers to its stock;*

   • *potential investors;*

- *other promoters;* and

- *creditors,* in certain situations. See *McCandless v. Furlaud,* 296 U.S. 140 (1935).

2. **Types of contracts:** Several parties may wish to be involved in the formation of a new corporation. The parties will include promoters, prospective shareholders and participants, stock subscribers, stock underwriters, lenders and lawyers. Agreements made in anticipation of the formation of a corporation may take a variety of forms.

- *Agreements between third parties and the promoters*, e.g., typical pre-incorporation agreements;

- *Agreements among promoters* with respect to the formation of the corporation;

- *Agreements among prospective shareholders*;

- *Share subscriptions*;

- *Underwriting agreements*; and

- *Agreements with professionals to render services*, e.g., lawyer and accountants.

3. **Contract liability:** Whether a promoter for a corporation yet to be formed is bound on a contract for the benefit of the corporation which he makes with a third person, turns on ***the terms of the contract and the intention of the parties*** under all the circumstances.

Example 1: A contracts to buy certain goods from T and signs it "XYZ Corp., by A, President." T knows that XYZ Corp. has not yet been formed. The corporation is never formed, and T sues A for breach of contract. A is not liable. If a contract is made by a promoter on behalf of a corporation which is known by the ***other party to be in the process of formation, and he agrees to look only to the corporation*** for payment, the ***promoter is not personally liable*** on the contract. *Quaker Hill, Inc. v. Parr,* 364 P.2d 1056 (Colo. 1961).

Note: If the facts are ambiguous and it is not clear whether the third party is looking only to the corporation-in-formation for payment, the courts tend to hold the promoter liable if the corporation is never formed.

Example 2: Promoter A signed a contract with T as "Edwin A. Boss, agent for a Minnesota corporation to be formed who will be the obligor." T sued A for nonperformance of the contract. A claimed that he disclosed who the corporation was and that the third party agreed to look only to the corporation and not to himself for payment. It was unclear at the time of trial whether the corporation was ever formed. In any event, if it was, it had no assets from which to pay T.

Held, the promoter was liable. The court held that **A would avoid liability only if T specifically agreed to hold someone other than A liable.** A was the **current** obligor when the contract was signed; a declaration that P "will" assume responsibility was insufficient to hold P liable. Moreover, there was no showing that any corporation, formed or not, had agreed to assume responsibility for the contract. *Stanley J. How & Assoc. v. Boss*, 222 F. Supp. 936 (S.D. Iowa 1963).

Example 3: An accounting firm (T) did tax and other work in helping promoter (A) to incorporate a business (P). T sent its bill to P; the bill was not paid. T then addressed the bill to A personally.

Held, the promoter (A) was liable. In the **absence of an agreement to look solely to the corporation for payment, the promoter is personally liable.** The court added that the promoter had the burden of proving an agreement to release him from liability and had failed to meet it. *Coopers & Lybrand v. Fox*, 758 P.2d 683 (Colo. Ct. App. 1988).

Example 4: A represents that he is president of P corporation, and signs an agreement under which P leases from T. However, T does not know that P is a corporation-in-formation which does not yet exist. T sues A personally for rent due under the lease.

Held, T may recover from A. It is presumed that the parties to every contract intend it to be an enforceable obligation. Usually, it may be presumed that an agent intends to bind his principal. In this case A signed the contract in the name of P, which did not exist, so no such inference is possible. A is personally liable for the tort of deceit based on A's misrepresentation concerning the existence of P and of his authority, or for the breach of his warranty as to the existence of a principal and his authority to act as agent. *Hagan v. Asa G. Candler, Inc.*, 5 S.E.2d 739 (Ga. 1939).

Note: The *Hagan* decision can be distinguished from the decision in *Quaker Hill*. In *Hagan*, the promoter did not disclose to T that the corporation he claimed to act for did not yet exist. In *Quaker Hill*, T knew that the corporation did not yet exist but agreed to look to the corporation for payment. The *Hagan* court followed the usual agency rule involving a non-existent principal--the agent is liable when he makes a contract as agent knowing that there is no principal in existence.

    a. Extinguishing promoter's liability: Even after the corporation is formed and *adopts a contract* on which th*e promoter was bound,* the promoter *is not released* from the contract unless the parties so provide, or unless there is a novation. (T agrees that P may be substituted as obligor for A).

    Example: Promoter A contracts with T for the benefit of corporation P, still to be formed. After it is formed, P adopts the contract and T agrees to accept P instead of A as the debtor. P's promise to pay is consideration for T's release of A and acceptance of P as promisor. This is a matter of contract law. The new agreement creates a *novation* in which P is substituted for A with T's agreement.

  4. Other theories: In addition to liability on the basis of the contract with T, a promoter can be liable on the following legal theories:

- *breach of warranty of authority*, as for example, by falsely claiming that the corporation was already in existence;

- *breach of implied warranty of existence of corporation or of authority from the corporation;*

- *breach of promise or warranty to form the corporation;*

- *breach of implied warranty to use best efforts to form the corporation;* or

- *fraud or misrepresentation.*

  5. Effect of theory of liability: The theory on which a promoter is held liable may determine the applicable statute of limitations and the extent of damages. See Hamilton, p. 252.

B. Corporate liability: A corporation is not liable on a contract made by its promoter for its benefit unless it takes some affirmative act to adopt the contract. This *affirmative act may be by express words or by inference from the corporation's acceptance of the contract benefits*. *Chartrand v. Barney's Club,* Inc., 380 F.2d 97 (9th Cir. 1967).

Note: In Example 3 under (C), *supra,* adoption by the corporation would probably not release A unless T consented to exchange the corporate obligation for A's liability.

Example: A, a promoter of P Publishing Co., engages T to solicit advertisements for P prior to its incorporation. The contract is for one year. P is incorporated and discharges T after six months. P never takes formal action through its board of directors to adopt the contract with T. P's stockholders and directors know of T's contract, and P pays T until his discharge. T sues P for breach of contract; P defends on the basis that it was not in existence at the time the contract was made and cannot be bound by acts of its promoters without adoption by the board of directors.

Held, T may recover on his contract from P. Although P is not liable on a contract made by A unless it takes some affirmative action to adopt it, the act of adoption need not be by express action of the board. Adoption may be **inferred** from its actions after incorporation. The court can infer that P adopted the contract by reason of the failure of its stockholders and directors to object, and by P's actions after incorporation. *McArthur v. Times Printing Co.,* 51 N.W. 216 (Minn. 1892).

1. **Comparison of ratification to adoption:** Ratification is an act by which the corporation approves and agrees to be bound by the actions of its agent. Ratification can be accomplished only by an existing principal. It is not possible so long as a corporate principal does not exist. Ratification causes the act of the principal to **relate back** to the **date of the Agent's contract with the third person.** See p. 73, *infra.* On the other hand, a corporation can **adopt** the acts of its Agent even though it was not in existence at the time those acts occurred. Under the theory of adoption, the effective date of the Agent's act is the date upon which the corporation adopts it, and not the date upon which the Agent performed it. This has important ramifications in determining whether the statute of limitations has run.

2. **Liability to promoter on restitution theory:** A corporation is not liable to a promoter for services performed by him before incorporation unless it makes an affirmative promise to pay. However, some courts have held a corporation liable on a quasi-contract or restitution theory even if it did not formally adopt the contract. This problem arises particularly with respect to work done by attorneys retained by the promoters to help in forming the corporation. The court in *David v. Southern Import Wine Co.,* 171 So. 180, 192 (La. Ct. App. 1936), allowed recovery on the theory of unjust enrichment when the corporation accepted the benefits of the promoter's services.

3. **Enforcement by corporation:** A corporation may enforce a contract made by its promoter on its behalf before incorporation, if the promoter is bound and has assigned his rights to the corporation, or if the corporation is intended by the parties to be a third party beneficiary of the contract.

CHAPTER 6

RATIFICATION

ChapterScope

Faced with some act by her agent which may exceed the bounds of authority or reflect an error in communication or interpretation, the principal has *two choices*: either to *reject the act* and face a dispute with the agent and/or the third party, or to *ratify the act* and proceed as though the act had been approved from the start. In this chapter, we will deal with the process of *ratification.* We will touch on the ways in which a principal ratifies, i.e., by words, conduct or silence. We will also study the rules governing ratification, as well as the limitations on the principal's power to ratify.

I. INTRODUCTION

A. Ratification: Under some circumstances, a principal will wish to *affirm the prior acts of agents and purported agents* which did not bind him at the time they were committed. A principal can only affirm acts which *were done or professedly done for his account.* If he does affirm these prior acts, he is said *to ratify them,* and they are given effect as though they were originally authorized by him. Ratification binds the principal to all persons who were or are affected by these acts. as of the date(s) on which the acts were committed (i.e., *ab initio*). Rest. (2d) § 82.

B. Rationale for doctrine: The best explanation for the doctrine of ratification is that it is "needed in the prosecution of business" because it helps to cure "minor defects in an agent's authority, minimizing technical defenses and preventing unnecessary law suits." Rest. (2d) § 82, comment d.

Example: P's unidentified foreman (A) hired T to haul stone. A told T that the work was being done for P. P provided triplicate slips on which T was to enter the weight of each load of stone, as well as other information. P received one copy of each slip. T presented a bill for the work to P. P told T he would pay him if T presented a sworn affidavit. P later refused to pay T. T sued P. P argued he had not ratified A's hiring of T, and that new consideration was needed to support ratification.

Held, P ratified A's hiring of T and was liable to pay T. Agency could not be established by A's statements alone. But the proof that P had furnished the weight slips, together with his affirmance of the work and his commitment to pay T if T supplied an affidavit, were sufficient to constitute ratification. The court added that **"ratification** *does not require a new consideration." Evans v. Ruth,* 195 A. 163 (Pa. Super. Ct. 1937).

II.   THE PRINCIPAL-AGENCY RELATIONSHIP AND RATIFICATION

A. Only disclosed or partially disclosed principal can ratify: Ratification is available only to disclosed or partially disclosed principals; it is not available to an undisclosed principal. Rest. (2d) § 85. If the agent for a partially disclosed principal describes his principal to a third person, only a principal fitting that description can ratify the transaction. Rest. (2d) § 85 comment c. If two or more persons fit that description equally (e.g., have the same name), only the one the agent intends to act for can ratify.

Example 1: A, a merchant, buys goods from T. He tells T that he is acting for "my principal." A later finds a customer, P, who writes to T, affirming the purchase for his account. P has ratified.

Example 2: A, a merchant, buys goods from T. He tells T that he is acting for "a merchant from London". A finds a customer, P, who is a Philadelphia merchant. P writes to T, affirming the transaction. There is no ratification. Rest. (2d) § 85, Illustrations 4 and 5.

B. Ratification possible without principal-agency relationship: A party may ratify the acts of another purporting to act on his behalf even though no principal-agency relationship exists between them.

C. Principal may ratify act outside of agent's authority: Ratification by the principal can occur even when the agent acts outside his authority, as long as he is acting or purports to be acting for the principal. The basis for this rule is the expectation of the third party that when an agent purports to act for a principal, the principal will ratify the agent's acts. Hynes, p. 455.

III.   METHODS OF RATIFICATION

A. By words, conduct, or silence: Ratification can be accomplished by the words or other conduct of the principal indicating his desire to be bound. *Silence can constitute ratification* in circumstances in which the principal has the opportunity to dispute or reject the agent's conduct or authority and fails to do so.

Example 1: Husband (A) and wife (P) are divorced. A tells florist that he and P will pay for the flowers at their son's upcoming wedding. Florist supplies the flowers, then calls P and asks her whether she liked the flowers "that you and your husband ordered". P says that she liked the flowers, but she does not say whether she authorized the purchase. P has ratified the purchase by her silence.

Example 2: A took a tractor to T's shop and authorized T to do major repairs. A did not disclose that P owned the tractor, nor did A state that he was acting on behalf of P. Later, P entered the shop and authorized some minor repairs on the same tractor. T sued P for payment of the major repairs. T claimed that P's conduct in authorizing the minor repairs constituted an affirmance of the major repairs.

Held, P did not ratify the major repairs, and so was not liable to pay for them. The court cited two reasons: (1) A did not purport to act as P's agent when A took the tractor in for repairs; and (2) P's act of paying for the minor repairs while saying nothing about the major repairs did not constitute ratification of the major repairs; T could just as reasonably assume that A would pay for the repairs. Because there was no discussion of P's liability, or of the cost of the major repairs, P's silence was equivocal and gave T no reason to believe that P was willing to pay for the major repairs. *Bruton v. Automatic Welding & Supply Corp.,* 513 P.2d 1122 (Alaska 1973).

1. **Ratification by delay in repudiation:** Even a slight delay in repudiating a transaction may result in ratification when the transaction is executed by an agent who is acting for a disclosed principal. The result may be different if the purported agent was a stranger to the person called upon to ratify. Rest. (2d) § 85, comment d.

B. **Employer's failure to discipline or apologize may constitute ratification:** A third party may wish to argue that an employer is liable for the wrongful acts of an employee because he fails to discipline the employee or to apologize for the employee's conduct. Some courts have held, however, that an employer's failure to discipline an employee, or to apologize for her conduct, will not ordinarily be enough to support a finding of ratification. In determining whether the employer's conduct constitutes ratification, the courts will look to the *seriousness of the employee's conduct and whether there are other plausible explanations for the employer's failure to act.*

Example 1: In *Manning v. Twin Falls Clinic & Hospital, Inc.,* 830 P.2d 1185 (Idaho 1992), the court did not find ratification. It held that an employer may have several reasons for refusing to discipline an employee. The employer may want the employee to learn from her own mistakes, or may reasonably conclude that there are better ways to modify the employee's behavior.

Example 2: In *Pinshaw v. Metropolitan Dist. Comm'n,* 604 N.E.2d 1321 (Mass. App. Ct. 1992), the court did find ratification. It held that the failure of a police officer's employer's to investigate complaints about the policeman's conduct, and its failure to discipline him for his improper conduct, could be considered evidence of ratification.

C. **Ratification by accepting benefits:** A principal can ratify the acts of her agent by ***accepting the benefits*** of the agent's transaction(s), e.g., a contract executed by the agent.

D. **Ratification by litigation:** A principal will be ***deemed to have ratified a transaction*** if she ***institutes a law suit*** (e.g., a law suit to enforce a contract) or ***asserts a defense*** which is based on the transaction (e.g., the defense of breach of contract by the third party.) *Hardware Mut. Casualty Co. v. Lieberman,* 39 F. Supp. 243 (D.N.J. 1941).

E. **Principal's failure to act:** Ratification may also result on the theory of estoppel when the principal fails to act. Rest. (2d) § 103. The principal may be estopped to deny that she has ratified. If a person commits an act for a principal who is incompetent to act, a statement by the principal after he becomes competent that the act was done for him, will operate as an estoppel with respect to third parties who changed their position in reliance on his competence. In other words, ratification by estoppel benefits only those who rely and are misled. Rest. (2d) § 103 comment a.

IV. RATIFICATION — PARTICULAR RULES

A. **Compliance with the equal dignities rule:** If the original act or transaction by the agent requires compliance with the equal dignities rule, then the ratification must comply with the rule as well. See *supra,* p. 3.

Example: Mother died and left her farm to her eight children as tenants in common. One of the eight children, A, orally agreed on behalf of all eight, to sell the property to T. When some of the other children refused to sell, T sued for specific performance. The other children argued that A lacked authority to agree to a sales contract, and that they had never ratified her conduct. They also argued that any ratification of the contract had to be in writing, because an agent's authority to contract to sell land must be in writing.

Held, as to two of the defendants, ratification was ineffective because they were not notified of the agreement; when they became aware of it, one objected and the other refused to sign. As to all the defendants, ratification was inapplicable. The Statute of Frauds requires that an agent conveying an interest in land must be authorized in writing. Therefore, oral ratification was ineffective. *Bradshaw v. McBride,* 649 P.2d 74 (Utah 1982).

1. **Equal dignities rule trumps ratification:** The equal dignities rule trumps ratification. Even where ratification would otherwise be effective, it ***will not be applied if*** the equal dignities rule has not been satisfied. However, some jurisdictions have modified or eliminated the equal dignities rule with respect to ***ratification between agent and principal.*** See *Rakestraw v. Rodrigues,* 500 P.2d 1401 (Cal. 1972).

B. **Effective ratification requires knowledge of facts:** An affirmance becomes a ratification only ***if the principal knows all the relevant facts*** at the time of affirmance. If, however, the principal ***is aware*** that he does not know all the facts and ***indicates a desire to affirm*** nevertheless, his affirmance will constitute a ratification.

Example 1: Union T sued employer P for wages due under its collective bargaining agreement with P. P's agent, A, was an association which had negotiated the contract. P had paid wages under its 1948 contract with T in order to avoid a strike, but refused to continue payments under a similar 1950 contract. P contended that A, the association which negotiated the contract, was not authorized to make either agreement, and that P did not have knowledge of all the material facts needed for ratification.

Held, P was liable to pay wages to T because P had ratified the contracts. P's intentions as to ratification do not control; its conduct does. P cannot operate under the contract by paying wages to prevent a strike, and then disaffirm it. P made payments under the 1948 agreement. This had the legal effect of a ratification by P. It also created apparent authority in A to negotiate the 1950 agreement for P. Even if P did not have full knowledge of all material facts, its past payments to T demonstrated P's ratification of the contract despite its lack of complete knowledge. *Lewis v. Cable,* 107 F. Supp. 196 (W.D. Pa. 1952); Rest. (2d) § 95.

Example 2: Husband (A) signed his name and his wife's (P's) name to promissory notes in favor of T. In a letter P wrote to T, she enclosed a check as payment toward the balance on "our account." She also said, "we will make payments to you to show good faith that we wish to satisfy our debt with you." P subsequently signed a pleading in which she admitted that she and her husband (A) had signed and delivered the promissory notes. In an amended answer, she denied that her signature was on the notes.

Held, wife (P) was sufficiently aware of the terms of the loan agreements to have effectively ratified them. Also, her answer and amended answer were evidence that P knew that her signature was effectively on the notes when she manifested an intent to ratify the agreement. *Southern Or. Prod. Credit Ass'n v. Patridge,* 691 P.2d 135 (Or. Ct. App. 1984).

C. Ratification affects entire contract, not just part: A   principal cannot affirm the agent's conduct in part only.

Example 1: A, a member of P's household, but not P's servant, delivered a load of coal to T, fulfilling an order from T to P. During the course of delivery, A broke a window in T's building. P presented a bill to T for the coal. T argued that by presenting the bill, P had ratified A's conduct in delivering the coal and in breaking the window. P answered that he had not ratified the breaking of the window, but only the delivery of the coal.

Held, P is responsible for the window; the ratification covers the entire transaction. A's activity in breaking the window was interconnected with his delivery of the coal. *Dempsey v. Chambers,* 28 N.E. 279 (Mass. 1891) (opinion by Judge Holmes).

Example 2: A participates in forging P's name on documents to acquire a loan. When P learns of the forgeries, she does not repudiate them. She also accepts the benefit arising from the loan and claims as her own property which secures the loan. P sues A for A's role in forging P's name. P argues that she has not ratified the forgeries.

Held, P ratified the forgeries, thereby relieving A of liability to P. "[R]atification of part of a transaction is deemed to be ratification of the whole transaction." *Rakestraw v. Rodrigues,* 500 P.2d 1401, 1404 (Cal. 1972).

D. Notice not required: Ratification ***does not require notice*** to either the third party or the agent. However, notice is ***useful evidence*** of ratification; without it, ratification may be difficult to prove. Also, if the third party does not receive notice of ratification, as a practical matter, it will be more difficult for the third party to assert his rights.

E. Ratification of agent's tortious conduct: A principal can ratify an agent's tortious conduct.

Example: P, a landlord, employed A to clean and empty a rental house of all furniture, clothes, toys, boxes, and rags, plus anything not part of the original house. A broke a window to the wrong house (T's house) and cleaned and removed all items from that house. A policeman investigating the incident spoke to P, who told him that he had employed A but that A had apparently gone to the wrong address. P assured the police officer that he would get in touch with T, return the furniture and compensate him for any damage. P failed to do so.

Held, P was liable to T for conversion. Even assuming that removal of the items from the wrong house was not within the scope of A's authority, P ratified the conduct when he told the police officer that the incident was a mistake and that he would return the furniture and compensate T for any damages. *Phipps v. Cohn,* 487 N.E.2d 428 (Ill. App. Ct. 1985).

F. Relation-back doctrine: A principal who ratifies a contract or transaction has the same liability as if he had authorized the agent to act for him when the contract or transaction originally occurred. This is known as the ***relation-back doctrine:*** i.e., the obligations of the principal ***relate back*** to the time of the original act. This principle has important ramifications in determining whether the statute of limitations has run.

Example: Without authority, A enters into a contract purportedly on behalf of P on January 1, 1991. The statute of limitations is six years. P ratifies the contract on February 1, 1992.

Held, the statute of limitations expires on January 1, 1997, six years from the date upon which A entered into the transaction. P's ratification relates back to January 1, 1991.

1. Rights of innocent third parties: The doctrine of *"relation back"* will not be allowed to defeat the rights of innocent third persons who have acted in the interim between transaction and ratification.

Example: Without authority, but purporting to be acting on behalf of P, A enters into a contract with T to sell P's land and records the contract. P's creditor subsequently attaches the land and records the attachment. P then affirms the contract executed by A and T. The rights of P's creditor are superior to T's. P is subject to liability on A's contract with T. Rest. (2d) § 101, comment c, Illustration 2.

2. Ratification after deadlines: If an act has to be performed by a certain date in order to create rights against a third party, an affirmance after that date is not effective against the third party.

Example: A rule requires that a complaint be filed no later than September 1. Principal's attorney, without authority, files the complaint on August 31. Principal learns of the filing and affirms it on September 2. The ratification is not timely. Rest. (2d) § 90.

V.   LIMITATIONS ON POWER TO RATIFY

A. **Material change in circumstances:** Ratification will not be effective if circumstances have changed materially between the time of the agent's transaction and the date upon which the principal ratifies.

Example: Without authority, but purporting to act on behalf of P, A contracts to sell P's house to T. The next day P's house burns down. P hastily ratifies the contract.

Held, T can elect to avoid liability because the situation has materially changed. It would be inequitable to require him to perform the contract by reason of P's ratification. Rest. (2d) § 89, Illustration 1.

B. **T withdraws before ratification:** To constitute an effective ratification, the affirmance must take place before the third party manifests his withdrawal from the transaction either to the agent or to the principal, and before the offer or agreement has terminated or been discharged. Rest. (2d) § 88.

Example: Purporting to act for P but without authority to do so, A enters into a contract with T on P's behalf. T discovers that A is not authorized and withdraws from the transaction. P then affirms the transaction.

Held, the affirmance does not constitute a ratification because T withdrew before P affirmed the transaction. Rest. (2d) § 88, comment a, Illustration 1.

C. **Transaction illegal:** A principal can affirm a transaction only if it is lawful at the time of affirmance. If a transaction was lawful at the time the purported agent entered into the contract but became unlawful thereafter, the principal may still be able to affirm it, but only if it does not violate public policy.

D. **Ratification requires legal capacity:** A principal can affirm a transaction only if he has legal capacity at the time of the affirmance. (See *supra,* p. 76.)

E. **Pre-incorporation agreements — adoption distinguished:** In order for ratification to be effective, the principal ***must have been in existence*** when the act or transaction occurred. Thus, an act done on behalf of a corporation not yet in existence cannot be ratified. However, when the corporation does come into existence, a pre-incorporation agreement may be ***adopted*** by the corporation. *McArthur v. Times Printing Co., supra,* p. 71. Unlike ratification, adoption has no retroactive effect. (See *supra,* p. 72.)

Note: If neither ratification nor adoption applies, the principal may still be liable under other theories, such as novation and assignment.

CHAPTER 7

RIGHTS AND LIABILITIES OF PARTIALLY DISCLOSED AND UNDISCLOSED PRINCIPALS

ChapterScope _____

As we have seen, principals generally fall into one of three categories: disclosed, partially disclosed, or undisclosed. In this chapter, we will explore in greater detail the rights and duties of each category. Before we do, it will be helpful to review the definition of each category:

■ **Disclosed principal:** The third party knows that the agent is acting for a principal whose identity is fully disclosed;

■ **Partially disclosed principal:** The third party knows that the agent is acting, or may be acting, for a principal, but does not know the identity of the principal;

■ **Undisclosed principal:** The third party does not know that any agency relationship exists, and assumes that the agent is acting on his own behalf.

I. GENERALLY

A. General rule: Generally, both undisclosed and partially disclosed principals have the same rights and liabilities on contracts made by their agents as disclosed principals.

1. **Personal liability of agent:** The agent for an undisclosed or partially disclosed principal *incurs personal liability* when he contracts with a third person. (See p. 64, *supra.*)

2. **Election of parties:** If both the principal and the agent may be held liable on a contract, the third person must *elect* which of the two to hold liable. Under the majority rule, he may not obtain judgments against both. (See p. 85, *infra.*)

3. **Examples applying rules:** The following examples will help the student to understand the different treatment of the three categories of principal.

   Example 1 (no principal exists): A contracts with T in his own name and for his own account—only A is liable on, and can enforce, the contract. There is no principal-agency relationship.

   Example 2 (undisclosed principal): A contracts with T on behalf of P, but neither the agency nor the principal is disclosed to T—either A or P, but not both, may be held liable. When T discovers that A was acting for P, he may elect which one to hold to the contract.

Example 3 (partially disclosed principal): A contracts with T on behalf of P after he discloses that he is acting as agent but without disclosing P's identity—again, either A or P, but not both, may be held liable. When T discovers P's identity, he may elect which one to hold.

Example 4 (disclosed principal): A contracts with T on behalf of P after disclosing both the agency and P's identity—only P may be held liable to T.

II.   UNDISCLOSED PRINCIPAL — RIGHTS AND LIABILITIES OF THE PARTIES

A. Definition: A principal is *"undisclosed"* if the third party has no notice that the agent is acting for a principal. Rest. (2d) § 4(3).

B. General rule: The *undisclosed principal* is liable on, and may enforce, any contract, oral or written, made on his behalf by his agent. (But see the limitations imposed by the *equal dignities rule,* pp. 3 and 76, *supra.*)

Example 1: P wants to buy some asphalt blocks from T. He does not think T will sell them to him personally because P and T are business competitors. P gives A money with which to buy the blocks from T. A buys the asphalt blocks and delivers them to P. The blocks are defective and P sues T for breach of warranty. T argues that he would not have sold the blocks to P if he had known P's identity at the time of the sale.

   Held, P may recover. When an agent contracts in his own name for an undisclosed principal, **both the agent and the undisclosed principal are liable on the contract and may enforce the contract.** It should be immaterial to T whether the action against him is brought by A or P. T intended to contract with A, but A could have assigned the contract to P. There was no misrepresentation by A. *Kelly Asphalt Block Co. v. Barber Asphalt Paving Co.,* 105 N.E. 88 (N.Y. 1914).

Note: Although T did not know that P was an undisclosed principal, there was no misrepresentation by A. Further, T did not rely on any consideration personal to A (e.g., A's credit). However, if Y had asked A whether he was acting as agent for someone and A had denied the agency or had misrepresented the identity of his principal, many courts would permit T to rescind the sale for fraud or mistake. *Casteel v. King,* 269 P.2d 529 (Or. 1954). In *Casteel,* specific performance was denied because P's conduct in tricking T into selling property to A constituted unclean hands.

Example 2 (negotiable instruments): An undisclosed principal is bound upon negotiable instruments executed by the agent for the principal, whether or not the principal is identified in the instrument. UCC § 3-402 (1990).

C. **Exceptions to rule:** In certain situations, an undisclosed principal is not liable on a contract.

1. **Sealed instruments:** Only the person whose seal appears on a sealed instrument may be held liable on the instrument. An undisclosed principal is not liable on a contract under seal even if the seal is not required by state law. *McMullen v. McMullen,* 145 So. 2d 568 (Fla. Dist. Ct. App. 1962). Similarly, the third party is not liable to an undisclosed principal when the contract is under seal. Rest. (2d) § 303.

2. **If third party would be prejudiced or disadvantaged:** An undisclosed principal cannot enforce a contract if the third party believed she was contracting with the agent only and will be prejudiced by being forced to deal with the principal. An undisclosed principal cannot enforce the contract if the third party will be disadvantaged or prejudiced, as for example, if the third party has relied on the personal credit or integrity of the agent.

   Example: P authorizes A to sell P's land to T by a warranty deed, but directs A not to disclose the agency to T. A contracts with T to give T a warranty deed to the land. T believes that A is the owner and refuses to accept title from P. P sues T for breach of the contract to buy the land. T's defense to P's suit is that the contract calls for a warranty deed signed by A, not one signed by P.

   Held, the defense is valid. The warranty of a grantor on a deed involves his personal integrity and his financial capacity to make the title to the property good in any event. Having contracted for a warranty by A, T cannot be compelled to accept a warranty from P, a person with whom he did not contract and in whom he lacks confidence. *Birmingham Matinee Club v. McCarty,* 44 So. 642 (Ala. 1907). (See *Kelly Asphalt Block Co. v. Barber Asphalt Paving Co., supra.*)

3. **Third party must not lose a right or a defense:** The third party may not be subjected to any greater liability to the undisclosed principal than to the agent. In a suit by the principal against the third party, the third party retains all the rights or defenses he would have against the agent.

Example: A buys securities from T for an undisclosed P. T's sale to A is valid because A is a broker, but a similar sale to P would violate state securities laws because P is a nonbroker who resides in a state in which the securities have not been qualified for sale. Subsequently, P sues to rescind the sale because it is prohibited under the state's blue sky laws.

Held, P may not rescind. The rights of P depend on the rights of A. Since the sale to A was lawful, and A would not be entitled to rescind, P may not rescind even though a sale to P would have been unlawful. *Howell v. First of Boston Int'l Corp.,* 34 N.E.2d 633 (Mass. 1941).

4. **When contract precludes existence of undisclosed principal:** If A's contract with T specifically establishes T's intent to treat A as the sole contracting party, or if it specifically precludes the possibility of a particular P or of any undisclosed P, then no one but A may enforce the agreement. See Rest. (2d) §§ 189, 303. See also *Arnold's of Miss. v. Clancy* 171 So. 2d 152, 154 (Miss. 1965). In *Arnold,* a clause in a lease which prohibited subleasing was held to preclude assignment to an undisclosed principal.

5. **Parol evidence rule:** The parol evidence rule will not prevent the parties to a written agreement from presenting evidence of the existence of a previously undisclosed or partially disclosed principal. The theory is that in these circumstances, parol evidence does not contradict the terms of a contract; it merely explains that an additional party (the principal), may also be liable. Of course, as discussed above, if a contract specifically precludes the existence of a principal and commits the agent only, parol evidence is not permitted to contradict the terms of the contract.

III. PARTIALLY DISCLOSED PRINCIPAL — RIGHTS AND LIABILITIES OF THE PARTIES

A. **Definition:** A principal is *partially disclosed* when the third party dealing with the agent has notice that the agent is acting, or may be acting, for a principal, but does not know the identity of the principal. (See **ChapterScope**, p. 81 *supra.*) Rest. (2d) § 4(2).

B. **General rule:** The rights and obligations of a partially disclosed principal are essentially the same as those of an undisclosed principal. (See p. 82, *supra.*)

IV. RIGHTS OF THIRD PERSONS — DOCTRINE OF ELECTION

A. **Doctrine of election:** When a third person contracts with an agent *who is acting for either an undisclosed or a partially disclosed principal* and later discovers both the existence of the agency relationship and the identity of the principal, the third person may enforce the contract *against the agent or against the principal, at his election*, but not against both. This is known as the doctrine of election.

1. **Majority view — only one judgment per contract:** The third person *may sue* both the agent and the principal, but she *may enter judgment only against one* of them. After suit is filed but before judgment is rendered, the third person must decide whether to enter judgment against the principal or the agent; she cannot obtain judgment against both. Rest. (2d) §§210, 210A, 337. The courts reason that the third person's right to sue the principal is a windfall—she never expected to be able to choose between the agent and the principal. Therefore, she should be forced to pursue her remedies against one or the other, but not both. (See p. 81, *supra*.)

   a. **Agency disputed:** If the existence of an agency is in dispute, no election is required by the third party until that issue is resolved. If P and A dispute the alleged agency relationship, a default judgment by T against A will not preclude a suit by T against P. T is not required to make an election before a determination is made as to the existence of the agency. *North Carolina Lumber Co. v. Spear Motor Co.*, 135 S.E. 115 (N.C. 1926).

   b. **Limitation on majority rule:** Obviously, the third party cannot be required to make an election until he knows *the identity of the principal.* If the third person does not learn the identity of the principal before she enters judgment, the judgment, if unsatisfied, will not bar a subsequent action against the principal. Rest. (2d) § 210.

   Example: A contracts with T on behalf of P without disclosing the agency. T sues A for breach of contract and enters judgment against A, but collects nothing. Then T discovers that A made the contract for the benefit of P. T now sues P for breach of contract. P's defense is T's judgment against A.

   Held, the defense is not valid. T can maintain the suit against P. The doctrine of election does not apply unless T knows the identities of both P and A. He can make no choice until he knew P's identity. Hence, T can sue P despite T's unsatisfied judgment against A, as long as T did not know P's identity when

T entered judgment against A. *Old Ben Coal Co. v. Universal Coal Co.,* 227 N.W. 210 (Mich. 1929).

c. Minority view — two judgments but only one satisfaction: Under the minority view, the third party may proceed to judgment against both the principal and the agent; he need not elect his remedies until one or the other satisfies his claims in full. The ***third party may recover judgments against both,*** but he may have only one satisfaction, i.e., he may collect the full amount only once.

i. Minority rule preferred: The minority rule is considered the better rule; there is no reason to prevent the third party from collecting from either the agent or the principal. *Grinder v. Bryans Road Bldg. & Supply Co.,* 432 A.2d 453 (Md. App. Ct. 1981).

Query: Under the minority rule, are the agent and principal jointly and severally liable, or are they liable only in the alternative? In *Old Ben Coal, supra,* the Michigan court held that they were liable in the alternative. The third party was able to sue both and recover judgment against both, but he could collect only from one.

d. English rule: Under the English rule, a judgment against the agent destroys any claim against the principal. This rule is not based on the theory of election of remedies. It is based on the theory of merger—the cause of action against the principal is merged in the judgment against the agent.

V. PAYMENT AND SET-OFF

What happens when an agent fails to turn over to the third party a payment made to him by an undisclosed principal and intended for the third party?

A. Majority rule—undisclosed principal does not have to pay twice: An undisclosed principal is not liable on a contract which his agent has made for him with a third person, if the principal pays or otherwise settles with the agent in good faith.

Example: P authorizes A to buy nylon yarn for P. P puts money in an account for A to use in paying T, but instructs A not to disclose the agency relationship. A buys nylon from T and gives it to P, but A overdraws the account for his own use. T is not paid. T learns of P and sues him.

Held, P is not liable. P paid A for the goods in advance. The majority of American decisions hold that a good faith payment or settlement by an undisclosed principal to his agent entitles the principal to a ***complete defense*** even against a third person who later discovers the principal's existence, and even if that person can establish that the agent acted within the scope of his authority and that the principal has benefited. *Senor v. Bangor Mills,* 211 F.2d 685, 689 (3d Cir. 1954).

1. **Minority rule—undisclosed principal may have to pay twice:** Under the minority view, an undisclosed principal must pay the third party, even if the principal has already given the agent the money with which to pay the third party.

    a. **Rationale for minority view:** According to the minority view, the principal is the person who initiates the transaction and enjoys the benefits of the agent's conduct. He is also in a better position to prevent the agent's misconduct than an innocent third party. Therefore, he should bear the burden of the agent's misconduct, rather than the third party. Under this view, the principal's settlement with the agent will not ordinarily relieve him of liability unless he does so in reasonable reliance on the conduct of the third person.

    b. **Exception to minority view:** If the third party indicates by his conduct that the agent has paid him and the principal reasonably relies on these indications and pays the agent in the belief that he is reimbursing him, the principal will not be liable to the third party, unless the principal's payment to the agent was induced by the agent's misrepresentations. Rest. (2d) § 208.

B. **Payments by third person to agent:** If the third person pays the agent before he learns of the undisclosed principal's existence, the principal cannot then collect from the third party. Rest. (2d) § 307 comment a, Illustration 1. This is a variation on the rule, *supra,* which precludes an undisclosed principal from enforcing a contract if the third party will be prejudiced or adversely affected.

C. **Third party's right to set off payments made to agent from amount due to principal:**

1. **Undisclosed principal:** The third party ***can set off against*** any amount owed to an undisclosed principal any sums the third party has already paid to the agent before learning of the principal's existence (as well as any other related claims by the third party against the agent), if the principal instructed the agent not to reveal the agency relationship.

2. **Disclosed or partially disclosed principal:** On the other hand, if the third party knew there was a principal (but necessarily not

the identity of the principal), then the third party ***cannot set off against*** the amount she owes the principal, any payments or claims against the agent. In *Branham v. Fullmer,* 181 N.W.2d 36 (Mich. Ct. App. 1970), the court held that when the third person has reason to know, or was on inquiry notice of, the existence of an agency relationship, he cannot set off claims he has against the agent to reduce the amount that he owes the principal.

a. **Exception—principal induces the third party to extend credit to the agent:** If the principal has entrusted the agent with his chattels in connection with the agency, or has otherwise caused the third person to extend credit to the agent, the third party can set off against amounts due to the principal, any amounts paid to the agent. Rest. (2d) § 306.

Chapter 8

PRINCIPAL'S LIABILITY FOR TORTS OF AN AGENT

ChapterScope

So far in this book, we have dealt with the basic nature of the agency-principal relationship and with the rights and liabilities of principal, agent and third party in the context of contracts and commercial transactions. In this chapter, we will discuss the consequences to the parties of the negligence and the intentional torts of the agent. A principal who exercises, or has the right to exercise detailed control over his agent is called a master or employer. An employer can be liable for the negligence, and, in some circumstances, the intentional torts, of his agent, even when the principal is not himself at fault. We will discuss the employer's liability for the negligent and intentional torts of his employees, the element of vicarious liability in partnerships and joint enterprises, the family car doctrine, the principal's liability for the acts of independent contractors, the borrowed servant doctrine, and the liability of a principal for the misrepresentations of his agent.

I. GENERAL RULES

A. Respondeat superior: Under many circumstances, a principal can be *liable vicariously for her agent's tort,* even when she herself is without fault. This is known as the *doctrine of respondeat superior.*

B. Master-servant relationship: The principal-agent relationship is a consensual relationship in which the agent acts on behalf of the principal and subject to the principal's control. The master-servant relationship requires that *the master (employer) exercise, or have the right to exercise, detailed control over the physical actions of the servant (employee).*

C. General rule: In the field of agency, one may be liable without fault for the acts of another *if:*

- *a master-servant relationship exists;* and

- the servant acts *within the scope of the servant's employment.*

In determining whether the servant is acting within the scope of his employment, we look at:

1. **Time and space limits:** whether the servant is substantially within the time and space limitations set forth by his master; and

2. **The master's interests:** whether the servant is furthering the master's interest or business and is not on a frolic of his own.

Example: Policeman, on patrol for X City, saw plaintiff at various places during his patrol. At one place, he encountered plaintiff and his son, who was drunk. Plaintiff told him they did not need assistance. In response to a radio operator's message that there were two cars blocking an intersection, policeman drove just outside the X City limits to investigate. Plaintiff, who was in one of the cars, told policeman that he would "whip his ass" if policeman did not return to X City. Policeman left, but then returned to get plaintiff's license for his incident report. After an exchange of words, policeman struck plaintiff, allegedly in self defense. Plaintiff sued X City as the policeman's employer. The city argued it wasn't liable because the policeman's act occurred outside the city limits and was not within the scope of his employment.

Held, the city was vicariously liable for the policeman's activities because the policeman was acting within the scope of his employment. Prior to the incident in question, there was no bad blood between the policeman and the plaintiff. All of the policeman's contacts with the plaintiff arose as a result of the policeman's performance of his duties. The radio operator instructed him to go to the intersection where the incident occurred. Therefore, the policeman's ***tortious conduct was so closely connected in time, place and causation to his employment duties that the risk of harm was attributable to his employer's business.*** *Lamkin v. Brooks,* 498 So. 2d 1068 (La. 1986).

   a. **Employee remains liable:** The employee is ***not relieved of liability*** simply because the employer can be held vicariously liable. If the injured party recovers from the employer for his injury, the employer has a cause of action against the employee for reimbursement (indemnification) of the amount paid by him. (See p. 94, *infra*.)

3. **Master may be liable for servant's intentional physical torts:** If the master can reasonably anticipate that her servant will commit an intentional tort, she may be held liable.

Example: A bouncer in a bar throws a customer out forcibly and injures him. Because bouncers often need to use force to expel unruly and inebriated customers, the owner of the bar can reasonably expect to be liable for the customer's injuries. On the other hand, if the bouncer takes out a pistol and shoots the customer, the owner will probably not be bound; he cannot reasonably anticipate this conduct by the bouncer; the bouncer is acting outside the scope of his employment.

4. **Application to partnerships and joint ventures:** Since, as we shall see, the rules of agency apply to partnerships, a partner may also be held vicariously liable for the torts of partnership employees or of her partners. So, too, may participants in a joint enterprise be held vicariously liable for the torts of the other joint venturers and their employees. Similarly, corporations or limited liability companies may be held vicariously liable for the torts of their employees.

5. **Application to owners of family cars:** In some states, the owner of a family car can also be liable for the negligence of family members who drive the car. (See p. 107, *infra.*)

6. **Independent contractor exception:** A principal will often be able to avoid tort liability if the person performing services can be classified as an independent contractor rather than an employee or servant. Because the principal typically does not control the details of the independent contractor's work, it would be unreasonable to impute the torts of the independent contractor to him.

   Example: E hires Ace Lawn Mowing Service to mow her lawn once a week. Ace supplies its own equipment and mows the lawn any time it wants. Ace will probably be viewed as an independent contractor and E will not be liable to a passerby who is injured by a stone thrown by Ace's lawn mower.

D. **The borrowed servant doctrine:** If a master has *loaned his servant to a special employer who has a greater opportunity to control the servant's work* than does the master, he will not be liable for those torts of the servant which are committed during the performance of services for the special employer. This is known as the borrowed servant doctrine. (See, p. 95, *infra.*)

II. MASTER'S LIABILITY FOR SERVANT'S NEGLIGENCE

A. **Doctrine of *respondeat superior*:** If a servant (employee) commits a tort within the scope of employment, the master (employer) will be held vicariously liable, under the doctrine of *respondeat superior* (let the master respond), *supra*.

   1. **Rationales supporting doctrine :** Several rationales support the doctrine of *respondeat superior*:

      a. **Entrepreneur theory:** Because the employer enjoys the benefits of the business and of the employee's labors, and because he controls the employee's actions, he should be responsible for the employee's tort as part of the cost of doing business.

b. "Deep pocket" theory: The employer is more financially able than the servant to assume the responsibility for the injury. This theory is flawed: masters who lack deep pockets are nonetheless liable, and masters with deep pockets are not liable if the servant acts outside the scope of employment.

c. "Economic efficiency" theory: Economic efficiency is defined as the exploitation of resources in such a way as to maximize value. It assumes that laws that help maximize value are good for society. This theory would hold that if X has a contract with A to sell A widgets for $1.00 and B is willing to pay him $10, contract law should allow or even encourage X to break the contract and to sell the widgets to B. Although X will be required to pay damages to A, there is a net gain to society as a whole.

   i. Application to *respondeat superior*: Making   masters vicariously liable for their servants' torts is economically efficient. If servants had to pay for their own torts, they would refuse to work at risky jobs. And injured parties would have to pay for their own injuries. By making masters liable, the enterprise goes forward, jobs are created, third parties are reimbursed for their injuries, and the enterprise pays for these societal benefits and still, hopefully, makes a profit. Also, because the master is able to control the servant's work, the master can take steps to avoid the loss. He is likely to do this if it costs less to take the safety steps than to pay liability insurance premiums or to reimburse injured parties. Masters can buy insurance more cheaply than their employees or innocent third parties, because they can limit the coverage to suit the risks of the enterprise. *See* Sykes, *The Economics of Vicarious Liability*, 93 YALE L. J. 1231 (1984).

2. Employer is liable under *respondeat superior* only if she controls or has the right to control the physical movements of her employee: The master-servant relationship is a subset of the principal-agency relationship. Thus, all servants are agents but not all agents are servants. For a master-servant relationship to exist, the employer must control, or at least have the right to control, the physical movements of the employee. If the principal cannot control the agent and cannot economically take the steps required to prevent a tort, she should not be held liable when the tort occurs.

Example: P employs A to sell washing machines. A gets a commission on sales and pays his own expenses. A employs other salesmen and gets a commission on their sales. A is not required to follow any particular rules in selling washing machines, but A must use P's contacts. While A is driving home with another salesman, A negligently collides with T's automobile. T sues P and A for damages.

Held, A is liable, but P is not. A is an agent but not a servant, and therefore, P is not liable for A's negligence. The right to control is the most important test. In the present case, P had little or no control over A's activities. By contrast, a master is responsible for the acts of a servant within the scope of the servant's employment if the master controls the servant's acts. *Stockwell v. Morris,* 22 P.2d 189 (Wyo. 1933).

Note: Some courts, on facts similar to the *Stockwell* case, would hold that A was a servant, making P liable for A's negligence. *Sinclair v. Perma-Maid Co.,* 26 A.2d 924 (Pa. 1942).

3. **Control creates liability even without employee relationship.** Liability can exist so long as the worker is working on behalf of the master and his physical actions are subject to the detailed control of the master, even when no true employment exists and the worker is unpaid.

Example: P washed his car with the help of his 16 year old nephew, A. A was an unpaid volunteer. They obtained water by the pailful from a faucet on the outside of P's house. P asked A to get more water and A did so. A spilled water on the sidewalk and the water froze. T slipped on the ice and was injured. T sued P for A's negligence on the theory of *respondeat superior.*

Held, P was liable, because the trial court could find that A was P's servant. *Heims v. Hanke,* 93 N.W.2d 455 (Wis. 1958).

4. **Servant by estoppel:** Even when a person is not his servant, a principal may be estopped to deny the servant relationship if she allows that person to look like her servant and a third person relies to his detriment.

Example: A was a motel franchisee of P. A used P's trade name and trademark. These appeared on numerous items at the motel. P engaged in a national advertising campaign which did not distinguish between A and P. T was familiar with the national advertising. T used P's directory to make a reservation to stay at A. While at A, T was assaulted. T sued P for A's poor security. P defended, claiming that A motel was not P's agent.

Held, although there was no actual principal-agency relationship, the jury should be allowed to decide whether P should be estopped from denying the relationship, because P let third parties believe A was P's agent. *Crinkley v. Holiday Inns, Inc.,* 844 F.2d 156 (4th Cir. 1988).

5. **Employer may be sued both separately and jointly:** The injured third party may sue the master directly based on ***respondeat superior.*** Or, the master and servant may be joined in the same suit. If the master pays a judgment, she may obtain indemnification from the servant because the servant is primarily liable for the tort. *See infra,* p. 101.

Note: If the master is not liable under the doctrine of ***respondeat superior*** for the servant's act, she may still be liable for her own negligence in ***hiring*** or ***retaining*** the servant.

a. **Intermediate supervisors:** The liability of the the owner/employer and of the the negligent employee to the injured person, does not carry over to the manager or intermediate supervisor of the employer. The supervisor is not liable unless his own negligence caused or contributed to the injury.

Example: Master (M) employs a servant (S1) to manage his lumber business. M also employs S2 and S3. S3 is killed at work through S2's negligence. At the time, M is with a customer and not present at the accident. W, S3's widow, brings suit against M and S1.

Held, W may recover from M, but not from S1, the manager. An intermediate supervisor should be liable only if his personal negligence caused or partly caused the injury. Any other rule would render the responsibility of a manager so onerous that few persons would accept his position. For this reason, the law limits ***respondeat superior*** liability to the negligent employee and the employer. *Brown & Sons Lumber Co. v. Sessler,* 163 S.W. 812 (Tenn. 1914).

6. **Punitive damages:**

a. **Majority view:** An injured plaintiff will often seek punitive damages from the employer in instances of employee negligence. Most courts allow a third party to collect punitive damages from an employer only if the employer himself is at fault. Several factors are used to assess the masters' fault:

i. **Authorization:** The master authorized the act and the way in which it should be done;

ii. **Recklessness in hiring/retention:** The agent was unfit for the job and the master was reckless in employing or retaining him;

iii. **Within scope of management position:** The agent was employed in a managerial capacity and was acting in the scope of his employment; or

iv. Ratification: The master or his managerial agent ratified or approved the act. Rest. (2d) of Torts § 909; Rest. (2d) of Agency § 217C.

Example: T was injured and T's son was killed by a truck negligently driven by M's employee, S. S was drunk at the time and had previously been convicted of drunk driving. M failed to find this previous conviction. S and other employee drivers sometimes reported to work drunk. S openly consumed alcohol while at work and periodically took alcohol with him when he made deliveries. Beer cans were frequently left in the truck. There was evidence that M's management either knew of these practices or could easily have discovered them. M's managers occasionally participated in drinking on the job. T sought to collect punitive damages from M.

Held, summary judgment for M was improper. A jury must decide whether to award punitive damages against M. The jury could have concluded that M authorized the drunk driving, or that S was unfit and M was reckless in employing or retaining him. *Johnson v. Rogers,* 763 P.2d 771 (Utah 1988).

b. Minority views: A few courts subject employers to punitive damages vicariously, i.e., they are liable without their own fault if the acts of the employee call for punitive damages.

B. Scope of employment: The general rule is that in order to subject a master to vicarious liable for her servant's torts, the *servant must be operating within the scope of his employment.* Otherwise, it would be cost-prohibitive for the master to enforce safe employee behavior. Whether a servant is acting within the scope of employment is ordinarily a question of fact for the jury. *Pyne v. Witmer,* 543 N.E.2d 1304 (Ill. 1989).

1. Factors to consider: In assessing whether to apply vicarious liability in a particular case, several factors must be considered:

- whether the servant was performing the *kind of work for which he was hired*;

- whether the servant was within the *space and time limitations* of her employment;

- whether the servant was *serving the master's purpose*;

- if force is intentionally used by the servant against another, whether the master could reasonably *expect the force*;

- whether the servant was using the ***tools or materials of the master***;

- whether the servant's act could be reasonably anticipated by the master in light of ***their past history***;

- whether the act is one ordinarily performed by ***servants similarly employed***;

- whether the ***same act has been entrusted*** to other servants;

- whether the act is ***similar to other acts previously authorized*** by the master;

- whether the act ***violates a criminal statute***.

a. **Whether the servant was performing the kind of work for which she was hired:** If the employee was doing the job she was hired to do, the employee was likely to be acting within the scope of her employment. Employers can reasonably anticipate that employees hired to do a certain job will perform only the activities related to that job. They can select, train and monitor employees in reliance on their knowledge that the employee will perform a certain task. When the employee performs a task which is completely unrelated to the task for which she was hired and which is completely unexpected by the employer, the employer should not be held liable. See Rest. (2d) § 228(1)(a).

Example: Master hires A as his bookkeeper. He hires a number of other people to unload his trucks. One day, one of the people unloading a truck is ill, and the bookkeeper decides on her own to help unload the truck. She drops an object on a passerby. The bookkeeper's conduct is outside the scope of her employment because the master hired others to unload trucks. The job of unloading trucks is completely unrelated to a bookkeeper's job, and the master could not reasonably anticipate that the bookkeeper would engage in a teamster's work. Cf. *White Oak Co v. Rivoux*, 102 N.E. 302 (Ohio 1913).

b. **Whether the servant was acting within the scope of her employment as measured by space and time.** The duties to be performed in a particular case will normally be fixed by the employer with reference to both time and place (e.g., "Review this document for me and give me your comments by noon tomorrow;" or "Load your truck with the order for ABC Foods and try to get it there by Friday afternoon;" or "you have three days to dig that trench and install the wiring." Whatever the instructions, an employee may choose to deviate from them. The issue then becomes: was her deviation a ***minor detour*** or was it a substantial *frolic?* If the servant's conduct occurs on a route that she was authorized to take, or only a short distance from it (**minor *detour***), the servant will probably have acted within the scope of her employment. Similarly, if the employee performs her work substantially within the time authorized, she will have acted within the scope of her employment. However, if she is removed from the limits of her employment, either in space or in time, she may be acting on a *frolic* of her own. In that case, she will be outside the scope of her employment and her employer will not be liable for her conduct. See Rest. (2d) § 228(1)(b),(2).

Example: Employee left work for a half-hour lunch but had not returned after almost 3 hours. He was supposed to pick up another employee after lunch and return to work. He had a collision after drinking at a bar. At the time, he was heading in a direction away from work. It was not clear whether he intended to return to work, and he was, in fact, far from work at the time of the accident.

Held, the employer was not liable because the employee was not within the scope of his employment. He was on a frolic which had not ended, and he had not returned to the limits of his employment. He was gone too long, was pursuing his own purpose, and had not reentered the time and place of his employment. Even if he was headed back to work, he was still too far from work and was pursuing his own objectives. *Prince v. Atchison, Topeka & Santa Fe Ry. Co.,* 395 N.E.2d 592 (Ill. App. Ct. 1979).

i. **Going and coming rule:** Most courts hold that an accident during the employee's travel to or from work (or for lunch during the work day), is not within the scope of employment. This conclusion is based on the theory that the employer has no "control" over the employee during those periods. However, the courts are divided. In *Robarge v. Bechtel Power Corp.,* 640 P.2d 211 (Ariz. Ct. App. 1982), the court held that generally, an employee is not within the scope of his employment when traveling to or from work **as a matter of law,** even if the employee is paid for that time. Some jurisdictions leave this issue for the jury in the same way as other scope of employment issues. In *Luth v. Rogers & Babler Constr. Co.,* 507 P.2d 761 (Alaska 1973), the court decided that it was improper to direct a verdict for an employee who was paid for commuting to and from work, when the employee negligently injured plaintiff while returning home from work.

c. **Whether the servant is serving the purpose of the master, at least in part:** If the servant *intends to act wholly for his own purposes* and not at all for the master's purposes, *the master is not liable* for the servant's tort upon a third person, even though the acts appear to be done for the master's account. The servant's intent to serve his own purposes is controlling, and the servant will be deemed to have abandoned his employment and to be **"on a frolic of his own."** Rest. (2d) § 235, comment a; § 228(1)(c).

Example 1: S delivers goods to Staten Island for his master, M. He is supposed to return to M's place of business on the west side of New York. However, S drives to the east side of town to visit X. S gives a ride in the truck to several children near X's house. Eventually S begins his return to M's place of business and tells the children to get off the truck. T is still on the truck when S starts it. T is injured and sues M. M contends that there is no liability because S was on a frolic of his own.

Held, M is not liable. S had abandoned his service to M when he gave the children a ride around town, so he was not acting within the scope of his employment. Although S intended to return the truck to M's place of business, the mere intent to return was not sufficient to restore him to the scope of his employment and render M liable for T's injuries. S was still far away from the route he should have traveled, and he was still using the truck to entertain the children. An objective act, not mere intent, is required to end the frolic and reenter the scope of employment. *Fiocco v. Carver,* 137 N.E. 309 (N.Y. 1922).

Example 2: M employs S to deliver articles. After making a delivery, S invites T to ride in M's delivery truck. T is injured in an accident caused by S's negligence. T's suit against M is dismissed because M did not give S authority to invite anyone to ride on the truck. The invitation by S was not within the scope of his employment. *Thomas v. Magnolia Petroleum Co.,* 9 S.W.2d 1 (Ark. 1928); Rest. (2d) § 242.

Note: Some courts have declined to apply the reasoning of the *Thomas* case and of the Restatement. Those jurisdictions have found the employer liable in cases with similar facts. They reason that **since M would be liable for S's negligence to a stranger in the event of an accident, M should also be liable to an invitee,** even if S was not authorized to invite others for a ride. *Meyer v. Blackman,* 381 P.2d 916 (Cal. 1963).

d. **Whether the servant is serving a dual purpose:** If the servant is furthering his master's business in part but also serving his own interests, he will generally be held to be acting within the scope of his employment.

Example 1: M directs his servant, S, to drive M's truck directly from point X to point Y and to deliver a load of lumber. S takes his wife with him, intending to drop her off on the way, but before reaching Y. Before reaching his wife's destination along the road to Y, S negligently injures T. M is liable to T under the dual-purpose rule. So long as *the business of the master is being furthered* by the act of the servant, it's not material that the servant also has another self-serving purpose. The master's business need not be the sole purpose of the servant's activity in order to make the master liable. Rest. (2d) § 236.

Example 2: T approached a vehicle to speak to the driver (S) about the security patrol dog in the back of S's car. S was employed by National Detective Agency, K-9 Division (M), as a security patrol guard. M had an unwritten regulation that no dog on security patrol was to be used for any other purpose. S wanted to show T how well the dog was trained and opened the car door to pull the dog to the front seat. The dog jumped out of the car and bit T. The trial court directed a verdict for M, holding that S was acting outside the scope of his employment as a matter of law.

Held, the trial judge erred in taking the case from the jury, even though S had broken M's rule. S could have been acting to further M's business by attempting to show residents in the area how well the dog was trained. On the other hand, S could have been trying to impress T for his own personal purposes. Since both inferences were possible, the jury should have been allowed to determine whether S was motivated either *"wholly or partially by an intention to promote his employer's interests."* *Meyers v. National Detective Agency, Inc.,* 281 A.2d 435 (D.C. 1971).

e. **Whether the degree of control exercised by the employer brings the servant's purpose within the scope of employment:** If an employer exercises sufficient control over his servant's activities, even the servant's personal activities may be viewed as within the scope of employment.

Example: Employer instructed its employees when to take their coffee breaks and where to smoke during their breaks. T walked into the smoking room with gasoline-soaked clothing, and was injured by the negligence of an employee who was smoking. T sued P.

Held, the lower court erred in dismissing the suit. The jury could reasonably have concluded that the employer assumed such control over its employees' smoking habits as to bring the employee's act within the scope of employment. *Landiorio v. Kriss & Senko Enters. Inc.,* 517 A.2d 530 (Pa. 1986).

2. **Liability for acts prohibited by employer:** Because, under ***the doctrine of respondeat superior,*** the employer is liable ***whether or not she is at fault,*** it follows that under some circumstances she may be liable even if she expressly ***forbids*** the acts, if the acts are done in furtherance of the employment. In this way, a gun store owner who expressly orders her clerk never to load a gun when showing it to a customer, may nevertheless be liable to a third parties who is injured when the clerk disobeys, on the theory that the clerk is furthering the employer's general business purpose of selling guns. Rest. (2d) § 230, Illustration 1.

   a. **Relevance to scope of employment:** The scope of employment may be such that the employer's rule prohibiting a particular activity will constitute evidence that it is not what the employee was hired to do, and thus was not for the employer's business purpose. For instance, the custodian of a private swimming pool was told not to allow any unauthorized persons to swim; when he disobeyed and allowed outsiders to use the pool, his act was outside the scope of employment, because he was hired for the purpose of keeping people out. *Gurley v. Southern Power Co.,* 90 S.E. 943 (N.C. 1916).

      i. **Unauthorized delegation by employee:** According to most courts, an employer is ***not automatically liable vicariously*** if the tort involved is committed by a person hired by the employee without permission, or by a person who is permitted by the employee to use the master's property without authorization. The employer will be vicariously liable only if the employee himself was negligent in hiring or bringing in the third person, e.g., if he should have known that the third person would not be able to do the job safely.

         Example: M instructs his truck driver, S, not to let anyone else drive the truck or even ride with him in it. Contrary to this instruction, S permits Y, a thirteen-year-old, not only to ride but also to drive the truck. While Y is driving and S is a passenger, Y negligently collides with T.

         Held, since M did not authorize S to let anyone else drive, M is liable only if S was himself negligent in either entrusting the truck to Y, or in supervising Y's driving. The issue of S's negligence is for the jury. *Potter v. Golden Rule Grocery Co.,* 84 S.W.2d 364 (Tenn. 1935).

b. Imputed contributory negligence:

i. Traditional rule: Under the traditional rule, if a master sues a third party for causing him injury, the ***contributory negligence of his servant will be imputed*** to him to reduce or eliminate his claim against the third person. The theory is that this is ***consistent with the imputation of vicarious liability*** when a third party sues the master for the servant's negligence. This is the view adopted by the Restatement. Rest. (2d) § 317.

ii. Modern view. Recently, a number of courts have *rejected* the notion that contributory negligence must be treated in the same way as negligence. For example, when T negligently collided with a car in which M was a passenger and S was the driver, the court refused to impute S's contributory negligence to M. It was not fair to prevent or reduce M's recovery for T's negligence simply because M might have deeper pockets than S. *Weber v. Stokely-Van Camp, Inc.,* 144 N.W.2d 540 (Minn. 1966). Other courts have rejected the imputation of contributory negligence on the ground that the employer as a passenger is not able to control the employee's contributory negligence. *State v. Popricki,* 456 N.Y.S.2d 850, 851 (N.Y. App. Div. 1982). See also *South Carolina Ins. Co. v. James C. Greene & Co,* 348 S.E.2d 617 (S.C. Ct. App. 1986). In the *Greene* case, the court refused to impute to the employer the negligence of an agent which contributed to the accident, in a suit by the employer against another agent. It should be noted that many of these cases involve the negligent operation of motor vehicles. In these cases, it's hard to find any degree of control by the employer over the acts of the servant-driver.

III. MASTER'S LIABILITY FOR SERVANT'S INTENTIONAL TORTS

A. General rule: A servant may be acting within the scope of her employment when she commits an intentional tort, although it is less likely that an intentional tort will fall within the scope of employment than a negligent tort.

B. Factors: The factors to consider in determining whether an intentional tort falls within the scope of employment include: (a) the ***extent of the***

wrong; (b) the *forseeability of the conduct*; and (c) whether the servant's *purpose was to serve the master*.

1. **The extent of the wrong:** An employer is *more likely to anticipate minor crimes than major ones.* For example, a gardener who drives a child off with a stick to keep the child out of his master's garden may be deemed to act within the scope of his employment. However, if the gardener were to shoot the child, no one would seriously suggest that the gardener was acting within the scope of his employment. Rest. (2d) § 231, comment a.; *Metzler v. Layton,* 25 N.E.2d 60 (Ill. 1939). In *Metzler,* the employee was found to be acting within the scope of his employment when he mistakenly injured plaintiff while defending his employer's property against robbers.

2. **Foreseeability of the conduct:** Recently, some courts have applied a *foreseeability rule* in cases of intentional torts. Under this rule, the employer is *liable for the intentional torts* of his employees *if they were reasonably foreseeable* or *"characteristic."*

   Example: A drunken Coast Guard sailor, while on his way back to his vessel, damaged T's drydock by tampering with the machinery that controlled the water level. Though there was no evidence that the sailor intended to serve his employer by his actions, his employer (the United States) was held liable. The court said that an employer should be liable for accidents which may be said to be characteristic of its employees' activities, and that this tort was "characteristic" of men serving in the Coast Guard, in view of the "proclivity of seamen to find solace for solitude by copious resort to the bottle when ashore." *Ira S. Bushey & Sons, Inc. v. United States,* 398 F.2d 167 (2d Cir. 1968).

   a. **Limits to foreseeability rule:** The foreseeability test in cases of *respondeat superior* is limited to torts which "may fairly be said to be characteristic" of the enterprise.

      Example 1: The court in *Whitson v. Oakland Unified Sch. Dist.,* 176 Cal. Rptr. 287, 291 (Ct. App. 1981), dismissed a suit against a school district by a female student who was raped by a custodian in his office. "[I]t defies every notion of fairness to say that rape is characteristic of school district activities." *The mere use of the employer's facilities for a tort does not impute liability to the employer.* See also *G.L. v. Kaiser Found. Hosps., Inc.,* 757 P.2d 1347 (Or. 1988), in which a hospital was not vicariously liable for a rape committed by a respiratory therapist.

Example 2: A different result was reached by the court in *Mary M. v. City of Los Angeles,* 814 P.2d 1341 (Cal. 1991). The court found that a police officer who stopped an individual on suspicion of drunken diving, made her take a field sobriety test, drove her home and then raped her, acted within the scope of his employment. The officer's initial actions were clearly within the scope of his employment. He simply went on to misuse his authority. The court distinguished police officers from other individuals who lack such expansive authority, citing *Rita M. v. Roman Catholic Archbishop,* 232 Cal. Rptr. 685, 690 (Ct. App. 1986). In that case, priests who allegedly seduced a teenage parishioner were found, as a matter of law, to be acting outside the scope of their employment.

3. **Employee's purpose:** A master may also be vicariously liable for a servant's intentional torts if the servant is "actuated, at least in part, by a purpose to serve the master." Rest. (2d) § 228(1)(c). Bar owners are frequently held liable for the excessive force used by bouncers in removing patrons on these grounds. Clearly, bouncers are furthering their master's business when they remove drunk or unruly patrons. (See p. 95, *supra.*)

Example 1: M company was hired by Bank to move Bank's lockers to a new location after Police had already moved the bank's money. M's employee, S, opened a locker, discovered some money and absconded with it.

     Held, S acted outside the scope of his employment. He was not furthering his master's business when he stole the money. *Bremen State Bank v. Hartford Accident & Indemnity Co.,* 427 F.2d 425 (7th Cir. 1970).

Example 2: S, a bartender, got into a fight with a patron (T) and beat him savagely, after S had shut off the engine to T's car. There was a history of animosity between S and T. The court found that the bartender had no need to remain in the lot once he had shut off the engine. He was no longer furthering his master's business and was acting outside the scope of his employment. *Maddex v. Ricca,* 258 F. Supp. 352 (D. Ariz. 1966).

Example 3: M employs S as a bartender. T enters and sits at the bar with his ex-wife, who is now married to S. T makes a statement which offends S, and S hits T with a bottle. T sues M for damages. M is liable because S was employed to keep order in the bar as well as tend bar. T's verbal attack on S was committed in the course of S's duties. The fact that S's actions were malicious and willful does not change the result. *Novick v. Gouldsberry,* 173 F.2d 496 (9th Cir. 1949).

    a. Debt collection: The ***employer may be liable if his employee attempts to collect a debt owed to the employer by T,*** and if in the process of collection, the employee commits the torts of assault, battery or false imprisonment.

    b. Special duty owed by some employers: Employers who owe a special and independent duty of protection to the public or to their customers may be liable even if the employee acts for purely personal motives. Rest. (2d) § 214. The employer's duty may be created by contract or by the nature of the employer's business. For instance, a common carrier owes its passengers a duty of reasonable care to protect them against torts by its employees. If an airline ticket agent attacks a passenger, even though solely for his own motives, the airline will still be liable on the grounds that it breached its direct duty of care. See also *Nazareth v. Herndon Ambulance Serv., Inc.,* 467 So. 2d 1076 (Fla. Dist. Ct. App. 1985), *review denied,* 478 So. 2d 53 (Fla. 1985). In *Nazareth,* the court found that a complaint against an ambulance service for rape committed by its ambulance attendant stated a good cause of action. The ambulance service qualified as a common carrier which owed an implied contractual duty of safe passage to its passengers.

C. Conduct authorized or ratified by master: Even if a servant's conduct is outside the usual scope of employment, the master may be ***vicariously liable if she authorized it or ratified it.*** *Novick v. Gouldsberry,* 173 F.2d 496, 500 (9th Cir. 1949). A master can also be ***vicariously liable for the unintended consequences of authorized acts.***

Example: M authorizes his servant S to take possession of a ship named "Peerless." There are two ships named "Peerless." S takes possession of the wrong ship "Peerless," owned by T. M is subject to liability for S's conduct because it was the consequence of an authorized act, even if unintended. Rest. (2d) § 215, comment a, b, Illustration 2.

IV. TORT LIABILITY IN PARTNERSHIP AND JOINT ENTERPRISE RELATIONSHIPS

A. Partnerships: Beginning with Chapter 12, we will discuss in detail the nature, elements and consequences of a partnership relationship. Here, we deal only with the liability of one partner for a tort committed by another partner. A partner is liable to third persons for torts committed by his partner when that partner is acting within the scope of the partnership business and in furtherance of the firm's business. UPA §§ 13, 15[1]. Partners owe each other a general fiduciary duty. For this reason, the UPA subjects partners to liability for the torts of their partners. This is the case even though in many instances a partner will not have the ability to control the activities of his partners in the same way as an employer can control his employees.

Example: P and A are partners operating a retail shoe store under the firm name, "P and A Shoe Co." The firm owns a pickup truck with which it gathers and delivers the firm's merchandise. While delivering shoes to a customer, A drives the firm truck negligently and injures T. T sues P for damages.

Held, T may recover. Each partner in a firm is an agent of the other partner or partners. A was driving the firm truck and was acting within the scope and in furtherance of the firm's business when he negligently injured T. The other partner, P, is liable for A's tort to T.

B. Joint enterprise: A joint enterprise is like a partnership, except that it is generally for a very short and specific purpose, such as a trip or a single transaction. If the requirements for a joint enterprise are met, the negligence of one "joint enterpriser" or "joint venturer" is imputed to the other.

1. Requirements for joint enterprise: To be labeled a joint enterprise, a relationship must contain *four ingredients*: (1) an *agreement,* express or implied, between the members; (2) a *common purpose,* to be carried out by the members; (3) a *common pecuniary interest* in that purpose; and (4) an *equal right of control* by each member of the enterprise.

a. Restatement definition: The Restatement of Torts defines a joint enterprise as "in the nature of a partnership," but with broader and more inclusive attributes. A partnership usually deals with a continuing relationship over many transactions, e.g., a law partnership, while a joint enterprise may be less formal, and more limited in time and purpose, e.g., an agreement to purchase a carload of wheat by two bakeries in the same city. Restatement of Torts (2d) §491, comment b.

b. Pecuniary interest: Because joint enterprises require a common pecuniary interest, the result is that a mere *social trip,* or a trip in which each member is pursuing his own *independent business interest,* is not a joint enterprise.

---

1. Uniform Partnership Act, adopted by 49 states. Section 305 of the Revised Uniform Partnership Act, released in 1994, retains the essential elements of UPA § 13.

i. **Sharing expenses:** The fact that two people share the expenses of a trip either for social purposes or because they intend to do business at the same destination, is not by itself enough to establish that they have a "common pecuniary or business purpose."

Example 1: Four people travelled together on a fishing trip. The driver negligently collided with T and was killed. The driver's estate filed a negligence action against T and T counterclaimed against the three passengers on the theory of joint enterprise—alleging that the driver's negligence should be imputed to them as members of a joint enterprise. Two of the passengers filed separate actions against T, and T counterclaimed on the theory of imputed liability in a joint enterprise.

Held, T's counterclaims against the passengers were dismissed. There was no joint enterprise because there was no common pecuniary or commercial interest. The fact that they had a ***common purpose in fishing was insufficient*** to subject the car passengers to vicarious liability for the driver's negligence on the theory of joint enterprise. *Easter v. McNabb,* 541 P.2d 604 (Idaho 1975).

Example 2: T gave X and Y, who were friends, permission to cut trees on T's property. X and Y wanted firewood for their homes. The first tree cut by X knocked down an overhead electrical power line and started a fire which caused damage to T. T sued X for negligence and X sued Y for contribution on a theory of joint enterprise liability.

Held, X's complaint against Y was dismissed because X and Y ***lacked a common business purpose.*** The fact that they both had an economic motive in obtaining firewood was not persuasive. They had no joint plans to sell the firewood; their purpose was purely ***personal.*** Therefore, no joint venture existed. *Maselli v. Ginner,* 809 P.2d 1181 (Idaho Ct. App. 1991).

c. **Joint right of control over auto:** When applied to auto trips, the requirement that each joint venturer have a partial right of control over the enterprise means that ***each must have some say in how the car is to be driven.*** In cases which find a "common business purpose," the facts usually show that each participant had at least a theoretical right of control over the car. This doesn't mean that each had the right, at any time, to grab the wheel and steer; it simply means that each was understood to have an equal say in such things as how fast the car would travel, what the route would be, how often and where they would stop, etc.

Example: X and Y plan an automobile journey for pleasure. X gets permission to use his father's car on the trip. X and Y take two friends with them. X and Y alternate driving. While Y is driving, he negligently kills T.

Held, X is liable for Y's negligence. "An enterprise is simply a project or undertaking, and a joint enterprise is simply one participated in by associates acting together. The basis of liability of one associate in a joint enterprise for the tort of another is equal privilege to control the method and means of accomplishing the common design." The control necessary for liability is not the actual steering of the wheel, but the equal authority in both X and Y to decide when and how to use the car. X and Y borrowed the car from X's father to take their friends riding. The friends were their guests, but neither X nor Y was a guest of the other, nor was either a mere passenger while the other was driving. X and Y had equal authority to decide where to go, how long to stay and who was to drive. *Howard v. Zimmermann,* 242 P. 131 (Kan. 1926).

Note: Many courts require a business purpose before they will find a joint enterprise. In those jurisdictions the *Howard* decision would not be followed, but liability might be found under the family car doctrine, *infra*.

V.   OWNER'S LIABILITY FOR OPERATION OF CAR

A. **The Family Car Doctrine:** Generally, relationships between the members of a family are not a basis for vicarious liability. Thus, parents are not, without more, vicariously liable for the torts of their children, and a spouse is not liable for the torts of his or her spouse. Some courts have developed an exception to this rule known as the "family car doctrine." Under this doctrine, when the *owner of an automobile lets a family member use his car, he is, in effect, treating that person's purpose as his own "business" and is vicariously liable.* This fiction has been *rejected by most courts.*

B. **Owner consent statutes:** By statute, however, about one-fourth of the states have enacted statutes which make the *owner of a car vicariously liable for the tort of anyone who uses his car with his consent.* These are called "owner consent statutes."

1. **Scope of consent:** Since the liability is based upon *"consent,"* if the use by the borrower (or *"bailee"* as he is usually called) goes

clearly **beyond** the scope of that consent, there is no liability by the owner or **bailor.** For instance, if the owner expressly forbids the bailee to drive on a highway, his disobedience would probably so exceed the scope of consent as to render the statute inapplicable.

2. **Use by sub-bailee:** If the bailee, without authorization by the owner, in turn lends the car to a third person (called a **"sub-bai-lee"**), is the owner liable for the sub-bailee's negligence? The courts are divided, but they are more likely to find statutory liability if the bailee is a passenger in the car driven by the sub-bailee.

   a. **Modern view:** The modern view favors imposing liability on the owner of the vehicle. *Shuck v. Means,* 226 N.W.2d 285 (Minn. 1974). In *Shuck,* the court held the defendant rent-a-car company liable when its customer allowed a third person to drive, even though the rental agreement prohibited the customer from allowing anyone else to drive unless the customer was a passenger.

C. **Non-statutory bailment:** In those states which do not impose liability on the owner either under the family automobile doctrine or under a consent statute, the **owner is generally liable only if the driver is in fact acting as his servant.**

D. **Direct negligence by bailor:** The vehicle owner may be liable for his own negligence in entrusting the vehicle to a bailee, if he knows or should know that the bailee may use it unsafely. But a car rental company was not liable for an accident caused when its customer drove a rented van which was twelve feet high into an overpass which measured less than twelve feet. The company did not know its customer lacked experience with large vehicles. *Littles v. Avis Rent-A-Car System,* 248 A.2d 837 (Pa. 1969).

   1. **Liability by rental car companies:** In about a dozen states, rental car companies are liable by statute for the negligent driving of persons who rent their cars. Hynes, p. 198.

E. **Insurance:** In many instances, the issue of liability is resolved by auto liability insurance. Almost all automobile insurance policies protect the named insured, as well as persons who use the vehicle with his permission. Hynes, p. 198.

VI. LIABILITY OF EMPLOYER FOR ACTS OF INDEPENDENT CONTRACTOR

A. **General rule:** Subject to a few exceptions discussed below, an **employer is not vicariously liable (liable without fault) for the acts of an independent contractor.**

1. **Rationale:** One reason for this rule is that the independent contractor, normally a person or firm with special skills, is more likely than a mere employee to have money and/or liability insurance. There is therefore less risk that a third person will be unable to recover for her injuries. In addition, the employer does not normally control the details of the independent contractor's work. He cannot as easily or economically take steps to improve the safety standards of the independent contractor, as he can with his own employees. Posner, p. 172.

B. **Definition of independent contractor:** The Restatement defines an independent contractor as "a person who contracts with another to do something for him but who is not controlled by the other nor subject to the other's right to control with respect to his physical conduct in the performance of the undertaking. He may or may not be an agent." Rest. (2d) § 2(3).

C. **Statutory definition of employee:** In determining the liability of the employer, we must first decide whether the person who renders him services is an *employee (servant)* or an *independent contractor.* The Restatement defines an employee as "an agent employed by a master to perform service in his affairs whose physical performance of the service is controlled or is subject to the right to control of the master." Rest. (2d) §§ 2(2); 220(1). Some statutes define "employee" differently from this typical agency definition. However, if there is no statutory definition, the term *"employee"* should be given its common law meaning. *Nationwide Mutual Ins. Co. v. Darden,* 503 U.S. 318 (1992).

D. **Factors used in determining whether an individual is an independent contractor or an employee:** The Restatement lists the following factors to be used in determining whether an individual is a servant or an independent contractor (Rest.(2d) § 220(2)(a)-(j)):

1. **Exercise of control:** The extent of control which, by the agreement, the master may exercise over the details of the work;

2. **Distinct occupation:** Whether or not the one employed is engaged in a distinct occupation or business;

3. **Nature of work:** The kind of occupation, with reference to whether, in the locality, the work is usually done under the direction of the employer or by a specialist without supervision;

4. **Skill required:** The skill required in the particular occupation;

5. **Who supplies the tools, etc.:** Whether the employer or the workman supplies the instrumentalities, tools, and the place of work;

6. **Duration of employment:** The length of time for which the person is employed;

7. **Payment method:** The method of payment, whether by the time or by the job;

8. **Part of employer's regular business:** Whether or not the work is a part of the regular business of the employer;

9. **Parties' belief:** Whether or not the parties believe they are creating the relation of master and servant;

10. **Principal in business:** Whether the principal is or is not in business.

   a. **Designation by parties may not be controlling:** The fact that the parties call a provider of services an "independent contractor" may be a factor in a court's decision to classify him as a servant or an independent contractor, but it is not controlling. *Sandrock v. Taylor*, 174 N.W.2d 186 (Neb. 1970). In *Sandrock*, the court held that an employer cannot "escape his liability under the doctrine of *respondeat superior* by a contract that expressly provides that the workman is an independent contractor, if in fact under the entire contract, the workman only possesses the same independence that employees in general enjoy."

E. **IRS 20-factor test:** The Internal Revenue Service has a vital interest in knowing whether an individual is an employee or an independent contractor. An employer has an obligation to withhold income taxes from remuneration paid to employees, but not, ordinarily, on compensation to independent contractors. Also, the employer must contribute to employee benefits in the case of his employees, but not of the independent contractors he deals with. The IRS has formulated a 20-factor test for determining whether a worker is an employee or an independent contractor. The answer depends essentially on the degree of employer control over the worker's performance, the extent of the employer's financial controls, and the underlying relationship between the parties.

F. **Application of factors:**

Example 1: P hired A to negotiate gas and oil leases for P. A had previously been an independent oil and gas broker for 26 years. P set maximum prices and durations for the leases, but otherwise gave A freedom to negotiate. P told A the vicinities in which P wanted to acquire leases, but did not give A directions about where to go or what routes to travel. A's schedule was up to him. P paid A $175 per day plus expenses, and A accounted to P at two-week intervals. A negligently injured T in an auto accident while working for P.

Held, P was not vicariously liable for A's act because A was an independent contractor. P lacked the right to control the means by which A accomplished his mission. P hired A to accomplish a particular result—to obtain leases for P. P lacked the ability to control A's physical movements. *Soderback v. Townsend,* 644 P.2d 640 (Or. Ct. App. 1982).

Example 2: P sold and installed carpeting. A bought P's installation business and installed the carpets P sold. P did not pay withholding tax on sums paid to A, and did not supervise A's work. The work in question required considerable skill. The work was done by installers who provided their own tools. Payment was measured by yards installed, and the work was on an "as needed" basis. A hired other independent installers, such as Sub-A, to complete jobs which he could not perform. After completing two installation jobs assigned to him by A, Sub-A got into an automobile accident with T.

Held, P was not liable to T because both A and Sub-A were independent contractors. Key factors were that carpet installers are skilled workers who routinely work without supervision; A and Sub-A had huge discretion in the performance of their tasks and did not report to anyone at P; they supplied their own equipment; they worked on an "as needed" basis; they were paid by the yard installed rather than on an hourly basis (so that there was less ability for P to control their work); and the parties believed they were creating an independent contractor relationship, as evidenced by the fact that both A and Sub-A paid taxes as the owners of an independent carpet installation business and P did not withhold social security or income taxes from their compensation. *Kane Furniture Corp. v. Miranda,* 506 So. 2d 1061 (Fla. Dist. Ct. App. 1987).

Example 3: A delivered newspapers for P. The agreement between A and P called A an "independent contractor." The contract was for a six month period, renewable at P's option. Either A or P could terminate the agreement without cause on 28 days' notice. P could terminate anytime if there were an unacceptable number of complaints, or if A failed to maintain acceptable subscriber relations. Each morning A drove to a point specified by P to load the papers. He then delivered the papers by a time specified by P, to addresses provided by P. A's car collided with T's motorcycle. T sued P on a theory of ***respondeat superior***.

Held, the jury should have been allowed to decide whether A was an employee or an independent contractor; a finding that A was an independent contractor as a matter of law was improper. Facts which supported the conclusion that A was an employee included:

- P involved itself in the details of delivery: P specified the pick-up and delivery site, and the manner in which the papers would be bagged and delivered.

- P received customer complaints and changes.

- A believed he was an employee.

- The community believes that people making newspaper deliveries are employees of a distributor.

- A had no delivery business distinct from his work for P.

- A did not purchase the papers from P and did not sell them for his own profit.

- P supplied the newspapers, and, although it did not supply the bags, rubber bands or transportation, it did specify the route.

- The length of the relationship between P and A was such that a jury could conclude that P had sufficient control over A to create an employer-employee relationship.

- P's right to terminate on 28 days' notice gave P control over A.

- Home delivery is a regular part of P's business and is critical to its survival.

- P supplied health and disability insurance to A.

In contrast, the facts supporting a conclusion that A was an independent contractor included:

- A owned his own car.

- A was subject to little supervision in his activities.

- A provided some of his own supplies.

Santiago v. Phoenix Newspapers, Inc., 794 P.2d 138 (Ariz. 1990).

1. **Importance of the control factor:** The skill required for performance of the services is not controlling; the key question is the ability of the employer to control and supervise the worker's conduct. Thus, a law firm associate who gets into an auto accident on the way to take a deposition ordinarily *does not subject his client to liability*. However, *the law partners* who authorized him to take the deposition and for whom he conducted the deposition, would be subject to liability for his negligence. (The members of the law firm would also be vicariously liable for his legal malpractice, if any.)

   Example: A negligently injured T while A was delivering pizzas for P. The issue on appeal was whether A could be considered an employee, subjecting P to vicarious liability, rather than an independent contractor.

   Several factors favored the conclusion that A was an independent contractor not subject to P's control: (1) A provided his own car, expenses and insurance; (2) A was paid on a commission basis; (3) A agreed to pay his own FICA and income taxes; (4) A provided his own worker's compensation coverage; and (5) A signed an agreement in which he acknowledged his status as an "independent contractor."

On the other hand, a number of factors pointed to a master-servant relationship giving P control over, or the **right to control,** A: (1) P told A the hours he was to work; (2) P told A where and when, and in what quantities, to deliver pizzas; (3) A collected the money shown on a bill prepared by P and delivered it to P (shortages were deducted from A's commission); and (4) P could terminate A's employment at any time and for any reason.

Held, The facts were equivocal and indecisive. A could reasonably be judged either an employee or an independent contractor. The court relied on the control test and commented that A had no discretion and had to follow P's directions as to when, where and to whom to deliver the pizzas. *Toyota Motor Sales U.S.A., Inc. v. Superior Court,* 269 Cal. Rptr. 647 (Ct. App. 1990).

Comment: The court did not conclude that A was an employee as a matter of law. It left that question to be resolved at a new trial. The court merely held that the trial court had erred in concluding, on the basis of the evidence, that a settlement based on a finding that A was an independent contractor was a good-faith settlement.

G. **Employer's supervisory ability:** To be held vicariously liable, the employer should have sufficient training to be able to supervise the worker's conduct.

Example: B's foreman supervises a group of men working on the reconstruction of a stairway for B. P, a master carpenter, sends A, a skilled cabinetmaker, to work under the direction of B's foreman. B is to pay P an agreed amount for A's work. A acts as the servant of B in building the stairway. Rest. (2d) § 227, Illustration 3.

1. **Rationale:** Although A's work as a cabinetmaker requires a great deal of skill and B might not be able to supervise her if she were working as a cabinetmaker, he does have sufficient skill to supervise her work in reconstructing the stairway, a simpler task than cabinetmaking. Also, since A is working for B for a week, B has an adequate opportunity to observe A's work and to take steps to prevent mishaps by her.

H. **Exceptions to the rule—liability of employers for the conduct of their independent contractors:** Notwithstanding the general rule, an employer can be liable for the torts of her independent contractor in four situations:

(1) when the activity is inherently dangerous;

(2) when the employer owes a nondelegable duty to a third person;

(3) when a third person contracts with the principal for services in the reasonable belief that the services will be rendered by the principal or his servants; and

(4) when the principal herself is negligent, e.g., in selecting or monitoring the performance of the independent contractor.

1. **Inherently dangerous activity:** Employers are vicariously liable for the torts of their independent contractor if the contractor's work is inherently dangerous.

   a. **Rationale:** This rule can be explained on the basis of economic cost efficiency. If the employer knows in advance that he will be held responsible, he will be more likely to take steps to assure safety or to obtain adequate insurance coverage. An employer can afford to take extensive safety measures at a smaller cost than the damage likely to be caused by his inherently dangerous activity. Besides, the principal is likely to have deeper pockets than the independent contractor, who may not have the resources to cover the cost of damages. Imposing liability on the employer when the work is inherently dangerous avoids the risk that the employer will purposely hire an impecunious independent contractor to shift the risk onto innocent third parties. Posner, Economic Analysis of Law 172 (3d ed. 1986).

   b. **Definition of "inherently dangerous":** An activity is inherently dangerous if it is dangerous when done normally. Thus, one who employs an independent contractor to do work which is likely to create a peculiar risk of harm to others unless special precautions are taken, is liable for physical harm caused to them by the failure of the contractor to exercise reasonable care in installing the precautions. Restatement (2d) of Torts §§ 416, 427. On the other hand, if the activity is dangerous only when done in some bizarre fashion, the employer will not be liable, because he would have no reason to take steps to prevent an injury which he could not reasonably foresee.

   Example: General contractor hired subcontractor P to install linoleum in customer's home. P hired A to do the job. A used a glue that was extremely flammable and ignored warnings on the can to open the windows and turn off the pilot light on the hot water heater in the customer's kitchen. There was an explosion. The customer's insurer paid for the damage caused to the house and sued P for indemnification.

   Held, P, the employer, was not liable for the negligence of its independent contractor, A. The installation of linoleum is not ordinarily or inherently hazardous. It becomes dangerous only if the installer misuses the glue. If the employer cannot reasonably anticipate that an activity will be dangerous, the cost of care may be too high to warrant requiring the employer to take additional precautions. *Hixon v. Sherwin-Williams Co.,* 671 F.2d 1005 (7th Cir. 1982).

c. Peculiar risk: P can be liable for the torts of its independent contractors if P knows, or has special reason to know, that the independent contractor's operation poses a *peculiar risk* of harm under the particular circumstances under which the work is to be done.

Example: The Good Humor Ice Cream Company (P) employed drivers in a traditional employer-employee relationship to drive trucks and to sell ice cream to children at street corners. P trained its drivers to refrain from selling at locations which would require children to cross busy intersections, and to assist children in crossing streets. P then changed its method of operation so that all its vendors became independent contractors. The drivers purchased their trucks with the help of financing from P, and were free to sell ice cream at any price and at any location they wanted. P ceased its safety training of the ice cream drivers. T's daughter was killed by an automobile as she attempted to cross the street to buy some ice cream from one of the trucks. T sued P, alleging that P should be liable because the activity in question was *inherently dangerous* or posed a *peculiar risk.* P argued that selling ice cream is not an inherently dangerous activity, and that it should not be held vicariously liable for the negligence of the independent-contractor-drivers.

Held, the jury should have been allowed to determine whether operation of the truck posed a peculiar risk to children. Summary judgment for P was improper, given P's role in the conversion of its vendors from employees to independent contractors and the integral role that the vendors played in P's operation. The court noted that *P was very much aware of the special danger posed by the operation of the ice cream trucks and that many of the vendors were not aware of this danger,* particularly since P had abandoned its prior safety training program. *Wilson v. Good Humor Corp.,* 757 F.2d 1293 (D.C. Cir. 1985).

2. Nondelegable duty: A nondelegable duty can arise at common law or by statute. A duty is said to be nondelegable when "the responsibility is so important to the community that the employer should not be permitted to transfer it to another." *Kleeman v. Rheingold,* 614 N.E.2d 712 (N.Y. 1993). If the employer with a nondelegable duty delegates the duty nevertheless to an independent contractor who performs carelessly, the employer will be vicariously liable. For example, a city, which has a duty to keep its streets in repair, cannot avoid liability by hiring a private company to do the work. Likewise, many of the duties of landowners (*e.g.*, the duty to keep the premises safe for business visitors) may not be delegated.

Example: P, an automobile owner, hires A, a mechanic, to fix her brakes. A does the work negligently, and three months later, P is in an accident caused by the bad brakes, injuring T.

Held, P is liable to T. P has a statutory duty to keep her brakes in good working order. This duty is so important that it cannot be delegated. P's statutory duty to keep the brakes in good order could be met by the use of "ordinary prudence." But since the contractor's acts are deemed to be those of P, if the contractor did not exercise ordinary prudence, P is liable. P could (and probably did) buy liability insurance to cover this liability, which stemmed from her own driving activity. *Maloney v. Rath,* 445 P.2d 513 (Cal. 1968).

a. **Statutes and common law define scope of nondelegable duties:** In determining whether an employer has a nondelegable duty, one must look to applicable statutes and to the common law to determine the scope of the employer's obligation. A particular employer may be permitted to delegate some duties and responsibilities, but not others. For example, a hospital may not delegate its duty to provide a safe environment for its patients and the general public, and it is therefore liable for injuries caused by slippery floors within its premises. However, it may delegate to doctors the task of providing safe anesthesia, and it is not vicariously liable for the doctors' negligence. *Menzie v. Windham Community Memorial Hosp.,* 774 F. Supp. 91, 98 (D. Conn. 1991).

i. **Sources of law:** By resort to common law and statutes, the courts can determine whether the employer has such an important obligation to the public that it may not delegate the responsibility to another.

Example: A law firm (P) hired an independent contractor (A) to serve process upon a defendant. A served the defendant's secretary rather than the defendant. The statute of limitations expired before the defendant could be served. The client sued P for malpractice. P argued that it could not be liable for A's negligence because A was an independent contractor. The court held that, for the protection of its client, P had a nondelegable duty to make sure that the defendant was properly served in a timely fashion. This duty could not be delegated to an independent contractor. *Kleeman v. Rheingold,* 614 N.E.2d 712 (N.Y. 1993).

3. **Vicarious liability based on third party's reasonable belief:** Some courts, particularly in cases involving hospitals, have allowed third persons to recover against employers when the ***third person reasonably believes that there is an employer-employee relationship,*** rather than an independent contractor relationship. Recovery has been permitted even when the parties stated in writing that they were creating an "independent contractor" relationship, and even when the employer did not retain much control over the worker.

   Example: A hospital hired a doctors' group to perform emergency room services. The contract specified that the group was working as an independent contractor and that the hospital did not retain control over how the group performed its services. The group set the fees for its services.

   Held, the hospital was vicariously liable because the patient came into the hospital without reliance on a particular physician and because the patient expected the hospital to deliver the emergency services. On the other hand, if the patient had engaged the services of a particular doctor who was responsible for admitting the patient, there would be no vicarious liability by the hospital. *Hardy v. Brantley, M.D.,* 471 So. 2d 358 (Miss. 1985).

4. **Employer's liability for its own negligence:** An employer can be liable for her own negligence in hiring or retaining, or in failing to supervise (where there is a duty to supervise), an independent contractor. Under these circumstance, the liability cannot be characterized as vicarious liability under the doctrine of ***respondeat superior.*** It is simply direct liability for one's own negligence. The principal who hires an independent contractor is particularly vulnerable if it retains extensive control over the contractor and fails to ensure that reasonable safety procedures are followed.

   Example 1: P hired an independent contractor (A) to construct a building. P drew up the building plans and the contract specifications and acted as the architectural supervisor. It also wrote the contracts which were agreed to by the other contractors. P could order A to terminate the services of any prime- or sub-contractor within 24 hours. P also retained the right to hire additional subcontractors and to assign their contracts to A for coordination with the other contractors. On a daily basis, P's representative interpreted the contract specifications and plans for A. T fell through the roof of the building and was injured. T sued P for negligence in failing to install and implement adequate safety precautions.

Held, the jury could properly conclude that P had retained such a high degree of control over the independent contractor (A) as to render P liable for P's own negligence in failing to insure that A implemented reasonable safety precautions. *Funk v. General Motors Corp.,* 220 N.W.2d 641 (Mich. 1974).

Example 2: A doctor (A) had privileges at P hospital to perform plastic surgery. A performed surgery on T. T claimed that A performed the operation negligently. T sued P hospital, alleging that P negligently gave hospital privileges to A. P's rules required that staff privileges be granted only to doctors who passed a thorough competence examination. P's rules also required an annual reassessment of a doctor's competence prior to his reappointment. Another doctor in the hospital had previously complained that A was not competent to perform plastic surgery. He had even threatened to resign if the situation continued. P argued it was entitled to judgment as a matter of law, because A was P's independent contractor.

Held, the hospital was not entitled to judgment as a matter of law. There was ample evidence that the hospital was negligent in granting staff privileges to A and in later retaining A to perform plastic surgery. *Park N. Gen. Hosp. v. Hickman,* 703 S.W.2d 262 (Tex. Ct. App. 1985).

5. **Exception to liability for dangerous activity:** The courts have created exceptions to the employer's liability in certain cases involving inherently dangerous activities and nondelegable duties. For example, the courts have **refused to find employers liable in suits by injured employees of the independent contractor.** The courts reason that workers' compensation programs protect the injured employees adequately. Moreover, the employers are indirectly subsidizing the workers' compensation insurance of the contractor's employees when they pay the contractor's fees. *Tauscher v. Puget Sound Power & Light Co.,* 635 P.2d 426, 430 (Wash. 1981); *New Mexico Elec. Serv. Co. v. Montanez,* 551 P.2d 634, 637 (N.M. 1976). In the *New Mexico* case, an oil well owner was not vicariously liable when an electrical contractor he had hired negligently failed to warn its employee of danger, leading to his injury. The court pointed out that if the oil well owner had used his own employees, he would have been protected from suit by the workers' compensation laws, and that it was unfair to subject him to greater liability for using an independent contractor to do the work.

VII. THE BORROWED SERVANT DOCTRINE

A. Definitions: Occasionally, we need to determine which of two or more masters a servant was working for when she negligently performed some act. This need arises most often when a servant hired by one master (the ***general employer)*** is loaned to another (the ***special employer)*** for a limited special purpose.

B. General rule: Generally, the courts hold that ***the servant remains the employee of the general employer who originally hired him.*** It's the general employer, and not the special employer, who is ordinarily held vicariously liable for the servant's negligence.

   1. Rationale: The general employer usually has the greater opportunity to observe the employee and his skills. He knows more about the employee and is in a better position to appreciate the risks posed by the servant's activity. Furthermore, the servant usually owes his primary allegiance to the general employer. His livelihood depends upon pleasing him rather than upon satisfying the special employer. When the work of the special employer is finished, the employee will return to the services of the general employer. Hynes, *Chaos and the Law of Borrowed Servant: An Argument for Consistency*, 14 THE JOURNAL OF LAW AND COMMERCE 1 (1994).

C. Tests used to transfer liability to the special principal: In some cases, the special employer will have enough control over the work of the employee to transfer liability to the special employer. To impose liability on the special employer, it must be shown that, as to the tortious act in question, the servant was under a primary duty of obedience to the special employer.

   1. Facts to look for: Factors which suggest a transfer of control and thereby impose liability on the special employer include:

- servant is an ***unskilled laborer***;

- servant is ***paid hourly***;

- general employer ***does not supply needed tools*** or other instrumentality;

- transfer is for an ***extended time or indefinite period***; and

- special employer has a ***right of discharge***.

   Example: General employer supplied a truck and driver to special employer. Special employer was to pay the driver at an hourly rate. Special employer's own employees loaded the truck, sealed it and sent the driver to a railroad terminal where special employer's employees unloaded the truck. While en route between the two special employer locations, the truck driver negligently injured T.

Held, General employer and not special employer was liable for the truck driver's negligence. In a famous opinion by Judge Cardozo, then on the New York Court of Appeals, the rule was stated as follows: "as long as the employee is *furthering the business of his general employer by the service rendered to another, there will be no inference of a new relation unless command has been surrendered,* and no inference of its surrender from the mere fact of its division." *Charles v. Barrett,* 135 N.E. 199, 200 (N.Y. 1922).

2. **Seventh Circuit transfer test:** The Seventh Circuit in *Green v. United States,* 709 F.2d 1158 (7th Cir. 1983) applied a similar analysis in holding the general employer liable. The court stated that a servant would be held to be the *employee of the general employer* rather than the special employer *unless all of the following four questions could be answered affirmatively:*

   a. **Employee consent:** Did the employee actually or impliedly consent to work for the special employer?

   b. **Whose work:** Was the employee performing the special employer's work at the time of the injury?

   c. **Right to control:** Did the special employer have the right to control the details of the work being performed? and

   d. **Beneficiary of work:** Was the work of the employee primarily for the benefit of the special employer?

   Example: The United States government (general employer) authorizes S, an Air Force surgeon, to be retrained in surgical procedures by working with special employer. S continues to be paid by the government during his training, under an unpaid fellowship from special employer. During his training, S operates negligently on T, and a malpractice suit is brought against the general employer. The government's defense is that S was a borrowed servant of the special employer and that vicarious liability was transferred to the special employer.

   Held, S was not transferred to the special employer and the government is liable. The presumption is that S remains an employee of the general employer (the government) rather than the special employer. The fact that S was working under the supervision of the special employer's physicians does not automatically make S a borrowed servant. Using the criteria above, the fourth requirement is not met; that is, S's training fellowship was primarily for the benefit of the general employer, not the special employer. The general employer would not have agreed to continue to pay S if it did not expect to benefit. The training suited the general employer's needs; S was in a highly skilled profession; S was a "fellow" not an employee; and S was to remain in training for a limited time. These facts show that neither employment nor liability was transferred to the special employer. *Green v. United States,* 709 F.2d 1158 (7th Cir. 1983).

3. **Right of special employer to control risk:** The special employer rather than the general employer will sometimes be held liable if the special employer can better predict and prevent accidents than the general employer., i.e., if he is in a better position to control the risk.

Example: General employer leases a crane and operator (S) to special employer for use in constructing a factory. Special employer's other employees give signals to S indicating when and in what direction the boom should be turned. S operates the crane negligently and injures T. T sues general employer for damages, contending that S is general employer's servant. General employer contends that S was special employer's servant at the time of T's injuries and that only special employer is responsible.

Held, General employer is not vicariously liable. The benefits test is not useful because both general and special employer's businesses benefited from the arrangement (general employer benefited by the lease arrangement; special employer benefited by the construction assistance). Under the right-to-control test, however, we conclude that S was under the special employer's exclusive control. The movement of the crane was being directed by special employer's foreman. S had knowledge to assist in the work only when directed by special employer's foreman, who knew how the construction was to progress. It is not material that S's negligent movement of the crane may have been contrary to a specific signal from special employer's foreman. Special employer had the exclusive right to direct all movements of the crane, and general employer did not. *Nepstad v. Lambert,* 50 N.W.2d 614 (Minn. 1951).

Note: In the *Nepstad* case, the general employer selected S for the job, paid S's wages and administered such matters as social security and workers' compensation in S's behalf. General employer could also direct the manner in which the crane was cared for. While these are elements of control, they were more remote than the special employer's control, which was the detailed, on-the-spot control of S's movements. S was responding to the commands and instructions of the special employer's foreman. Thus special employer, and not general employer, was liable for S's negligent crane operation.

D. Dual liability: Under the minority view, which prevails at least in Pennsylvania, both employers can be held liable for a borrowed servant's negligence. However, these cases are frequently decided on special facts which show that the servant's work *directly benefited both employers.*

Example: General employer allows special employer to use general employer's truck for one week in special employer's gasoline business. Special employer agrees that after one week, special employer may buy or lease the truck. General employer's license plates are on the truck, and general employer pays the driver, S. During the week, S demonstrates and operates the truck with the intent to make the sale of the truck to special employer, but he does so by performing tasks with the truck for special employer's business. While S is unloading the truck for one of special employer's customers, S negligently causes gasoline to overflow from the truck. The gasoline explodes, killing T. Suit is brought against both general and special employers.

Held, both general and special employers are vicariously liable for S's negligence. The act which caused the explosion was performed on behalf of both employers. S was promoting general employer's interest by manipulating the machinery of the truck to demonstrate its ability to cause gasoline to flow efficiently. If the mechanism on the tank would not discharge the gasoline, special employer would not buy the truck. S was also acting for special employer at the time of the explosion by delivering gasoline to its customer. Thus, S's negligent conduct was performed for both employers. *Gordon v. S. M. Byers Motor Car Co.,* 164 A. 334 (Pa. 1932).

1. **Dual liability rejected by majority:** Most courts reject the dual liability approach in favor of the more traditional borrowed servant analysis, which requires that the servant be deemed the employee of either the general employer or the special employer, but not of both.

   Example: General employer leased a crane and driver (S) to special employer. S's negligent crane operation injured T, one of special employer's employees. T was entitled to worker's compensation benefits from special employer. T also brought a tort action against general employer. T argued for dual liability.

   Held, the dual liability approach was rejected. The dual liability approach would require the courts to decide if each employer retained sufficient control to make it liable. The courts would have to determine what minimal level of responsibility would make each employer responsible. Because T's claim against the special employer is limited to a worker's compensation claim, the general employer could be liable even though it had little control and could not require contribution from the special employer. The court affirmed a judgment in favor of the general employer. *DePratt v. Sergio*, 306 N.W.2d 62 (Wis. 1981).

VIII. PRINCIPAL'S LIABILITY FOR AGENT'S FRAUDULENT MISREPRESENTATIONS

A. No master-servant relationship required: Because society has an interest in discouraging deceit in business transactions, it imposes liability upon the principal for the fraud or deceit of his agent. A master-servant relationship need not exist for a principal to be liable. ***The agent need only be actually or apparently authorized, or have the inherent authority, to act for the principal.***

B. Misrepresentation: This term refers to a wide variety of tortious conduct. Courts use the terms ***"misrepresentation," "fraud"*** and ***"deceit"*** interchangeably to mean essentially the same thing. At common law, the cause of action for misrepresentation or fraud was called the tort of deceit. See, *Emanuel* on *Torts*, "Misrepresentation."

1. **Requirements:** The following elements are required to establish deceit or misrepresentation:

   - ***False statement*** of a material fact;

   - ***Knowledge*** by the person making the statement that it is false (known as ***scienter*** or ***culpable state of mind)***;

   - ***Intent to deceive***—some courts still require that the agent have the intent to deceive, but a number of courts now require only a negligent misrepresentation (some limit liability for negligent misrepresentation to business relationships and/or to a limited class of third persons, e.g., only those the agent intends to deceive);

   - ***Justifiable reliance*** on the statement; and

   - ***Damage*** stemming from the reliance.

   Note: The agent's conduct may be both tortious and criminal, as in the next Example.

   Example: Attorney (A), representing P, negotiated a settlement of an automobile lawsuit against D. A received a check from D's insurer, forged P's endorsement and absconded with the proceeds of the settlement. A also discontinued the lawsuit. When P learned what A had done, he tried to reinstate the lawsuit against D.

   Held, P could not reinstate the lawsuit because he was bound by the fraudulent actions of his A. D bargained in good faith with A and had no reason to suspect his behavior was deceitful. **When one of two innocent parties must suffer as a result of A's fraud, the one who accredited him (the P) must bear the loss.** The fact that A's conduct was criminal and violated his obligation to P does not relieve P of liability. *Rothman v. Fillette,* 469 A.2d 543 (Pa. 1983).

C. Innocent misrepresentation: If the agent's misrepresentation is innocent there is no liability by the principal in tort, but the third person who justifiably relied on it may be able to rescind the contract, p. 126, *infra.*

D. Employer liability: An employer is liable for a servant's misrepresentation or deceit if the misrepresentation:

- *is made in the course of employment,* and

- *is authorized or apparently authorized, or is within the agent's power* to make for the principal. Rest. (2d) § 257.

1. Authorized: A statement is authorized if the agent has reason to believe from his principal's conduct that the principal wants the statement to be made even though it is not true.

2. Apparently authorized: A representation is apparently authorized if the third party to the transaction reasonably believes, as a result of conduct for which the principal is responsible, that the agent is authorized by the principal to make the representation as made. Rest. (2d) § 257, comment a.

    a. Derives from law of contracts: The theory under which a principal is held liable for the representations of his agent, both authorized and apparently authorized, originates not from the law of agency and the principle of **respondeat superior**; but from the theory which imposes underlying **liability upon authorized or apparently authorized contracts.** Rest. (2d) § 257, comment a.

Example: P operates an automobile repair garage. T drives his automobile into the garage and asks P to remove a front wheel, replace a washer on the axle, pack it with grease and replace the wheel. S, who is not a servant of P, but who wants employment with P, says, "Just drive over here and I'll be glad to do that for you." P hears S but remains silent. Believing that S is one of P's mechanics, T does as directed, and S makes the repairs. However, S fails to secure the front wheel tightly to the axle but negligently represents to T that the car is "as good and safe as new." T drives away, but the wheel comes off and T is injured. T sues P for damages.

Held, T may recover. By permitting S to represent himself to T as an employee of P, P held S out as being an employee. When P permitted S to work on T's car, P was representing to T that S was working within the scope of his employment. On these facts T could reasonably conclude that S was an employee of P, acting within the scope of his employment. The negligent misrepresentation of the car's safety made by S was clearly within the apparent scope of his employment. P is liable to T for S's misrepresentation. Rest. (2d) §§ 261, 266, Illustration 2.

3. **Within the inherent power of the agent:** A representation is within the inherent power of the agent if it is usually within the scope of similar general agency relationships. To recover against the principal for the agent's fraudulent misrepresentations, the third person must reasonably believe that the agent has authority to make the representation, *supra,* p. 124. Even an undisclosed principal may be liable if a general agent makes misrepresentations within the scope of his powers.

4. **Exculpatory clauses:** A *principal may be able to relieve himself of liability* in damages for his agent's fraudulent misrepresentations if the agreement with the third person contains a sufficiently specific exculpatory clause. Generally, these clauses will *not relieve the agent of liability* to the third person. *Glendale Realty, Inc. v. Johnson,* 495 P.2d 1375 (Wash. Ct. App. 1972).

Example 1: In negotiating to sell a building, seller's (P's) agent (A) fraudulently misrepresented the condition of an oil burner. Believing A, T purchased the building. The sales agreement contained an exculpatory clause stating that P had made no representation as to the physical condition of the building or as to services. T sued P and A for misrepresentation.

Held, P was not liable because the exculpatory clause was specific enough to cover the representations made by A. In effect, the exculpatory clause rendered the representation nonexistent as to P. T still had a cause of action against A because the exculpatory provision, by its express language, did not protect A. *Wittenberg v. Robinov,* 173 N.E.2d 868 (N.Y. 1961).

a. **Third party cannot rely:** Some courts hold that a third person who has agreed to an exculpatory clause should not be entitled to rely on the representations of the agent and should be barred from asserting claims against the principal on the theory that forewarned is forearmed. *Danann Realty Corp. v. Harris,* 157 N.E.2d 597 (N.Y. 1959). On the other hand, because the third party can always sue the agent, his claim against the agent should not be foreclosed by the existence of the exculpatory clause, although the clause may prevent him from showing that he relied on the agent's authority to make the statement for the principal. *Wittenberg v. Robinov, supra.*

Example 2: Seller's (P's) agent (A) showed buyer (T) certain property, erroneously but honestly, believing it to be property P had authorized him to sell. The sales agreement contained an exculpatory clause stating that T waived reliance upon any representation not contained in the agreement.

Held, P was liable for damages. "[D]espite the provision, the purchaser was justified in believing that the agent had authority to show and sell property of the principal . . . ." *Eamoe v. Big Bear Land & Water Co.,* 220 P.2d 408 (Cal. Dist. Ct. App. 1950).

Note: If A's representations had been as to the quality of the land, P would not have been liable.

5. **Action for rescission:** If the agent's representations were not actually or apparently authorized or within the agent's inherent authority, the principal will not be liable to the third person, p. 124, *supra.* However, the third person will be able to rescind the transaction, unless the principal has changed his position before learning of the fraud. Change of position is a defense if the agent did not have the power to bind the principal. Change of position is not a defense if the principal was liable for the misrepresentations. Rest. (2d) § 259.

   a. **Exculpatory clause does not affect rescission:** The existence of an exculpatory clause will not affect the third person's right to rescind. *Dembowski v. Central Constr. Co.,* 185 N.W.2d 461 (Neb. 1971).

   b. **Principal's refusal to rescind may be ratification of fraud:** If the third person notifies the principal of the agent's fraud and seeks to rescind the contract but the principal refuses, the principal may be held to have ratified the contract and then become liable for damages. See *Light v. Chandler Improvement Co.,* 261 P. 969 (Ariz. 1928).

CHAPTER 9

RIGHTS AND LIABILITIES OF AGENTS IN TORT

ChapterScope ━━━━━━━━━━━━━━━━━━━━━━━━━━━━━━

The previous chapter analyzed the ***principal's liability*** for the agent's torts. This chapter discusses the ***agent's*** rights and liabilities in tort. We discuss the right of third parties to recover against the agent, the agent's right to recover against third parties, and the agent's obligation to indemnify his principal for the damages recovered against him by third parties. We also cover the right of the servant to recover from his employer for work-related injuries, usually through workers' compensation. In general:

■ The agent must ***indemnify*** (reimburse) the principal for damages the principal must pay to third parties for the agent's tort.

■ The employer is liable to the agent or servant for ***work-related injuries*** (this obligation is normally met through workers compensation insurance). By statute, the employer's liability to his employee ends when the employee is covered by workers' compensation.

■ The servant is liable to ***third persons*** for injuries resulting from the servant's own torts, whether or not the principal is also liable under ***respondeat superior.*** The servant may not assert as a defense the fact that he was acting for someone else, i.e., his master.

■ A ***third person who commits a tort against the servant,*** is liable to the servant for his injuries.

━━

I. PRINCIPAL'S RIGHT TO INDEMNIFICATION

A. General rule: If a principal has been held ***vicariously liable to third parties for the agent's tort, the agent must indemnify*** (reimburse) the principal. The agent has a duty to indemnify the principal whether she was acting as a servant or an independent contractor.

Example: Master (M) is riding in the rear seat of an automobile driven by his chauffeur, Servant (S). S negligently injures T. T sues both M and S for his injuries. M enters a cross-complaint against S, seeking judgment for any amount T recovers against M.

Held, T may recover from M and S; M may recover on his cross-complaint against S. M is liable for the negligent acts of S which are performed within the scope of his employment under the doctrine of ***respondeat superior.*** Since S negligently injured T, S is also liable to T. As between M and S, M has a right to be made whole (indemnified) for any loss which has been imposed upon him due to S's negligence. See Rest. (2d) § 401.

Note: A servant who negligently uses a tool or instrument supplied by the master, causing injuries to the master, is liable to the master for damages. For instance: M hires S as a chauffeur. S drives M's car negligently while M is riding in the rear seat. M is injured and the car is damaged. M may recover damages from S for injuries to himself and his car.

B. Contribution by joint tortfeasors distinguished: The obligation of a servant to his master is different from the liability of one joint tortfeasor to another. Joint tortfeasors are two or more persons who are the proximate cause of the plaintiff's harm. Their responsibility is considered "indivisible," and each is liable for the entire harm. Their liability is said to be "joint and several." At common law, there was no right of contribution by one tortfeasor to another. Today, however, most states permit contribution among joint tortfeasors by statute. (See, e.g., 740 Ill. Comp. Stat. 100/0.01 *et seq.*) The contribution amount is typically determined by the tortfeasors' allocable share of fault.

   1. **Different theory in master-servant indemnification:** A principal is not considered the joint tortfeasor of an agent who commits a tort unless the principal's own negligence is also a proximate cause of the injury. For this reason, when a master or principal obtains indemnification from a servant or agent who has committed a tort, she is entitled to full recovery rather than only a share. The reason for this distinction is that the master or principal is not herself negligent; her liability is based strictly on the fault of her servant or agent.

C. Failure to follow instructions: The principal also has the right to indemnity from an agent for any loss caused by the agent's failure to follow instructions.

Example: P instructs A to sell certain goods without any warranties. If A sells the goods with a warranty and P is held liable on that warranty, P may recover her losses from A.

D. Federal employees excepted: Under the Federal Tort Claims Act, the *federal government is precluded from seeking indemnity* from its employees for their negligence.

Example: S, a government employee, negligently injures T while driving a government car. T sues the government under the Federal Tort Claims Act. The government files a third party complaint against S, asking indemnity from S if it is found liable to T. The court finds that the accident was caused by S's negligence while S acted within the scope of his employment.

   Held, the government is not entitled to indemnification from S under the Federal Tort Claims Act, even though the government is liable to T only as a result of S's negligence. The Federal Tort Claims Act imposed liability on the federal government for the negligence of its employees, placing the federal government in the same position as any private employer. However, the Act imposed no liability on the part of federal employees themselves. When the government sues an employee, it commits its tremendous resources to haul him into court and imposes a discipline on him second only to discharge. The financial burden to the employee, the loss of his working time, and the effect on his efficiency and morale must be considered. Congress was silent on the issue of employee indemnity and the courts should not impose it by judicial decision. Selection of the most appropriate policy, considering all the circumstances, should be left to Congress, which makes the laws, rather than to the courts, which interpret them. *United States v. Gilman,* 347 U.S. 507 (1954).

II. INJURIES TO SERVANT WHILE EMPLOYED— WORKERS' COMPENSATION

A. **Introductory note:** Originally, most laws dealing with compensation to employees for injuries suffered in the course of their employment were called "workmen's compensation" laws. In keeping with the trend toward the elimination of sexist terminology in the law, many states now call these laws "workers' compensation" laws.

B. **Traditional view:** Under the common law, a master was liable for the injuries of a servant only if the master's negligence was the cause of the injuries. A master could defend a suit by a servant on one of the following grounds:

1. **Fellow servant rule:** The master was *not* liable for injuries caused an employee by another employee, ***so long as the master used ordinary care in hiring the "fellow servant."*** However, the master was liable if the negligence was that of an employee who worked in a different department than the injured employee. The rationale for the underlying rule, and for the exception, is that ***workers who work together*** or in proximity to each other can observe the level of care and precaution taken by their fellows and are in a better position than the employer to protect themselves against carelessness;

2. **Assumption of the risk:** By accepting the job in the first place, the employee assumed the risk of injury in the course of his employment; and

3. **Contributory negligence:** The injured employee was himself negligent and, therefore, could not recover on the theory of contributory negligence.

C. Modern view: Today, the harshness of the common law rules has been eliminated by statutes.

1. **Federal Employers Liability Act:** This act applies to interstate carriers. It eliminates both the fellow servant rule and the defense of assumption of the risk by employees. *Tiller v. Atlantic Coast Line R.R. Co.,* 318 U.S. 54 (1943).

2. **Workers' compensation laws:** All states have adopted laws under which employees are awarded compensation for accidental injury occurring within the scope of employment.

   a. **Purpose:** Workers' compensation laws serve a vital social and economic purpose. Injuries to employees occur in every business. In the absence of an organized compensation system, the worker who is injured is thrown on his own resources. He may find that his employer has no funds with which to compensate him or his dependents for his injuries. It's important to have in place a system the employee can depend upon. The cost of this system should be borne by the employers. They enjoy the fruits of the employees' labors and they are better able to afford it.

   b. **Scope:** Coverage under workers' compensation laws varies from state to state. Generally, the terms "employee" and "scope of employment" are usually construed more broadly than under the doctrine of ***respondeat superior***. As a result, many accidents are covered by workers compensation that would not be covered under ***respondeat superior***. Furthermore, coverage is not limited to accidents, but includes occupational diseases. A disease is covered if the job caused an unusual degree of exposure to harmful conditions, or greater exposure than in other jobs. Even if an employee's pre-existing condition made her particularly susceptible to the disease, it will usually be covered if increased exposure on the job contributed to her illness. Larson's Workmen's Compensation Law § 41.00 (1996).

   Example: Employee suffered an inflammation of the tissue between his ribs and sternum (costochondritis) as a result of lifting heavy rolls of cloth averaging a total of 20,000 pounds a day.

   Held, the employee was entitled to recover under the workers' compensation statute because his condition was clearly characteristic of his employment. *Thomason v. Fiber Indus.,* 336 S.E.2d 632 (N.C. Ct. App. 1985).

   i. **Rational for broader scope:** Employees generally recover substantially less under workers' compensation than they would recover in a tort action based on the same facts and the same injuries. This is one of the reasons the workers' compensation laws are designed to expand upon coverage by enlarging the definitions of such terms as "employee" and "scope of employment." Under workers' compensation, employers pay into a fund and an injured employee can recover for his injury on the basis of an award which is based upon prefixed schedules. No recovery is permitted for emotional distress or punitive damages. In addition, under workers' compensation law, an employer is liable only to a finite number of scheduled employees, whereas under *respondeat superior*, an employer is potentially liable to an infinite number of third persons. *Luth v. Rogers & Babler Constr. Co.,* 507 P.2d 761, 764 (Alaska 1973).

Examples: A police officer who shot himself while unholstering his pistol at home after work was held to be acting within the course of his employment because the employer did not provide any place on its premises for unloading and storing weapons. *City of Harrisburg v. Workmen's Compensation Appeal Board,* 616 A.2d 1369 (Pa. 1992). Similarly, an employee injured while playing for his employer's softball team was acting within the course of his employment when the employer paid a share of the rental fee for the field and provided the bats and balls. *LeSuer-Johnson v. Rollins-Burdick Hunter of Alaska,* 808 P.2d 266 (Alaska 1991).

c. **Defenses abolished:** The elements of negligence, assumption of the risk and foreseeability of the injury do not affect recovery under workers' compensation statutes. An injured employee is covered so long as he is injured on the job and is within the scope of employment, whether or not his employer or his fellow employees are the cause of his accident.

Example: An unusual hurricane caused a wall to fall on S while at work. S was entitled to workers' compensation because S's injury arose out of his employment and occurred at the place where he worked (the wall). *Caswell's Case,* 26 N.E.2d 328 (Mass. 1940).

d. **Recovery:** Under most workers' compensation statutes, a state agency awards compensation for the injury. The award is paid either by a commercial carrier or out of a state fund. Usually, the award precludes any other legal action by the employee against the employer or another employee. N.Y. Work. Comp. Law § 29 (6) (McKinney 1996); 820 Ill. Comp. Stat. 305/5(a).

III.   AGENT'S LIABILITY TO THIRD PERSONS

A. General rule: An agent or servant who commits a tort is personally liable to an injured third person, even though she was acting for her principal or master and was within the scope of employment at the time.

Example 1: P sends her chauffeur, S, to the store to buy groceries. S drives off alone and negligently injures T. T may recover from S. The fact that S was acting within the scope of his employment makes P also liable to T, but it does not relieve S of his liability for the tort. Rest. (2d) § 343.

Example 2: Suppose in the example above, P accompanies S and directs S to strike and injure T. The same rule applies as in **Example 1** and makes S liable for injuring T. However, in this case, the tort of battery is intentional, rather than negligent. P and S are joint tortfeasors and are jointly and severally liable to T.

B. Fraud: An agent or independent contractor may be liable to third persons if he *knowingly* assists in the commission of fraud or duress by his principal. However, if the agent has no knowledge of the fraud intended by his principal, he is not liable. Rest. (2d) § 348.

Example: P tells S to sell a lamp which P represents as a valuable antique. As P knows, but S does not, the lamp is a cheap modern imitation. S sells the lamp to T as an antique. S is not liable to T. Rest. (2d) § 348, Illustration 3.

C. Defense of privilege: If the agent is acting within the scope of employment for her principal, and the principal would be privileged to do the act, then the agent is also privileged. Rest. (2d) § 345.

Example: P has a right of way which permits P to drive his trucks over T's land. P's servant, A, acting for P, drives P's truck over the right of way. T may not recover from A for trespass. Of course, if A had not been acting for P, then A would have been liable to T for trespass. The right of way in P's favor is extended to her agents and servants while they act for P, and constitutes a good defense to the trespass. Rest. (2d) § 345, Illustration 1.

IV.   THIRD PERSON'S LIABILITY TO AGENT OR SERVANT

A. Contract liability: An agent who makes a contract with a third person for the account of his principal has no cause of action in contract or tort against the third person to recover the commission which agent was to receive for making the contract.

Example: P hires A to sell P's land. P agrees to pay A a commission of 10% of the sale price. A finds a buyer, T. P and T sign a sales contract. T refuses to perform and is released by P, who sells the land to another person. A sues T for breach of contract and claims damages to the extent of his commission.

Held, A may not recover. A negotiated the contract, which was signed by P and T. As to that transaction, there is no privity of contract between A and T. The only privity extending to A is A's privity with his principal, P, who agreed to pay A the 10% commission. A made no contract with T, so A has no right to recover for T's breach of contract. *Gibson Land Auction Co. v. Brittain,* 110 S.E. 82 (N.C. 1921); Rest. (2d) § 372(2).

B. Tort liability: If a third party injures a principal's agent, only the injured agent, not the principal, may sue the third party.

1. **Interference with advantageous relations:** A third person who wrongfully causes the servant's or agent's discharge is liable to the servant or agent in tort for interfering with his advantageous relation.

   Example: P is in the construction business, and S is one of his sheet metal workers. T is a casualty insurance company which insures P against damages for personal injuries to employees. A metal splinter flies into S's eye in the course of his employment and causes serious injury. T offers to settle with S for his injury for $50, but S refuses. T then insists that P discharge S as a condition to T's continuing P's casualty insurance policy. P discharges S, and S sues T for its conduct in causing S to be discharged from his job.

   Held, S may recover. Whether $50 is a fair and reasonable settlement should be settled in court. The question should not be settled by the use of economic compulsion such as T attempted to exert in this case. To force S to choose between losing his job and accepting what to him appeared to be an inadequate settlement for a personal injury was a form of extortion which the law cannot countenance. T's conduct is a tort as to S for which T is liable to S in damages. *U.S. Fidelity & Guaranty Co. v. Millonas,* 89 So. 732 (Ala. 1921).

CHAPTER 10

CRIMINAL RESPONSIBILITY OF PRINCIPAL AND AGENT

ChapterScope

Two or more persons can be liable in connection with the same crime. They may, for example, be co-conspirators. Co-conspirators are two or more people who form **an agreement** to commit either **an unlawful act** or **a lawful act by unlawful means.** The prosecution must prove the agreement, the unlawful objective, and a culpable intent (**mens rea).** Unless the principal in the ordinary agency relationship has participated with the agent to form a criminal conspiracy, he is not likely to be charged as a co-conspirator. A person may also be liable as **an accessory.** An **accessory before the fact** is one who aids and abets in the commission of a crime, but does not himself commit the crime. He need not be present at the crime. An **accessory after the fact** is one who does not participate in the crime itself but who furnishes assistance to the perpetrator after the crime is committed, e.g., by hiding him or impeding his arrest. It's easy to see that a principal can readily appear to be an accessory if the agent commits a crime in the course of his employment. One may also be an **accomplice** to a crime. An accomplice is anyone who **aids, abets, encourages or assists another** to commit a crime. As an accomplice, he is himself liable for the crime. Again, it's not difficult to see that a principal can easily be labelled the accomplice of an agent who commits a crime in the course of his employment. In this chapter, we will consider not these basic elements of **criminal law,** but the principles **of agency law** which may cause a principal to become liable for the crimes of his agent.

I. INTRODUCTION

A. Generally: The doctrine of **respondeat superior,** by itself, is not applicable to crimes. It deals with the **civil liability** of principals for the acts of their agents, **not with criminal matters.** A principal is not criminally liable for the crimes of his agent or servant unless he has previously **authorized** or **assented** to those acts (in which case, he will be liable not because he is a principal under agency law, but because he is a co-conspirator, an accessory or an accomplice).

B. Purpose of agency: By definition, a true agency can exist only for a lawful purpose. An agency created for the purpose of committing a crime is void as against public policy and becomes, instead, a criminal conspiracy.

C. Exception: Many criminal statutes dealing with regulatory offenses impose liability without fault. A principal may be prosecuted criminally under these statutes for the acts of his agents, *infra.*

D. Civil liability. In the same way as he may be liable to third parties for the torts of his agent, a principal may be liable *civilly* for injuries to third parties caused by the criminal acts of his agent committed within the scope of employment. See *supra,* p. 89.

E. Corporations: A corporation may be held responsible criminally for the acts of its officers or agents because it can only act through such officers or agents. The public has an interest in compelling the managers of corporations to control their employees so as to discourage the commission of crimes.

II. CRIMINAL RESPONSIBILITY OF PRINCIPAL FOR ACTS OF AGENT

A. General rule: A principal is not ordinarily liable for the criminal acts of her agent or servant unless she has previously authorized or assented to such acts, even though the agent or servant was acting within the scope of employment.

B. Exceptions: A principal is liable without criminal intent or negligence under various regulatory statutes. Regulatory criminal statutes often impose liability without fault. These statutes often involve matters such as public morals, health, peace and safety. The following examples demonstrate circumstances under which the principal may be held liable.

Example 1: A statute makes it a criminal offense to sell intoxicating liquor to a minor. P operates a nightclub, and his bartender, S, sells liquor to a minor. P and S are arrested. S argues that he was acting only as P's agent. P contends that he did not personally sell the liquor, and that he had given S specific orders not to sell liquor to minors.

Held, the defenses are not valid. S did the act prohibited, so he is criminally liable under the statute. S's belief that the minor was of legal drinking age is no defense. P's criminal responsibility represents an exception to the general rule that one person is not criminally liable for a criminal act committed by another person. The act in this case is a crime only because the statute so declares. If P were not criminally responsible for the acts of his agent, the purpose of the law could not be realized. P could ignore the law and simply say, "I told him not to do it," if charged with a violation. *Mo Yaen v. State,* 163 P. 135 (Ariz. 1917).

Example 2: P's employee sold mislabeled motor oil. At the time, P was away from the station, was not aware of the activity and did not condone it.

Held, P's conviction was affirmed. The legislature intended to impose strict liability irrespective of fault. Statutes controlling the *mis-*

labeling of products are among the regulatory statutes which impose liability on individuals without criminal intent. This is one area in which employers can be held liable for the criminal activity of their employees. *People v. Travers,* 124 Cal. Rptr. 728, 729 (Ct. App. 1975).

Example 3: P owns land on which he operates a feed yard for cattle. The operation is conducted wholly through P's employees. The employees dump refuse from the animals in a creek, thereby polluting the water and creating a public nuisance. Under the applicable statute, P is criminally liable even though he did not know of the pollution and had instructed his servants not to pollute the stream.

C. Partnerships: Partnerships are different from true agencies in that the partners are working towards a common purpose with a common economic interest in the outcome. In a true agency, the employee/servant is serving the interest of his principal. Though his purpose may be the same, his economic interest is usually substantially different from the principal's.

1. **General rule: authorization required:** In the absence of a statute imposing vicarious criminal liability, partners have generally not been held criminally liable for the crimes of their partners if they did not authorize or participate in the criminal act. *United States v. Quinn*, 141 F. Supp. 622 (S.D.N.Y. 1956). However, as with employers, a partner may be liable if the statute in question eliminates the need to prove criminal intent.

2. **Vicarious criminal liability imposed by statute:** A   statute may be written in such a way as to impose criminal liability for a partner's act on the partnership as a unit. Typically, the statute defines "person" to include a "partnership," and requires the partner who commits the crime to have acted with the criminal intent specified in the statute. *People v. Smithtown General Hospital,* 399 N.Y.S.2d 993 (N.Y. Sup. Ct. 1977). In *Smithtown,* a general partnership operated an entire hospital. The partnership was indicted for allowing an unauthorized person to perform surgery on a nonconsenting patient and for falsifying the hospital records to cover it up. The court refused to dismiss the indictment. It rejected the argument that a general partnership could not be liable as a whole for the crime of one partner. It relied on the need to regulate the partnership, and not simply the individual partner, in order to protect the public interest. The *Smithtown* case is somewhat unusual in that it involved a hospital, a business which elicits special protective instincts on the part of the judiciary.

    a. **Non-participating partners:** The earlier cases refused to impose statutory penalties against partners who did not participate in the commission of the crime. See, e.g., *Schreiber & Sons v. Charles Sharpless & Sons,* 6 F. 175 (E.D. Pa. 1881). The more modern cases impose statutory criminal penalties against non-participating partners. For example, in *Calvey v. United States,* 448 F.2d 177 (6th Cir. 1971), a partner's property was assessed for a tax fraud penalty incurred by her co-partner. The modern cases rely on § 13 of the Uniform Partnership Act, which provides.

> Where, by any wrongful act or omission of any partner acting in the ordinary course of the business of the partnership or with the authority of his co-partners, loss or injury is caused to any person, not being a partner in the partnership, or any penalty is incurred, the partnership is liable therefor to the same extent as the partner so acting or omitting to act.

The underlying intent of this provision is carried over into Section 305 of the Revised Uniform Partnership Act of 1994.

D. Independent contractors: A principal is not liable for the criminal acts of an independent contractor if she has no control over the criminal act, even though the act may have been done within the scope of employment.

Example: P University employs A, an independent contractor, to design and construct a heating and cooling plant. A is responsible for inspecting and testing all materials and workmanship, and has authority to reject anything defective. Sub-A, a mechanical contractor working under A, has responsibility to conduct tests of the oil system in the plant. During installation of the system, Sub-A directs P University's plant supervisor to turn on the oil pumps to test the system. Sub-A then performs additional work, but never directs the plant supervisor to turn the system off. As a result, the oil overflows into a river. Criminal charges are brought against P University for discharging oil into the river.

Held, P University is not criminally liable. At the time of the incident, P University had not accepted the new power system. A and Sub-A were independent contractors and P University did not control their conduct. All construction was planned and arranged by A, and all tests of the power system were conducted by Sub-A. University was not in control of the oil leak at any time. When P University's plant supervisor turned on the oil pump, it was at the direction of Sub-A, and the plant supervisor became a borrowed servant of Sub-A at that time. See *supra,* p. 119. The plant supervisor, who had not been instructed in the mechanics of the system, could not be expected to turn off the system without specific orders from Sub-A. When the principal does everything that a reasonable, prudent person could be expected to do, no liability is imposed. Even though the statute involved was a strict liability statute, in the absence of a showing that the university exercised some control over the individuals involved, there could be no criminal responsibility. *United States v. Georgetown Univ.*, 331 F. Supp. 69 (D.D.C. 1971).

1. **Rationale behind decision:** The court explained: "In cases like the one here involving strict liability, while not requiring the usual element of criminal intent, they do necessitate some element of control by those indicted. . . . When one is not in control of facilities which lead to a violation of statutes like those in the case at bar, the ultimate result or damage to persons or property should be examined in the light of the Congressional policy to impose strict liability upon only those corporations or individuals who have it peculiarly within their power through the exercise of due diligence to protect the public." Id., p. 73.

III. CRIMINAL LIABILITY OF CORPORATIONS AND THEIR AGENTS

A. **Traditional view:** Under the early common law, a corporation could not be charged with a crime. The courts reasoned that because corporations were not natural persons, but fictions of the law, they could not possess the criminal intent required for crimes. *Commonwealth v. Illinois Central R.R. Co.*, 153 S.W. 459 (Ky. 1913); Henn & Alexander, Laws of Corporations 480 (3d ed. 1983).

B. **Modern view:** Today, a corporation may be held criminally liable for the acts of its agent, provided the corporation authorized the agent to act for it in the *particular* activity which resulted in the crime. The agent's criminal acts and intent are imputed to the corporation. The factors to be considered in determining whether the corporation is criminally responsible include:

- "the extent of control and authority exercised by the agent or corporate officer over and within the corporation;

- the extent and manner to which corporate funds were used in the commission of the crime; and

- whether there is a repeated pattern of criminal conduct tending to indicate corporation toleration or ratification of the agent's acts." *Commonwealth v. Beneficial Fin. Co.*, 275 N.E.2d 33, 86 (Mass. 1971).

1. **Application:** Corporations have been held criminally liable in libel, assault and battery, involuntary manslaughter based on negligence, and other crimes requiring specific intent. The intent of the

agent or officer of the corporation who commits the crime while acting within the scope of his authority is imputed to the corporation.

Example: A truck owned by a corporation ran over two children as they descended from a school bus. The corporation was indicted for manslaughter. The corporation moved to dismiss the indictment, arguing that it could not be indicted for a serious crime which required either an evil intent or a violation of social policy.

Held, the corporation was subject to indictment for manslaughter under the statute. The legislature contemplated that corporations could be fined for commission of all classes of crimes. *Commonwealth v. Fortner LP Gas Co., Inc.,* 610 S.W.2d 941 (Ky. Ct. App. 1980).

2. **Rationale:** If corporations were immune from criminal prosecution, the state would be unable to enforce much of the great body of criminal legislation designed to protect the general public; the legislation would be rendered ineffective.

C. **Liability of corporate agent:** The agent of a corporation who commits an offense for the benefit of the corporation may be held personally liable for his crime, even though the act was within the scope of the agent's employment and even if the corporation itself could not be convicted of that offense.

D. **Liability of corporate officer:** Usually, a corporate officer will be held personally liable for the crimes of the corporation only if it is shown that the acts were done by her, at her direction or with her approval.

Chapter 11

TERMINATION OF THE AGENCY RELATIONSHIP

ChapterScope

In this chapter, we deal with the methods by which an agency relationship may be terminated or dissolved. The relationship may be terminated by *agreement of the parties,* by the *unilateral decision of one* of the parties, as the consequence of *a party's breach*, or *by operation of law.* The termination of an agency relationship affects not only the principal and agent, but also third parties who have been affected by the relationship. We give special attention to the impact of termination on agencies coupled with an interest.

I. INTRODUCTION

A. **General rule of unrestricted power to terminate:** As we have seen, an agency is a consensual relationship between at least two parties. Generally, the relationship can be terminated by either the agent or the principal at any time.

   1. **Exception for agency coupled with an interest:** If, however, the agent's power is coupled with an interest (e.g., she has paid consideration for her power), then the principal cannot terminate her interest.

   2. **Principal's liability for wrongful termination:** Even if an agent is functioning under a long term contract, the principal may prematurely terminate the agency relationship. However, the principal will be liable to the agent in an action for breach of contract. If the agent is employed at will, the principal may fire her, but the principal may be liable to her in a tort action if his actions are in violation of some public policy. In these cases, the principal may have the *power to fire her,* but not the *right* to fire her.

B. **Notice of termination:**

   1. **Notice between principal and agent:** No particular form of notice is required as between principal and agent. As long as one party clearly manifests his intention to terminate to the other, the agency is over.

   2. **Notice to third parties:** When the agent has continuing authority (i.e., the authority of a *general agent*), the agent's *apparent* authority continues unless third parties are notified of the termination. To terminate the agent's apparent authority, the principal

must notify third persons of the termination of the relationship. Notice is usually not required if the agent had authority for one transaction only (i.e., authority as a ***special agent***), or if the agency is terminated by operation of law.

C. Termination by operation of law: The agency can be terminated by operation of law. Some of the events which qualify to terminate an agency relationship are the death, incapacity, or bankruptcy of the principal or agent.

II. TERMINATION BY WILL OF THE PRINCIPAL OR AGENT

A. Methods of termination by will: Termination by will occurs if either the principal or agent notifies the other that the agency is terminated, or if an agreed-upon event or contingency occurs, such as the completion of the agent's task. Rest. (2d) §§ 117, 134.

1. **Termination by notification to the principal or agent:** The agency relationship terminates whenever either the agent or principal notifies the other that the relationship is terminated. No special form of notification is required. As long as one party manifests to the other that he does not want the agency relationship to continue, it is terminated.

   Example 1: A hears from T, a friend of P, that P has terminated A's authority. A's authority is terminated even if it was given to him in writing and under seal. Rest. (2d) § 119, comment a, Illustrations 1-3. Note that A's apparent authority may still continue, *infra*.

   Example 2: P employs A as a salesman and tells A that he will place all important notices on a company bulletin board. He directs A to come to the office and check the board every Wednesday. P posts a notice on the bulletin board terminating A's employment. A's employment is terminated on the Wednesday following posting, whether or not A sees the notice. See Rest. (2d) § 119, Illustration 6.

   Example 3: P authorizes A to sell his car. A sees T driving the car around town with a new license plate. A should infer that P has sold or disposed of the car and that his authority to sell it has terminated. Rest. (2d) § 108(1).

2. **Termination by contractual contingency:** The agreement creating the agency relationship may specify that the agent's authority will terminate upon the happening of an event. If so, then the occurrence of that event terminates the agent's authority without the need for further action by the principal. Similarly, if the agency has

a particular goal or objective, e.g., to sell a particular piece of real property, accomplishment of the objective will terminate the agency relationship. It's reasonable to infer that the parties would not want the agency to continue once its purpose has been achieved.

B. Liability of principal for wrongful termination: A principal may be liable for terminating the agency in breach of the agency contract (unless the agent has violated a fiduciary duty), or for terminating the agency in violation of an important public policy.

1. **Contractual rights of agent:** If an agent has a long-term contract, the principal still has the *power* to fire him and thereby terminate the agency relationship. However, the principal will be liable to the agent in damages for breach of contract. Even without a formal contract, the agent may have a cause of action for breach if he has been given assurance that he will not be fired except for cause and he is fired without good cause. *Pugh v. See's Candies, Inc.,* 250 Cal. Rptr. 195 (Ct. App. 1988).

   a. **Agent's breach of fiduciary duties:** A principal will not be liable for firing an agent in violation of their contractual arrangement if the agent has *breached his fiduciary duty.*

   Example: P Corporation hired A to manage its mines. A was to keep P Corp. informed of all management activities, to act for P Corp.'s benefit, to be guided by P Corp.'s suggestions and to use its best efforts to maintain a certain level of coal production. If either party breached, the other could terminate upon 60 days' notice to give the defaulting party an opportunity to cure its breach. A tried to pressure a potential buyer of P's stock to change some provisions of the stock purchase agreement. To put pressure on the stock buyer, A attempted to prevent P Corp. from using certain real estate. A also refused to replace topsoil which it had removed from P's property, even though A was enjoined by a restraining order from interfering with P Corp.'s use of the property. A's attorney also tried to interfere with the renewal of P Corp.'s mining permit. A sued P for terminating A's authority without notice.

   Held, if A violated its fiduciary duty to its principal, P Corp., it could be fired at any time, notwithstanding the 60 day notice provision. The determination whether A had breached its fiduciary duty to P Corp. was an issue for the jury. *Union Miniere, S.A. v. Parday Corp.,* 521 N.E.2d 700 (Ind. Ct. App. 1988).

2. **Termination in violation of public policy:** If the agent or servant has no contract, she can be fired at any time for any reason or

for no reason at all. If, however, she is fired for a reason that contravenes public policy, the agent or employee may have a cause of action for the tort of wrongful discharge.

Example: P hired A to drive its trucks. State regulations limited shifts to 10 hours, followed by at least eight hours of rest. They also required drivers to keep logs of their travel. P required A to drive in excess of 10 hours. P also required A to falsify the logs to show that A had worked no more than 10 hours. Upon A's refusal to violate the regulations, he was told that his pay would be reduced by at least 50%. A sued P.

Held, A had a cause of action against P for wrongful discharge. The pay reduction was tantamount to a dismissal. Even as an at-will employee, A could not be discharged for reasons which violated public policy. Violation of the regulations in question could violate the state's highway safety rules. Therefore, the state had a strong public interest in deterring wrongful discharges. *Coman v. Thomas Mfg. Co.,* 381 S.E.2d 445 (N.C. 1989).

a. **Discharge effective even when irrational:** An employee can be fired even for irrational reasons, as long as the discharge does not violate public policy. For example, an employee may be discharged for planning to attend law school at night, even though continued education is an important societal goal. *Scroghan v. Kraftco Corp.,* 551 S.W.2d 811 (Ky. Ct. App. 1977). The court determined that whether an employee attended night school was essentially a private matter. On the other hand, discharging an employee for serving on a jury does violate the public policy of ensuring that people will serve on juries. An employee discharged for serving would have a cause of action for wrongful discharge. *Nees v. Hocks,* 536 P.2d 512 (Or. 1975).

III. NOTICE TO THIRD PERSONS

A. **General agency and special agency distinguished:** A general agent has authority to perform a continuous series of acts, p. 140, *supra.* A special agent only has authority to perform a specific act or series of acts, p. 140, *supra.* A special agent's authority exhausts itself upon the completion of the specific act for which the agency was created.

1. **Notice required for general agency:** A principal who has hired a general agent must inform third persons that the agent's authority has terminated. Otherwise, the general agent can continue to

deal with third persons on the strength of the agent's continuing apparent authority.

a. **Apparent authority after termination:** Even after the agency terminates by action of the parties, the authority of a general agent is *presumed to continue* until third parties who have dealt or done business with the agent are given actual notice of the termination of the agency. In the absence of notice, the principal is *estopped* to deny the existence of the agency with respect to third parties.

Example: A, P's purchasing agent, regularly buys materials from T. A's employment is terminated, but no notice is given to T. A then purchases materials from X. Many officers of X hold the same offices in T. Although P had never himself purchased from X, P was held liable for A's purchases because the officers of X knew of A's agency through their prior dealings with A on behalf of T. Since P would be estopped to deny A's agency while dealing with T, P is also estopped to deny A's agency while dealing with the same persons as officers of X. *Montana Reservoir & Irrigation Co. v. Utah Junk Co.*, 228 P. 201 (Utah 1924).

2. **Usually no notice required for special agency:** In general, no notice need be given to third persons concerning the termination of the authority of a special agent.

a. **Apparent authority of special agent:** The apparent authority of a special agent who has authority only to do a single act terminates with the completion of that act or the termination of actual authority, unless:

- the principal has *specially accredited* the agent to the third person;

- the agent has *begun to deal* with the third person, as the principal is aware;

- the agent possesses *indicia of authority* entrusted to her by the principal and shown by her to the third person; or

- the *principal has told the agent* to represent that the agency has not terminated and the agent has so represented. Rest. (2d) § 132.

Example: P hired A to sell certain real estate. T offered A $13,500. P accepted T's offer, signed the sales contract, and gave the contract to A. The contract provided that T must pay the earnest money in four days or the contract would be void. The next day, P received a higher offer and phoned A. P claimed that he told A the deal with T was off. A said that their communication was not so clear-cut. Two days later, T signed the contract and delivered it and the earnest money to A. A accepted the money. P claimed it was not bound by T's acceptance because P told A the deal was off before T accepted the contract. T sued P for specific performance.

Held, P was obligated to sell the property to T pursuant to the sales contract. A's apparent authority did not terminate until T received notice of the termination. P had entrusted A with authority by giving A the signed sales contract. Furthermore, T had begun to deal with A. Because T signed the contract before receiving notice of the termination of A's authority, the contract was binding on P and specifically enforceable by T. *Moore v. Marks,* 278 S.W.2d 659 (Ark. 1955).

B. Form of notice:

1. **Persons doing business:** The principal must give ***actual notice*** to all persons who have been dealing with him through his general agent that the agency has been terminated. Rest. (2d) §§ 135-136. Otherwise, the third persons will be able to hold the principal liable unless they know, have reason to know, or should know, that the principal does not consent to have the agent act for him.

    Example: P, an insurance company, makes A its general agent to write insurance policies. A writes a policy on T's house. Thereafter, and without notifying T, P revokes A's agency. Before T has notice or knowledge of the revocation, A writes another insurance policy on T's vacation home as agent for P. T's second house is destroyed by fire, and T sues P on the later policy issued by A.

    Held, T may recover. T dealt with A as P's general agent, so T had a right to rely on the continuation of that general agency until he was given actual notice by P that the agency and A's authority had been terminated. T relied on the continuation of the agency and made a contract with A in P's name. The policy issued by A to T under these circumstances is binding on P because P is estopped to assert that the agency was terminated.

    a. **Knowledge of termination:** If the person dealing with the agent learns of the termination of the agent's authority on her own, the principal is not liable to the third person even though the principal fails to perform his duty to give notice. The reason is that the third person cannot be misled by the appearance of an agency when she knows that there is no agency.

2. **Persons with knowledge of the agency:** In the case of people who know about the general agency but who have had no actual

dealings with the principal through the agency, the principal need give only **reasonable notice.** Notice in a newspaper of general circulation is sufficient. This is sometimes known as **constructive notice.** Rest. (2d) § 136(3).

3. **Unknown persons:** *No notice of termination* is required to persons who do not know of the agency and have had no dealings with the principal through the agency.

C. **When notice is not required:** Notice to third persons is not required when the agency is terminated by such events as (these are considered events which terminate the relationship by *operation of law*):

- death of the principal;

- legal incapacity of the principal or agent;

- destruction or disposition of the subject matter of the agency;

- existence of, or change in, law making performance of the object of the agency illegal; or

- war. (See *infra*, p. 149.)

IV. AGENCY COUPLED WITH AN INTEREST

A. **Agency irrevocable:** An agency coupled with an interest exists when the agent has a *vested interest* in the subject matter of the agency and is given authority to exercise a power over the subject matter. In contrast to the usual agency, an agency coupled with an interest *cannot be revoked.* Whereas in a usual agency the principal can terminate the agency by breaching the contract (though the principal will remain liable in damages), in an agency which is coupled with an interest, the principal may not terminate the agency even if he attempts to do so by breaching the contract.

1. **Example of agency coupled with interest:** An agency coupled with an interest can occur when the agent is given his agency power as *security* for an obligation, or in connection with the agent's part ownership of, or part interest in, some asset.

2. **Not true agency:** Technically, an agency coupled with an interest is not a true agency because the agent acts for his own interests or in the interest of some third person, rather than for his principal. The agreement between the parties is simply couched in agency terms.

B. **Requirements:** An agency coupled with an interest requires:

1. **Security:** Agency power is granted to the agent as security for the protection of the agent or of a third person; and

2. **Consideration:** The agent gives consideration for the agency power. Rest. (2d) § 138.

Example 1: P, through A, obtains a 99 year lease on land. A also loans $200,000 to P to construct a building costing $250,000 on the site. P's lease is subject to forfeiture in the event of default in payment of rent, taxes, insurance or other charges, or should the character or reputation of the building become unsound through faulty management, or should the building be used for unlawful purposes. In consideration for A's services and loan, P gives A a 20 year rent-free lease on the second floor of the building, and appoints A the exclusive agent to manage it. The contract between P and A provides that A's appointment is irrevocable for the period of A's lease. A is to collect all rents and pay all expenses and to be paid commissions on transactions. Subsequently, P assigns its interests to New P, who takes with knowledge of A's interest. P's loan to A is paid in full. New P now seeks to exclude A from management of the building, contending that A's agency may be revoked at any time.

Held, A is entitled to an injunction enforcing his agreement with P, which was assigned to New P. A had a valuable beneficial interest in New P's building—a 20 year lease. That interest would be subject to destruction or forfeiture if the building were not managed properly and the provisions of the 99 year lease were not met. The right to manage the building was given to A as a means of preserving A's interest. A had a power (to manage the building) coupled with an interest (the 20 year lease) and the agency is not revocable. *Lane Mortgage Co. v. Crenshaw,* 269 P. 672 (Cal. Ct. App. 1928).

Note: If A merely held an agency to manage the building for 20 years without also having a leasehold interest, that agency would be revocable. The fact that A was entitled to a commission for management services would not be such an interest as to make the agency irrevocable because damages at law would be an adequate remedy. However, A had a 20 year lease, and money damages would be insufficient to compensate A for the loss of that interest in land. This created an agency coupled with an interest which was irrevocable.

Example 2: P hired A to manage 17 hotels. The contract provided that P could terminate the contract 60 days after providing written notice of breach, if A failed to cure the breach within the 60 days. P sought to terminate A's services as manager, alleging A's expenses exceeded budget allocations. A argued its agency power was coupled with an interest which could not be terminated at the will of the principal.

Held, A did not have a power coupled with an interest, and P could terminate the relationship. To constitute a power coupled with an interest "[t]he agency must be created for the **benefit of the agent** in order to protect some title or right in the subject of the agency or secure some performance to him." The fact that A was to receive a management fee does not create a power coupled with an interest so as to make the agency irrevocable. *Woolley v. Embassy Suites, Inc.,* 278 Cal. Rptr. 719 (Ct. App. 1991).

Note: Unlike *Woolley,* in *Lane,* the agent had a 20 year leasehold interest which was being protected by its power to manage the property. Without its management authority, its leasehold interest would be rendered valueless. In *Woolley,* the agent had no interest in the property except to manage it; nor had it paid anything in consideration of its power.

C. **Agency to sell:** When an agent is authorized to sell or manage property and receive a commission for his services, his interest in the subject matter of the agency is not sufficient to make the agency irrevocable.

Example: P hired A to manage a citrus grove. The contract provided A could manage the property for five years, renewable for subsequent five year periods unless either party served the other with notice of intention not to renew. The agreement also stated it was "binding upon the heirs, personal representatives, successors and assigns of the respective parties." P sold the property to New P, who attempted to terminate A's services. A contended that the agreement was binding upon New P and continued to maintain the groves. New P then brought an action for declaratory judgment, trespass, conversion and other relief.

Held, the agency power was not coupled with an interest, so New P could terminate the relationship. Since the management agreement did not give A any proprietary interest in the fruit or the property but merely the right to receive commissions, there was no agency coupled with an interest, and New P had the right to terminate the contract at any time, subject to its liability to pay damages. The court also held that A had a lien upon the property and the produce from the property, to secure the recovery of any expenses incurred and any compensation earned in performance of the agreements. *Peacock v. American Agronomics Corp.,* 422 So. 2d 55 (Fla. Dist. Ct. App. 1982).

D. **Not revoked by death or incapacity:** An agency coupled with an interest is **not terminated** by revocation of the creator of the power; nor by the incapacity of the creator or the holder of the power; nor by the death of the holder of the power; nor, by the death of the creator, if the power was created to secure an obligation which by its terms does not terminate at the death of the creator. Rest. (2d) § 139.

E. **Attempted revocation:** If the principal attempts to revoke an agency coupled with an interest, the principal's actions have no legal effect. The agent may sue for specific performance of an actual or implied promise not to revoke.

  1. **Effect of agent's fraud:** If the agency coupled with an interest is obtained by the agent through fraud or duress, the principal may *rescind* the agency so long as the rescission does not affect the rights of an innocent third party.

V. TERMINATION OF AGENCY BY OPERATION OF LAW

A. **General rule:** With those exceptions which we will describe, if an agency is terminated by operation of law, all third persons are presumed to have notice of the termination and need not receive actual notice. Examples of ways in which an agency relationship can be terminated by operation of law include:

  1. **Death of the principal:** The agency terminates on the principal's death without notice to the agent. However, if the agent has duties that extend into the management of the decedent's affairs after his death, he may be able to bind the estate. Rest. (2d) § 120, Caveat. Also, a bank has authority to pay checks drawn by the decedent or his agent before his death and until it receives actual notice of his death; and a bank in which a check is deposited by the holder has authority to continue with the collection process until it receives notice of the holder's death. Rest. (2d) § 120; UCC § 4-405.

     Example: P gives A a power of attorney authorizing A to sell P's house. P dies, which is unknown to A and T. A sells P's house to T. P's estate is not bound by A's sale to T because A's power to bind P terminated at P's death. It does not matter that neither A nor T knew of P's death.

  2. **Death of the agent:** The agent's death terminates the agency without more. Recall, however, that in the case of an agency coupled with an interest, the power of the deceased agent survives in his representatives, *supra.* Rest. (2d) § 121.

  3. **Incapacity of the agent or principal:** The Restatement provides that the incapacity of the principal or the agent operates in the same way as the death of either. Rest. (2d) § 122. See p. 151, *infra,* for a further discussion of incapacity.

4. **Bankruptcy of the agent:** The question which controls upon the agent's bankruptcy is whether the agent should understand or realize that the state of his affairs would lead the principal not to wish him to exercise his authority as agent any further. If so, the agency terminates. The question is a subjective one and the answer will depend on the facts of each case. For example, a principal may believe that the impairment of the agent's credit will impair his own credit. Or the principal may believe that the agent's lack of credit will not adversely affect either the principal or the agency. For example, a client may not wish to discharge his lawyer if the lawyer files in bankruptcy. Rest. (2d) § 113.

5. **Bankruptcy of the principal:** Bankruptcy of the principal terminates the agent's authority to bind the principal as to those matters and transactions which the agent should understand the principal no longer wishes him to handle, ***but only*** if the agent has notice of the bankruptcy. Rest. (2d) § 114. Until he has notice, the agent continues to have authority to bind the principal personally, although management of the principal's assets may pass to the trustee in bankruptcy. Rest. (2d) § 114, comment c.

6. **Loss or destruction of the subject matter of the agency:** Unless the parties otherwise agree, destruction of the agency's subject matter, or the end of the principal's interest in the subject matter, will terminate the agency. Notice to the agent may or may not be necessary, depending on the prior manifestations of the principal to the agent. Rest. (2d) § 110.

   Example 1: P gives A, a real estate broker, exclusive authority to sell Blackacre. Without telling A, P conveys Blackacre to X. A contracts to sell Blackacre to T. A is authorized to do so and P is liable to A and T. Rest. (2d) § 110, Illustration 3.

   Example 2: Same facts as **Example 1,** except that A's authority is not exclusive and A knows that P is negotiating with prospective buyers himself. A's authority terminates when P conveys to X. Rest. (2d) § 110, Illustration 4.

7. **Impossibility of performance of the subject of the agency:** Several of the illustrations of impossibility in the Restatement duplicate matters we have already discussed. They are: destruction of the subject matter and loss by the principal of his interest in the subject matter. Two other illustrations are: the death or loss of capacity of a third party with whom the agent is negotiating; and a change of law or circumstances which would negate the intent of the principal in authorizing the agency. Rest. (2d) § 124.

a. Change in law: A change in law of which *the agent has notice*, which makes the object of the agency illegal, or a change in law or circumstance materially affecting the execution of the agency if the agent should infer that the principal, if he knew of the change, would not want her to continue. Rest. (2d) § 116.

b. War: If the agent has notice of war, if conditions are so changed by the outbreak of war that he should infer that if the principal knew of the facts, he would not consent to continuation of the agency. Rest. (2d) § 115.

B. Incapacity of principal: Permanent incapacity of the principal terminates the agent's authority. It is basically equivalent to the death of the principal. However, if the incapacity is only temporary, the agent's authority is suspended during the period of incapacity. Any action taken by the agent during the period of incapacity is voidable at the option of the principal. Rest. (2d) § 122.

Example: Decedent P gave his son A a power of attorney authorizing him "to do any and every act, and exercise any and every power" that he could exercise through any other person. P lapsed into a coma caused by a stroke shortly before he died. While P was in a coma, A purchased flower bonds. Flower bonds are used to pay federal estate taxes, but they must be owned by the decedent at the time of his death. The government claimed that P did not own them at the time of his death because A's power had terminated when P went into a coma. The government further argued that P could have given A a durable power of attorney if he had chosen. A durable power would continue during any period of disability; his failure to use a durable power caused his authority to terminate when he became incapacitated. (Almost all states have statutes which authorize the creation of durable powers of attorney which do not terminate upon the incapacity of the maker of the power.)

Held, P owned the bonds when he died, so his estate could use them to pay federal estate taxes. The court refused to accept the Restatement position that an agent necessarily loses his authority when his principal loses capacity under circumstances which make it difficult or impossible to tell whether the incapacity is permanent or temporary. The court stated that the Restatement position leaves the agent in a quandary. How is he to determine whether his principal's incapacity is temporary or permanent? *Campbell v. United States,* 657 F.2d 1174 (Ct. Cl. 1981). Moreover, the estate's offer to pay federal estate taxes with the bonds ratified the agent's actions in purchasing the bonds.

1. **New York Rule:** The principal's mental incapacity deprives the agent of authority only when the agent *learns that the incapacity is permanent*; otherwise, the agent's actions are merely voidable at the option of the principal.

CHAPTER 12

ANALYSIS OF PARTNERSHIP

ChapterScope ▬▬▬▬▬▬▬▬▬▬▬▬▬▬▬▬▬▬▬▬▬▬▬

In this chapter, we introduce the subject of partnership law, which we cover in the rest of this book. We discuss the various uniform acts adopted by the National Conference of Commissioners on Uniform State Laws, as well as statutes adopted by the various states. We define the terms which occur most frequently in the analysis of fact patterns concerning partnerships, and we introduce the various kinds of partnerships. We also list the ingredients which must be analyzed when you, the student, are confronted with fact patterns in which partnership issues may be lurking.

▬▬▬

I. BASIS OF PARTNERSHIP LAW

In analyzing a fact situation which suggests that a partnership may be involved, the student should recognize that the law of partnership is essentially statutory in nature. The statutes deal with general partnerships and limited partnerships. We will cover both in detail. The law of partnership therefore differs from the law of agency, which was developed and is still controlled essentially by the common law. It is important to note, however, that since partners are agents of each other, a knowledge of the law of agency is often crucial to analyzing the relations of partners to each other and to third parties.

A. Uniform Partnership Act: The Uniform Partnership Act (UPA), was initially approved by the Conference of Commissioners on Uniform State Laws in 1914. The UPA codified the common law of partnership. Today, all the states except Louisiana have adopted some version of the Act. The District of Columbia, Guam, and the Virgin Islands have also adopted the UPA. In addition, seven states have adopted a version of the Revised Uniform Partnership Act (RUPA), adopted in 1994.

B. Uniform Limited Partnership Act: In addition to the traditional general partnership, with its historical origins in the common law and modern basis in the UPA, all states permit some form of *limited partnership.* The concept of limited partnership is wholly a creature of statute. The original basis for the concept was the Uniform Limited Partnership Act (ULPA), adopted in 1916. The original Act is still the law in a few states.

C. Revised Uniform Limited Partnership Act: In 1976 the Revised Uniform Limited Partnership Act (RULPA) was approved. The RULPA was amended in 1985.

1. **Purpose:** The RULPA was designed to clarify or fill in gaps in the ULPA. For a full discussion, see *infra,* p. 288.

D. **Limited Liability Company Statutes:** The limited liability company is a new entrant into the world of business organizations. Virtually all states have now adopted their own Limited Liability Company statutes. In 1994 the Uniform Limited Liability Company Act was approved by the National Conference of Commissioners. It is too early to tell how the states will respond to the codification contained in the uniform Act.

E. **Limited Liability Partnership Statutes:** A number of states have adopted limited liability partnership statutes. To date there is no uniform limited liability partnership statute.

II. EXPLANATION OF TERMS

Partnership law uses special terms to describe partnerships and to classify partners. The student must be familiar with these terms to understand fact patterns and to write lawyer-like answers to examination questions.

A. **Kinds of partnerships:** Sometimes, a partnership is classified according to the kind of work it does. The classification may affect the authority of partners to act for the partnership.

1. **Trading partnership:** This is the name given to a partnership engaged in the buying and selling of commodities for profit. Each partner has implied authority (see p. 47, *supra*) to borrow money on behalf of the partnership, to execute negotiable instruments, and to buy or sell property for the firm in the course of the firm's business.

2. **Non-trading partnership:** This is the name for a partnership which renders a service, such as a law firm or an architectural firm. Usually partners in a non-trading partnership do not have authority to borrow money for the firm or to bind the firm by executing negotiable instruments.

B. **Classification of partners:** The members of a partnership may be classified by various terms, each describing the status or the function of the partner within the partnership.

1. **Dormant or silent partner:** A partner whose name is not used in the business and who is not active in the business, but is nevertheless a full partner.

2. **Incoming partner:** A person who enters an established partnership. He is not personally liable for old obligations unless he

assumes them, but his partnership shares are liable for all existing partnership debts.

3. **Retiring partner:** A person who leaves an established partnership and ceases to be a partner. She remains personally liable for partnership obligations incurred while she was a partner, but is not liable for new ones, unless she failed to give proper notice of retirement. If she fails to give adequate notice, she may be *liable by estoppel.*

4. **Surviving partners:** The partners who *remain after the dissolution* of the partnership as the result of the death or retirement of a partner or some other event requiring dissolution. Following dissolution, the surviving partners may liquidate or "wind up" the business. They may also elect to continue the partnership business, provided they have not wrongfully caused the dissolution. The business may also be continued by a sale to some or all of the surviving partners, or to third parties, or through a buyout of the retiring partner's interest. Continuation of the business is often governed and facilitated by a contract among the partners, called a partnership agreement.

5. **Continuing partner:** A partner who participates in the continuing business after dissolution of a partnership because of the death or retirement of a former partner.

6. **Partner by estoppel:** A person who is not a true partner, but who becomes liable for the debts or obligations of the partnership because she *consented or permitted herself* to be *"held out"* as a partner in such a way as to induce a third person to *change his position* to his detriment in *reasonable reliance* on her actions. A partner by estoppel may also be called an *"ostensible partner"* or *"apparent partner."*

III. ANALYSIS OF PARTNERSHIP PROBLEMS

In applying a logical and systematic analysis to a partnership problem, we must follow the structure of the applicable partnership act. The following issues may be present in any given factual situation. We discuss each issue at the pages cited.

A. **Formation:** The first question is whether a partnership actually exists, and whether the requirements for its formation have been met, *infra,* pp. 158, 168.

Note: The partnership relationship may be confused with many other relationships which share some of the qualities of a partnership but have different structure and consequences. Some of these are: bailment (*supra,* p. 13), escrow agreements (*supra,* p. 12), sale, trust, or joint venture (*supra,* p. 13).

B. Partnership property: In some cases, we must decide whether the property used in the partnership belongs to the partnership or to the individual partners, *infra,* p. 175.

C. Nature of partners property rights: We must recognize and define the rights of the individual partners to partnership property, and the rights of the personal creditors of an individual partner to the assets of the partner and of the partnership, *infra,* p. 185.

D. Relation to third parties: We must next consider the rights and liabilities of third parties who deal with the partnership, especially those arising through contract or tort, *infra,* p. 202.

E. Relation of partners to each other: A partner must respect not only his obligations to third parties, but also his obligations to his partners. Partners owe each other a ***fiduciary duty.*** They may maintain an action for an accounting for breach of that duty, *infra,* p. 204.

F. Termination of partnership: If the partnership has come to an end, a determination must be made of the individual property rights and liabilities arising from the dissolution, as well as the steps required in the wind up of the partnership. We must also determine how partnership assets should be distributed and partner liabilities assessed, *infra,* p. 234.

G. Limited partnerships: We must determine whether we are dealing with a general partnership or a limited partnership, which is wholly a statutory creation. A limited partnership allows the limited partner to limit his liability to the amount of his capital contribution, so long as the limited partner does not participate in the management of the business, *infra,* p. 288.

H. Limited liability companies: The limited liability company is a relatively new introduction to the world of commerce. It was designed as a ***hybrid between the corporation and the partnership.*** The members of limited liability companies receive favorable partnership-like tax treatment, while also enjoying the limited liability available to corporate stockholders. They can achieve these ends without sacrificing the right (as they would in a limited partnership) of participating in control of the business. See *infra,* p. 317.

I. Limited liability partnerships: These entities were created by statute to allow a partner to enjoy limited liability from some tort claims, at least so long as the partner does not supervise or control the business of the tortfeasor-partnership. Like limited liability company members but unlike partners in a limited partnership, partners in a limited liability partnership can secure this limitation on liability without sacrificing their right to participate in the control of the business. See *infra,* p. 314.

CHAPTER 13

NATURE OF A PARTNERSHIP

ChapterScope

It's not always clear whether you're dealing with a partnership or with another form of legal entity. Our purpose in this chapter is to teach you the basic elements which distinguish partnerships from other business organizations. We will cover who has the capacity to be a partner; how to distinguish a partnership from a corporation; what makes a partnership different from a joint venture, a mining partnership, a joint stock association, a business trust and a non-profit association. We will also discuss the differences among a general partnership, a limited liability company and a limited partnership. Lastly, we will outline the tests for determining whether a partnership exists at all.

I. ELEMENTS OF A PARTNERSHIP

A. Partnership defined: "A partnership is an association of two or more persons to carry on as co-owners a business for profit." UPA § 6. The elements of this definition are discussed below.

1. **Association:** This defines the state of mind under which the partners must enter the partnership, i.e.,—*voluntarily.* Under the concept of *delectus personae ("choice of persons"),* no one can be a partner without her *own consent*, nor can she be a partner without the consent of those with whom she is to become a partner. This *consent to associate* as partners may be oral, but it is more usually expressed in formal written Articles of Partnership. Compare partner by estoppel, *infra,* p. 253.

2. **Two or more persons:** Although this factor is common to many other relationships, it does serve to distinguish a partnership from a sole proprietorship.

3. **To carry on a business:** The partners must intend to conduct a business, but it is possible for a partnership to exist before the business is actually established.

   Example: A and B agree to become partners to conduct a retail shoe business. Each contributes $5,000, and they lease a building for the business. They argue violently and decide not to proceed further. A and B are partners. The partnership exists for the purposes of an accounting, and for the process of dissolution and winding up, even though the retail shoe business never began.

4. **Co-owners of the business:** The partners must be co-owners of the business, but they need not be equal partners. This factor distinguishes a partnership from an employment relationship. Even though an employee may be paid a salary geared to the profits of the business, he is not a co-owner of the business.

5. **Profit motive:** The partners must intend to profit from the business. An association for the sole purpose of promoting an ideology, to further particular religious beliefs, or to establish a lodge or hospital for social or charitable purposes is not a partnership.

II. CAPACITY TO BECOME A PARTNER

A. **Capacity:** Any natural person who has the *capacity to contract* has the capacity to become a partner. (See capacity of corporations, *infra*).

Example 1: A, an *infant,* and B, an *adult*, agree to become partners in a book store. A contributes $500 to the capital assets of the firm. The firm becomes indebted to C, a publisher. C sues "A and B, co-partners doing business as A and B Co." What are A's rights? Only A can use the infancy defense. A's contracts are not void but only voidable. A may join in paying C or he may disaffirm any personal liability to C. However, the firm's assets, including A's contribution, may be reached by C to satisfy his claims. B is personally liable to C. (B is also bound on the partnership agreement unless and until it is disaffirmed by A.)

Example 2: A, an *insane* person, and B, an *adult*, agree to become partners. If A has been adjudicated insane, there is no partnership because A's contract is void. If A has not been adjudicated insane, and there was no notice to B or third persons of A's insanity, then the partnership is valid and binding on A, so long as no advantage has been taken of A in the contract. The contract will also be enforceable as to any contribution A has made to the firm.

1. **Corporation as partner:** Nothing in partnership law prevents corporations from being partners. Bromberg & Ripstein on Partnership § 2.04(e), at 2:23. Under traditional corporate law, however, it was *ultra vires* (outside the corporation's authority) for a corporation to become a partner, because the association with others would partly remove corporate control from the corporation's board of directors.

   a. **Modern rule:** Today, *ultra vires* is not a recognized ground for invalidating corporate action in most states. Indeed, many states, through statutes or court decisions, now allow corporations to become partners; e.g., Del. Code Ann., tit. 8, § 122 (11). In those states where corporations still cannot become partners, the restrictions can generally be avoided by forming a joint venture between the corporation and others.

b. Corporation as joint venturer: A corporation has implied authority to enter into a joint venture involving a business enterprise in which profits and losses are shared with others, so long as the enterprise is reasonably related to the corporation's authorized business. *Phillips v. Playboy Music Inc.,* 424 F. Supp. 1148, 1152-53 (N.D. Miss. 1976). Corporations will commit to joint ventures more readily than to partnerships, because a joint venture is generally more limited in time and purpose.

Example: *X partnership* was engaged in business as a marine contractor. X possessed some of the necessary facilities and equipment but not the necessary capital. Nolan, the head of X, approached Doyle, the president of **Y *corporation***, which was engaged in the general contracting business, specializing in road and sewer repair. X and Y entered into an agreement in which Y would bid on dredging contracts and X would do the actual work on successful bids. All profits in excess of $5,000 would be divided equally between X and Y. Y agreed to supply the necessary financing and also the money necessary to recondition X's equipment and to pay for performance bonds. The sums advanced for X's account were to be repaid to Y out of X's share of the profits. The agreement between X and Y was not in writing. After a dispute arose, Y claimed that it was not liable for breach because the contract to do marine dredging exceeded its corporate powers and because a corporation lacks the power to enter into a partnership agreement.

Held, Y's defenses are not valid. The functions of the parties were separate and distinct: X was to do the dredging; Y was merely to enter into the contract and supply the money. The defense of *ultra vires* is abolished. Finally, a corporation has the capacity to enter into a contract for the sharing of profits in a joint venture. The dredging of the canal was but an isolated transaction and did not constitute an agreement "to carry on as co-owners of a business for profits" within the meaning of the Uniform Partnership Act. *Nolan v. J. & M. Doyle Co.,* 13 A.2d 59 (Pa. 1940).

2. Trustee as partner: A trustee may become a partner, if permitted by the trust agreement.

III. AGGREGATE VS. ENTITY THEORY

A. Aggregate theory: Subject to some exceptions, the Uniform Partnership Act follows the ***aggregate theory*** of partnership. Under this approach, a partnership is viewed as a collection of individuals with a common purpose, rather than as a separate legal entity. This theory controls partners' liabilities and duties. Under the aggregate theory, each partner is personally liable for all the debts of the partnership.

1. Application to workers' compensation laws: Under Workers' Compensation laws, the individual managing partners are employers; they are not viewed as separate from the partnership itself. Therefore, they are immune from personal liability for employee injuries. *Swiezynski v. Civiello*, 489 A.2d 634 (N.H. 1985). See also *Mazzuchelli v. Silberberg*, 148 A.2d 8, 11 (N.J. 1959). In the *Mazzuchelli* case, the plaintiff was prevented from recovering from the managing partner in tort; because he was the employee of the managing partner, he was limited to coverage under the workers' compensation laws.

Example: ABC Partnership consisted of three partners: A, B, and C. ABC Partnership bought a property title insurance policy from T, a title insurance company. Thereafter, partners A and B sold their entire interests to C and a new partner, D. This terminated ABC Partnership and created CD Partnership. CD Partnership then sued the title insurance company, T, when defects appeared in title to the insured property. T argued that it was not liable to CD Partnership because T had issued its policy to ABC Partnership. CD Partnership argued that the partnerships had the same purpose (the acquisition and development of real estate); therefore, T should be liable under the policy.

Held, T was not liable under the insurance policy. A new partnership was created when the partnership interests were sold. Under the aggregate theory, the partnership consists simply of individual partners. There is no continuity of entity; when the partners change, the entity changes. A and B did not simply assign their right to receive the profits of the business (assignment alone would not have resulted in a dissolution of the partnership). UPA § 27. They assigned all their right to participate in the management of the partnership. Under UPA §§ 29 and 41, any change in the make-up of the partnership results in the dissolution of the old partnership and the creation of a new one. *Fairway Dev. Co. v. Title Ins. Co. of Minnesota*, 621 F. Supp. 120 (N.D. Ohio 1985).

B. Entity theory: The entity theory views the partnership as a separate legal entity. In the following circumstances, the Uniform Partnership Act follows the entity theory, contrary to its general adoption of the aggregate theory *(supra)*:

- The partnership is **bound by a partner's admission.** UPA § 11.

- The partnership is **charged with knowledge of, or notice to, a partner,** except for fraud committed by the partner. UPA § 12.

- **Conveyance of a partner's interest in the profits does not dissolve** the partnership. UPA § 27.

- A partner's interest is **subject to a charging order** in favor of the partner's judgment creditor. UPA § 28.

- The partnership is **not terminated by dissolution** (the partnership continues until winding up is completed). UPA § 30.

- Matters related to the **holding and conveyancing of property.** UPA §§ 10, 24-26.

- Matters relating to the rights of creditors in connection with the **marshalling and distribution of assets** when partnership property is in possession of a court or when a partner is insolvent. UPA § 40(h), (i).

C. **Entity theory adopted by RUPA:** The Revised Uniform Partnership Act (RUPA), *supra,* p. 153, **adopts the entity theory** of partnerships. RUPA § 201. RUPA was designed in part to reverse the result in the *Fairway* case, *supra.* Examples of the application of the entity theory under RUPA include:

- **Property acquired** by the partnership becomes property of the partnership and not of the partners individually. RUPA § 203.

- The partnership **may sue and be sued** in the partnership name. RUPA § 307(a).

- A **judgment against the partnership** is not a judgment against any individual partner; the assets of the individual partner cannot be reached or levied upon unless there is a separate judgment against the partner individually. RUPA § 307(c).

- A **partner can sue the partnership** in tort or contract. He is not limited to an action for dissolution or for an accounting as under the UPA. RUPA § 405(b).

- The **partnership** may sue a partner for violation of the partnership agreement, or for **violation of a duty to the partnership,** which causes harm to the partnership. "This provision is new and reflects the entity theory of partnership." RUPA § 405, comment 1.

IV. DISTINGUISHING PARTNERSHIP FROM CORPORATION

A. Corporation as a legal entity: The UPA for most purposes considers a partnership as a collection of individuals (the aggregate theory) rather than as a separate legal entity (the entity theory). A corporation, however, is deemed under the law of all states to be a legal entity, wholly separate from its owners, the shareholders. This distinction is important for issues of liability and taxes. (For more on Corporations, see *Emanuel* on *Corporations*.)

1. **Effect on taxation:** Because they are not traditionally considered separate legal entities, partnerships are not separate taxable entities, and all partnership income and deductions flow through, and are taxed, to the individual partners. In contrast, the shareholders of corporations pay taxes twice: first, the ***corporation is required to pay taxes*** on the corporate income, and then the corporate shareholders must pay taxes on the same income when it is distributed to them as dividends. Deductions are trapped at the corporate level, and shareholders usually cannot take advantage of them. Corporations can sometimes limit their tax at the corporate level by making deductible payments, e.g., reasonable salaries to officers and other employees. (Corporations with a limited number of stockholders may qualify as ***S Corporations.*** In these corporations, the income is taxed as though it were the income of the shareholders rather the corporation. The effect is the same as for partnerships. Corporations which do not qualify as S Corporations are known as ***C Corporations***.)

2. **Personal liability for debts:** Partners are ***personally liable*** for all partnership debts. A partner with actual or apparent authority to act for the partnership can obligate the other partners to a partnership debt. On the other hand, the ***corporate entity and not the individual shareholder is liable*** for the corporate debts. Corporate shareholders generally risk only their investment and are not personally liable for the debts of the corporation. (Rarely, shareholders may be personally liable when a court ***pierces the corporate veil.*** This may happen if the corporation and its shareholders are viewed as interchangeable, if corporate formalities are not observed, or, sometimes, if the corporation is undercapitalized.)

   a. **Significance of differences in personal liability:** The advantage of corporate limited liability is sometimes overrated, especially in small businesses. Most owners of small corporations cannot obtain loans without their ***personal guarantees*** and/or without giving the lender a security interest in the business. The corporate form may not help avoid liability in these cases. Also, the officers of all corporations may be held personally liable by the IRS for such claims as failure to withhold and pay taxes on wages. To reduce the exposure to shareholders and directors, most businesses, corporate or partnership, ***can obtain insurance*** against potential tort and fiduciary claims. The main advantage in incorporating is to achieve protection from liability from suppliers and small lenders who do not insist on personal guarantees or other security, and from tort claimants when liability exceeds the insurance coverage. W. Klein & J. Coffee, Jr., *Business Organization and Finance* 139-42 (Foundation Press 6th ed. 1996).

V. ASSOCIATIONS OTHER THAN PARTNERSHIPS AND CORPORATIONS

A. Kinds of associations: The following eight associations or business organizations are similar to partnerships in some respects, but they must be distinguished.

1. **Joint venture:** A joint venture is a form of business association created by two or more co-owners for a limited or specific purpose and duration, whereas a general partnership has broader purposes and is continuous. Further, in a partnership each partner is a general agent of her partners, but in a joint venture there is no such general agency; usually, the duties and responsibilities of each joint venturer are spelled out in great and specific detail in a joint venture agreement.

   a. **Distinction between partnership and joint venture:** A partnership consists of two or more persons who associate to carry on as co-owners a business for profit. A joint venture is like a partnership in that it has two or more participants who are co-owners and have the same business purpose for profit, but it usually is limited to one particular enterprise. The line between partners and joint venturers in a particular enterprise is often unclear, and sometimes those who intend to form a joint venture may be found to have formed a partnership. This is not usually critical because the same rules often govern both. Joint ventures, however, usually have narrower purposes than partnerships; as a result, a joint venturer may have less actual and apparent authority to bind his co-venturer than a partner has to bind his partners. R&G, p. 454.

Example: Two Texas cities owned undivided ownership interests in a nuclear electric-generating project, together with two private entities ("Project"). The private entities managed the Project. Each city transmitted and sold its own portion of the generated electricity through its own electricity distribution system. Neither city could share its profits with the other, and neither was liable for the other's costs. Each city earned money from the Project. Texas sought to tax the cities' interests in the Project. The cities claimed exemption under the state's constitution, which exempts from taxation city property held only for public purposes. Texas claimed that the cities' interests constituted a partnership or a joint venture and that the cities therefore were taxable.

Held, the Project was neither a partnership nor a joint venture, and thus neither city could be taxed. The Project was not a partnership because there was no proof that the participants intended to share profits as co-owners of the business. The participants in the Project simply owned an undivided interest as tenants in common. Under UPA § 7(2), this is insufficient to establish a partnership. A joint venture requires the following elements: (1) mutual right of control; (2) community of interest; (3) agreements to share profits as principals; and (4) agreement to share losses, costs and expenses. Because in this case there was no agreement to share profits, the Project was not taxable as a joint venture. *State v. Houston Lighting & Power Co.,* 609 S.W.2d 263 (Tex. Civ. App. 1980).

2. **Mining partnership:** Mining partnerships are creatures of American common law in those states which have developed extensive mining activity (e.g., Colorado, Pennsylvania, West Virginia, Kentucky, Texas). These partnerships deal only with the commercial operation of mining claims. A mining partnership requires: 1) a common and concurrent interest in real property; 2) joint operation of the mining claim; and 3) the sharing of profits and losses. R&G, pp. 436-37. A mining partnership differs from the ordinary trading partnership in several ways:

   a. **Voluntary association:** There is no ***delectus personae*** (choice of persons) as there is in a general partnership. Only the co-owners who work a mine may become mining partners.

   b. **Authority of partners:** Mining partners have less authority to bind the partnership than do general partners. *Blocker Exploration Co. v. Frontier Exploration, Inc.,* 740 P.2d 983 (Colo. 1987). For example, without an agreement to the contrary or the consent of a majority of the partners, a mining partner does not have the authority to borrow money in the firm name. R&G, p. 436.

c. Right to assign interest: Unlike an ordinary partner, a partner in a mining partnership can assign not only his share of the profits but also his right to participate in running the business.

d. Termination: The death or bankruptcy of a partner does not dissolve a mining partnership, whereas under UPA § 31 either of these events would precipitate the dissolution of a general partnership.

3. **Joint stock association:** The business organization known as a joint stock association, or joint stock company, became popular in the late 18th century, when it was difficult to obtain a corporate charter. A joint stock association could be formed by a contract among investors without special legislation.

   a. Partnership distinguished: A joint stock association has the following characteristics which differentiate it from a partnership:

   i. Transferable stock: Shares of stock representing ownership in joint stock associations are transferable without the consent of other owners, whereas partners must consent to the admission of new partners.

   ii. Management: A joint stock association is managed by officers or directors elected by the shareholders. The individual shareholders cannot act for the association in the way that individual partners can act for the partnership.

   iii. Continuous existence: A joint stock association continues until it is formally dissolved according to its articles of association or by a court order for good cause, whereas a number of events will dissolve a partnership (UPA § 31), e.g., the death of a partner.

   iv. Ownership: Ownership is usually distributed among a large number of shareholders, whereas a partnership often has only a few partners.

   Note 1: These distinctions are sometimes difficult to make in a particular case. For instance, the partners in a partnership may agree that their shares are freely transferable, but that does not, without additional indicia, render the partnership a joint stock association. Also, many law firms now have hundreds of partners and they still qualify as partnerships.

Note 2: The differences between joint stock associations and partnerships do not extend to limits on liability. The owners of a joint stock association are ***subject to personal liability*** in the same way as partners. For that reason, joint stock associations are seldom used today; corporations or limited liability companies are formed instead.

4. **Business or Massachusetts trust:** The business trust, often called a Massachusetts trust, is created when investors transfer capital to a governing group of trustees. The trust agreement lists the trustees' powers and duties. Each investor receives a ***transferable*** certificate. The trust does not dissolve if an investor transfers a certificate, dies, goes bankrupt or becomes insane. The trustees own the business property. If the investors do not reserve the right to control the trust management, they are not personally liable. However, if the investors can remove or elect trustees, there is sufficient control to make the investors personally liable. *Goldwater v. Oltman,* 292 P. 624 (Cal. 1930).

   a. **Partnership distinguished:** Unlike a partnership, a business trust must pay income taxes as a separately taxable entity. The investors in the trust do not enjoy the flow-through element of partnerships which enables partnership income to be taxed only once, i.e., at the level of the individual partner.

   b. **Personal liability:** The trustees of a business trust are personally liable on contracts made for the trust, unless the third-party contracts specifically provide otherwise. *Larson v. Sylvester,* 185 N.E. 44 (Mass. 1933); *Schumann-Heink v. Folsom,* 159 N.E. 250 (Ill. 1927).

5. **Limited partnership (LP):** In this business form, the limited partner can limit her liability to the amount of her capital contribution. However, to obtain this protection, she must renounce her right to participate in management. The partnership is managed by at least one general partner, who is personally liable. Like general partnerships, LP's do not pay income taxes at the partnership level, and the partners can take business losses and deductions on their personal returns. See *infra,* p. 288.

6. **Limited liability company (LLC):** Limited liability company members may limit their liability to their capital contributions even though they participate in the management of the business. LLC members also enjoy the partnership-like tax benefits of one level of taxation and the flow-through of losses and deductions. See *infra,* p. 317.

7. **Limited liability partnership (LLP):** In those jurisdictions which recognize these partnerships, the liability of LLP partners is limited to their capital investment in connection with the tort claims of employees and partners who are not under their supervision and control. However, the partners have unlimited liability for contract claims. As in a limited partnership or an LLC, the partners in a limited liability partnership enjoy the benefits of one level of taxation and the flow-through of losses and deductions to the partners. See *infra*, p. 293.

8. **Non-profit association:** An unincorporated, non-profit association may exist for any purpose. Members of a non-profit association are personally liable on organization undertakings only if they authorized or ratified them.

    a. **Partnership distinguished:** Since a non-profit association does not conduct a business for profit, it cannot, by definition, be a partnership. Membership in a non-profit association does not impose personal liability on a member unless she authorized or ratified the undertaking on which liability is claimed. In contrast, in a partnership, all partners may be held personally liable for partnership obligations.

VI. TESTS FOR DETERMINING EXISTENCE OF A PARTNERSHIP

A. **Generally:** A partnership arises only when there is a ***contract*** among the associates that a partnership shall exist. The contract may be express or implied, oral or written, formal or informal. *Rizika v. Potter,* 72 N.Y.S.2d 372 (N.Y. Sup. Ct. 1947).

B. **Factors considered:** No single test standing alone is conclusive in deciding whether or not there is a partnership. The usual tests for determining the existence of a partnership include: (i) the parties' ***intention;*** (ii) whether there is ***co-ownership*** of the business; and (iii) whether ***profits are shared***.

1. **Dealings with third parties:** Persons who are not partners as to each other cannot be partners as to third persons (other than by estoppel). UPA § 7(1).

    Example: A and B are lawyers who share offices; each has his own clients and takes care of his own law practice. They have no intention of being partners, but both use stationery which reads "A & B, Attorneys at Law" at the top of each page. A becomes liable to a client, P, for his negligence in the handling of a legal matter. P sues both A and B. P cannot recover from B if B's liability is premised on the existence of a partnership with A. A true partnership can only be created by the partners by contract between themselves. However, P may be able to recover from B on the theory of estoppel. A ***"partnership by estoppel"*** is not a true partnership. But if B acted so as to lead P to believe reasonably that A was his partner, B is liable as though A and B were in fact partners. The use of the common letterhead, which seems to hold A and B out as partners, may estop B from denying that a partnership exists with A. B would be held liable to P based on estoppel. UPA §§ 7(1), 16; see, also, *infra,* p. 210.

2. **Intention of the parties:** If the parties intend a partnership, they will usually be able to manifest their intent well enough to communicate it to third parties. But even if they do not intend a partnership, they may nevertheless find that the world will deem them to have created one. In other words, the parties' intention is not always determinative. A court may find that a partnership exists even if the parties did not intend to form a partnership. In *Kaufman-Brown Potato Co. v. Long,* 182 F.2d 594 (9th Cir. 1950), the court found that P, who had loaned money to a partnership, was a partner and not a creditor. The issue arose when the firm went bankrupt. P had advanced more money than was required by the loan agreement, had made recommendations about partnership operations, was entitled to repayment from sales before expenses were deducted, and had a right to inspect the books. The combination of those facts showed that P was a partner, not a creditor. See also *Fenwick v. Unemployment Compensation Comm'n,* 44 A.2d 172 (N.J. 1945).

3. **Co-ownership of the business:** If two individuals own a business together, share in control of the business, agree to split profits and losses, and participate in a series of transactions directed toward creating business profits, a court is likely to hold that the relationship is a partnership. However, a partnership does not necessarily exist because two persons own a property jointly and share in the costs and profits of the property.

Example 1: A and B own land jointly. They agree to build a warehouse on the land, rent it, and divide the income equally. They do this, and after a year, divide their profits. The relationship between A and B is probably not a partnership, but a joint venture. There appeared to be no intention by A and B to become partners. There was an agreement to share profits, and they were co-owners of the undivided profits. But these facts, standing alone, did not create a partnership. However, if A and B ***intended to become partners,*** then it would not be unreasonable or contrary to authority to find that A and B were conducting a business as partners. UPA § 7(2); see also *Brown v. Miller,* 141 P.2d 682 (Colo. 1943).

Example 2: X and Y jointly owned some aircraft which they leased to XY Corporation. They believed that the aircraft leasing business would usually have losses, but that they would benefit from favorable tax deductions and credits. They agreed they would usually split business losses 50-50. X contributed more than half the money, but Y handled all details concerning purchase and operation of the aircraft. X had a right to inspect the books and records but never did so. Lease payments were deposited into a bank account named "the X & Y Jet Account." Y deposited a check into this account after forging X's endorsement on the check. Y then used the proceeds of the check for his own benefit. X sued the collecting bank for conversion. The bank argued that X and Y were partners and that Y, as X's partner, had authority to endorse the check for partnership business. X claimed that he and Y were simply co-owners and not partners because they did not intend to form a partnership.

Held, the business was a partnership, and Y had the authority to endorse X's name. X's claim against the bank failed. X and Y conceded that they co-owned the leasing business. Each participated in the control of the venture. They also shared profits, which is *prima facie* evidence of a partnership in the business. Finally, they engaged in a series of transactions designed to make a profit. X and Y purchased six aircraft together and carried out their leasing operation with the aim of realizing tax benefits. *In re Flight Transp. Corp. Sec. Litigation,* 669 F. Supp. 284 (D. Minn. 1985), *aff'd,* 825 F.2d 1249 (8th Cir. 1987), *cert. denied,* 485 U.S. 936 (1988).

4. **Right to income:** The sharing of gross receipts ("gross returns") does not of itself establish a partnership.

Example: A and B each owns an undivided one-half interest in twelve dairy cows. They agree that A will take care of six at his farm, and B will take care of the other six. The milk produced by all the cows will be sold to M, who will pay half the sale price to A and half to B. This is not a partnership. There must be an intent to share in "profits" for a partnership to exist. Profits exist only when costs and expenses have been paid before distribution takes place. "Gross returns" or "gross receipts" include money or goods which should be used to pay expenses and money or goods which may become profits only if the business is prosperous. UPA § 7(3); See *Moore v. Du Bard,* 29 N.W.2d 94 (Mich. 1947).

a. **Presumption of partnership:** The sharing of profits makes out a ***prima facie*** case of partnership.

Example: A sues B for a partnership accounting, alleging that the parties are operating a business and sharing the profits equally. A does not allege that A and B are partners. B moves to dismiss on the ground that the complaint fails to allege a partnership, an essential element of the complaint. The court should overrule the motion. Although the sharing of profits alone does not conclusively establish a partnership, the allegation of a profit-sharing arrangement is enough to constitute a ***prima facie*** claim of partnership from which the court can properly infer the existence of a partnership until the contrary is shown (e.g., that the profit-sharing arrangement was in payment of a pre-existing debt or annuity, or pursuant to an employment contract). Thus, A's complaint states a cause of action. UPA § 7(4).

b. **Rebutting the presumption:** The ***prima facie*** case of partnership shown by the sharing of profits is overcome by showing that the profits were received as ***payment of a debt***, ***interest on a debt***, ***wages***, ***rent***, an ***annuity*** to a deceased partner's spouse or representative, or in payment of ***business goodwill*** or other property, by installments or otherwise.

Example 1 (payment of a debt): A owns and operates a retail shoe store and owes B $5,000. They agree that each month A will pay all business expenses, and then will pay B one-half of the remaining profits as an installment on the debt. This sharing of profits is merely a convenient method of paying A's debt to B; B receives the profits merely as part payment of the debt. Without more, this overcomes the ***prima facie*** case of partnership inferred from the profit sharing arrangement. UPA § 7(4)(a).

Example 2 (payment of a debt): A milk distributor bought milk from a dairy. The distributor maintained an account payable to the dairy averaging $20,000 to $25,000. Sometimes the dairy billed the distributor's customers directly and credited the payments to the distributor's account. When the distributor sold its stock to a new company, the dairy agreed not to press for payment of the account payable if the account did not exceed the average of $20-25,000. There was no express agreement to share profits or losses. Neither the dairy nor its officers had any interest in the distributor, nor did the distributor in the dairy. An employee of the milk distributor drove a vehicle negligently, killing a man. His widow sued the dairy upon a theory of joint venture and upon a theory of common enterprise with the distributor. She claimed that the dairy's actions in bankrolling the distributor to the extent of the account payable balance was really a division of profits. Therefore, there was a joint venture, and the dairy should be vicariously liable for the negligence of the distributor's employee.

Held, the dairy was not liable because there was no joint venture or common enterprise. The account payable is evidence of a debtor-creditor relationship between the dairy and the distributor. Furthermore, there was no evidence that the parties combined their property and money to further the venture, as is typical of a joint venture. *Werkmeister v. Robinson Dairy, Inc.,* 669 P.2d 1042 (Colo. Ct. App. 1983).

Example 3 (payment of interest on a debt): X and Y loaned a stock brokerage firm $2.5 million in securities. By agreement, they were to receive 40% of the firm's profits as interest, but not less than $100,000 nor more than $500,000. The agreement gave X and Y the right, among others, to veto any business of the firm believed injurious, to inspect the firm's books, to buy up to 50% of the firm, and to force each partner of the firm to resign. In addition, the firm's partners assigned their interests to X and Y, and the agreement set the partners' compensation. The firm's creditors sued X and Y, seeking to hold them liable as partners.

Held, X and Y were not firm partners, so were not liable to the firm's creditors. Sharing profits is only one consideration in determining whether there is a partnership. It is not decisive when the sharing is adopted merely as a device to pay a debt, wages or interest on a loan. X's and Y's other rights were security measures designed to protect their loan to the firm. It does not matter that the loan was of securities rather than cash. X and Y had no affirmative control of the business even with the rights described. X and Y were not partners of the business. *Martin v. Peyton,* 158 N.E. 77 (N.Y. 1927); see also R&G, pp. 258-260.

Example 4 (payment of wages or rent): Dr. X agreed to treat Dr. Y's patients while Dr. Y was away. Dr. X used Dr. Y's office. Dr. X was to keep 30% of the fees collected from insured patients, and all the fees collected from non-insured patients. Dr. X had the authority to use Dr. Y's prescription pads, office equipment and staff while Dr. Y was away. Dr. X committed malpractice on a patient, and the patient died. The patient's estate sued Dr. Y on the ground that Dr. Y and Dr. X were partners.

Held, the doctors were not partners. The agreement to give Dr. X 30% of the fees generated on some patients was merely a method of providing compensation to Dr. X. Dr. X had no voice in the management of the enterprise and had no obligation to bear any losses of the practice. There was also no partnership by estoppel, since Dr. Y did not represent or hold out Dr. X as his partner. The court held, however, that Dr. X was Dr. Y's employee, making Dr. Y vicariously liable for Dr. X's negligence. *Impastato v. De Girolamo,* 459 N.Y.S.2d 512 (N.Y. Sup. Ct. 1983).

Example 5 (payment of an annuity to a deceased partner's spouse or representative): Partners A, B and C agree that upon the death of a partner, the surviving spouse will receive a fixed percentage of the profits from the deceased partner's share of the business for a period of five years. This does not create a partnership with the recipient spouse, since she has no control of the business and is not intended to become a partner. Furthermore, she is not to share in the losses.

Example 6 (payment for goodwill of a business or other property): X sells Y a machine. The price is a share of Y's profits from using it. There is no partnership between X and Y. If, however, X participates in the control of the business, or X and Y intend a partnership, a partnership may exist.

C. **Rules for determining the existence of a partnership (UPA § 7):** In summary, UPA § 7 provides the following four elements which may or may not, in the individual case, suggest whether a partnership exists:

1. **Third person's perspective:** Persons who are not partners as to each other are not partners as to third persons, except by estoppel.

2. **Co-ownership of property:** The existence of a joint tenancy, tenancy in common, tenancy by the entireties, joint property, common property, or part ownership, does not of itself establish a partnership, even if the co-owners share in profits from the property.

3. **Sharing of profits:** The sharing of gross returns does not of itself establish a partnership, even if the persons sharing them co-own the property creating the returns.

   a. **Profit sharing as evidence of partnership:** Receipt of a share of a business's profits is *prima facie* evidence that the recipient is a partner, but no inference shall be drawn if the profits were received in payment of:

   - *a loan* by installments or otherwise;

   - *wages* to an employee *or rent* to a landlord;

   - *an annuity* to a widow or representative of a *deceased partner;*

   - *interest on a loan,* even if the amount of payment varies with the business's profits; or

- ***consideration for the sale of good-will*** of a business or other property by installments or otherwise.

Note: This section permits a person to loan money to a partnership and to take a share of its profits *in lieu* of interest without running serious risk of being considered a partner.

CHAPTER 14

PARTNERSHIP PROPERTY

ChapterScope

Because a partnership is made up of two or more individuals, it's often difficult to tell exactly where the interests of the individual partners end and the interests of the partnership begin. In this chapter, we will discuss how to tell whether property is partnership property. We will also discuss how to convey title to real estate to a partnership and how a partnership transfers title to its real estate. We will also cover the provisions of the RPA and the RUPA which deal with the conveyancing of partnership real estate.

I. HOW TO DETERMINE WHETHER PROPERTY IS OWNED BY AN INDIVIDUAL PARTNER OR BY THE PARTNERSHIP

A. **Intention of the parties controls:** Whether particular property belongs to an individual partner or to the partnership is primarily a question of the *intention* of the partners.

Example: A and B form AB Partnership. They open a partnership bank account, and each takes $5,000 from his individual bank account and deposits it the partnership account. They then lease a store for a year and spend $5,000 for inventory. The assets of A and B, and of the AB partnership, should be classified as follows: the partnership's bank account, the store lease and the inventory are partnership property. This was the result intended by A and B, and nothing appears to the contrary. Any funds remaining in their individual accounts remain the personal property of A and B, in the absence of any showing of intent to make these funds part of the partnership assets. UPA § 8(1); see also *Fortugno v. Hudson Manure Co.*, 144 A.2d 207 (N.J. Super. Ct. App. Div. 1958).

1. **Statute of frauds:** Whenever there is a *partnership transaction involving land*, the student must be alert to a possible issue involving the *statute of frauds*. If a partner intends to contribute her land and *transfer title* to the partnership, the transfer must be in writing. If a partner permits the partnership to use her property for *less than a year*, there is no need to comply with the statute. In most states, a lease of land from one partner to the partnership for *a period of more than one year requires a writing.*

a. **Dealing in land:** Under the majority rule, no writing is necessary to create a partnership which is organized and intended to deal in real estate. Under the minority view, a partnership created to **deal in real estate** must have a written partnership agreement. However, even in those states which follow this minority rule, when the parties have operated the business in a way which confirms that they intended and have performed pursuant to a contract, the requirement of a writing is waived. *In re Estate of Schaefer,* 241 N.W.2d 607 (Wis. 1976).

2. **Evidence of intention:** If the intention of the partners is not clear, the following factors will help to determine if the property is partnership property:

   a. **Source of funds:** If a purchase is made with partnership funds or credit, that fact itself may warrant the conclusion that the property belongs to the partnership. UPA § 8(2).

      Example: A and B are equal partners in a real estate business. They purchase survivors' life insurance to provide the surviving partner with funds necessary to wind up or continue the business. A and B consult an insurance broker who tells them, erroneously, that the proceeds cannot be made payable to the partnership. Therefore, A and B each makes the policy on his life payable to his own estate. Partnership funds pay all premiums. When A dies, A's widow claims all proceeds from A's insurance, and B sues, claiming that the insurance policies and proceeds are partnership assets.

      Held, the property is a partnership asset. Property acquired with partnership funds is considered partnership property, unless a contrary intention appears. Although this presumption is not controlling here (because the partners indiscriminately used partnership funds to pay individual obligations, as well as partnership obligations), the fact that the partners told the insurance broker that they wanted the insurance for the business indicates that they intended the property to belong to the partnership. The only evidence that the insurance policies should not belong to the partnership is the fact that they were made payable separately to the estate of each partner. That circumstance is explained by the erroneous advice they received from their insurance broker. Since the insurance policies were to benefit the partnership, A's widow is entitled only to A's share from the partnership, which is one-half of the partnership assets. *Quinn v. Leidinger,* 152 A. 249 (N.J. Ch. 1930), *aff'd,* 160 A. 537 (1932); see also *Block v. Mylish,* 41 A.2d 731 (Pa. 1945).

b. Business records: If the books and records maintained by the partnership show the property to be a partnership asset, that fact has substantial weight, especially when this fact is known to all the partners.

c. Use: The use, occupancy or possession of realty by the partnership is not determinative of ownership because the property may have been loaned to the partnership, but it does have evidentiary impact to be used with other factors.

d. Title: The fact that record title of land is in the name of the partnership is affirmative evidence, but ***not*** conclusive, because title may have been transferred for convenience or other reasons.

e. Taxes: Payment of taxes, repairs or insurance, and deduction of the same items on the partnership's tax return, are evidence of partnership property. If the property is owned solely by an individual partner, the partnership lacks an insurable interest in it. Co-ownership gives both owners an insurable interest. R&G, p. 332.

f. Payment for improvements: Improvements to property at partnership expense are evidence of ownership, but are not conclusive.

g. Mortgage expense: Payment of a mortgage or other encumbrance by the partnership evidences ownership, but it is not conclusive.

Example: X acquired land with his own funds. He then wrote to his brother Y and urged him to go into partnership with him. They agreed to split the profits 50-50. Y, a carpenter, moved his family to the property and built a cabin for himself on the property. With partnership funds, Y built six other cabins on the property. Y contributed all the labor to the project; X contributed no labor to the project. Y died and his widow claimed that she was entitled to half the value of the business, including the fair market value of the land. X claimed that she had no interest in the land because he had only loaned the property to the partnership.

Held, Y's widow was entitled to half the entire value of the business, including the value of the land. The property was partnership property because partnership funds were used to pay for the buildings and the taxes on the property. *Cyrus v. Cyrus,* 64 N.W.2d 538 (Minn. 1954).

Note: Because the brothers agreed to split profits 50-50, it is likely the brothers conceived of their contributions as being roughly equal. Their intent was apparently that Y should contribute all the labor and X should contribute the value of the land as well as the use of the land and his interest in the partnership funds. Under these facts, the court's decision was correct.

B. Partnership property (UPA § 8): UPA § 8 provides the following rules for distinguishing partnership property from individual property:

- All property originally brought into the partnership stock or business, or subsequently acquired on account of the partnership, is partnership property.

- Unless a contrary intention appears, property acquired with partnership funds is partnership property.

- Title to real property can be acquired in the partnership name; after acquisition, it must be conveyed in the partnership name.

- Conveyance by any person to a partnership in the partnership name conveys the entire estate of that person, unless a contrary intent appears.

C. RUPA rules for determining whether property is partnership property or individual property:

1. **Presumption if purchased with partnership funds:** Property purchased with partnership assets is ***presumed*** to be partnership property, whether or not acquired in the name of the partnership. RUPA § 204(c).

   a. **Presumption if title is not acquired in partnership name:** Property acquired in the name of a partner is ***presumed*** to be the partner's separate property even if it is used for partnership purposes, if the instrument transferring title does not indicate the person's capacity as a partner or the existence of the partnership, and if no partnership funds are used to acquire the property. RUPA § 204(d).

   b. **Irrebuttable presumption on use of name:** Property is ***deemed*** to be partnership property if the conveyance is to (a) the partnership in its name or (b) one or two partners in their capacity as partners, provided the instrument conveying title discloses the partnership's name. This is ***not*** a rebuttable presumption. RUPA § 204(b) and comment 3.

      i. **Caveat:** However, the RUPA draftsmen provide the following caveat: if property is conveyed to a third party who does not know that it is partnership property, by a partner, without any indication of his capacity as partner or of the existence of the partnership, the third party takes title free of any claims by the partnership.

II.   TITLE IN PARTNERSHIP PROPERTY

A. **Real property and personal property distinction:** At common law only individual partners could hold title to realty, because the courts did not recognize the partnership as a legal person. A partnership could, however, hold legal title to personalty. Under UPA § 8(3), *supra,* title to real property may now be acquired in the partnership name and, if so acquired, must be conveyed in the same partnership name.

Example: A and B are partners doing business as Acme Iron Works. A and B sign a specifically enforceable contract to buy land from T. T conveys title to Acme Iron Works in exchange for partnership funds. At common law, T still holds the legal title to the land and the partners, A and B, have the equitable title. Under UPA § 8(3), both legal and equitable title vest in the partnership, Acme Iron Works.

B. **Title in partner:** A partner or partners may hold property *in trust* for the partnership, if the parties intend to treat the property as partnership property.

Example: A, B and C, partners, authorize A to use firm funds to buy land from T, which A does. T's deed recites A as sole grantee, although the partners intend that the land be partnership property. The legal title to the land is in the name of the grantee, A, but A holds title in trust for the partnership. The firm may have A declared a trustee for its benefit, and may compel A to convey the land to the partnership. *Cyrus v. Cyrus,* 64 N.W.2d 538, 543 (Minn. 1954).

Note: Suppose in the example above, A knows that B and C expect her to use the firm's funds and to take title in the name of the partnership, but, instead, uses her own money and takes title in her own name. The result would be the same as in the *Cyrus* case. The reason is that A breached her fiduciary duty to the firm when she bought the land in her own name, even though she used her own funds. The firm may have A declared a constructive trustee for the partnership by tendering the purchase price to A.

C. **Words of inheritance used in conveyance:** Words of inheritance are not essential to pass a fee simple estate in land under UPA § 8(4).

All that's required is that the conveyance be to the partnership in the partnership name.

Example: A and B are partners doing business as A and B Co. T conveys land by deed to "A and B Co." The partnership acquires fee simple title. At common law, the words of inheritance, "and his heirs" or "and their heirs," were necessary to pass a fee simple estate in land. That is changed by UPA § 8(4), and the partnership acquires fee simple title.

III. CONVEYING PARTNERSHIP REAL PROPERTY

A. **General rule:** Any partner may convey real property held in the partnership name *if the conveyance is within the scope of the firm's business.* The conveyance of partnership real estate is covered by UPA § 10.

Example 1: A and B are partners engaged in buying and selling cattle, and in buying and trading real estate. Land is conveyed to "A and Company" the name under which A and B are doing business. The conveyance is in the regular course of business of the firm, and the land is "stock in trade," not the office building they occupy. B sells the land to T, and signs the deed as "A and Company by B." A and the partnership may not set aside the deed on the ground that B had no authority to sign it. This is because: (i) title to the land was held in the firm name; (ii) the land was stock in trade available to be bought and sold in the course of the firm's business; and (iii) B is a general agent of the partnership and is authorized to sign the firm name for the purpose of carrying on the partnership business.

Example 2: Assume the same facts as in the previous example, except that the land is the office building in which the firm conducts its business and not stock in trade. Unless B has actual authority to convey it, the firm can recover the land from T. UPA § 9(2).

Example 3: Assume the same facts as in the last example, except that T subsequently conveys the land to a *bona fide purchaser* (a good-faith purchaser for value without notice), who had no knowledge of B's lack of authority and who paid T for the land. The firm may not be able to recover the land. When title passes from T to a *bona fide* purchaser, the firm's right to recover it is terminated. UPA § 10(1). The partnership and the other partner, A, will have to find their remedy against B through an action for an accounting.

1. **Title in partnership name, transfer in individual name:** A partner *with authority* to convey partnership real property held in the firm name *will convey equitable title* to the property if he

signs the deed in his own name rather than the firm name. UPA § 10(2).

Example: A and B are partners doing business in real property and hold a parcel of land under the firm name of "A and Company." Either partner has authority to convey this parcel. B sells the parcel to T, and signs the deed "B." The record will show that the land was transferred to "A and Company" as grantee, and that it is now conveyed to T by grantor "B." There is a break in the chain of record title. T acquires the equitable title. He has a cause of action against the partners and the firm to compel A or B to sign a deed with "A and Company" as grantor to perfect the record title in T.

2. **Title in individual partner or trustee:** If title is held in the name of one or more partners or in the name of a trustee for the partnership, a conveyance by a partner either in his own name or the partnership name, passes the equitable interest of the partnership, provided the partner has ***actual or apparent authority to convey partnership real property.*** UPA § 10(4), 9(1).

Example: T holds title to parcels of land in trust for the partnership, A, B and C Company. This means the legal title is in T and the equitable title is in the partnership. Each partner is authorized to convey partnership land. A deeds a parcel to P, and signs the deed "A." P has the equitable interest in the land. He has a right to compel T to convey the legal title to him. UPA § 10(4).

3. **Title in less than all partners' names:** When real property of the partnership is held in the name of less than all the partners, and the firm interest does not appear of record, the partner(s) of record may convey title to the land, but ***if the partner(s) lack actual or apparent authority to convey, the partnership may recover the property*** from the purchaser, unless the purchaser is a holder for value without notice (i.e., a bona fide purchaser). UPA § 10(3), 9(1).

Example: A, B and C are partners. No partner is authorized to convey land without joining all partners in the conveyance. A deed intended to convey land to the firm names the grantees as "A and B and their heirs." Without authority from C or the partnership, A and B sign a deed conveying the land to T. If T was a ***bona fide purchaser*** (a good-faith purchaser for value without notice), then the partnership cannot recover the land. If T was not a bona fide purchaser (i.e., he knew that the land belonged to the partnership and that A and B were not authorized to convey title), then the partnership can recover the land.

Note: If the name or title of *the grantor* in a proposed deed is not the same as the name of the *grantee* in the most immediate prior deed, the purchaser is on notice of a possible defect in title and may lose his status as a *bona fide purchaser*. For example, if the prior deed is to "A & B", the purchaser is on notice not to accept a deed from "Acme Iron Works."

4. **Title in all partners' names:** If title is in the name of all the partners, a conveyance executed by all of them will pass complete title to the grantee.

   Example: A, B and C are copartners doing business as "A and Company." Land is firm property held under a deed in which the grantee appears as "A, B and C and their heirs." All three sign a deed as grantors to T and his heirs. The deed conveys all the interest of the firm and all the interests of the partners. UPA § 10(5).

B. **UPA provisions on transfers of real property:** UPA § 10 divides transfers of real property by partners and partnerships as follows:

   1. **Title is in the partnership name and is conveyed by a partner in the partnership name:** This is covered in UPA § 10(1).

   2. **Title is in the partnership name and the conveyance is executed by a partner in his individual name:** This situation is covered by UPA § 10(2).

   3. **Title is in the name of one or more, but not all, of the partners, and the record title does not disclose the interest of the partnership:** This is dealt with in UPA § 10(3).

   4. **Title is in the name of one or more of the partners, or in a trustee for the partnership, and the conveyance is in the partnership name:** This circumstance is covered in UPA § 10(4).

   5. **Title is in the names of all the partners:** This situation is covered by UPA § 10(5).

C. **RUPA provisions on transfers:** The RUPA provisions deal with transfers in ways which are different from the treatment in the RUPA. The underlying change is the introduction of an optional statement of partnership authority specifying the names of partners who are authorized to execute instruments transferring real property held in the name of the partnership. The certificate can be recorded and can grant supplementary authority to, or limit the authority of, a partner. RUPA § 303, comment 1. The goal of the statement is to facilitate the transfer of real property held in the name of the partnership. § 303, comment 2.

   1. **Title is in partnership name:** Subject to the effect of the recorded statement of partnership authority, partnership property held in

the name of the partnership may be transferred by a conveyance executed by any partner in the partnership name. RUPA § 302(a)(1).

2. **Title is in one or more partners with indication of partnership:** If title is in the name of one or more partners under an instrument which indicates that there is a partnership, but without specifying the name of the partnership, title may be transferred by a conveyance executed by the partners in whose name the property is held. RUPA § 302(a)(2).

   Example: Title is conveyed to "A & B, partners." A and B do business as partners in "AB Productions," but the deed makes no mention of the firm name. A and B may convey title by executing the deed in their own names.

3. **Title is in name of partner with no indication of partnership:** If title is held in the name of a partner *without any indication in the instrument of conveyance* of his capacity as partner or that a partnership exists, the partner named in the instrument may execute an instrument conveying title. RUPA § 302(a)(3).

   Example: Title is conveyed to "A", without any indication that he is a partner in AB Productions or any mention of the partnership. A can convey the partnership's interest by a deed executed in his individual name.

4. **When partnership may recover property:** The ability of the partnership to recover property transferred by a partner is severely limited by the RUPA. A partnership may recover partnership property from a transferee only if it proves that the execution of the conveyance *did not bind the partnership*. RUPA § 302(b) Whether the partnership is bound is determined by RUPA § 301, which applies general principles of agency law. Under § 301, each partner is the agent of the partnership for the purpose of its regular business. Each partner may bind the partnership in the business except with respect to a third party who knew that the partner did not have the authority to do a specific act. Under this reasoning, the partnership may recover real property transferred by a partner *only if it is not bound by the act of the partner and*

   - as to a transferee for value from a partner when there is no indication of partnership and no indication of the transferor's status as a partner in the prior deed, the partnership proves that the transferee knew or received notification (a) that the property was partnership property and (b) that the transferor-partner had no authority to bind the partnership. RUPA § 302(b)(2); and

- as to a transferee for value from a partner when the title is in the partnership name, or when title is in the name of a partner but the deed indicates the existence of a partnership and/or the transferor's status as a partner, the partnership proves that the transferee know or received notice that the partner who executed the instrument lacked authority to bind the partnership. RUPA § 302(b)(1).

   a. **Recovery from subsequent transferees:** A partnership cannot recover property from a subsequent transferee if the partnership could not have recovered the property from an earlier transferee of the property. RUPA § 302(c).

5. **Statement of authority to transfer real property (RUPA § 303):** RUPA § 303 is unlike anything in the UPA. It permits but does not require a partnership to execute and record a document listing the names of a partner or partners authorized to transfer real property held in the partnership name. It also allows the partnership to limit or expand the authority of partners to enter into transactions for the partnership. The document is called a statement of partnership authority.

   a. **Purpose:** The purpose of RUPA § 303 is to facilitate transfers of partnership property, particularly real property.

   b. **Statement of Authority:** Under § 303, a *recorded statement of authority* to convey real property is *conclusive* in favor of a transferee for value *without actual knowledge* of facts or circumstances which modify or contradict the statement. A transferee is deemed to know the limitations on a partner's authority if the limitations are recorded in accordance with RUPA § 303. A transferee with actual knowledge of the limits of a partner's authority is bound whether or not there is a recorded statement limiting the partner's authority.

CHAPTER 15

PROPERTY RIGHTS OF A PARTNER

ChapterScope ▬▬▬▬▬▬▬▬▬▬▬▬▬▬▬▬▬▬▬▬▬▬

In this chapter, we discuss the relationship between a partner and the property of the partnership. What are the partner's rights in partnership property? What kind of interest does a partner have in a specific partnership asset? Why is real property owned by a partnership treated as personalty? Can a partner sell his interest in a specific piece of partnership real estate? Can a partner assign his entire interest in the partnership? What are the rights of her assignee? How does a creditor reach the interests or property of a partner? What is a charging order? How does a judgment creditor arrange a foreclosure sale of a partner's interest? Who may buy at the sale? All of these questions, as well as several other subsidiary issues, are discussed in this chapter.

▬▬▬▬▬▬▬▬▬▬▬▬▬▬▬▬▬▬▬▬▬▬

I. EXTENT OF PARTNER'S PROPERTY RIGHTS

A. **Generally:** Membership in a partnership carries with it a number of property rights. UPA § 24 summarizes these rights as follows:

1. A partner's interest in specific partnership property.

2. Her interest in the partnership.

3. Her right to participate in partnership management.

II. PARTNER'S INTEREST IN SPECIFIC PARTNERSHIP PROPERTY—TENANCY IN PARTNERSHIP

A. **Nature of interest:** A partnership may own or possess property in the same way as an individual. It may, for example, take title to a piece of real property. Under the UPA, each partner will be a co-owner of the real property with his partners, as well as of all other specific partnership property. He is said to hold as a tenant in partnership. This reflects the aggregate theory of partnership discussed earlier; see *supra,* p. 161. UPA § 25(1). The creditor of any one partner can levy on the partner's interest in the partnership, but not on any specific partnership property.

1. **Rejected by RUPA:** Tenancy in partnership is abolished in the RUPA. RUPA § 501. Under this provision, a partner is not co-owner of partnership property. She has no interest which can be transferred, either voluntarily or involuntarily. The RUPA provision adopts the entity theory of partnership, under which property taken

by the partnership is the property of the partnership as a whole and not of the partners individually. Under this theory, the partnership property is not subject to execution by a partner's personal creditors, though the creditors may seek a charging order to reach a partner's interest in the partnership, p. 162 *supra*.

B. Tenancy in partnership description: All the partners together own all the partnership property. Their tenancy has some characteristics of a joint tenancy and some characteristics of a tenancy in common, but it is not exactly like either. It is wholly *sui generis,* different from every other tenancy. Under UPA § 25(1), it is called ***"tenancy in partnership."*** *Lueth v. Goodknecht,* 177 N.E. 690 (Ill. 1931).

Example: A, B and C form a partnership to operate a retail haberdashery. They buy a building and set up shop with an inventory of shirts, ties, socks and other items. Every item of personalty belongs to the three of them as tenants in the partnership, as does the building. They have a common interest in the going business and its profits and losses.

C. Possession of partnership property: Subject to any agreement to the contrary, each partner has an ***equal right with his partners to possess partnership property for partnership purposes.*** The other partners must consent to possession for any purpose which is not a partnership purpose. UPA § 25(2)(a).

D. Power of disposition of partnership property: Three   concepts must be identified respecting the power of partners to dispose of partnership property:

1. **If all partners act as a unit:** All the partners ***acting together as a unit*** have the power to dispose of partnership property in the same way as any sole owner may dispose of his property.

2. **If one partner acts as agent:** Any ***single partner, acting as agent*** for the partnership and within the scope of the firm's business, may dispose of any partnership asset, on the theory that all the partners have consented to that agency.

3. **Assignment of individual interest.** An attempt on the part of any partner to dispose of ***her individual interest*** in specific partnership property is ineffective, because the individual interest or right of a partner is ***not assignable,*** except in connection with the assignment of all the partners' rights in the property, or if the other partners consent to the transfer. UPA § 25(2)(b).

Example: A and B are partners. As security for a personal loan, A gives T a mortgage on land owned by the partnership. B knows of the mortgage and does not object. After mortgage payments are in default, T begins foreclosure proceedings. B then brings the present suit contending that T's mortgage is void as an assignment of partnership property under UPA § 25(2)(b). T claims that the mortgage is a transfer of A's right to possession of partnership property for a non-partnership purpose with the consent of the other partner, permissible under UPA § 25(2)(a).

Held, T may proceed with foreclosure because although A had no power to assign his ***interest in any part or unit of the partnership property,*** he effectively assigned his entire ***partnership interest*** as represented by the property as a whole. The mortgage is an assignment which, unless qualified, transfers the whole interest of the transferor. Although the UPA prohibits an assignment of A's rights in any specific property, it does not prohibit assignment of a partner's entire interest in the partnership. Therefore, T has a security interest in the land to the extent of A's interest in the land. A's interest was one-half of the partnership's value after the settlement of partnership accounts. B's tacit consent is not an agreement that the entire partnership be mortgaged, but only that A's interest be mortgaged. *Stroebel-Polasky Co. v. Slachta,* 308 N.W.2d 273 (Mich. Ct. App. 1981).

4. **Partners' consent to assignment of specific partnership property by individual partner:** A partner may assign her interest in specific partnership property with the consent of all the other partners. UPA § 25(2)(b).

Example: A partnership agreement gave A the power to purchase the other partners' interests in partnership real estate at specified prices. Another partner, B, loaned A money. To secure the debt, A gave B a deed of trust conveying partnership real estate to B. After A took bankruptcy, the bankruptcy trustee tried to have the transfer to B set aside. B argued that the other partners impliedly consented to the transfer when they did not object.

Held, A's assignment to B, though not effective as an assignment of his interest in specific partnership property, was valid as an assignment of A's undivided partnership interest—his right to his share of the profits and surplus, if any, after the partnership affairs had been resolved. The other partners did not impliedly consent to the partnership property transfer. The property was assigned as security for A's individual debts, which was not a partnership purpose. The other partners would not voluntarily relinquish their property to help A satisfy his personal debts. Though A had the power to purchase the other partners' interests in the property at specified prices, it does not follow that he had the authority to effect a partition by other means, such as assignment of his interest in the property. *In re Decker,* 295 F. Supp. 501 (W.D. Va. 1969), *aff'd sub nom. Woodson v. Gilmer,* 420 F.2d 378 (4th Cir. 1970).

a. **Why consent to assign is required:** UPA § 25(2)(b), preventing assignment of a partner's interest in specific property without the consent of her partners, is designed (i) to prevent outside interference in partnership affairs; (ii) to protect the interests of other partners and creditors in ensuring that partnership assets are applied to partnership debts; and (iii) to avoid the problems inherent in assigning a value to a partner's beneficial interest in the property.

5. **Partner's creditor may not attach partnership property:** An individual partner's creditor has no right to attach or levy an execution against specific partnership property. UPA § 25(2)(c).

Example: A and B are partners. A's individual creditor, T, takes judgment against A and levies a writ of execution against one of the partnership trucks. T threatens to sell the truck to satisfy the judgment. The partnership may enjoin the sale of the truck. This is consistent with the general rule: ***If a person cannot transfer a property interest voluntarily, that interest cannot be taken by a creditor involuntarily.*** A cannot transfer her interest in the partnership truck by herself. UPA § 25(2)(c) denies T the right to subject A's interest to attachment or execution. T has no means of reaching specific partnership property, but he can reach A's interest in the partnership by a charging order as provided in UPA § 28, *infra* p. 195.

a. **Rights of creditor of corporation when corporation is a partner:** The judgment creditor of a corporation which is in a partnership with others has no greater ability to attach the corporation's interest in specific property than the judgment creditor of an individual partner.

Example: Creditor obtained a money judgment against X Corp. X Corp. did not have sufficient assets to pay Creditor. X Corp. was a partner with Y in XY Partnership. Creditor attempted to force Y to pay X Corp.'s debt and asked the court to liquidate X Corp.'s interest in XY Partnership if X did not pay.

Held, Creditor cannot reach partnership assets of X Corp. To proceed against a judgment debtor-partner, a creditor must obtain a charging order under UPA § 28(1). "Even then, the creditor cannot reach partnership assets but can only reach the debtor's share of profits from the partnership." *Atlantic Mobile Homes, Inc. v. LeFever,* 481 So. 2d 1002 (Fla. Dist. Ct. App. 1986).

6. **Death of a partner:** When a partner dies, the surviving partners acquire her interest in all partnership property. Her heirs acquire her interest in the partnership.

Example: A and B are partners in a jewelry store. A dies without a will, leaving H as his sole statutory heir. Title to the store's jewelry is in B, the surviving partner, for the purpose of winding up the partnership's affairs.

  a. **No greater rights in death than in life:** Because A's interest in partnership property was not transferable during her life, neither A's will nor descent statutes can transfer A's interest in partnership property to anyone other than A's surviving partners. Title to the property was in the partnership, and after A's death, it is now in the surviving partner, B.

  b. **Interest is chose in action:** A's partnership interest consisted of a chose in action (the right to have the firm property applied to pay firm debts, and to a division of the surplus, if any). This chose in action passed to A's statutory heir upon his death.

      i. **Rights and duties of survivor:** It is the right and duty of the surviving partner, B, to apply the specific partnership property to the settlement of the firm's accounts and to divide the profits between B and H when the partnership affairs are settled. If B dies before that is done, title to the partnership property passes to B's administrator for the sole purpose of winding up the affairs of the partnership and dividing the profits after firm debts are paid. UPA § 25(d).

E. **RUPA view — partner not co-owner of partnership property:** RUPA abolishes the concept of tenancy in partnership adopted by UPA § 25(1). In its place it adopts the entity theory (see pp. 161 and 162, *supra*). The partnership as an entity, not the individual partners, owns the partnership property. This compels the same treatment of creditors as in UPA § 25(2)(c): a partner's personal creditors cannot attach an individual partner's interest in the partnership. A partner's personal creditors have to obtain a charging order to reach the partner's transferable interest in the partnership. RUPA § 501, comment.

III. NATURE OF THE PARTNER'S INTEREST IN THE PARTNERSHIP

A. **Generally:** If we conceive of a partnership as having an existence separate from its members, it's easy to understand that a partner's basic interest in the partnership is her share of the profits and surplus. This interest is the same as personal property. UPA § 26.

B. Nature of interest: The interest of a partner in the partnership, in its business, its property and its management, is a *right to share* in its operations and its profits and surplus. A partner owns no specific divisible interest in any one partnership property or asset. The partnership owns the property or asset as a separate business unit. UPA §§ 8, 26.

Example: A and B each owns a one-half interest in AB partnership. The books of the partnership show a negative financial position of $90,000. A wants to sell her partnership interest because of the resulting personal liability. S agrees to assume A's position in the partnership on condition that A and B each pay $21,000 into the partnership account. Further, S agrees to assume personal liability for all *past* partnership debts (this step is not required under the UPA). The major creditor of the firm, a bank, agrees to release A from personal liability and look to S for payment of A's share of past losses. A conveys her interest in the partnership by quitclaim deed to S. Later S and B discover that the partnership bookkeeper has embezzled $68,000 from AB partnership by forging checks, and the firm recovers that amount from the bank which honored the forged checks. A claims one-half of the amount recovered, arguing that the agreement between A and S did not cover firm assets which were unknown when her partnership interest was sold, and that A's deed conveyed only listed physical assets.

Held, A may not recover. A conveyed her entire interest in the *partnership.* She had no specific individual interest to convey in the then unknown claim against the bank. That claim was a partnership asset, not A's personal asset. *Putnam v. Shoaf,* 620 S.W.2d 510 (Tenn. Ct. App. 1981).

1. **Conversion of real property into personalty:** The right of a partner to share in firm profits is personal property, and includes the doctrine of *"out and out conversion"* into personalty of real property acquired by the firm. Under that doctrine, when any property, including real property, is acquired by the partnership with partnership funds for partnership purposes, it becomes personal property for *all* purposes. *Wharf v. Wharf,* 137 N.E. 446 (Ill. 1922).

☞ **Exam question:** A and B are equal partners in the trading firm of "A, B & Co." The firm is engaged in buying and selling leather goods. The firm owes X $5,000, Y $10,000 and Z $20,000. A has loaned the firm $6,000 and has contributed $8,000 to the firm. B has loaned the firm $7,000 and has contributed $4,000 to the firm. Firm assets consist of a stock of leather goods worth $40,000 and land worth $50,000. What is the interest of each of the partners?

Answer: Each partner has a right to share in the profits and surplus of the partnership. They have the right to secure payment of the firm's debts to its creditors, X, Y and Z. Next, A's advance of $6,000 and B's advance of $7,000 will be repaid to them (with interest if so agreed), and then A's contribution of $8,000 and B's contribution of $4,000 (with interest if so agreed) will be repaid. Finally, A and B would make an equal division of what is left of the firm property, i.e., the remaining profits and surplus. The value of each partner's interest in the partnership is the value of one-half the profits or surplus after all partnership debts are paid and all accounts between the partners have been settled.

Here's the calculation: The firm's assets total $90,000: $40,000 in leather goods and $50,000 in land. The firm's liabilities total $60,000: $35,000 to general creditors, $13,000 in partners' advances, and $12,000 in partners' contributions. $90,000 in assets less $60,000 in liabilities leaves a surplus of $30,000. Of this sum, A and B are each entitled to $15,000. This calculation presupposes a sale of the assets for cash. Under UPA § 26 all partnership real property is considered converted into cash or personal property.

2. **Distribution at death:** The death of a partner functions to cause a dissolution of the partnership. On dissolution, the partnership is not terminated, but continues until the winding up of partnership affairs is completed. During the process of dissolution, the interest of each partner is considered ***personal property,*** even if the distributable partnership assets consist of real property.

    a. **General rules:** The courts have adopted the following rules regarding distribution of a partnership interest on a partner's death:

    - title to the firm realty vests in the surviving partner(s), or if none, in the deceased partner's personal representative;

    - the deceased partner's interest is only a share in the profits and surplus, and is personal property;

    - a deceased partner's interest in specific partnership property is not subject to dower, curtesy, or allowance to the next of kin; and

    - the debts of the partnership are to be paid and the surplus paid in cash or cash equivalent to the partners; the heirs of the deceased partner receive his share.

    Example: A, B, C and D are partners doing business as ABCD Partnership. The partnership acquires three tracts of land. Two of the tracts are acquired in the name "A, B, C, D doing business as ABCD Partnership." The third tract is acquired in the names of A, B, C and D only, without any reference to the partnership. All three tracts are acquired with partnership funds for partnership purposes. A dies and each partner's share is calculated. The calculation shows a surplus which includes all three tracts of land. A's heirs claim that the surplus should be treated as real property.

Held, an interest in partnership real estate is considered personal property, and must be distributed as such. Based upon this principle, and the fact that a partner has no right to specific property, but only to the surplus after all property is converted into cash and debts are paid, the partnership real property is treated and distributed as personal property. *Cultra v. Cultra,* 221 S.W.2d 533 (Tenn. 1949).

IV. ASSIGNMENT OF PARTNER'S INTEREST IN THE PARTNERSHIP

A. **Rules controlling assignment:** UPA § 27 provides the following two rules to govern assignment of a partner's interest, and the effect of an assignment on dissolution:

1. **No dissolution on assignment:** A partner's conveyance of her interest in the partnership does not dissolve the partnership. In the absence of a contrary agreement, the partnership continues as before. The assignee may not interfere in the partnership's management, may not require any information or account of partnership transactions, and may not even inspect the partnership books. Of course, the partners may enter into an agreement modifying these results.

   a. **Assignee receives assignor's interest in profits:** The assignee is entitled to receive the profits which the assigning partner would receive, as determined by the provisions of the partnership agreement and the agreement between the assignor and the assignee.

2. **Interest of assignee on dissolution:** In case of a dissolution of the partnership, the assignee is entitled to receive his assignor's interest. He may require an account, but only from the date of the last account agreed to by all the partners.

B. **Effect of assignment:** The effect of an assignment of her interest by a partner is to give the assignee few rights except to share in the profits of the partnership, if any. The assignee occupies only a small part of the assignor's shoes.

1. **UPA changes common law rule:** At common law, if a partner assigned her interest in the partnership, the partnership would be required to dissolve. Under UPA § 27(1), an assignment or conveyance of a partner's interest in the partnership *does not cause a dissolution*, whether the assignment is to another partner or to a third person.

2. **Limited rights of assignee:** In the absence of agreement to the contrary, the assignee of a partner's interest in the partnership has *only* the right which the partner had to *participate in the firm's profits.* The assignee has: (i) no right to be a partner of the continuing firm; (ii) no right to participate in running the business; and (iii) no right to any information concerning the business or to an inspection of the firm books.

   a. **Basis for rule:** Under general contract law, rights which are wholly personal are not assignable. For example, an author may not assign his contractual right to write a book. Similarly, most of the rights of a partner are personal and cannot be assigned. These include: the right to be a partner, to participate in the management of the firm, to receive confidential information about the firm's transactions, and to inspect the firm books. By contrast, the right to receive profits is impersonal and may be assigned, in the same way as the writer in our example can assign his right to receive royalty payments.

      Example: A, B and C are equal partners in a trading firm. At the end of each month the books are balanced and the profits are determined. C assigns all of his right, title and interest in the partnership to D. At the end of the first month following the assignment, the firm's profits are $900. The assignment of C's interest in the partnership gives D the right to receive the amount which C, had he remained a partner, would have received in profits. Thus, D has a right to $300.

   b. **Assignee is bound by existing partnership contract:** The articles of partnership are a binding contract among the partners. If, in the example above, the articles provided that the firm would continue for three years following C's assignment, D would have no right to terminate the contract before the termination date. On the other hand, if the partnership were one *at will,* or *if the term of the partnership had expired*, then D could ask to have the partnership dissolved by decree of court. UPA § 32(2). The UPA describes this remedy as *equitable*.

      i. **Right to accounting:** Upon the court's decree of dissolution, D would have a right to an accounting from the time of the last firm account and, the right to participate in all surplus after payment of the firm's debts and after settlement of the partners' accounts among themselves. UPA § 27(2).

Example: Assignee loaned $800,000 to Partner. As security for the loan, Partner assigned all his rights to income and profits from the XYZ partnership. When Partner defaulted on the loan, Assignee sent notice to the XYZ partnership of his rights as an assignee. For a while, the partnership made payments to Assignee. Then they stopped making monthly payments to him and declared a commission of $877,000 to another partner, Z. As a result, there was no money left to make payments to Assignee. Assignee claimed that his rights as an assignee had been violated.

Held, since Assignee was not a partner, he had no right to participate in management decisions and no right to inspect the partnership books. He only had the right to receive partnership profits and surplus, *if any*. UPA §§ 26, 27. Because all the partners agreed to pay the commission to Z, Assignee could not complain.

Dissent: The majority's interpretation allows the partnership to deprive an assignee of his right to receive his share of the profits and surplus even when the partners operate in bad faith. The trial court should have held a hearing to determine whether the partnership decision to pay a commission was made in good faith. *Bauer v. Blomfield Co./ Holden Joint Venture,* 849 P.2d 1365 (Alaska 1993).

ii. **No right to interfere in partnership affairs:** In partnerships at will, assignees who are aggrieved have the right to petition for a dissolution of the partnership under UPA § 32(2). However, in partnerships for a term, many courts hold that until the term expires, assignees have no right to obtain judicial intervention in partnership affairs, even when the partners operate in bad faith to spend partnership assets so as to deprive the assignees of their share of the partnership profits and surplus. Furthermore, in the absence of agreement, there is no right to pre-dissolution distributions in a partnership.

c. **Consent to assignee's becoming a partner:** The   assignee may become a partner with the consent of the other partners. Consent is necessary because of the personal nature of the partnership relation *(delectus personae), supra.*

V. DEFINITION AND ANALYSIS OF CHARGING ORDER

Introductory note: As we have seen (p. 188, *supra*), a creditor may not attach partnership assets to obtain payment of a partner's personal debt. The creditor's only remedy is to obtain a ***charging order*** against the debtor-partner's interest in the partnership.

A. **Partner's interest subject to charging order:** UPA § 28 provides the following three rules in connection with charging orders:

   1. **Partner's interest is chargeable with partner's debt:** On application of a partner's judgment creditor, the court may charge the debtor-partner's interest with payment of the unsatisfied amount of the judgment debt, together with interest. The court may also appoint a receiver of his share of the profits or of other money due him, and may also make all other orders, directions, accounts and inquiries which the circumstances of the case may require.

   2. **Redemption by charged partner or purchase by other partners:** The judgment debtor-partner may redeem her partnership interest at any time before foreclosure.

      a. **Right of purchase at sale:** If the court orders a sale of the debtor-partner's interest, any partner(s) may purchase it with separate property, or with partnership property, provided all non-charged partners consent. Purchase at the sale will not cause a dissolution of the partnership.

   3. **Exemptions preserved:** The partner whose interest is being charged is not deprived of her exemptions or homestead rights in the interest charged.

B. **Charging order explained:** The UPA's "charging order" provision is taken from the English Partnership Act. It replaces attachment of partnership property by a partner's creditor. Attachment and execution are prohibited by UPA § 25(c). Under a charging order, a partner's separate interest, represented by his right to participate in the firm's net profits and surplus, if any, may be reached by his individual creditor without interfering with the continuation of the firm business.

Example: A, B and C are equal partners in a firm. T, A's individual creditor, has a judgment for $2,000 against A. The partnership has six months before its term will expire. Under UPA § 28(1), T may apply to the court for an order charging A's interest in the partnership with payment of the judgment. A copy of the order will be served on A and on each of the other partners. The order directs the firm and the partners to pay T any profits due A, and makes the partners responsible for the payment. Suppose the profits of the firm are $1,200 per month and that

$400 is therefore due and payable to each of the three partners. Each month, A's share—$400—is payable to T under the charging order. After five months T is paid in full, disregarding costs and interest. If the judgment is not satisfied when the term of the partnership expires, T may apply to the court for an order dissolving the firm and for an accounting. The balance due would be paid to T out of the surplus, if any, after the winding-up process was complete.

Note: The charging order procedure is the ***exclusive remedy*** of a judgment creditor seeking to satisfy a judgment against a partner out of the partner's interest in the partnership assets. A judgment creditor of one partner has no right to attach partnership assets or property. UPA § 25(2)(c). *Weisinger v. Rae,* 188 N.Y.S.2d 10 (N.Y. Sup. Ct.), *aff'd,* 190 N.Y.S.2d 621 (N.Y. App. Div. 1959).

1. **Court-ordered sale:** As we have seen, under UPA § 28(1), a court may order a sale of a partner's interest, and the proceeds used to pay a judgment against her. In that event, any other partner has a right to purchase the interest with his separate funds. Firm funds may also be used to make the purchase if all the partners agree. The purchase may be made in either way without causing a dissolution of the partnership.

    a. **No foreclosure if proceeds will satisfy judgment:** Generally, a court will not order a foreclosure unless proceeds from the charged interest are not likely to satisfy the creditor within a reasonable time. *City of New York v. Bencivenga,* 169 N.Y.S.2d 515, 519-20 (N.Y. Sup. Ct. 1955).

    b. **Effect of foreclosure:** The creditor who receives a charging order does not become the owner of the partner's interest except after purchase of the interest at a sale following an order of foreclosure by the court. If the creditor buys the interest at the foreclosure sale, he may cause the dissolution of the partnership, ***if the partnership is at will***. ***To prevent dissolution*** of a partnership at will, the partners may agree to make the creditor a partner. The creditor cannot become a partner without consent of all the other partners.

2. **Effect on debtor-partner:** While the charging order is in effect, the partner affected by the charge continues in the business, except for his right to distribution and withdrawals.

    Example: A and B entered into a limited partnership. A was the general partner and B the limited partner. B sued A for mismanaging the partnership and for misappropriating partnership funds. Pending resolution of that claim, the trial court appointed a receiver to manage the partnership. A had been unable to pay his share of partnership obligations. After A signed promissory notes to B, B paid the partnership's obligations, including A's portion. When A did not pay the notes, B sued A and won. To satisfy those judgments, B obtained a charging order directing the sheriff to sell A's interest in the partnership. B bought A's interest at a public sale for $2,500, and the receiver was discharged. A then sued B. A's claims included: (1) that B had failed to show that a sale of A's interest was necessary; (2) that it was inequitable to sell partnership property while the partnership was in receivership; (3) that a partner's interest in a partnership is not subject to a sale unless there is an accounting to show the interest's value; (4) that the price paid for the interest was inadequate; and (5) that the sale violated a prohibition in the partnership agreement against assignment of a partnership interest.

Held, all of A's claims are rejected. (1) The creditor need not show that a sale is necessary to obtain an order of sale—only that his judgment is unsatisfied. (2) Although the partnership was in receivership, B was entitled to request a sale to satisfy his judgment. A could have avoided the charging order or limited its effect by paying off the judgment, but he did not do so. (3) No accounting was necessary as a condition to B's obtaining a judgment creditor's charging order. UPA § 28 does not require an accounting before a charging order is given effect. (4) The fact that the sale was public made it unnecessary for the trial court to determine if the price was adequate. (5) Although there was a provision in the partnership agreement precluding assignment of a partner's interest, the trial court had the power to enter a charging order.

When B bought all A's interest, B was entitled to all future profits from the business. However, once the receiver was discharged, A still had the right to participate in the management of the partnership, until the partnership was dissolved. *Tupper v. Kroc,* 494 P.2d 1275 (Nev. 1972).

3. **Exemptions:** If *partnership property* is attached in connection with a *claim against the partnership*, neither the partnership nor any of the partners can claim any right under the homestead or exemption laws. A partner may not claim exemptions or homestead rights in specific partnership property, but a partner may claim her exemptions or homestead rights, if the rights exist under applicable law, in her interest in the partnership. UPA §§ 25(2)(c) and 28(3).

4. **Payment by debtor:** The debtor-partner may pay off the debt charged against his partnership interest at any time before the court orders his interest foreclosed. UPA § 28(2).

CHAPTER 16

RELATIONS OF PARTNERS TO PERSONS DEALING WITH THE PARTNERSHIP

ChapterScope

One of the critical features of a general partnership is that each partner is an *agent of the partnership* for purposes of the partnership business. This means that each partner can bind the business to acts committed by him in *carrying out the usual business of the partnership*. We will discuss the nature of this agency, as well as the limitations imposed on it. We will also discuss *what happens when partners disagree.* We will cover the rules for determining when the partnership is responsible to third parties for the acts of a partner, both in contract and in tort. We will discuss the concept of joint and several liability when a partner commits a wrongful act or a breach of trust; and of joint liability when a partner or the partnership is bound in contract. We will also take up partnership by estoppel; and, finally, we will deal with how the law treats the liability of a new partner who joins a partnership which is already in existence.

I. AUTHORITY OF THE PARTNERS TO BIND THE PARTNERSHIP

A. **Partner is agent of partnership as to partnership business (UPA § 9):** The authority of the partners to bind the partnership, as well as the limits on their authority, are set forth in UPA § 9. The full text of this provision is as follows:

> (1) Every partner is an agent of the partnership for the purpose of its business, and the act of every partner, including the execution in the partnership name, of any instrument, for apparently carrying on in the usual way the business of the partnership of which he is a member binds the partnership, unless the partner so acting has in fact no authority to act for the partnership in the particular matter, and the person with whom he is dealing knows or has knowledge of the fact that he has no such authority.

> (2) An act of a partner which is not apparently for the carrying on of the business of the partnership in the usual way does not bind the partnership unless authorized by the other partners.

> (3) Unless authorized by the other partners or unless they have abandoned the business, one or more but less than all the partners have no authority to:

> > (a) Assign the partnership property in trust for creditors or on the assignee's promise to pay the debts of the partnership,

(b) Dispose of the good-will of the business,

(c) Do any other act which would make it impossible to carry on the ordinary business of a partnership,

(d) Confess a judgment,

(e) Submit a partnership claim or liability to arbitration or reference.

(4) No act of a partner in contravention of a restriction on authority shall bind the partnership to persons having knowledge of the restriction.

1. Applies the law of agency to partnerships: UPA § 9 is substantially a codification of common law agency principles as applied to partnerships. These principles have been discussed earlier in the chapters on Agency.

B. Agency of partner: When a partner in a general partnership acts for the firm, she acts for herself as a principal and for her partner(s) as a general agent.

1. Scope of authority: If the partner's act is within the scope of the partnership business, then her act will bind both the partnership and the other partners, even if the act is a tort or a breach of contract.

Example 1 (acts within the scope): A, B and C are partners. A executes a five year lease for certain premises with T. T sues A, B and C for rent due under the lease. The defense is that A did not have authority to bind the partnership to the lease.

Held, T may recover. The issue is whether A bound the partnership. UPA § 9(1) states that every partner is the partnership's agent "for apparently carrying on in the usual way the business of the partnership." The partnership needed a place to carry on its business, and a five year lease is not unusual. The partnership had previously leased the same premises under a five year lease. Thus, A had implied authority to execute the lease. This act bound the partnership in the absence of knowledge by T that A's authority was more limited. *Lawer v. Kline,* 270 P. 1077 (Wyo. 1928).

Example 2 (acts outside the scope): A and B are partners. B uses the partnership automobile for personal business which is wholly unconnected with the firm's business. B is negligent in his driving and injures T. B is liable to T, but A is not. B was "on a frolic of his own" and did not bind his partner, A. It is immaterial that the firm's automobile happened to be involved. UPA §§ 9(1), 13; *Bunnell v. Vrooman,* 145 N.E. 58 (Mass. 1924).

2. Apparent authority: Whether a partner's act constitutes an "apparent carrying on of the firm business in the usual way" depends on the **nature of the business** and the circumstances surrounding the act.

Example 1: A and B are partners in a trading firm. A signs the firm name as an accommodation indorser on T's note to a bank. Neither B nor the firm is liable on the indorsement. The general rule is that a partner does not have implied or apparent authority to bind the firm or his partners on surety or guaranty contracts. Nothing appears in these facts to take the case out of the general rule. However, if the partnership business is the buying and selling of negotiable paper, and one of its usual business functions is indorsing negotiable paper, then an indorsement by one partner will bind the others and the partnership. *Jamestown Banking Co. v. Conneaut Lake Dock & Dredge Co.,* 14 A.2d 325 (Pa. 1940); *First Nat'l Bank v. Farson,* 123 N.E. 490 (N.Y. 1919).

Example 2: A and B operated AB partnership. The partnership sold radio time for the corporation which owned radio station X. A was president of station X, and A and B each owned one-half of its stock. Station X and AB partnership agreed to provide T with two 15-minute segments of radio time daily so long as the radio station franchise remained in force. T paid $100,000 for this broadcast time. Due in part to labor problems, station X was shut down and could not provide T with the agreed-upon broadcast times. To make up for the breach of contract, A, purporting to act for AB partnership, signed a $40,000 promissory note payable to T. A executed the note, in part, in return for T's promise not to sue station X. B claimed that he was not liable on the note because he had not authorized A to execute the note.

Held, B was not liable on the note. A had neither the actual nor the apparent authority to execute the promissory note. AB partnership sold time on a radio station. The acts of borrowing money or executing notes were not incidental to the transaction of this business. There was nothing to show that transacting the partnership business required "periodic or continuous or frequent purchasing" or that it made "frequent resort to borrowing a necessity . . . ." T failed to meet his **burden of proof** that executing a promissory note was within the apparent purpose of AB partnership. *Burns v. Gonzalez,* 439 S.W.2d 128 (Tex. Civ. App. 1969).

a. Limitations of authority: In addition to those acts enumerated in UPA § 9, the following acts are not generally considered to be within the apparent authority of a partner:

- contracts of suretyship and guaranty;

- payment of separate debts of a partner with partnership assets;

- stock subscriptions; and

- gratuitous undertakings, such as giving away the firm's property.

   b. Authority limitations by agreement: A partnership agreement prohibiting certain specified acts does not bind third persons who do not know of the restrictions. But third persons who know of the restrictions are bound. UPA § 9(4).

3. **Partners disagree and partnership evenly split:** If the partners are evenly divided on an issue which is connected to and arises out of ordinary partnership business, one partner can bind the partnership to a third person even if the third person is aware of the split between the partners.

   Example: A and B formed AB partnership to sell groceries. T regularly sold bread to AB partnership. A advised T that A would not be liable for any additional sales of bread by T to AB partnership. B continued to buy bread for the partnership. Finally, A and B dissolved the partnership. A used partnership assets and over $7,000 of his own money to pay partnership bills, except for $171.04 owed to T. T sought to recover the cost of his bread from A. A claimed that the purchase in question was unauthorized because he, as a 50% partner, had opposed the purchase. Furthermore, A claimed that T knew that the purchase was unauthorized.

   Held, A was liable to T. Both A and B had equal rights in the management and conduct of the business. (Under UPA § 18(e), unless the partnership agreement provides otherwise, each partner has an equal voice in business management, regardless of his percentage share of the profits.) Therefore, A could not restrict B's rights to continue to purchase bread, an act which was in the ordinary operation of the partnership. "The partnership being a going concern, activities within the scope of the business should not be limited, save by the expressed will of the majority deciding a disputed question; half of the members are not a majority." *National Biscuit Co. v. Stroud,* 106 S.E.2d 692 (N.C. 1959).

   Note: In light of the court's holding in *Stroud,* A could have protected himself only by dissolving the partnership sooner.

   a. Effect of disagreement as between partners: However, as between the partners themselves, if the partners are evenly split and one partner decides to enter into a ***new contract*** over the other's objections, his actions will be viewed as unauthorized. The result is that the objecting partner is not liable to reimburse the partner who acts despite the objections.

Example: A and B operated the AB trash collection partnership. A proposed to B that they hire T, but B refused. A hired T anyway. A later sued B for reimbursement of A's personal expenses in paying T's salary.

Held, B was not obligated to reimburse A. B had equal rights in the management of the business, and A had no right to hire the employee over B's objection. "[I]f the partners are equally divided, those who forbid a change must have their way." *Summers v. Dooley,* 481 P.2d 318 (Idaho 1971).

Analysis of cases: The rule to be developed from these cases is that in an equally divided partnership, an objecting partner may be liable to third persons if an equal partner acts over his objection, but he will not be liable to reimburse a partner who has charged the business over his objection.

4. **When unanimous decision required:** Under UPA § 9(3), unless the partnership business has been abandoned or the partners have otherwise previously agreed, ***all*** the partners must agree jointly to bind the firm to the following acts:

- assign all the firm property, even if the assignee promises to assume and pay the partnership's debts (the reason for this rule is that the assignment would make it impossible to carry on the firm's business);

- dispose of the firm's good will;

- commit any act which makes it impossible to carry on the firm's business;

- confess a judgment; or

- submit a partnership claim or liability to arbitration.

II. RESPONSIBILITY OF THE PARTNERSHIP TO THIRD PERSONS

A. **UPA provisions:** The UPA provides the following rules regarding the ability of a partner to bind the partnership to third parties.

1. **Partnership bound by admission of partner (UPA § 11):** The partnership is bound by an admission or representation made by any partner concerning partnership affairs within the scope of his authority.

2. **Partnership charged with knowledge of or notice to partner (UPA § 12):** The partnership has notice or knowledge of the following: (a) notice to any partner of any matter relating to partnership affairs; (b) knowledge of the partner acting for the partnership in a particular matter, acquired while he was a partner or "then present to his mind"; and (c) the knowledge of any other partner who reasonably could and should have communicated it to the acting partner. However, if the partner commits or consents to a fraud on the partnership, the partnership will be deemed not to have such notice or knowledge.

3. **Partnership bound by partner's wrongful act (UPA § 13):** If a partner who acts in the partnership's ordinary course of business or with the authority of his partners (1) incurs a penalty or (2) causes loss or injury to a non-partner, by his wrongful act or omission the partnership, is liable to the same extent as the partner himself.

4. **Partnership bound by partner's breach of trust (UPA § 14):** The partnership must make good the loss:

   a. **Misapplication by partner:** when one partner acting within the scope of his apparent authority receives a third person's money or property and misapplies it; and

   b. **Misapplication while in partnership custody:** when the partnership receives a third person's money or property in the course of its business and any partner misapplies it while it is in the partnership's custody.

B. **Partnership's civil liability for partners' acts:** Each partner is liable for any injury to a third person caused by a partner's wrongful acts committed *within the scope of the partnership business and in furtherance of the business*. This applies to professional partnerships as well as to general partnerships.

Example 1: A and B are partners in the practice of law. A negligently tells his client, T, that some real property is free from encumbrances when it is not. T sues A and B for damages. If A's negligent act injured T, A's act binds A's partner, B. B is liable in the same way as A because the act of giving an opinion on an abstract of title is within the scope and in furtherance of the business of lawyers.

Example 2: D is a partner in a law firm with A, B and C. Unknown to A, B and C, T, D's client, gives $28,000 to D to invest for her. For a period, D sends interest to T, but later D embezzles the money. T sues A, B and C to recover the money D embezzled. The court held that T may not recover from A, B, or C because D was not acting on a matter within the scope of the law firm's business. Investment of a client's money is not part of the usual practice of law. A, B and C did not know of D's actions or approve of them. *Rouse v. Pollard,* 18 A.2d 5 (N.J. Ch.), *aff'd,* 21 A.2d 801 (N.J. 1941).

1. **Liability expanded:** A few courts have taken a broader view of the term, "acting in the ordinary course of the business of the partnership", at least, as applied to law firms (UPA § 13). For instance, in *Cook v. Brundidge, Fountain, Elliott & Churchill,* 533 S.W.2d 751 (Tex. 1976), the court reversed a summary judgment for the defendant law firm. The court held that there was a question of fact whether a law firm partner had apparent authority to invest a client's money. One authority suggests that the newer cases require a different approach because the scope of a contemporary law practice has expanded since the *Rouse* decision. R&G, p. 310.

2. **Partnership liability to partner:** UPA § 13 states that a partnership is liable to a ***non-partner*** for injuries caused by a partner's wrongful act. Many courts have expanded on this concept and have found a partnership liable ***to a partner in tort***, even if the partner is also a defendant.

   Example: A is one of eight partners who operate a coal mine. The partnership "hires" A's truck to haul coal to a railroad tipple. While A's truck is being serviced at a gasoline station operated by the partnership, an employee's negligence causes gasoline to ignite and destroy the truck. A sues the partnership and its partners (including himself as partner) for the loss of his truck. The defense is that A cannot maintain a suit against his partners for his own damages.

   Held, A may recover from his partners, but A must bear his proportionate share of the loss, as partner. A partner who has paid a partnership obligation out of his own funds may obtain contribution from his partners. Further, if a partner negligently damages the property of another partner, he will be liable to the partner whose property was damaged. In this case A's truck was being used under a contract with the partnership, and the partnership should bear the loss because it was destroyed through the negligence of partnership employees. A did not contribute his truck to the partnership with the intent that A should assume the risk of loss. *Smith v. Hensley,* 354 S.W.2d 744 (Ky. 1962).

3. **Partnership liability for breach of fiduciary duty:** When a partner breaches a fiduciary duty, the partnership is liable in the following situations:

Example 1: The partnership, while acting as agent for another, *colludes with a third party* to secure a secret profit at the principal's expense.

Example 2: A partner, while acting as fiduciary to a third party, *breaches her fiduciary duty* to that party in order to benefit the partnership.

Example 3: A partner participates in a breach of fiduciary duty *by a third party*.

4. **Partnership liability for breach of trust:**

   a. **Breach of trust by partner:** If a *partner misapplies funds* received by him or by the partnership from a third person within the scope of the partnership business, the other partners and the partnership must make good the loss. UPA § 14(a).

      Example: A and B are partners in the business of managing and investing funds for third parties. Within the scope of that business, A receives a check from T for $5,000. He is directed to invest the proceeds in first mortgages on real property. A deposits the check in his own individual account and spends it in riotous living. A received the $5,000 within the scope of the firm's business. The wrongful breach of trust by A is binding on B and on the partnership and all three may be held liable to T. UPA § 14(a).

   b. **Breach of trust by partnership:** If the partnership receives either money or property of a third person, and it is misapplied by a partner while in the custody of the partnership, the partnership must make good the loss. UPA § 14(b).

      Example: A and B are partners whose business it is to invest money belonging to others. T delivers $5,000 to the firm. The money is deposited in AB Partnership's bank account. A withdraws $3,000 from this account for his personal use. There is no money in this account other than the money supplied by T. A loses all of the $3,000 betting on the horse races. T sues for his loss, naming "A and B, copartners doing business as AB Partnership". It was the duty of each partner and the firm to preserve and make proper investments of the money received from T. A breached that duty; A was acting for B and the firm as well as for himself. Hence, A's act makes both B and the partnership liable with A for T's loss. UPA § 14(b).

5. **Partnership liability for intentional torts:** Partnership liability for the torts of its partners is based on the theory of *respondeat superior.* (See *supra*, p. 89.) *Intentional* torts are *less likely* to be

viewed as within the scope of the partnership business than are **negligent torts**. However, a partnership may be liable for a partner's intentional tort when the tort represents a breach of a legal duty.

Example: Dr. B is one of 30 doctors who comprise a medical partnership called Clinic. H and W, husband and wife, and their children are Clinic patients. Dr. B is the doctor who treats them. He allegedly has an affair with W, causing W to separate from H. H sues Clinic for alienation of affections. Clinic moves for summary judgment, arguing it is not liable for Dr. B's acts.

Held, Clinic may be liable for Dr. B's acts. Clinic has a duty to exercise ordinary care to protect patients from harm resulting from the tortious conduct of persons on its premises. Clinic also owes a duty to the families of its patients to exercise ordinary care to prevent tortious interference with family relations. If the Clinic partnership knew or should have known of Dr. B's conduct, there might be a duty to investigate and take action. Facts relating to these issues must be determined at trial. *Kelsey-Seybold Clinic v. Maclay*, 466 S.W.2d 716 (Tex. 1971).

a. **Misrepresentation:** A partnership is liable for a partner's misrepresentations made in the course of selling the partnership's product.

b. **Punitive damages:** Most jurisdictions will not impose vicarious liability against a partnership or an innocent partner for the willful conduct of another partner. Generally, the courts will impose punitive damages against the willful actor's partner *only if the partner authorized or ratified* the conduct, or was responsible for it in some other way. See, e.g., *Duncan v. Henington*, 835 P.2d 816 (N.M. 1992). A few jurisdictions do allow punitive damages even against an innocent partner who did not authorize or ratify the intentional tort. *See*, e.g., *Blue v. Rose*, 786 F.2d 349 (8th Cir. 1986) (applying Missouri law). *See*, also, Michael A. Rosenhouse, Annotation, *Derivative Liability of Partner for Punitive Damages for Wrongful Act of Copartner*, 14 A.L.R. 4th 1335 (1981).

C. **Criminal liability of partnership:** The U.S. Supreme Court has ruled that if a common-carrier partnership violates an ICC regulation (i.e., regulating interstate transportation of dangerous articles), the partnership may be criminally liable as a separate entity, and a fine may be levied on its assets. *United States v. A & P Trucking Co.*, 358 U.S. 121 (1958).

III. LIABILITY OF THE PARTNERS

A. **Nature of partner's liability (UPA § 15):** UPA § 15 sets forth the concept of joint and several liability. It provides that all partners are liable:

(a) ***jointly and severally*** for everything chargeable to the partnership under UPA § 13 (***wrongful acts***) and UPA § 14 (***breaches of trust***); and

(b) ***jointly*** for all of the partnership's ***other debts and obligations***. However, any ***partner may separately agree*** to perform a partnership contract.

B. **Tort and breach of trust liability:** Individual partners are ***jointly and severally liable*** for any torts or breaches of trust committed by any partner within the scope of the partnership business. UPA § 15(a).

Example: A and B are partners in the steel business. A uses the firm's truck to deliver steel to a customer. On the same trip, he takes a friend to a party. A drives the truck negligently and injures T. T sues A, B and the partnership.

Held, T may recover. When a partner is acting both for the firm (within the scope of its business) and for himself, his negligence makes the other partners and the partnership jointly and severally liable.

1. **Joint and several liability:** If we refer to the Example above, we conclude that A and B owe the obligation to pay T's damages as a partnership unit, and that T can satisfy that obligation out of the partnership property. Also, A severally and individually owes that same obligation to T; and T can satisfy A's obligation out of any property A owns individually. Also, B severally and individually owes the same obligation to T; and T can satisfy B's obligation out of any assets B owns individually. See *Evans v. Thompson,* 121 F. Supp. 46 (W.D. Ark. 1954).

2. **Procedure for tort or breach of trust claim against partner:** The effect of joint and several liability of the partners in the Example above is that T may sue A and B together, or he may sue A alone or B alone. If the assets of one partner are insufficient to pay a claim, the tort claimant can proceed against the other partner even if that partner was not at fault. Some states today require that a creditor cannot proceed against the assets of an individual partner, until he has exhausted the partnership's assets. See, e.g., *Cunard Line Ltd. v. Abney,* 540 F. Supp. 657, 660 (S.D.N.Y. 1982). See also Gregory and Hurst, Cases and Materials on Agency and Partnership 317 (2d ed. 1990).

a. Failure to identify the partner as a partner: Joint and several liability also means that a creditor can name a partner in his summons and complaint without designating him as "a partner," and still subject the partner's individual assets to liability.

Example: T brought a medical malpractice action against Dr. A and Dr. B, partners, for their negligence in treating T. The jury found that Dr. B was guilty of negligence but Dr. A was not. Dr. A claimed that the court lacked jurisdiction to render a judgment against him. He argued that the plaintiff's summons named him and Dr. B, although it did not designate him as Dr. B's partner.

Held, T could enforce the judgment against Dr. A individually because he was jointly and severally liable. T did not have to name Dr. A as a partner to collect from him as an individual. *Zuckerman v. Antenucci,* 478 N.Y.S.2d 578 (N.Y. Sup. Ct. 1984).

C. Contract liability:

1. **Majority view:** The majority view distinguishes between tort liability and contract liability. It limits *joint liability* to contract claims while applying joint and several liability to tort claims. Thus, at common law and under UPA § 15(b), partners are *only jointly liable* for the partnership's contractual obligations and debts. The partners are neither severally nor jointly and severally liable.

2. **Minority view:** A substantial number of states have modified section 15(b) by statute. The result in these states is that all partners are *jointly and severally liable* for all partnership debts, including contract indebtedness.

D. Substantive effect of joint liability: The effect of joint liability in contract claims, as distinguished from joint and several liability in tort claims, is that the partners *as a partnership unit,* not singly and individually, owe the obligation to the creditor. The major consequence of this distinction is in *the joinder of defendants* and other procedural matters.

1. **Joinder of all partners required:** At common law, the creditor *had to join all partners in a suit,* except if a partner had died or was outside the jurisdiction. See R&G, pp. 316-17; UPA § 36, *infra,* p. 254.

2. **Joinder of all partners not required:** By statute in some jurisdictions, joinder of all partners is no longer required. In these jurisdictions, under the doctrine of *merger,* a creditor who sues one of the partners on a contract claim may not pursue the other partners' assets, even if his claim is unsatisfied.

a. **Requirement in contract claims that partnership assets be exhausted before creditor can proceed against partners' individual assets:** The judgment creditor of a partnership must first attempt to recover from the partnership's assets. If those assets are insufficient, the creditor may then proceed against the property of individual partners who were served with process in the proceeding against the partnership. *Dayco Corp. v. Fred T. Roberts and Co.,* 472 A.2d 780, 784 (Conn. 1984).

Example: T sued ABC partnership and its partner, A, as guarantors on a note. T's action was started after the partnership had dissolved but while it was still winding up. A stipulated to the entry of judgment against ABC. T then obtained summary judgment against A as partner, based on the judgment against ABC. A then claimed that the judgment against ABC was void because the lawsuit was brought after the partnership was dissolved. A also claimed that there was no right by T to proceed against him as an individual partner, because T's claim was based only upon a judgment against the partnership.

Held, a partnership may be sued following dissolution but before the partnership is wound up, and A was jointly liable as a partner of ABC. After a partnership's judgment creditor exhausts the partnership's assets, he can pursue the partners' individual assets. *Commonwealth Capital Inv. Corp. v. McElmurry,* 302 N.W.2d 222 (Mich. Ct. App. 1980).

Note: Inasmuch as A had personally been served with the complaint in the original suit and had stipulated to the entry of judgment against ABC, he could hardly claim that the summary judgment against him violated due process.

i. **Exception for jurisdictions where partners are jointly and severally liable to contract creditors:** In those jurisdictions which have made partners jointly and severally liable to contract creditors, the creditor may pursue individual partners' assets without first exhausting the partnership assets. See *Head v. Henry Tyler Constr. Corp.,* 539 So. 2d 196 (Ala. 1988).

3. **Effect of a release:** In most states the release of any joint obligor is a release of all joint obligors. However, in those jurisdictions in which partners are jointly and severally liable for the partnership's contractual obligations, a ***release of one partner does not effect*** a release of the other partners. The other partners remain liable for any unpaid portion of the obligation. See Hynes, pp. 601-602.

E. RUPA makes partners jointly and severally liable on all claims against the partnership: Under RUPA § 306 partners are jointly and severally liable *on all creditor claims*. However, under this provision, a partnership creditor must exhaust his remedies against partnership assets before proceeding against the assets of any individual partner. By requiring the exhaustion of partnership assets, the RUPA differs from the approach in many jurisdictions.

IV. PARTNER BY ESTOPPEL

A. Generally: The concept of partnership by estoppel is developed in UPA § 16. Under this provision, when a *person represents himself*, or consents to have another represent him, as a *partner in an existing partnership*, or as *acting as a partner* with one or more persons who are not actually partners, he is liable to any third party to whom the representation has been made and who has, on the faith of such representation, given credit to the actual or apparent partnership. If he makes the representation, or consents to its being made, *publicly*, he is liable to the party giving credit, even if the apparent partner does not know of the communication to such party.

1. **Resulting partnership liability:** When a partnership liability results from his representation, he is liable as though he were an actual member of the partnership. UPA § 16(1)(a).

2. **No resulting partnership liability:** When no partnership liability results, he is jointly liable with any other persons who consents to the contract or representation, but if there is no such other person, then he is liable separately. UPA § 16(1)(b).

3. **Representation creates agency:** When a person has been represented to be a partner, he becomes an agent of those who consent to the representation. The result is that, by estoppel, he can bind those persons to third parties who rely upon the representation, as though he were a partner. If all the members of an existing partnership consent to the representation, a partnership act or obligation results; in all other cases the act becomes the joint act or obligation only of the person acting and the persons consenting to the representation. UPA § 16(2).

B. Definition of "partner by estoppel": A "partner by estoppel" is sometimes called an "ostensible partner" or "apparent partner." The term is used when there has been a *holding out* of someone as a partner and *reasonable reliance* by a third party on that representation, *causing injury to the third party*. In that case, the law imposes liability as though the person held out as a partner were in fact a partner. The concept may arise in both contract and tort situations.

Note: A partner by estoppel is not a true partner in fact or in law because she has not entered into a partnership agreement. Thus, a partner by estoppel has no right to manage the business or assert any of the rights of a true partner.

1. **Elements of partnership by estoppel:** The elements necessary to impose personal liability by estoppel on an individual are a question of fact for the jury. They are:

    a. **Holding out:** there is a *holding out* of the individual as partner;

    b. **Consent of individual required:** The act of holding out was done by the would-be partner either *directly or with his consent*;

    c. **Knowledge of insured party:** the injured third person *knew of such holding out*;

    d. **Reliance to third party's detriment:** the third person *reasonably relied* on the holding out to his detriment.

    Example: In 1975, A committed legal malpractice in representing T by falsely telling T that a bank would not foreclose on T's property. A sent letters to T on stationery bearing the names "A and B." T paid for A's services by a check made payable to A alone; however, three years earlier, T had paid for A's services by a check made payable to B. T sued B, claiming that B was vicariously liable for A's malpractice because, by virtue of the letterhead and the previous payment, he was A's partner by estoppel. (There was no evidence that A and B were partners in an actual partnership.)

    Held, B was not liable as a partner by estoppel. The 1975 check was made payable to A alone. This suggests B did not hold himself out as a partner, nor did B consent to A's holding him out as a partner. In addition, T did not rely on B's being a partner of A. The court added that use of stationery with both names, even if done with B's consent, was too slender a reed on which to base a finding that the consent element was present. *Brown v. Gerstein,* 460 N.E.2d 1043 (Mass. App. Ct. 1984).

C. **Consent to being held out as a partner can be implied from silence:** Although the *Brown* court held that there was no implication of consent simply from the use of a two-name letterhead, consent to a holding out can be inferred if A tells a third person that B is his partner and B does or says nothing when he could easily deny it.

Example: A and B met with T. A, a masonry contractor, had been T's customer for about a year and had always paid his bills on time. A introduced B as his partner and told T that he wanted to discontinue his own account and start an account under the name "X Masonry" and do business on a larger scale. B stood there and said nothing. T sent invoices to X Masonry. Those invoices were paid by checks bearing the name X Masonry and in very small type the additional words "a division of the Y Fireplace Corp." T's employees did not notice the fine print. When T tried to collect the unpaid balance from B personally, B said that Y Fireplace Corp. was a corporation and that he was not liable personally. When T told B, "you told me you and A were partners," B replied, "I call everybody I go into business with a partner no matter what the deal is."

Held, B was liable as A's partner by estoppel. His acts were sufficient to lead a reasonable person to believe that he and A were partners. B should have denied the statements A made in his presence to avoid misleading T. B's silence constituted an **adoptive admission.** T relied on B as A's partner when he extended credit. *J&J Builders Supply v. Caffin,* 56 Cal. Rptr. 365 (Cal. Ct. App. 1967). See also *Anderson Hay & Grain Co. v. Dunn,* 467 P.2d 5, 7 (N.M. 1970). The *Anderson* case held that a defendant's failure to tell T that he was not a partner when T demanded payment of a debt, and his payment to T when he was told that payments were past due, would cause a reasonable and prudent person to believe that defendant was a partner.

D. The third person must rely on the holding out: Based on the wording of UPA § 16(1), a **minority** of courts have held that reliance is not necessary to estoppel if the holding out was public. See, e.g., *Brown & Bigelow v. Roy,* 132 N.E.2d 755 (Ohio Ct. App. 1955). However, the **majority** of courts require reliance even on a public representation. One manifestation of reliance is the extension of credit in the belief that the ostensible partner was a partner in fact, whether the holding out was done publicly or privately.

Example (majority view): A had an account at T's business in his own name and the trade name of Y Investment Company. T delivered materials to A but was not paid. T sought a judgment against B. He testified that the business name certificate filed in the County Clerk's office listed B as one of the partners of Y Investment Company. T had not known of the county clerk's records when he extended credit to A or that B had once been connected to Y Investment Company. In fact, at the time that T extended credit to A, B was no longer connected to the business, though B was still listed on the county clerk's records as a partner.

Held, B was not liable on the theory of partnership by estoppel because T had not relied on the records in the clerk's office. "It would indeed be illogical to assume that the Legislature intended that reliance upon the representation is essential where the representation is made directly to the creditor but not essential where the representation occurs through public filing." *Riesen Lumber & Millwork Co. v. Simonelli,* 237 A.2d 303 (N.J. Super. Ct. Law Div. 1967).

E. RUPA requires reliance even when the representation is made in a public manner: Under RUPA § 308, even if the representation is made publicly, the purported partner is liable only if the third person relies upon the purported partnership. RUPA clarifies what UPA § 16 intended to accomplish by stating that when the representation is made publicly, by or with the consent of the purported partner, liability exists if the third person relies on the public representation, even if the purported partner is not aware the he is being held out to the third person as a partner.

V. LIABILITY OF INCOMING PARTNER

A. Generally: What happens when a person who has not been a partner becomes admitted as a partner? UPA § 17 provides that a person admitted as a partner into an existing partnership is liable for all those obligations of the partnership which exist at the time of his admission as though he had been a partner when the obligations were incurred. However, his liability for these prior obligations is limited to the partnership assets, including his investment in the partnership, and does not extend to his own individual assets.

B. Partnership dissolved at common law: Under the common law, the addition of a new partner dissolved the old partnership.

Example: A, B and C are partners and T is their creditor. The firm then takes in a new partner, D. Under the common law view, there is an entirely new partnership, A, B, C and D. The new firm has taken over the assets of the old firm, and no assets now belong to the old firm of A, B and C. Also, T, the creditor of the old firm, has no right to recover out of the assets of the new firm. T must proceed against A, B and C individually to collect the money due him.

C. Present law under UPA: The UPA does not specifically state whether the addition of a new partner dissolves the old partnership. However, it does modify the common law view by providing that creditors may continue to look for satisfaction of their debts to the partnership assets as they move from the old partnership to the new partnership, including the capital contribution of the new partner. The *new partner is not personally liable* for partnership debts incurred before his admission to the partnership. UPA § 17.

1. **Incoming partner is not personally liable, but her investment may be used to satisfy old partnership debts:** The purpose of UPA § 17, is to clarify the liability of an incoming partner and the rights of creditors of the old and new firms. The creditors can reach *all the assets of the partnership*, including any *investment made by the new partner* in the partnership. But the incoming partner is protected against *personal* liability for partnership obligations which arose before he became a partner.

2. **Exceptions:** There are a number of exceptions to the UPA provisions freeing the incoming partner from personal liability for existing debts of the partnership. The incoming partner may be held personally liable for partnership obligations which predated his entry into the partnership when:

   a. **Prior holding out:** There was a "holding out" of the incoming partner as a partner when the debt was incurred;

   b. **Agreement to pay:** The incoming partner agreed *for a consideration* to pay existing debts; or

   c. **Novation:** There was a novation. A novation is an agreement among three parties, the creditor, the new partner and the partnership (or retiring partner). In a novation, all three agree to modify the existing obligations.

   Example 1: The creditor may agree to release a retiring partner from liability in consideration for the assumption of liability by the incoming partner. The incoming partner may agree to the novation as part of the consideration for an interest in the partnership.

   Example 2: A and B are partners doing business as X Lumber Company. The company becomes liable to T. Thereafter C becomes a partner and manager. C acknowledges the partnership debt to T. T sues C personally for the partnership debt owing to him.

   Held, T may not recover. There was no "holding out" of C as a partner when A and B incurred the debt to T. In the *absence of a holding out, an incoming partner is liable to creditors of the old partnership only when the new partner agrees to pay the creditors.* The agreement to pay *must be founded on consideration.* In this case there was no such agreement. C, who became manager of the partnership acknowledged the partnership debt to T, but that did not make C personally liable. *Wolff v. Madden,* 33 P. 975 (Wash. 1893).

D. Present law under RUPA: The RUPA adopts essentially the same position as the UPA. The addition of a new partner does not result in either a dissociation or a dissolution of the partnership. RUPA §§ 601, 801. See *infra* p. 236. Existing partners continue to be liable jointly and severally for partnership obligations, as does the partnership unit itself. RUPA § 306(a). New partners are liable only for those obligations incurred after they join the partnership. RUPA § 306(b).

CHAPTER 17

RELATIONSHIPS BETWEEN PARTNERS

ChapterScope

Once a partnership is organized, each partner has rights and obligations which are unique to the partnership form of business organization. The basic rights of a partner are: to be repaid his debts and expenses in behalf of the partnership, to be indemnified for payments made by him in the conduct of the partnership business, to participate in management, to receive an accounting of the partnership business, and to share in the profits. His principal duties are: to share in partnership losses, to give information to his partners on all items and transactions affecting the partnership, to act for the partnership with good faith and loyalty, not to exploit a partnership opportunity, to account for personal profits as a consequence of the partnership, not to compete with the partnership, to make full disclosure of any personal dealings with the partnership, and to manage partnership affairs with reasonable care. In this Chapter, we will examine all of these rights and duties in detail. We will also consider the fiduciary duties of a partner during and following dissolution, as well as in a partnership at will.

I. RIGHTS OF PARTNERS

Because a partnership is a consensual relationship, the partners may establish rights and obligations among themselves by the terms of their agreement or articles of partnership. These terms bind the partners and the partnership itself; and they are enforceable in court. The UPA's provisions governing the rights among the partners is superseded by any contrary agreement of the parties.

A. Rules determining rights and duties of partners (UPA § 18): UPA § 18 provides the following rules regarding partners' rights and duties in relation to the partnership, subject to any modification agreed upon between them:

1. **Right to be repaid, duty to pay losses:** Each partner shall be repaid his capital and advances to the partnership and shall share equally in the profits and surplus remaining after all liabilities are satisfied, including liabilities to partners; each partner must contribute towards the losses, whether of capital or otherwise, sustained by the partnership, according to his share in the profits.

2. **Right to indemnification:** The partnership must indemnify every partner for payments made and personal liabilities reasonably incurred by him in the conduct of the partnership business, or in the preservation of the partnership business or property.

3. **Right to payment of interest on contributions exceeding capital:** A partner who pays or advances for the partnership more than the amount of capital he agreed to contribute, must be paid interest from the date of the payment or advance.

4. **Right to interest on capital if repaid late:** A partner is not entitled to interest on his capital unless and until the date for repayment of the capital has passed.

5. **Equal right to manage:** All partners have equal rights in the management and conduct of the partnership business.

6. **No right to wages except during wind-up by surviving partner:** No partner is entitled to be paid for acting in the partnership business, except that a surviving partner is entitled to reasonable compensation for winding up the partnership affairs.

7. **Right to choose partners:** No person can become a member of a partnership without the consent of all the partners.

8. **Majority rule controls ordinary business, but all partners must agree to acts outside agreement:** A *majority* of partners may decide ordinary matters connected with the partnership business; but *all* partners must agree to any act that contravenes any agreement between the partners. (Emphasis added).

B. **Right to share assets on liquidation:** Upon liquidation, after a solvent partnership pays all partnership debts, it must pay each partner as follows:

1. **Advances:** After partnership debts are paid, partners' advances are then repaid with *interest upon each advance from the time it was made.*

   a. **Distinguishing advances and loans from capital contributions:** Partner advances and loans must be distinguished from capital contributions for the purposes of distribution of assets.

   Example: A and B formed a partnership to develop real estate. Each partner contributed $4,900 in capital. The partners agreed that additional capital contributions would be made equally. A Inc., a corporation chaired by A in which A was a minority shareholder, advanced $196,000 to the partnership. A promissory note to repay only $8,800 was executed and delivered, but the partnership's books carried the whole $196,000 as a loan. A Inc. sued B for failure to make payments on the $196,000 loan. B argued that the amounts paid by A constituted A's capital contribution rather than a loan, and that no loan payments were due.

Held, A Inc.'s $196,000 payment was an advance or loan to the partnership and not a capital contribution. Even if B were correct in arguing that the payments by A Inc. were really made by A personally, they should still be viewed as loans rather than a capital contribution. A contribution by a partner in excess of an agreed-upon amount is treated as a loan or advance. *Jack C. Keir, Inc. v. Robinson & Keir Partnership*, 560 A.2d 957 (Vt. 1989). In reaching the conclusion that the payments should be treated as loans rather than a capital contribution, the court relied on *Nogueras v. Maisel & Assocs. of Michigan*, 369 N.W.2d 492 (Mich. Ct. App. 1985), which held that a partner's **payments could be either loans or capital contributions, depending upon the parties' intentions.** The *Nogueras* court held that the **payments involved were loans even in the absence of a formally-executed note.**

b. **Significance of loan v. capital contribution:** If a partner's payments to the partnership are a loan, then the lender-partner is a creditor of the partnership and the partnership must repay the loan before repaying the partners' capital contributions. In addition, if the payment is a loan, then the partnership may owe the lender interest.

2. **Right to repayment of capital:** After repayment of partners' advances, with interest, the liquidating partnership must repay each partners' capital contribution, with **interest only from the time it was due for repayment.** Usually capital contributions consist only of the initial capital contributed when the partnership was formed. However, if the partners agree, subsequent additions or withdrawals can change the original capital account of each partner. **Changes in the capital accounts will not affect the partners' profit percentages** previously agreed upon between the parties, unless the agreement is modified.

Example: A and B were partners. They agreed to share profits equally. The partnership then gave A a house worth $23,000, in exchange for a reduction in A's capital account of $23,000. A died and the partnership dissolved. A's widow sued B for an accounting and division of partnership property. B claimed that A's widow was only entitled to 1/8 of the partnership property since that was the ratio of A's capital to the firm's total capital following the transfer of the house.

Held, B must share partnership profits equally with A's widow. Although A's capital account was properly reduced because they agreed to reduce it, the capital account adjustment had no bearing on the division of profits. A's widow was entitled to 1/2 the partnership's profits remaining after payments to creditors and repayment of the partners' capital. Partners divide profits equally unless they agree otherwise. UPA § 18(a). In this case, there was no agreement to the contrary. It is not likely that A would have agreed to reduce his profit share from 1/2 to 1/8 in a partnership then worth $300,000 when he reduced his capital account by only $23,000. *Mahan v. Mahan,* 489 P.2d 1197 (Ariz. 1971).

3. **Right to share profits:** After repayment of partners' advances and capital (including interest when required), proportionate shares of any profits remaining are then distributed among the partners.

    Example: A and B are solvent partners with no partnership debts. The firm has $10,000 in cash. Each contributed $1,000 to capital and a $1,500 loan as an advance. The balance is profit. If they agree to dissolve, they will distribute the $10,000 in this manner: each will get $1,500 with interest from the time the advances were paid to the firm, then each will be paid his $1,000 in capital, with interest from the time they agreed it should be paid, and the balance of the cash will be divided equally between them.

    a. **Profits to be shared equally:** Even if the capital contributions are uneven, profits are to be divided evenly unless the partnership agreement provides otherwise. UPA § 18(a), *supra.*

C. **Duty to share losses:** If the partnership shows a loss, in the absence of a specific agreement to the contrary by the partners, ***the loss must be shared in the same proportion as profits.***

    Example: A and B formed a partnership to purchase and log timber. A advanced $26,000 to buy the timber. B agreed to log the timber. They agreed to split the profits equally; no provision was made for losses. There was no agreement that B would be compensated for his services. The partnership lost money. A sued B to indemnify him for half the partnership's losses.

    Held, B must reimburse A for one-half the partnership's losses. Since there was no provision regarding losses, the partners were required to share losses in the same ratio as profits—in this case 50-50. UPA § 18(a). Furthermore, since there was no agreement to compensate B for his services, he was not entitled to compensation. UPA § 18(f). *Richert v. Handly,* 330 P.2d 1079, 1080-81 (Wash. 1958).

    1. **Avoiding the result in *Richert*:** The rule requiring equal sharing of losses is subject to contrary agreement between the partners. The partnership agreement can provide that the partner who contributes services need not pay a share of the losses proportionate to the cash contributed by another partner. Alternatively, the agreement can attach a value to the contribution of services and designate that

value as a capital contribution. Thus, if one partner contributes $10,000 in cash and the other partner contributes $10,000 in services, the latter will not have to come up with any cash to reimburse the former when the partnership goes belly up (assuming the cash contributor loses no more than the amount of his original investment). Each partner will lose her entire contribution. The partner who contributes cash will lose her cash contribution of $10,000 and the partner who contributes services will lose the value of her services. See *Kovacik v. Reed*, 315 P.2d 314 (Cal. 1957).

D. Right to reimbursement for expenses: Each partner is entitled to be reimbursed for expenses reasonably incurred on behalf of the partnership.

Example: A and B are partners who buy and sell used cars. They sell a car to T on credit. The next day, T calls the firm and tells them that he is abandoning the car at a certain place in the city. A hires a truck to tow the car and pays the charges out of her own pocket because the firm money had been locked in the safe for the night. The expense was incurred by A in the ordinary conduct of the firm business, and it was necessary to preserve the firm's property. A is entitled to reimburse herself out of partnership funds.

E. Right to indemnification for liabilities: Each partner can obtain indemnification for liabilities reasonably incurred in the ordinary *and proper* conduct of the business. However, if a partner commits an act of fraud or negligence, she cannot obtain indemnification from her innocent co-partners.

Example: A and B formed a joint venture to convert an apartment building into a residential cooperative. They agreed that B's only role was to provide the cash needed to buy the building. A, who had experience in cooperative conversions, was to form a cooperative corporation, take title to the building in the corporation, and renovate part of the building. A began selling shares in the cooperative. A told the purchasers that the cooperative corporation would secure a tax abatement; however, A failed to complete the renovations required to obtain the certificate of tax abatement. The tenants sued A, charging him with fraud. The trial court found that A had committed fraud by promising to complete renovations in time to get the tax abatement without having any intention to do so. A brought a claim for indemnification against B.

Held, A was not entitled to indemnification from B because A committed the fraud and B was entirely innocent. If the tenants had brought suit against both A and B, B would have been liable to the tenants along with A because public interest requires that even innocent partners compensate third parties for the unlawful actions of their agents when they are apparently taken on the innocent partner's behalf. However, as between A and B, there is no public interest which requires that the innocent partner should indemnify the culpable one. *Gramercy Equities Corp. v. Dumont,* 531 N.E.2d 629 (N.Y. 1988).

1. **Negligence compared:** If a partner is liable to a third person because of her negligence, she will be treated in the same way as a partner who commits a fraud—she will not be able to obtain indemnification from her innocent partners. See Bromberg & Ripstein on Partnership § 4.07(h) (1996); *Flynn v. Reaves,* 218 S.E.2d 661 (Ga. Ct. App. 1975). In *Flynn,* a partner who was guilty of malpractice was not permitted to recover any contribution from his innocent co-partners.

   Example: A and B, partners, sold an apartment complex to T. A negligently failed to disclose to T known defects in the boiler system. T sued both A and B. B, who had nothing to do with the sale and was entirely innocent, cross-claimed for indemnification from A. A argued that B had benefited from A's misrepresentation because the partnership received a higher price for the apartment complex than it would have if A had not made the misrepresentation.

   Held, B is entitled to indemnification from A for B's liability to T resulting from A's misrepresentation. If A had proved that the partnership received more money as a result of his misrepresentations, B's recovery would have been reduced by the amount of B's benefit. However, A did not prove the partnership received more money because of A's misrepresentation. *Eichberger v. Reid,* 728 S.W.2d 533 (Ky. 1987).

F. **Right to participate in management:** In the absence of agreement to the contrary, each partner has the same right as every other partner to control and manage the partnership business. UPA § 18(e).

1. **Making decisions:** Under UPA § 18(h) a *majority in number* of the partners can determine firm action over *ordinary partnership affairs,* without regard to the comparative investments which the partners have in the firm. For instance, a majority in number will govern in matters such as borrowing money, approving accounts, hiring employees and collecting debts. However, a *unanimous* decision is required to change the following:

   - the firm's capital;

   - the articles of partnership;

   - the scope of the partnership's business; or

- the firm's place of business.

Example: A, B and C are a trading partnership in which A has a two-thirds interest, and B and C each has a one-sixth interest. Profits and losses are shared according to the same fractions. Nothing is said in the articles of partnership about voting or control of the firm's business affairs. During a partners' meeting B and C vote in favor of the partnership's borrowing $10,000 from the partnership's bank, but A votes against it. The majority vote of B and C in favor of the loan is binding both on the partnership and on all of the partners. If either B or C executes a promissory note and the money is paid to the firm, the partnership and all its members, including A, will be bound on the note. This is so even if A tells the bank not to loan the money and states that he will not pay if the loan is made. The only way A can prevent liability on the note is to dissolve the partnership. He must do this by withdrawing before the note is executed and by notifying the bank of his withdrawal .

a.   **Partnership evenly split:** As between the partners, if the partners are evenly split and one partner enters into a new contract over another's objection, the contracting partner's actions will be viewed as unauthorized. *Summers v. Dooley,* 481 P.2d 318 (Idaho 1971), *supra,* p. 201.

Example: A and B were corporate officers and shareholders of CSI. A and B separately formed a partnership which leased land to CSI. Subsequently, A resigned his position with CSI and joined CSI's competitor. A demanded that B, as his partner, negotiate an increase in the amount of rent CSI paid to the partnership. B did not do so because he thought that CSI was paying as much as it could afford. A sued B.

   Held, B was not liable to A. Unless a specific agreement provides otherwise, when partners are evenly split over ordinary business operations, the one opposing a change must have his way. A's remedy was to dissolve the partnership. *Covalt v. High,* 675 P.2d 999 (N.M. Ct. App. 1983), *cert. denied,* 674 P.2d 521 (N.M. 1984).

G. **Right to compensation:** No partner is *entitled to compensation* for his work for the firm, except from the distribution of profits, unless the partners agree otherwise or unless the payments are to a surviving partner for his services in winding up the business. UPA § 18(f). In order for a partner to receive extra compensation, there must be an express or implied agreement of the partners authorizing it.

Example 1: A and B are equal partners in several successful real estate partnerships in Pennsylvania. B moves to Florida, works two or three days per week for six months, and then retires. A works the usual time. On dissolution of the partnership, A seeks compensation for the period A worked full time and B did little work.

Held, A may not recover additional compensation. A did not render extraordinary services. A only continued to run the business as it had been run previously. There was no express or implied agreement that A should be compensated for his services. *Altman v. Altman,* 653 F.2d 755 (3d Cir. 1981); see also *Hurst v. Hurst,* 344 P.2d 1001, 1003 (Ariz. 1959).

Example 2: A and B were partners who built and operated a fishing lodge. Initially, they agreed to contribute an equal amount of cash. They also agreed that each would contribute personal services according to his own expertise. Later, they signed two agreements which A drafted. A claimed these documents modified the original agreement in that A would do more in the construction phase and would manage the lodge for the first season. These extra services were in lieu of a further cash contribution. B claimed he did not knowingly agree to the arrangement and that he did not agree to compensate A for A's services. Upon dissolution of the partnership, A claimed he was entitled to be paid the value of his architectural and managerial services as a non-cash capital contribution to the partnership.

Held, A was not entitled to payment for the value of these services. A's services were not a capital contribution because the lower court did not find that the partners had agreed to treat A's services as capital contributions or as services requiring remuneration. Without that finding, A was not entitled to be paid for his services. A partner contributing only personal services is not entitled to have his services construed as partnership capital upon dissolution, in the absence of an agreement to the contrary. Also, no partner is entitled to be paid for acting in the partnership business (except that a surviving partner is entitled to reasonable compensation for his services in winding up the partnership affairs), unless the partners have previously agreed to the payment. *Schymanski v. Conventz,* 674 P.2d 281 (Alaska 1983).

1. **Wage payments to a partner's children, compensation for winding up:** Payment to a partner's children for services the children render to the partnership is not treated as compensation paid to the partner if the partnership benefits from the expense and the other partners acquiesce to the payments.

   Example: Brothers A and B operated a family farm as a partnership. They split the profits 50-50 and deposited all proceeds in a joint checking account from which all expenses were paid. Initially, both brothers were active in the partnership. However, B suffered a stroke and could not work full-time. The partners hired B's children occasionally to perform necessary farm chores. The partnership dissolved, and A sought to reduce the capital returned to B by the amount of wages paid to B's children. B sued A. A argued that B was not entitled to wages for his own services under UPA § 18(f), and that B's children were also not entitled because their work was only in lieu of his own. A also claimed that A was entitled to payment for winding up the partnership's affairs.

Held, B's children were entitled to wage payments from the partnership because the partnership benefited by obtaining a tax deduction for the payments and because A had acquiesced to the payments. Thus, the payments did not reduce B's capital account. A was not entitled to payment for winding up the affairs of the partnership because he was not a ***surviving partner*** under UPA § 18(f) since B was not dead. *Mehl v. Mehl,* 786 P.2d 1173 (Mont. 1990).

Note: Most courts construe the term ***surviving partner*** narrowly to mean a partner who survives after the death of the other partners, and not a partner involved in the dissolution of a partnership for reasons other than the death of the other partners. See, e.g., *Chazan v. Most,* 25 Cal. Rptr. 864 (Cal. Dist. Ct. App. 1962).

H. Right to choose partners: In the absence of a partnership agreement to the contrary, no one may become a partner without the consent of all the partners. This means that every person has a ***right to choose*** the person(s) who will be his partner ***(delectus personae).*** UPA § 18(g).

Example: A partnership agreement gave the executive committee power regarding "all questions of firm policy." The agreement also permitted the admission and separation of partners by majority agreement. A provision of the agreement permitted amendment by majority vote. The firm merged with another firm over the objection of Partner A. The merger was approved only by the executive committee without the consent of all partners. As a result of the merger, A lost his position as sole chairman of the firm's Washington office. A sued the firm, claiming that the merger violated the UPA rule giving all partners an equal voice in management [UPA § 18(e)] and the UPA rule requiring unanimous consent for admission of a new partner [UPA § 18(g)].

Held, the merger violated neither section 18(e) nor section 18(g). Under the partnership agreement, only a majority was required to approve the admission of new partners, and the executive committee had power regarding "all questions of firm policy." Since UPA §§ 18(e) and (g) are subject to contrary agreement by the partners, the executive committee had the power to conclude the merger over partner A's objection. *Day v. Sidley & Austin,* 394 F. Supp. 986, 992 (D.D.C. 1975).

I. Right of a partner to an accounting (UPA § 22):

1. **Accounting explained:** The right to an accounting encompasses a review of all transactions of the partnership and of the partners. It is an equitable action adjudicated by a master or referee appointed by the court. The master or referee determines the amount owed or due each partner after each partner presents his claims and is examined under oath. The master or referee's decision is subject to court approval or review. UPA § 22 provides that every partner shall have the right to a formal account as to partnership affairs under certain circumstances.

2. **Basis for accounting:** A partner may request an accounting:

   • **Wrongfully excluded:** If his co-partners wrongfully exclude him from the partnership business or possession of its property;

   • **Provided in agreement:** If the right exists under the terms of any agreement;

   • **Provided by UPA § 21:** If any partner has derived a benefit *without the consent of the other partners* from any transaction connected with the formation, conduct or liquidation of the partnership, or from any use of its property;

   • **Other circumstances:** Whenever other circumstances render the account just and reasonable.

3. **Old rule:** Prior to the formulation of UPA §§ 21 and 22, a partner *did not have a right to an accounting unless the partnership was in dissolution.* The reason for rejecting the right to any other accounting was that each partner had access to the firm's books and property and therefore could learn for himself the status of the firm's business. Bromberg & Ripstein on Partnership § 6.08 (1996). However, the right of access was often of theoretical value only, and the UPA rules were designed to protect partners who might be maltreated by their other partners.

4. **Rule under the UPA:** UPA § 43 preserves the right of a partner to an accounting when the partnership is dissolved. In addition, UPA § 22 expands the right to an accounting in those instances in which a partner is wrongfully excluded from the business; or the right is contained in a partnership agreement; or another partner is required to account to all partners for wrongful gains; or whenever other circumstances make an accounting just and reasonable. (*supra.*)

5. **Accounting is generally required before a partner can bring an action at law against another partner:** Generally, an action for an accounting is a prerequisite to an action at law

between the partners. An exception to this general rule, occurs when "the damages belong exclusively to one partner and not the firm and can be assessed without taking an account of the partnership business and without inquiry as to the profits and losses or expenses of the firm or adjustment of any claims arising out of the business involved." *Marcus v. Green*, 300 N.E.2d 512, 519 (Ill. App. Ct. 1973).

II. PARTNERS' FIDUCIARY DUTIES TO ONE ANOTHER

A. Partnership books (UPA § 19): This section provides that the partnership books shall be kept (subject to any contrary agreement) at the partnership's principal place of business, and that every partner shall at all times have access to and may inspect and copy any of them.

B. Duty of partners to render information (UPA § 20): This section provides that partners must render on demand true and full information of all things affecting the partnership, to any partner or to the legal representative of any deceased or legally disabled partner.

1. Liability of partner who keeps the books negligently: A partner who is responsible for maintaining the company books and records has a duty to maintain them with due care. In dissolution, the court may resolve any dispute between the partners as to the income earned by the partnership, against the partner responsible for the books and records, if that partner has failed to exercise due care. *Couri v. Couri*, 447 N.E.2d 334 (Ill. 1983). In *Couri, the* managing partner had responsibility for maintaining records of the business; his failure to do so was a breach of his fiduciary duty to his partner.

C. Partner accountable as a fiduciary (UPA § 21): As we have seen, this section provides that *every partner must account to the partnership for any benefit* derived by him from partnership transactions *without the other partners' consent* or from any use of its property. He must also hold as trustee any profits derived by him from the transaction. (*supra.*) This section also applies to the personal representatives of deceased partners who were the last surviving partners and who are liquidating the partnership.

D. Duty of good faith and loyalty: Every partner owes the fiduciary duties of *utmost good faith* and *loyalty* to the partnership and to her partners. She must account to them for all secret profits received by her within the scope of the partnership's business.

Example: A and B are partners in the business of road contracting. B learns that C wants to hire subcontractors for some road building work. The work is within the business of AB partnership, which is in a position to bid on the work. However, B obtains the subcontract from C for himself individually and not for the partnership. B fulfills the subcontract for C and makes a profit. A sues B to compel B to account to their partnership for the secret profit.

Held, B breached his duty to the partnership and must account for his profits. Partners occupy a position of trust and confidence far above the ordinary standard of trade morality in their dealings with each other.

Of course, if B had offered the work to the partnership and the partnership had decided that it could not perform the work, then B could have performed the subcontract individually without breaching his duty of loyalty. See *Shrader v. Downing,* 140 P. 558 (Wash. 1914); *Van Hooser v. Keenon,* 271 S.W.2d 270 (Ky. 1954).

1. **Duty on leaving the partnership:** Even when a partner plans to leave a partnership, she must not be dishonest to her fellow partners about her plans. In addition, she must not take steps to compete with her former firm until she has separated from the partnership.

   Example: A and B were partners in a law firm. They arranged to open their own practice and to take with them some of their associates. A was asked on three occasions by other partners whether he was leaving, and on on each occasion A denied that he planned to leave. Finally, after giving formal notice to the firm of their plan to leave, A and B began soliciting the firm's clients. They delayed telling their former partners the names of all the clients they had solicited. Also, their solicitation failed to make clear to the clients that the clients had a choice of staying with the old firm or going to A and B's new firm.

   Held, A and B breached their fiduciary duty to their former firm. They had an obligation to be candid with the firm about their plans. Moreover, they should have provided a full list of the clients whom they had solicited. Finally, their letter to the clients was one-sided and failed to give clients a fair choice between the old firm and the firm formed by A and B. The burden was on A and B to prove that the clients would have moved to the AB firm without their solicitations. *Meehan v. Shaughnessy,* 535 N.E.2d 1255 (Mass. 1989).

2. **Duty not to exploit partnership opportunity:** A partner or co-venturer has a responsibility not to exploit a partnership opportunity for his personal gain or individual advantage *Meinhard v.*

Salmon, 164 N.E. 545 (N.Y. 1928), p. 19 *supra*. We saw this principle in our discussion of Agency, p. 19 *supra*.

3. **Duty to account for personal profits:** Money (or property) which a partner receives personally from transactions connected with the firm's business is held by him **in trust,** as a fiduciary for the firm and not as a mere debtor to the firm. UPA § 21. (*supra*.) The partner must account to the other partners for any money or property received.

   Example: A, B and C are partners. C places money received for the firm into her personal bank account. A and B sue to compel C, who is insolvent, to hold the bank account in trust for the partnership. They will succeed under UPA § 21. When C received the money, she held it not as a mere debtor to the partnership, but as a **constructive trustee** with a fiduciary obligation to hold the money solely for the firm. So long as the property can be traced and located *in specie,* then the property is held in trust for the partnership, which is the equitable owner.

   a. **Importance of debtor/trustee distinction:** An ordinary debtor has no specific obligation to hold any of his assets for the account of his creditor. A judgment against an ordinary debtor is often ineffective because the money or property sought belongs to the debtor, and he may claim it as exempt or go into bankruptcy, where other creditors have equal or superior rights to it. Thus, UPA § 21 gives the partnership added protection by impressing a trust on the money or property.

   b. **Breach of joint venture agreement:** When a joint venturer breaches her fiduciary duty to her co-venturer, in the same way as in a partnership, the joint venturer holds profits in trust, and a court may order the joint venturer to account to the other for profits received.

   Example: A and the B agreed to purchase some property, subdivide it and sell it at a profit. A gave B one-half the purchase price. B then bought the property, contributing the other half of the purchase price, and recorded a deed which did not include A in the title. A moved from the area and empowered his brother to act as his agent. A's brother twice offered to purchase B's half interest. Both times B falsely informed him that the property had already been sold, and offered to repay A his original investment. A sued B to recover A's investment plus interest. B claimed that A had abandoned his investment.

   Held, the parties had entered into a joint venture, so partnership principles apply. A is entitled to an accounting, and to a return on his investment plus interest. He is also entitled to have the property held in a constructive trust. *Rust v. Kelly,* 741 P.2d 786 (Mont. 1987).

4. **Duty not to compete:** A partner ***cannot compete*** with her partnership in transactions within the scope of the partnership business. However, a partner is not prevented from earning money in other ventures, provided those ventures do not conflict with her fiduciary duties to the partnership.

Example: A and B are partners operating a business of buying and selling farm machinery. A individually operates a shoe store and a dairy farm, and he occasionally creates a valuable invention. A earns money from all these enterprises. B may not compel A to account for profits from A's other businesses. None of these businesses is within the scope of the partnership machinery-sales business, and none interferes with A's duties of loyalty and good faith to B. Cf. *Lipinski v. Lipinski,* 35 N.W.2d 708 (Minn. 1949).

E. **Duty of full disclosure:** In addition to the duties of good faith and loyalty, a partner has a ***fiduciary duty to disclose to her partners any personal dealings with the partnership.***

Example 1: Partner A purchased property from the partnership without telling his partners. A claimed that he had no duty to make disclosure because the purchase was at a fair price.

Held, A breached his fiduciary duty by failing to inform the other partners of his purchase of partnership property regardless of his claim that it was at a fair price. *Marsh v. Gentry,* 642 S.W.2d 574 (Ky. 1982). If a sale of partnership property were permitted without disclosure, the other partners would be deprived of their opportunity to secure a higher price. Moreover, the other partners may not have wanted to sell the property at all.

Example 2: A and B were partners in the development and operation of a casino. A was a sophisticated investor and had access to the partnership's financial data. A sold his interest in the casino to B. A subsequently sued B, alleging that in negotiating the purchase, B had withheld information that would have enabled A to negotiate on an equal footing with B. A particularly complained about B's failure to provide A with a financial projection which was based on financial data A had seen.

Held, A could not recover from B because B's omissions were not material, given A's sophistication and his access to a large amount of partnership financial data. Although B argued that ordinary fiduciary principles should not apply when partners are dealing with one another at arms' length, the court declined to decide the case on that basis. *Walter v. Holiday Inns, Inc.*, 985 F.2d 1232 (3d Cir. 1993).

F. Liability for mismanagement: Partners may be liable to the other partners for mismanagement. They are not liable for ordinary negligence in management, but only if they willfully disregard their duty, commit fraud, or commit "culpable negligence." This standard is akin to the liability of a corporate director. See *Wyler v. Feuer,* 149 Cal. Rptr. 626, 632-33 (Cal. Ct. App. 1978) The *Wyler* court applied the business judgment rule usually applied to corporations and held the managing partner of a limited partnership should not be liable for good faith mistakes. The theory is that partners require some latitude in exercising judgment on behalf of the partnership. *See* Bromberg & Ripstein on Partnership § 6.07, at 6:86. Bromberg and Ripstein argue that a director, as a paid agent, should have a higher standard of liability than a partner.

Example: A was a partner with the BCD law firm. Under the firm's pension plan, pension payments would end when and if the firm dissolved without a successor entity. Four months after the plan was adopted, A retired to Florida and began receiving pension payments. Several months later the firm merged with another firm. The merger was a disaster, and the merged firm later dissolved without a successor firm. At that point, A's benefit payments ceased, and A sued the members of the firm's managing counsel on the ground that they had acted unreasonably in merging with the other firm.

Held, the law firm partners owed no fiduciary duty to A since he was no longer a partner. Even if they did, partners are not liable for mere negligence in the firm's operation. In the same way as corporate directors, they are shielded from liability for mere negligence. The court rejected A's argument that the counsel was liable to him under UPA § 9(3)(c). This provision states "[u]nless authorized by the other partners or unless they have abandoned the business, . . . less than all the partners have no authority to . . . [d]o any . . . act which would make it impossible to carry on the [partnership's] ordinary business . . . ." The provision was not intended to make partners liable for their negligence to persons with whom the firm transacts business (such as a retired partner like A), but to limit the liability of one partner for the unauthorized actions of other partners. *Bane v. Ferguson,* 890 F.2d 11 (7th Cir. 1989).

G. Fiduciary duties after dissolution: A partner's fiduciary duty continues after dissolution, during the winding-up period.

Example: A and B were partners performing auditing services. They agreed to split their profits 50-50. After the business grew, they hired independent contractors (auditors) to do the auditing work. A, who generated 80% of the partnership revenues, became unhappy with having to split the profits evenly with B. He wrote a letter to B dissolving the partnership. During the winding-up phase, B and A agreed that the auditors would be told that the partnership was dissolved but they would be asked to continue to work on partnership accounts. A unilaterally contracted with the auditors to do work for his newly formed auditing firm. A also solicited firm clients and established new contracts with them for his new firm. B sued A, claiming that A had breached his fiduciary duty to B.

Held, A breached his fiduciary duty to B. "Even after dissolution of a partnership, both partners continue to have a fiduciary duty to the other partner that continues until the partnership assets have been divided and the liabilities have been satisfied." *Steeby v. Fial,* 765 P.2d 1081, 1084 (Colo. Ct. App. 1988).

H. Scope of fiduciary duty: Because each partner is accountable to her partners as a fiduciary, she must:

- keep accounts or books of partnership transactions in which she is involved or of which she has knowledge; this does not mean that each partner is charged with the physical maintenance of the books—only that she must ensure that the maintenance of the books is assigned to someone competent to maintain them (in the partnership agreement, the partners may designate the managing partner or some other partner as the person who has sole responsibility for maintaining the books of the partnership);

- disclose to other partners her personal dealings with the partnership;

- render true and full information to the other partners;

- submit her activities and transactions in the execution of partnership business to financial review; and

- answer to her partners for any breach of fiduciary duty.

I. Altering fiduciary duty in the partnership agreement: Though it cannot be eliminated entirely, a partner's fiduciary duty to her partners can be reduced through a provision in the partnership agreement.

Example: The CD partnership agreement stated, "Each partner shall be free to enter into business and other transactions for his or her own separate individual account even though such business or other transaction may be in conflict with and/or competition with the business of this partnership . . . it being the intention and agreement that any partner will be free to deal on his or her own account to the same extent and with the same force and effect as if he or she were not and never had been members of this partnership." A partnership meeting was held to consider purchasing some property. Decision on the purchase was deferred. Two partners of the CD partnership, A and B, then formed a separate partnership and purchased the property. One of the other CD partners demanded that the partnership be given the opportunity to purchase a 50% interest in the property.

Held, the CD partnership had no right to purchase an interest in the property because A and B had not breached their fiduciary duty of loyalty as defined by the partnership agreement. "From a fiduciary aspect, the permissible boundaries of intra-partnership competition, [under the partnership agreement], are limited only after the" partnership actually acquires property. Had A and B "pirated an existing partnership asset or used partnership funds or encumbered. . . [CD] financially, our decision would be different." *Singer v. Singer,* 634 P.2d 766 (Okla. Ct. App. 1981).

J. **Fiduciary duties under RUPA:** Under RUPA § 404, the only fiduciary duties owed by a partner are the ***duties of loyalty*** and the ***duty of care.***

   1. **Limits on duty of loyalty:** The partner's duty of loyalty to the partnership and to the other partners is limited to:

      - accounting to the partnership and holding as a trustee any property, profit or benefit derived in conducting and/or winding up the partnership business, or from using partnership property, or from appropriating a partnership opportunity;

      - refraining from dealing with the partnership in either the conduct or winding up of the partnership, or from dealing with any party having an interest adverse to the partnership; and

      - refraining from competing with the partnership before its dissolution.

   2. **Limits on duty of care:** A partner's duty of care to the partnership in conducting the partnership business and in winding it up is limited to refraining from engaging in grossly negligent or reckless conduct, intentional misconduct, or a knowing violation of the law.

   3. **Conduct furthering a partner's own business allowed under RUPA:** A partner does not violate the RUPA standards simply because her conduct furthers her own business. RUPA § 404(e). Therefore, a partner can lend money to, or transact other business with, the partnership just as an outsider could, subject to other applicable law. RUPA § 404(f).

   4. **Limiting fiduciary duties by agreement:** Neither the duty of loyalty nor the duty of care may be entirely waived or eliminated in

the partnership agreement. However, by partnership agreement and after full disclosure to all partners, the duty of loyalty can be limited to specific activities or categories of activities if the provisions are not manifestly unreasonable. Likewise, the duty of care can be reasonably reduced. RUPA § 103, comments 5, 6; RUPA § 404, comments 2, 3.

III. PARTNERSHIP AT WILL

A. **Continuation of partnership beyond fixed term (UPA § 23):** UPA § 23 provides substantially as follows:

1. **Rights and duties remain the same if consistent with a partnership at will:** When a partnership for a *fixed term* or for a *particular undertaking* is continued *after the termination of the term* or undertaking without any express agreement, the partners' rights and duties *remain the same* as they were at the termination, so far as is consistent with a *partnership at will*.

2. **Evidence of continuation:** A *continuation of the business* by the partners, or by those partners who habitually acted for the business during the term, without any settlement or liquidation of the partnership affairs, is *prima facie evidence* of a continuation of the partnership.

B. **Continuing the partnership:** When a partnership is created to last a definite or fixed time or for a specific undertaking, but is continued after the expiration of that period or after completion of the undertaking, it becomes a partnership at will and is subject to termination at any time.

1. **Deceased partner:** UPA § 23 refers only to the acts of living partners and has no application to the continuation of a business by a surviving partner and/or the representative of a deceased partner. *Tucker v. Tucker,* 87 A.2d 650, 654 (Pa. 1952). *See,* also *infra,* p. 240.

CHAPTER 18

DISSOLUTION AND WINDING UP

ChapterScope

Unlike corporations, partnerships do not enjoy perpetual life. They may be at will or for a stated term. In any event, there is a need to anticipate the process by which they will terminate. This process usually involves three successive steps: dissolution, winding up, and, finally, termination itself. In this chapter, we will discuss the meaning of each of these terms and the steps under which they are carried out. We will review the events which cause non-judicial dissolution, both under the UPA and the RUPA, and the ways in which dissolution may be accomplished in the courts. We will cover in detail the winding-up process following dissolution, including the partners' authority to bind one another and their right to contribution from each other. We will then review what happens to the partnership following dissolution, including the requirements for notice to third parties, the liability of the partners following dissolution, and who has the right to conduct the winding-up process. Finally, we will discuss the problem of competition for the business of the partnership among the outgoing partners.

I. TERMINOLOGY

A. **Dissolution defined:** The *dissolution* of a partnership is the change in the relation of the partners caused by any partner's ***ceasing to be associated*** in the carrying on (***as distinguished from the winding up***) of the business. UPA § 29.

B. **Partnership not terminated by dissolution:** The partnership ***does not terminate on dissolution***, but continues until the winding up of partnership affairs is completed. UPA § 30.

C. **Explanation of terms:** The terms ***dissolution, winding up*** and ***termination*** must be understood as they are used in the UPA.

1. **Dissolution:** This is the point in time when the partners cease to carry on the partnership business as a going concern, or when any partner ceases to be associated with the business. Dissolution does not end the partnership; it continues until the winding up of partnership affairs is completed.

2. **Winding up:** This refers to the series of transactions following dissolution which settle all partnership affairs and bring to an end all partnership items requiring resolution.

3. **Termination:** The point in time when all partnership affairs have been wound up and settled. The partnership continues until termination. UPA § 30.

Example: A and B are equal partners and operate a shirt factory. On Oct. 31, 1988, A and B contract to sell their business to T. The contract is to be effective that same day. A and B gather the firm assets, pay all firm debts, repay all advances and contributions made by them to the partnership, and inventory all remaining goods and materials. The winding up process is completed, and T pays A and B the contract price in full on Dec. 31, 1988. On these facts, the partnership was dissolved on Oct. 31, 1988; the period from Oct. 31 to Dec. 31, 1988 was the winding up period; and Dec. 31, 1988 was the date of termination of the partnership. For purposes of winding up (suing and being sued, paying debts, etc.) the partnership continued to exist until Dec. 31, 1988.

II. DISSOLUTION CAUSES IN GENERAL

A. **Dissolution by agreement:** A partnership is created by contract and can be dissolved by agreement without formal court proceedings. The courts will enforce the agreement during its term. However, generally, an agreement to enter into a partnership *at will or for an indefinite period will not be specifically enforced,* because any party may dissolve the partnership at any time. A contrary result was reached in a case involving an option to purchase a share in an existing partnership. *Jones v. Styles,* 109 So. 2d 713 (Ala. 1959).

B. **Causes of dissolution — UPA § 31:** UPA § 31 sets forth the circumstances which cause the dissolution of a partnership:

1. **Without violating the terms of any agreement between the partners:**

   • termination of the specified term or particular undertaking specified in the agreement;

   • the express will of any partner when no definite term or particular undertaking is specified;

   • the express will of all the partners who have not assigned their interests or suffered them to be charged for their separate debts, either before or after the termination of any specified term or particular undertaking; or

   • expulsion of any partner from the business *bona fide* in accordance with a power of expulsion conferred by the agreement between the partners.

2. **In contravention of the agreement between the partners:** If the circumstances do not permit a dissolution under any other provision of UPA § 31, dissolution may be caused by the express will of any partner at any time.

3. **Unlawful act or event:** If any event makes it unlawful for the partnership business to be carried on or for the members to carry it on in partnership, the partnership is dissolved.

4. **Death of partner:** Death of any partner dissolves the partnership.

5. **Bankruptcy:** Bankruptcy of any partner or of the partnership dissolves the partnership.

6. **Court decree:** Decree of court under UPA § 32 ("dissolution by decree of court") dissolves the partnership.

C. **RUPA rules for dissociation, dissolution and termination:**
   RUPA § 601 lists 10 events which can cause a partner's *dissociation* from a partnership. The RUPA treatment is substantially different from the treatment under the UPA. Unlike *dissolution* under the UPA, a *dissociation* under RUPA does not automatically precipitate a winding up and termination of the partnership. This change is consistent with the *entity theory of partnership* followed by RUPA. (See, *supra*, p. 162.) RUPA anticipates that most dissociations will result in a buy-out of the dissociated partners' interest. RUPA § 801, comment 1. Only certain dissociations, listed in RUPA § 801, will cause the partnership to dissolve, wind up, and then terminate.

   1. **Events which cause dissociation under RUPA:** The 10 events which cause dissociation under RUPA § 601 are substantially as follows RUPA § 601:

      • *receipt by the partnership* of notice of a partner's express will to withdraw as a partner, upon the date of notice or at a later date specified in the notice;

      • *occurrence of an event* specified in the partnership agreement as causing a partner's dissociation;

      • *expulsion of a partner* pursuant to the partnership agreement;

      • *the partner's expulsion by the unanimous vote* of the other partners if:

         • it is unlawful to carry on the partnership business with that partner; or

         • all or substantially all of the partner's interest in the partnership has been transferred, except for a transfer for security purposes, or except for a court order charging the partner's interest, which has not been foreclosed; or

- with respect to a corporate partner: (a) the partnership notifies the corporate partner that it will be expelled because it has filed a certificate of dissolution or the equivalent, or its charter has been revoked, or the jurisdiction of its incorporation has suspended its right to conduct business; and (b) the dissolution certificate is not revoked or there is no reinstatement of the charter or right to conduct business within 90 days after the notice; or

- a partnership that is itself a partner has been dissolved and its business is being wound up;

- *judicial expulsion* of the partner on application of the partnership or another partner, because:

  - the partner engaged in wrongful conduct that adversely and materially affected the partnership business; or

  - the partner willfully or persistently committed a material breach of the partnership agreement or a duty owed under RUPA Section 404 (i.e. — "general standards of partner's conduct"); or

  - a partner acted in the partnership business in a way which makes it not reasonably practicable to carry on the business in partnership with that partner;

- *the partner's:*

  - becoming a debtor in bankruptcy;

  - executing an assignment for the benefit of creditors;

  - seeking, consenting to, or acquiescing in the appointment of a trustee, receiver, or liquidator of that partner or of all or substantially all of that partner's property; or

  - failing, within 90 days after the appointment, to have vacated or stayed, the appointment of a trustee, receiver, or liquidator of the partner or of all or substantially all of the partner's property, obtained without the partner's consent or acquiescence, or failing within 90 days after the expiration of a stay to have the appointment vacated;

- *in the case of a partner who is an individual:*

  - the partner's death;

  - the appointment of a guardian or general conservator for the partner; or

- a judicial determination that the partner has otherwise become incapable of performing the partner's duties under the partnership agreement;

- *in the case of a partner that is a trust* or a trustee acting as partner by virtue of being a trustee of a trust, distribution of the trust's entire transferable interest in the partnership, but not merely by reason of the substitution of a successor trustee;

- *in the case of a partner that is an estate* or an estate's personal representative acting as a partner for the estate, distribution of the estate's entire transferable interest in the partnership, but not merely by reason of the substitution of a successor personal representative; or

- *termination of a partner* who is not an individual, partnership, corporation, trust, or estate.

2. **Events which cause dissolution under RUPA:** RUPA § 801 describes six events that will cause a partnership to dissolve, substantially as follows (if any of these events occurs, the partnership must be wound up):

- *in a partnership at will,* the partnership receives notice from a partner (other than a partner who is dissociated under RUPA Section 601(2) through (10)), of that partner's express will to withdraw as a partner, effective immediately or on a later date specified by the partner;

- *in a partnership for a definite term* or particular undertaking:

  - the expiration of 90 days after a partner's dissociation by death or otherwise under RUPA Section 601(6) through (10) or wrongful dissociation under § 602(b), *unless* before that time a majority in interest of the remaining partners, including partners who have rightfully dissociated pursuant to (RUPA) Section 602(b)(2)(i), agree to continue the partnership;

  - the express will of all of the partners to wind up the partnership business; or

  - the expiration of the term or the completion of the undertaking;

- *an event agreed to* in the partnership agreement resulting in the winding up of the partnership business;

- *an event that makes it unlawful* for all or substantially all of the partnership's business to be continued, but a cure of illegality within 90 days after notice to the partnership of the event is effective retroactively to the date of the event for purposes of this section;

- *on application by a partner,* a judicial determination that:

  - the economic purpose of the partnership is likely to be unreasonably frustrated;

  - another partner has engaged in conduct relating to the partnership business which makes it not reasonably practicable to carry on the partnership's business with that partner; or

  - it is not otherwise reasonably practicable to carry on the partnership business in conformity with the partnership agreement.

- *on application by a transferee* of a partner's transferable interest, a judicial determination that it is equitable to wind up the partnership business:

  - after the expiration of the term or completion of the undertaking, if the partnership was for a definite term or particular undertaking at the time of the transfer or entry of any charging order that gave rise to the transfer; or

  - at any time, if the partnership was a partnership at will at the time of the transfer or entry of any charging order that gave rise to the transfer.

3. **Partnership continuation until wind-up completion:** Under RUPA, even after dissolution, a partnership continues until the winding-up phase is completed, RUPA § 802. At any time after dissolution, all of the partners, including a dissociating partner other than a wrongfully dissociating partner, can waive the right to have the partnership's business wound up and terminated. In the latter event:

- the partnership resumes carrying on the business as if dissolution had never occurred;

- but the rights of a third party arising out of conduct in reliance on the dissolution before that third party receives notice of the waiver of dissolution by the partners may not be adversely affected.

III. NON-JUDICIAL DISSOLUTION

Under the UPA, *nonjudicial partnership dissolution* may occur through such events as expiration of the partnership's term, action by the partners, illegality, death or bankruptcy. A continuation clause in the partnership agreement may provide that the partnership will continue despite any or all of these events.

A. Dissolution by partner's act or will: Dissolution of a partnership is caused *without violating the contract or articles of partnership* by any of the following:

- *expiration of the term* for which it is to exist;

- the express *will of any partner* when it is a *partnership at will*;

- the express *will of all the partners* who have not assigned their interests or allowed them to be charged for their separate debts; or

- *the expulsion of a partner* according to the terms of the partnership agreement.

1. **Dissolution by will of individual partner:** Any partner has the *power,* (but, if his act is in breach of the agreement, not the *right*), to dissolve the partnership at any time.

    Example 1: A, B, C and D form a partnership to lease certain real estate for profit. After the partnership operates for 13 years, A writes to her partners: "I am terminating the partnership . . . ." Meetings among the partners do not produce a plan for liquidation and A brings suit. A dies during the litigation, and B, C and D contend that the partnership is dissolved as of A's death, not when she wrote the letter.

    Held, A dissolved the partnership by her letter. No justification was necessary for her action. Although the death of a partner dissolves the partnership under UPA § 31(4), it may also be dissolved "by the express will of any partner" under UPA § 31(1)(b), so long as the partner's action does not violate any partnership agreement. The partnership was not for a definite term, and there was no "particular undertaking" specified in the partnership agreement. A "particular undertaking" is one capable of being completed at some foreseeable time in the future. The business of leasing property may continue indefinitely, so there is nothing "particular" about it. Thus, A's letter dissolved the partnership. *Girard Bank v. Haley,* 332 A.2d 443 (Pa. 1975).

    Example 2: A and B agree to be partners for five years. After two years, and in violation of the agreement, A withdraws from the partnership and refuses to perform his partnership obligations. This dissolves the partnership. The relationship between partners is of a consensual nature involving general agency. No one can be compelled to remain in the relationship, even though to withdraw from it may constitute a breach of contract. In this case A could not withdraw from and dissolve the partnership without breaching the articles of partnership. For that breach, A may be liable to B for damages, but that does not prevent A from exercising his power to dissolve the firm. *Engelbrecht v. McCullough,* 292 P.2d 845 (Ariz. 1956); UPA §§ 31(2), 38(2).

2. **Power of court to order specific performance of partnership agreement:** Regardless of a party's power to dissolve a partnership, a court may order specific enforcement of a partnership agreement when (a) no personal services are involved; and (b) legal remedies are inadequate.

   Example: A Corp. (A) and B Corp. (B) formed a joint venture to develop and market a small pump for implantation below the skin for the administering of drugs. The joint venture's president met with T, who was to design valves for the joint venture. The president and T could not get along and reached a dead end. In light of their failure to get along, B worked out an arrangement between B and T. B did not hide what it was doing from A. A sought judicial dissolution of the partnership. A complained that B had breached its fiduciary obligation by usurping business opportunity and control from A and the joint venture.

   Held, partnership law will be applied to the joint venture. A was not entitled to judicial dissolution because B did not materially breach its agreement obligations. Although A was seeking dissolution, the trial court could order the joint venture to continue if both parties to the venture were corporations, and if legal remedies were found to be inadequate and no personal services were involved. If no specific performance was ordered on remand, the court could find that dissolution had already taken place by virtue of A's breach (A had failed to provide B with technical assistance and had denied B access to the venture's books and records). Under those circumstances, B could continue the venture upon paying A the value of A's interest, less any damages caused by A's breach, and by indemnifying A against future liabilities. *Infusaid Corp. v. Intermedics Infusaid, Inc,* 739 F.2d 661 (1st Cir. 1984).

3. **Requirement of good faith:** Many courts require that the party who exercises the power to terminate a partnership at will act in good faith because of the fiduciary relation of the partners.

   Example: A and B formed a partnership to operate a linen business. The partnership agreement provided no definite term for the partnership's duration. The parties agreed that all obligations were to be repaid from profits. A corporation controlled by A loaned the partnership money, and the partnership, after heavy losses, began to show a profit. A sought to dissolve the partnership. B resisted, contending that the agreement impliedly created a partnership for such period of time as was necessary for the partners to recoup their investment. B also argued that A was attempting to dissolve the partnership in bad faith by using his superior financial position to appropriate the business now that it was profitable. B argued that A would try to buy the business at dissolution for a low price (other buyers might not be interested because A's corporation held a demand note for $47,000). Then, A would be able to operate the business without adequately compensating B.

Held, the partnership was not for a term. There was no agreement, express or implied, for the partnership to continue for any period of time. Therefore, A had the right to dissolve the partnership under UPA § 31. The court added, however, that if A dissolved the partnership in bad faith in order to appropriate the partnership benefits for himself without adequately compensating B, he would be liable in damages to B. His liability would be based on having wrongfully excluded B from the partnership business opportunity. *Page v. Page,* 359 P.2d 41 (Cal. 1961).

4. **Rights of remaining partners if dissolution contravenes agreement:** If a partner causes dissolution in contravention of a partnership agreement, e.g., by causing it to dissolve prior to the expiration of its term, the remaining partners may buy out the retiring partner's interest, indemnify her against partnership liabilities, and thereafter continue the business. *Straus v. Straus,* 94 N.W.2d 679 (Minn. 1959).

B. **Dissolution for illegality:** If the business of the partnership becomes illegal, or it becomes illegal for a member to remain a partner, then the partnership is dissolved. UPA § 31(3).

Example 1: A and B are partners in the business of selling liquors. The state in which the business is being conducted passes a prohibition law making the business illegal. The partnership is thereby dissolved.

Example 2: A and B are partners in the practice of law. A is elected to the bench of the court of general jurisdiction. The election makes it illegal for A to practice law. This dissolves the partnership.

C. **Dissolution for death or bankruptcy:** A partnership is dissolved by any partner's death, or by the bankruptcy of any partner or of the partnership. The bankruptcy dissolution applies to a proceeding under chapter 7 of the Bankruptcy Act, which provides for business liquidation, but not to a partnership reorganization under chapter 11 of the Act. *In re Safren, infra,* p. 284.

1. **Bankruptcy of partner:** When a partner is adjudicated bankrupt in chapter 7, his interest in the partnership passes to his trustee in bankruptcy. He is then disabled from conducting the partnership business or from acting as the partnership's agent; and the partnership is thus dissolved.

2. **Bankruptcy of partnership:** When the partnership becomes bankrupt under Chapter 7, all partnership assets pass to the trustee in bankruptcy, and the firm is enjoined from continuing its business, thereby causing dissolution. Bankruptcy of the partnership does not necessarily mean the individual partners are insolvent or that they must declare bankruptcy.

   Example: H and W, partners, assign their partnership assets to a trustee for the benefit of creditors. Thereafter, creditors file an involuntary bankruptcy petition against the partnership and H and W individually.

   Held, the bankruptcy petition filed against H and W individually is dismissed. The bankruptcy of the partnership, by itself, does not constitute an act of bankruptcy by the individual partners. Dismissal against the individuals does not injure partnership creditors because the partners continue to be personally liable, and creditors can obtain ***in personam*** judgments against the individual partners for partnership debts. Furthermore, any transfer of property by partners must be ***bona fide,*** without intent to hinder, delay or defraud creditors; otherwise, the transfer may be undone. *In re Jercyn Dress Shop,* 516 F.2d 864 (2d Cir. 1975).

D. **Effect of continuation clauses on dissolution:** Partners can alter the UPA provisions regarding the rights and duties of each with respect to dissolution, winding up, and distribution of assets. For example, the partners can provide that ***death or retirement will not cause*** a dissolution of the partnership.

   Example: Dr. A, Dr. B and Dr. C formed a three-person medical partnership to practice radiology. Their partnership agreement provided that the partnership would continue until dissolved. It also provided that the death or retirement of any partner would not dissolve the partnership. Any retiring partner was required to give the remaining partners six months notice of his intent to withdraw. The retiring partner could then obtain certain planned distributions. The agreement also limited post-retirement competition. Dr. A and Dr. B sued to dissolve the partnership. They claimed that they could dissolve the partnership by filing the action and thereby circumvent the requirements of the continuation clause.

Held, Dr.'s A and B had the **power** to dissolve the partnership by electing to withdraw as partners, which they did by filing the lawsuit. However, they did not have the **right** to dissolve the partnership without complying with the terms of the partnership agreement. Dr.'s A and B were liable to Dr. C for violating the six-month notice provision, and they had to honor the noncompetition agreement and distribution plan. Dr. C was entitled to continue the partnership and to settle the affairs of the partnership in accordance with the partnership agreement. He was also entitled to recover for any damage he incurred as a result of the breach of the notice provision. *Hunter v. Straube,* 543 P.2d 278 (Or. 1975).

Note: The UPA gives partners the power to dissolve a partnership even though the partnership agreement provides otherwise. However, as in **Hunter,** the partners can determine the effect of the dissolution through a continuation clause.

IV.   PARTNERSHIP DISSOLUTION BY COURT

A. **Dissolution by decree of court — UPA § 32:** UPA § 32 provides the following regarding judicial dissolution of a partnership:

- On application by or for a partner the court will decree a dissolution whenever:

  - a partner has been declared a lunatic in any judicial proceeding or is shown to be of unsound mind;

  - a partner becomes in any other way incapable of performing his part of the partnership contract;

  - a partner has been guilty of such conduct as tends to prejudice the business;

  - a partner wilfully or persistently commits a breach of the partnership agreement, or otherwise conducts himself in matters relating to the partnership business that it is not reasonably practicable to carry on the business in partnership with him;

  - the partnership business can only be carried on at a loss; or

  - other circumstances render a dissolution equitable.

- On the application of the purchaser of a partner's interest under (UPA) section 27 ("assignment of partners interest") or section 28 ("partner's interest subject to charging order"):

  - after the termination of the specified term or particular undertaking;

- at any time, if the partnership was a partnership at will when the interest was assigned or when the charging order was issued.

B. Causes for judicial dissolution: A court may dissolve a partnership in the following situations.

1. **In general:** A court "shall decree" a dissolution of a partnership when the plaintiff would have grounds for rescinding the partnership agreement for any of the following reasons (UPA § 32):

   - a partner is unable to perform his partnership duties;

   - a partner materially breaches the partnership agreement;

   - a partner's conduct makes it impracticable to continue the firm's business with him as partner;

   - the business can be carried on only at a loss; or

   - considering all circumstances, a dissolution is equitable to the partners.

2. **Other specific grounds:** In addition to the causes listed under UPA § 32, the following have been held by the courts to constitute sufficient cause for a decree of dissolution: habitual drunkenness; permanent paralysis; excluding a partner from a voice in the firm management; fraudulent retention by a partner of partnership funds; consistent neglect of partnership duties; refusal of an accounting as required by the partnership articles; and constant dissension among the partners sufficient to endanger seriously the good will, property and business of the partnership.

3. **Insufficient grounds:** By contrast, the following have been found insufficient to justify a decree of dissolution: mere differences of opinion; slight losses caused by errors in judgment; and, even paying a partner's own debts with firm funds when it did not affect the partnership business.

   Example: The A & Co. partnership consisted of 10 partners, but it was dominated by A. Under the partnership agreement, A was in control of all aspects of the business except the admission of new members. New members could be admitted by majority vote. At a meeting, A proposed that the firm accountant be admitted as a partner. Seven of the 10 partners voted against the proposal and it was rejected. In a fit of pique, A called a special meeting and reduced the salaries of the seven dissenters by 50%. He subsequently relented and distributed the full amounts owed. The dissenters sued for dissolution under UPA § 32(1)(c) and (d) (relying on the express will of partners and their right to expel A. They claimed the right to continue the profitable partnership business under the name A & Co.

Held, A's conduct, though improper, was not so serious as to warrant dissolution. His ill-advised and short-lived attempt to reduce the salaries of the seven dissenters did not constitute gross misconduct warranting dissolution of the partnership, particularly since the partnership continued to make money for all the partners. A's control of the aspects of the partnership business other than the admission of new members was provided for under the partnership agreement and was not a basis for dissolution under UPA§ 32. *Potter v. Brown,* 195 A. 901, 903-04 (Pa. 1938). See also *Infusaid Corp. v. Intermedics Infusaid, Inc,* 739 F.2d 661 (1st Cir. 1984), discussed *supra,* p. 241.

4. **Dissolution by creditor:** If a partner assigns his partnership interest (UPA § 27), or his interest has been sold under a charging order (UPA § 28), and either (a) the partnership is one at will or (b) the term of the partnership has expired, then the assignee or purchaser may obtain a decree of dissolution. UPA § 32(2).

Example: A, B and C are equal partners conducting a trading partnership at will. T takes judgment against A on a separate debt and gets a charging order on A's interest. Then T applies for a decree dissolving the partnership so that there can be a winding up and an accounting to determine the value, if any, of A's interest in the partnership. The court should grant the decree. The firm is a partnership *at will,* which means that any partner can at any time dissolve the partnership without liability for breach of contract. If the debtor-partner has a right to dissolve the partnership, then his judgment creditor also has that right under UPA § 32(2). However, T cannot achieve dissolution himself; he can obtain dissolution only by a court decree, even though A himself could have dissolved the firm without applying to the court.

V. PARTNERS' AUTHORITY TO BIND ONE ANOTHER AFTER PARTNERSHIP DISSOLUTION

A. **General effect of dissolution on partner's authority (UPA § 33):** Except as necessary to wind up partnership affairs or to complete transactions, dissolution terminates all authority of any partner to act for the partnership:

1. **With respect to the partners:**

   • when the dissolution is not by the act, bankruptcy or death of a partner; or

- (a) if dissolution is by the act of a partner, the authority is terminated only when the partner acting for the partnership knew of the act causing dissolution; and (b) if dissolution is by the death or bankruptcy of a partner, the partner acting for the partnership knew or had notice of the death or bankruptcy causing dissolution. (UPA § 34.)

2. **With respect to persons not partners:** UPA § 33(2) refers us to § 35 for these provisions. We discuss § 35 in detail beginning at p. 249.

B. **Right of partner to contribution from co-partners after dissolution — UPA § 34:** When the dissolution is caused by a partner's act, death or bankruptcy, each partner must contribute to the partnership his share of any liability created by any partner acting for the partnership as if the partnership had not been dissolved unless:

- the dissolution is by act of any partner, and the partner acting for the partnership knew of the resulting dissolution, or

- the dissolution is by a partner's death or bankruptcy, and the partner acting for the partnership knew or had notice of the death or bankruptcy.

C. **General rule for termination of authority:** Generally, dissolution terminates any partner's authority to act as agent for the partnership or for the other partners, except to wind up the partnership affairs.

Example: A, B and C are equal partners who buy, sell and install heaters and coolers. The partnership is created for a five year term. At a meeting of the partners on the last day of the term, all agree to discontinue the partnership, and to assist in winding up the firm's business.

Problem 1: Following the meeting, A installs a heater for X and pays the firm employees who help in the installation with partnership funds. This is in accordance with a contract made by the firm *before its dissolution*. These acts bind the firm and B and C. A's installation of the heater is performance of a contract for which the firm is liable and is part of the winding up process. His act created no new or different obligation for the firm or the partners.

Problem 2: Following the meeting, B executes a partnership promissory note, due in one year, to Y for $1,000 to cover the cost of a heater purchased from Y. The firm had agreed to execute this promissory note for the heater before it dissolved. The firm and the partners are bound on the note. Every partnership is bound to carry out its executory contracts. B's signature of the firm name on the promissory note is not taking on any new debt, but is merely performing an already existing contract. It is part of the winding up process.

Problem 3: At the time of the meeting, the partnership owes Z some money, currently due, and no agreement has been made to pay it. C then executes a promissory note payable "on demand" covering the amount due and signs it as "A, B & C Co. by C." A, B and the partnership are not bound on the note. Execution and delivery of the promissory note is not part of winding up. It is the assumption of an entirely new and different obligation than existed at the time of the dissolution. Of course, A, B, C and the partnership all owe the money and all are still bound to pay it, but the promissory note is an entirely new contract which C had no authority to make after dissolution. The instrument gives Z a power he did not have before: the power to transfer the note to a holder in due course and cut off all defenses that the partners and the firm might have had against Z. During the winding up period each partner is limited to reducing the firm assets to cash, to paying outstanding obligations, and to performing existing contracts; he may not enter into new contracts.

D. Authority to sell partnership assets: Winding up the partnership involves liquidating all assets to pay firm creditors, and distributing any surplus to the partners. The winding-up partners are authorized only to sell firm inventory already on hand.

E. Other authority: A winding-up partner is also authorized to:

1. **Audit:** Employ an accountant to audit the partnership books;

2. **Litigate:** Compromise or litigate claims by or against the partnership; and

3. **Insure:** Renew or obtain insurance for partnership property and collect proceeds from insurance policies.

F. Acting partner unaware of dissolution binds other partners and has right to contribution: If a partner acting for the partnership does so without knowledge of dissolution caused by the act of another partner, or without knowledge or notice of the death or bankruptcy of a partner, all the partners are bound to each other by the acting partner's act within the scope of the partnership business. UPA § 34. The acting partner has a right to contribution from the other partners.

Example: A, B and C are partners operating a dairy business that buys and sells milk and dairy cows. The business is a partnership at will. C's principal job is to buy dairy cows. A and B decide to terminate the partnership, effective immediately. On the following day, without knowledge of the dissolution by A and B, C buys three dairy cows for the firm from T, and agrees that the firm will pay T within ten days. A and B refuse to receive the cows as firm property and do not permit C to pay for them from firm funds. C pays T out of his own separate funds. On the accounting among the partners, A and B must contribute their share of the money C paid to T.

G. Actions by partner which are not necessary to wind up the partnership affairs: If, after dissolution, the winding-up partner enters into new transactions which are for his own benefit and are not necessary for winding up the partnership affairs, the other partners will not be liable.

Example: A, B and C were partners. The partnership borrowed money from a bank, giving stock as security for the loan. A signed the note for the loan. The loan proceeds were to be for partnership purposes. Then the partnership was dissolved. At the time of dissolution the stock held by the bank as security well exceeded the loan's value. A had the old note marked "paid by renewal" and signed a new loan. The new loan charged higher interest and added $13,500 to the indebtedness. The stock held as security later declined in value and the bank eventually sold it when the loan was not repaid. A claimed that B and C should share in the liability on the loan and make up for the loss attributable to the decline in the value of the stock.

Held, B and C as departing partners had no obligation to share in partnership losses incurred after they left the partnership. A had an obligation to pay off creditors after dissolution. If he had promptly liquidated, the stock would have been worth more than enough to pay off the loan. Consequently, the loan renewal was really a new loan made to him personally. This conclusion is reinforced by the fact that the loan increased the prior indebtedness and was made at a higher rate of interest. Put simply, the "loan renewal" was not necessary to wind up the partnership affairs because the stock collateral was sufficient to discharge the partnership indebtedness. *Houstoun v. Albury,* 436 So. 2d 224 (Fla. Dist. Ct. App. 1983).

H. Responsibility of partner winding up partnership: A partner who winds up a partnership must do so as expeditiously as possible and must give her fellow partners a final accounting. Failure to do so constitutes a breach of fiduciary duty. *Tucker v. Ellbogen,* 793 P.2d 592 (Colo. Ct. App. 1989), *cert. denied,* (1990).

VI. PARTNERS' AUTHORITY TO BIND PARTNERSHIP AFTER DISSOLUTION

A. Power of partner to bind partnership to third persons after dissolution — UPA § 35: Except as provided in Paragraph (3) below, a partner can bind the partnership following dissolution:

(1) (a) by any act appropriate for winding up partnership affairs or completing unfinished transactions;

    (b) by any transaction which would bind the partnership if dissolution had not taken place, provided the other party to the transaction:

        had extended credit to the partnership prior to dissolution and had no knowledge or notice of the dissolution; or

        though he had not extended credit, nevertheless knew of the partnership prior to dissolution and had no knowledge or notice of dissolution; and the fact of dissolution had not been advertised in a newspaper of general circulation in the partnership's regular place of business (or in each place, if more than one).

(2) a partner's liability under Paragraph (1)(b) above shall be satisfied out of partnership assets alone when that partner, prior to dissolution, had been

    unknown as a partner to the person with whom the contract is made; and

    so far unknown and inactive in partnership affairs that the business reputation of the partnership could not be said to have been in any degree due to his connection with it.

(3) The partnership is not bound by any act of a partner after dissolution

    if the partnership dissolved because it is unlawful to carry on the business, unless the act is proper for winding-up partnership affairs; or

    if the partner has become bankrupt; or

    if the partner has no authority to wind-up partnership affairs; ***except by a transaction with one who:***

    (i)   had extended credit to the partnership prior to dissolution and had no knowledge or notice of the partner's want of authority; or

    (ii) had not extended credit to the partnership prior to dissolution, and had no knowledge or notice of the partner's want of authority; and the fact of his want of authority has not been advertised in a newspaper of general circulation in the place in which the partnership business was regularly carried on.

(4) any person who, after dissolution, represents himself, or consents to being represented, as a partner in a partnership engaged in carrying on business is liable under § 16 as a partner by estoppel. *Supra,* 210.

B. Partnership bound by acts appropriate to winding up or completing unfinished transactions: The partner acting for the partnership in winding up its affairs can bind the partnership when she performs acts appropriate to the winding-up or completes transactions which were unfinished at the dissolution. UPA § 35(1)(a).

1. **Exceptions:** The only exceptions to her power to bind the partnership occur when:

   a. **Illegality:** the partnership is dissolved because it is unlawful to carry on partnership business (but even then the partnership may be bound if the proposed act is not itself illegal and is appropriate to winding up partnership affairs);

   b. **Bankruptcy:** the partnership is dissolved because the partnership has become bankrupt; or

   c. **No authority to wind up:** the partner had no authority to wind up the affairs (except by a transaction with a third person who had previously extended credit to the partnership and did not know that the person lacked authority or who, though he had not extended credit to the partnership, did not know that the partner lacked authority *and* her lack of authority had not been properly advertised in a paper of general circulation).

2. **Winding-up partner can bind partnership by cancelling insurance:** A winding-up partner can cancel existing partnership insurance. Her cancellation will bind the partnership even if the other partners do not know of the cancellation.

   Example: A and B formed a partnership. They obtained liability insurance. The partnership subsequently dissolved, and A was given the power to wind up the partnership affairs. The insurance company knew of the dissolution. Unknown to B, A cancelled the partnership's insurance and collected the unused premiums. Thereafter, a painting subcontractor was injured at one of the partnership's residential projects. He sued the partnership and the individual partners. A and B and the partnership demanded that the insurance company provide a defense under the policy. The insurance company agreed but reserved all its rights. It then filed an action seeking a declaratory judgment that the policy was cancelled as to the partners individually and as to the partnership.

   Held, the policy had been cancelled as to the partners individually and as to the partnership. A had the power to cancel it. A's action was appropriate for winding up partnership affairs. B was bound even though he did not know that A had cancelled the policy. *Jefferson Ins. Co. of New York v. Curle,* 771 S.W.2d 424 (Tenn. Ct. App. 1989).

C. Binding partnership during wind-up when third person fails to receive proper notice of the dissolution: Transactions not appropriate for winding up may nevertheless ***bind the partnership if notice of the dissolution is not given*** to persons who later extend credit to the partnership. The extent of the notice required depends upon the prior relationship of those persons to the partnership. Three classes of persons may be affected by the dissolution of a partnership: persons who previously dealt with the firm; persons who knew of the firm but had not dealt with it before dissolution; and persons who neither knew of the firm nor had dealt with it.

1. **Persons previously dealing with firm:** The partnership and the partners are liable to persons who have previously dealt with the firm and who extend credit to the partnership after it is dissolved, without actual knowledge of the dissolution.

   Example: A, B and C are partners in a trading partnership that bought and sold well-drilling equipment. T has been selling equipment to the firm on credit for several years. The partnership is dissolved by expiration of the term for which it was to exist. T has no knowledge or notice of the dissolution, and sells a well-drilling rig to A on credit for the firm. The money is not paid when due and T sues.

   Held, A, B and C and their firm are liable to T for the debt. A had no actual authority to bind either the firm or B or C after dissolution because dissolution terminated A's authority as a general agent. However, liability will be based on ***apparent authority.*** A had been a general agent, and T had dealt with the firm through A. T had a right to rely on the continuation of A's agency in the absence of actual knowledge of dissolution. Further, there was a duty to give actual notice to T of the dissolution. Without such notice, there was ***apparent authority*** in A to continue to act for the firm.

   a. **Information sufficient to impart knowledge or notice:** If a creditor who dealt with a partnership before dissolution is notified that ***the partnership has incorporated,*** the former partners have no liability for obligations created by the new corporation.

      Example: A and B operated a partnership known as Long Island Sound. T had extended credit to the partnership. The partnership incorporated in 1979. Although T did not receive formal notice of the partnership's incorporation, it accepted checks for two years from Long Island Sound Systems, Inc. T sued A and B personally for payment of debts incurred by the corporation.

Held, T's receipt of corporate checks over a two year period was sufficient notice of partnership dissolution to relieve A and B of liability for debts incurred by the successor corporation. *Jensen Sound Laboratories v. Long,* 447 N.E.2d 464 (Ill. App. Ct. 1983).

2. **Persons with knowledge of the firm but who had not previously dealt with it:** If persons who know of the partnership but have not dealt with it, extend credit to the dissolved partnership, without knowledge or notice of the dissolution, and the dissolution has not been advertised in a newspaper in general circulation in the partnership's place of business, then the partnership and the partners are liable to those persons. UPA § 35(1)(b)(II).

Example: A, B and C are partners in a trading firm that buys and sells newsprint and stationery. T has heard of the partnership but has never done business with it. The firm is dissolved by agreement among the partners and immediately thereafter a notice is placed in the local newspaper that the "A, B, C Company" has been dissolved. T does not see the newspaper notice and knows nothing of the dissolution. A buys paper from T on credit for the partnership.

Held, neither B, C, nor the partnership is liable to T. T knew of the firm, but only a person who has dealt with the firm is entitled to *actual* notice of dissolution. T was entitled only to reasonable notice. The requirement is satisfied by an advertisement in a local newspaper of general circulation.

3. **Persons without any knowledge of firm:** Persons who have not dealt with the partnership and have not known of it, are not entitled to any notice of dissolution, and they cannot hold the partnership liable for credit extended to it after it has been dissolved.

D. **Estoppel:** No one can be liable as a partner by estoppel unless he has held himself out as a partner, or has consented to another's holding him out as his partner.

Example: A, B and C are partners who advertise under the firm name "A and B Company." C is a "dormant" partner who is not known generally to be a firm member. The firm is dissolved, but no notice of the dissolution is published. T, who never heard of the partnership, sees an advertisement for "A and B Company" after the dissolution. T believes that A and B are partners of the firm, but does not know that C is a partner. T sells goods to A on credit for the partnership. A had no authority to bind the firm because the transaction was not part of the winding up process. Nevertheless, partners A and B and the partnership can still be liable on a theory of estoppel. UPA § 35(4). Only those who have held themselves out, or consented to another's holding them out, as partners can be estopped. A and B are estopped to deny that they are partners with respect to T, because they held themselves out as partners. Therefore, A, B and the partnership are liable as if there had been no dissolution. On the other hand, T did not know that C was a partner, and cannot claim estoppel against C. The result is that although T has a claim against the partnership, including C's interest in it, he has no claim against C individually.

1. **Effect of bankruptcy or illegality:** If the dissolution is effectuated by bankruptcy or by the illegality of the partnership, the firm is not liable by estoppel. UPA § 35(3).

E. **Power of a partner to bind the partnership after dissociation under RUPA § 702:** RUPA § 702 significantly alters UPA § 35. Under § 702, for a period of two years after a partner dissociates from a partnership without resulting in a dissolution and winding up of the partnership, the partnership is bound by an act of the dissociated partner which would have bound the partnership before dissociation, but only if the other party to the transaction:

- reasonably believed that the dissociated partner was still a partner;

- did not have notice of the partner's dissociation; and

- is not deemed to have constructive knowledge under RUPA § 303(e) (which provides that a recorded statement can define a partner's authority to transfer real estate) or notice under RUPA § 704(c) (which provides that third parties are deemed to have notice of filed statements of dissociation 90 days after they are filed).

F. **RUPA § 804—Partner's power to bind the partnership after dissolution:** RUPA § 804 provides that after dissolution, the partnership is bound, if the act of the winding up partner is appropriate for winding up the partnership business, or if the act would have bound the partnership under § 301 before dissolution, *if the other party to the transaction had no notice of the dissolution.* § 301 is the provision which adopts the notion that each partner is the agent of the partnership for the purpose of its business and limits the ability of a partner to enter into transactions which are not actually or apparently authorized by the other partners.

VII. PARTNER'S LIABILITY UPON DISSOLUTION

A. **UPA § 36—Partner's liability upon dissolution:** UPA § 36 provides substantially as follows:

- the partnership's dissolution does not by itself discharge the existing liability of any partner.

- a partner is discharged from an existing liability upon partnership dissolution by a release agreement among himself, the relevant partnership creditor and the continuing partner(s); the release agreement may be inferred from the course of dealing between the creditor who knows of the dissolution and the continuing partner(s).

- if someone assumes the existing obligations of a dissolved partnership, the partners whose obligations have been assumed shall be discharged from liability to any of the partnership's creditors who, knowing of the assumption agreement, consent to a material alteration in the nature or time of payment of the obligations.

- A deceased partner's individual property shall be liable for all of the partnership obligations incurred while he was a partner, subject to the prior payment of his separate debts.

B. General rule of partners' liability on dissolution: Dissolution of a partnership does not affect the existing liabilities of either a partner or the partnership.

Example 1: Partners A and B owed T for merchandise purchased. Thereafter, A and B dissolved their partnership. Upon dissolution, B retained all the partnership's assets and assumed liability for all partnership debts. A informs T of the terms and conditions of the dissolution, and asks T to collect his debt at once. Although B is solvent at that time and is able to pay, T does not attempt to collect the debt. Subsequently, B becomes insolvent and T attempts to collect the debt from A.

Held, A is liable to T. The mere retirement of a partner, the assumption of debts by another who continues the business, and notice to creditors, do not discharge the retiring partner from personal liability on those debts. It would not be just to impose on creditors the duty of suing the continuing partner on the demand of the retiring partner, in the absence of special circumstances not present here. A's notice to T and his instructions to sue did not create a legal obligation upon T to proceed at once to collect the debt. *Faricy v. J.S. Brown Mercantile Co.,* 288 P. 639 (Colo. 1930).

Note: In the *Faricy* case, if the creditor had extended the time for payment, A might have lost the right to pay the debt at once and to sue B while B was still solvent. Therefore, if the creditor had agreed to extend the obligation, A would no longer be responsible for the debt.

Example 2: A and B are partners owing a partnership debt to T. The firm is dissolved and then T sues "A and B, copartners doing business as A and B Company." After personal service, judgment is taken against A, B and the firm. The dissolution of a partnership has no effect upon the existing liabilities of the partners or the partnership. Hence,

A, B and the firm continue to owe the debt jointly. T can satisfy the debt out of partnership property, or he may proceed against the separate properties of A or B. UPA § 36(1).

Example 3: A, B and C, partners in a trading firm, owe T $5,000. The partnership is dissolved and T sues the partners and the firm. Service of process is made on A, but B and C are outside the jurisdiction and are not served. A statute makes service on A valid as to A's property and as to partnership property. T has a right to judgment against A and the partnership. With judgment against A personally, T may levy upon A's separate property as well as partnership property.

Note: The constitutionality of this procedure may be justified on three grounds:

- the partnership is an entity which owns the partnership property, and service on one of the partners is service on the partnership;

- A is the agent of the partnership and of the other partners for purposes of process and binding the partnership property and the interests in the partnership of the other partners; and

- jurisdiction over one partner gives the court power to compel him to apply firm property to the payment of firm debts.

C. Assumption of obligations by another does not automatically release outgoing partner: Though those who continue the business after dissolution assume partnership debts, the outgoing partner(s) are not discharged unless (a) there is a **novation** (an agreement between the continuing partner(s) and the creditor to release the outgoing partner(s) from liability); or (b) the creditor and a continuing partner ***materially alter the nature or time of payment*** of the existing obligation.

Example 1: A and B were partners in the construction business. They were building a house for T. A and B dissolved their partnership. A and B each offered to complete the contract individually. T elected to have B do so. B assumed the partnership's obligations. Though B had the obligation to pay the materialmen, T prepaid and overpaid B, and T did not insist that B use the money to pay the materialmen before using the money himself. T ended up having to pay the materialmen himself. T sued A and B for breach of the construction contract. A contended that T's conduct amounted to a change in the material provisions of the agreement which relieved A of liability.

Held, B, but not A, was liable to T. T agreed to change the nature and time of ***T's payment to B,*** rather than of the payment due from the partnership to T. Nonetheless, this change constituted a ***material*** alteration of the agreement with the partnership, and A was discharged from liability as a former partner. *Munn v. Scalera,* 436 A.2d 18 (Conn. 1980).

Note: The key issue in determining whether a change is material enough to discharge a former partner is whether the withdrawing partner has been disadvantaged by the change.

Example 2: A and B were partners operating a delicatessen. They leased their store from T. B transferred his partnership interest to C. In return, the new partnership, and A and C individually, agreed to assume all liabilities and to indemnify B. T received notice that B was no longer on the lease. T was introduced to C as a new partner, and T did not object to the change or request that B remain liable. Subsequently, T and A added to the lease in order to rent more space to the deli. The new space was at a different price from the old. When the deli failed to pay rent, T sued B for breach of the lease. B argued that the partnership had dissolved and B had been released from liability. T argued that B had merely assigned his right to receive the profits and that there had been no dissolution. T also argued that even if there had been a dissolution, the dissolution would not automatically discharge B in the absence of T's agreement or a material change in the nature of the partnership obligations.

Held, B was not liable to T. B did not merely assign his right to profits to C; B withdrew fully, and the partnership dissolved by express will of a partner. Furthermore, T by his conduct impliedly consented to the discharge of B's liability. This constituted an implied novation under UPA § 36(2). Alternatively, the change in the lease was material enough to relieve B of liability. *Wester & Co. v. Nestle,* 669 P.2d 1046 (Colo. Ct. App. 1983).

1. **Withdrawing partner may become liable under assumption agreement:** As discussed above, under the doctrine of *merger,* a creditor who sues only one of two partners on a joint claim and whose claim is unsatisfied may not proceed against the other joint obligor. However, in the absence of a novation, if the continuing partner assumes the obligations of the dissolved partnership, the withdrawing partner will still be liable as a surety if the assuming partner defaults. *B-OK, Inc. v. Storey,* 485 P.2d 987 (Wash. 1971).

D. **Effect of partner's death:** When a partnership is dissolved because of a partner's death, the following rules apply:

1. **Debts:** The deceased partner's *estate is liable for partnership debts* after the deceased partner's separate debts are paid. This changes the common law rule which released a joint debtor's estate from liability. UPA § 36(4).

2. **Personal service contract:** A contract to render personal services to a partnership, such as an employment contract, is ***terminated upon the dissolution resulting from the partner's death.***

   Example: A and B are partners operating a retail clothing store. The partnership employs T as assistant manager under a five year written contract. A dies two years later, and B sells the business without making any provision for the continued employment of T. T may not maintain suit for breach of his employment contract. A's death dissolved the partnership. The dissolution by death released both T and the partnership from further performance of the employment contract. *Shumate v. Sohon,* 12 F.2d 825 (D.C. Cir. 1926).

E. **RUPA § 703:** RUPA § 703 is similar to UPA § 36 in its provisions regarding the liability of the dissociating partner for the preexisting obligations of the partnership. It defines the circumstances under which the dissociating partner is liable for new partnership obligations when creditors are not notified of the dissociation, in the same manner as in RUPA § 702, *supra,* p. 254.

VIII. RIGHT TO WIND UP THE PARTNERSHIP

A. **Right to wind up:** unless otherwise agreed, those partners who have not wrongfully dissolved the partnership, or the legal representative of the last surviving partner, provided he is not bankrupt, may wind up the partnership affairs; further, any partner, his legal representative or his assignee, upon cause shown, may obtain winding up by the court. UPA § 37.

B. **The process of winding up:**

1. **Dispute between partners regarding winding up:** All partners who have not caused the dissolution of the partnership, as well as the last surviving partner's legal representative, may wind up the partnership affairs. Any partner who shows good cause can petition to have the court appoint a receiver to wind up the partnership affairs. If more than one partner is involved in winding up the partnership and there is a dispute concerning the partnership's ordinary affairs, it is to be ***resolved by majority vote.***

   Example: A, B and C were partners pursuant to an informal oral agreement to own and run a racehorse. A, B and C owned 50%, 25% and 25% respectively. The partners agreed that C would be the horse's trainer. Following a race in which the horse fell, A and B sent a letter to C in which they told him that he was relieved of his employment as trainer and that they wanted him to turn the horse over to A and B. A and B wanted to continue to race the horse under a new trainer; C wanted to liquidate the partnership and sell the horse without running him again. The court found that the letter from A and B to C dissolved the partnership. (*See* UPA § 31(1)(b).) Both sides wanted to control the horse during wind-up.

Held, A and B could control the winding up phase since, barring an injury, running the horse would be likely to result in maximizing his value. The court noted that the horse was fit and that the parties had planned on running him through his three-year-old season. The court's decision was based on UPA § 37, under which a court may let a partner who shows good cause wind up the partnership affairs. The court rejected A's and B's claim that since they controlled a majority interest, they were entitled to decide what to do with the horse. The court said that UPA § 18 gave the majority the power to decide only **ordinary** matters, and what to do with the partnership's only asset was hardly an ordinary matter. The court also rejected C's argument that the partnership agreement incorporated a custom entitling the trainer to decide what to do with the horse during any period in which he participated in ownership. The court said that it could find no evidence of such a custom. *Paciaroni v. Crane,* 408 A.2d 946 (Del. Ch. 1979).

2. **Dissolution by bankruptcy; right of remaining partner(s) to wind up:** If a partner dissolves the firm by declaring bankruptcy, then the remaining partner(s) may wind up the firm's affairs. Recall, however (*supra*, p. 242) that a petition under chapter 11 of the Bankruptcy Act by a corporate partner does not cause a dissolution of the partnership.

3. **Dissolution by death; right of surviving partner(s) to wind up:** If a partnership is dissolved by a partner's death, the surviving partner(s) may wind up the partnership affairs. If the firm's affairs have not been wound up when the last surviving partner dies, then his executor or administrator may wind up the firm affairs.

   a. **Dissolution by death; right of remaining partner(s) to convey partnership real property:** Under the UPA all partnership real property is personalty as between the partners. Hence, all the partnership's property is **personal property**. Upon dissolution caused by a partner's death, the partnership property passes to the surviving partner(s). These partners have power to convey title to the land during the process of winding up.

   Example 1: A, B and C are partners who buy and sell land. Title to the land is in the partnership's name. A dies and the land must be sold to pay firm debts. Either B or C may convey good title to the land by selling it and signing the deed in the partnership name, "by B" or "by C".

Example 2: Assume the same facts as in the previous example, except that title is in the name of A only. Neither B nor C may pass good record title. A dies and no one has authority to sign his name. If B sells the land during wind-up, even though the record title is not complete, the purchaser will receive equitable title with a right to require A's heirs or devisees to sign a proper deed.

4. **Right to compensation for winding up the partnership:** At common law, except for extraordinary services, the surviving partner was not entitled to compensation for winding up the partnership affairs. Under UPA § 18(f), a person winding up the partnership is *not entitled to payment for winding up, except if he is the surviving partner* after the death of his copartner(s) or if the other partners have *expressly or impliedly agreed* that the winding-up partner should be compensated. *Kennedy v. Kennedy,* 433 N.E.2d 1247 (Mass. App. Ct. 1982) The *Kennedy* case held that a partner is not entitled to compensation for work done in the partnership business after dissolution; the term "surviving partner" means only a partner who survives his deceased partner(s). See *Lee v. Dahlin,* 159 A.2d 679 (Pa. 1960). In *Lee,* the surviving partner forfeited his right to compensation for winding up because he wrongfully used partnership funds and property. Claims for wages in continuing the business should be distinguished from claims for wages for winding up the partnership.

   a. **Right to compensation if partner continues business by agreement, rather than winding up:** If the partners agree to allow one partner to continue the business, as opposed to winding it up, there is some authority for the proposition that the *continuing partner may be entitled to compensation* for his services. *Lange v. Bartlett,* 360 N.W.2d 702 (Wis. Ct. App. 1984). See *infra,* p. 276.

   b. **Basis of compensation during wind up:** In the absence of contrary agreement, a winding up partner is entitled to share in profits earned during the winding up period in accordance with the partnership agreement. She is not entitled to compensation for her work on the basis of the number of matters she may have handled.

   Example: A was a partner in a law firm. After the partnership dissolved, A continued to work on over 150 cases to wind up the partnership. A claimed that he was entitled to compensation based on the amount of time he had spent working on these cases.

Held, A was not entitled to compensation for his services; he was only entitled to his share of the profits as specified in the partnership agreement. *Resnick v. Kaplan,* 434 A.2d 582 (Md. Ct. Spec. App. 1981).

Note: A was not a "surviving" partner, so he was not entitled to compensation under UPA § 18(f), which is interpreted to apply only to a partner who survives the death of his partner(s).

IX. COMPETING WITH FORMER PARTNERS AFTER DISSOLUTION

A. **Competing with former partners:** After dissolution, in general partners can compete with their former partners provided they do not breach a non-competition agreement or take former partnership assets for their own use. Bromberg and Ripstein on Partnership § 7.12, at 7:111 (1996). If the partners agree that a partner can take their former clients and receive compensation from them, the former partners may not share in that compensation.

Example: A, B and C were attorneys and shareholders in a professional service corporation. A had previously operated independently and later joined B and C. The corporation operated basically as a partnership. Serious differences arose between A and B. A and B agreed that A would no longer be a member of the firm. A and C agreed that "whatever is yours [A's] is yours and whatever is ours is ours." A took with him the file of a client named T. C noticed that T's file was missing and he called A, who acknowledged that he had the file. T decided to retain A. After the conclusion of litigation for T, the B and C firm sued A for a share of the profits from T's case.

Held, the court applied partnership law and determined that A did not breach his fiduciary duty, and did not have to share the T profits with B and C. A and C's agreement that "whatever is yours is yours and whatever is ours is ours" did not allocate duties for winding up; instead it effected an instant wind-up. Consequently, when A took the T file, he did not breach any fiduciary duty because none was owed. The court noted that A might have breached the A-C contract by physically taking the T file, but that no claim had been brought for breach of contract. *Marr v. Langhoff,* 589 A.2d 470 (Md. 1991).

X.   DISTRIBUTION OF PARTNERSHIP PROPERTY UPON DISSOLUTION

A. **Rights of partners to application of partnership property — UPA § 38:** Unless the partners agree otherwise, when dissolution is caused by any circumstance that does not contravene the partnership agreement, each partner may have the partnership property applied to discharge its liabilities, and may receive his share of the surplus in cash. But if dissolution is caused by the proper expulsion of a partner, who is then discharged from partnership liabilities either by agreement or by payment under UPA § 36(2), the expelled partner will receive in cash only the net amount due him from the partnership. UPA § 38(1).

B. **Rights of partners to distribution of partnership property:** UPA § 38(1) deals with two distinct rights of the partners on dissolution:

- every partner has the right to have the partnership property applied to the payment of partnership debts; and

- every partner has the right to be paid *in cash* the net amount owing to him out of the surplus after all partnership accounts are settled. This presupposes that all assets of the partnership will be reduced to cash and distributed as such.

Example: Brothers A, B, and C formed a partnership to operate two feed mills. There was no partnership agreement and the partnership was at will. A and B served C with a notice of dissolution and wind-up of the partnership. The dissolution was not wrongful. C requested that the court order a sale of partnership property and that he be paid the fair market value of his interest from the sale. A and B could bid at the sale and then continue the partnership under a new partnership. Instead, the trial court ordered an in-kind distribution of assets.

Held, the trial court erred in ordering an in-kind distribution; it should have ordered a sale of the assets and the payment of C's interest in cash. Under UPA § 38(1), unless otherwise agreed, when dissolution does not contravene the partnership agreement, each partner is entitled to have the partnership property applied to discharge its liabilities and the surplus paid to the partners in *cash.* The partners had made no contrary agreement, and C was entitled to have the partnership debts paid and to receive his share of the surplus in cash. *Dreifuerst v. Dreifuerst,* 280 N.W.2d 335 (Wis. Ct. App. 1979).

C. **Right of partners to have partnership assets used to discharge partnership liabilities:** Every partner has a right to have firm property applied to the payment of partnership debts because every partner is personally liable for all partnership debts. The partner's individual liability is discharged to the extent that partnership property is applied for his account to the payment of partnership debts.

1. **Rules for distribution after dissolution:** UPA § 40 provides that the following rules apply in settling accounts between the partners after dissolution. The rules may be changed or modified by agreement of the partners.

   a. **Partnership assets:** The assets of the partnership are:

      - the partnership property,

      - the partners' contributions necessary to pay all the liabilities specified in the next paragraph.

   b. **Order for paying liabilities:** The partnership pays its liabilities in the following order:

      - debts due to non-partner creditors,

      - debts due to partners other than for capital and profits,

      - debts due to partners in respect of capital,

      - debts due to partners in respect of profits.

   c. **Application of assets to debts:** Partnership property is applied before partners contributions to satisfy partnership liabilities.

   d. **Contribution towards payment of liabilities:** To ensure payment of any liabilities not paid out of partnership assets, partners must contribute (according to their share of profits), the amount necessary to satisfy the liabilities. If any, but not all, of the partners are insolvent, or, not being subject to process, refuse to contribute, the other partners must make up the amount necessary to pay liabilities, according to the relative proportions in which they share the profits.

      - An assignee for the benefit of creditors or any court-appointed person may enforce the contributions described in the paragraph above.

      - Any partner or his legal representative may enforce the contributions specified above, to the extent of the amount which he has paid in excess of his share of the liability.

      - The individual property of a deceased partner shall be liable for the contributions specified above.

   e. **When court has possession of partnership property:** When a court possesses for distribution both partnership property and the individual properties of the partners, partnership creditors have priority on partnership property and separate creditors on individual property. The rights of lien or secured creditors remain unchanged. However, in federal bankruptcy proceedings, partnership creditors are now on a par with individual unsecured creditors in making claims against a partner's personal assets. See *infra*, p. 266.

f. Partner in bankruptcy: When a partner has become bankrupt or his estate is insolvent, his separate property is applied to pay debts in the following order:

- debts due to his separate creditors,

- debts due to partnership creditors,

- debts due to partners by way of contribution.

2. Distribution of assets: Winding up includes reducing the partnership assets to cash and distributing the money.

a. Partnership assets: Partnership assets include not only the partnership property, but also the obligation of the partners to contribute to the payment of the firm's liabilities, including the actual contribution for such purpose when it is made.

Example: A, B and C are partners. A has $5,000 in personal assets and $15,000 in personal debts. B has $500 in assets and owes $30,000. C has $50,000 in assets and owes $5,000. The partnership has $5,000 in assets and $40,000 in debts. The firm owes $35,000 more than is covered by its assets. A and B are insolvent because their personal liabilities exceed their assets. After C pays his individual debt of $5,000, C still has $45,000 in assets. That is sufficient to pay the remaining $35,000 in firm debts. Both C and the partnership are solvent and their assets will be used to satisfy the partnership debts.

b. Order of asset distribution if partnership is solvent: When a solvent partnership is dissolved, its assets are reduced to cash, which is then used to pay partnership liabilities and claims in this order:

- Partnership creditors, except partners;

- Advances or loans due the partners;

- Capital contributed by the partners; and

- Profits due the partners out of surplus.

3. Insufficient assets: If the partnership assets are insufficient to pay the partnership creditors, then the ***partners must contribute***

to pay the creditors in the same proportion in which they share profits.

a. **Partners' rights of contribution:** In the absence of agreement to the contrary, each partner must contribute to pay partnership debts in the same proportion in which she shares profits. If any partner is compelled to pay more than her share, then she will have a right of contribution against each of the other partners.

Example: A, B and C are equal partners conducting a retail business. At the end of two years they decide to dissolve because of continuous losses. They owe X $9,000 and Y $6,000. They sell all the partnership assets for $7,500. From this amount they pay X $4,500 and Y $3,000. They still owe a total of $7,500. The rights of the parties are as follows:

Partners' rights: The partnership has a right to require each partner to contribute his share of the liabilities, in this case one third of $7,500. A, B and C should contribute $2,500 each. If any of them is compelled to pay more than $2,500, then he would have a right of contribution against each of the other partners for the excess paid.

Creditor's rights: Each creditor has a cause of action against the partners for the amount still due him. He can take judgment against all the partners and collect part from each partner or the entire amount from any one partner.

b. **Loans by partners:** If the partnership assets are insufficient to repay all the advances or loans made by partners, then the ***partners must contribute to make up those obligations*** in the same proportion as they share profits. *Richert v. Handly,* 330 P.2d 1079 (Wash. 1958). See, *supra,* p. 219 for a discussion of this issue.

c. **Partner insolvent or outside jurisdiction:** If a partner who is liable for contributions is outside the jurisdiction and refuses to contribute, or if a partner is insolvent, the other partners must pay the shortage according to their proportionate shares, but they can enforce their rights against the missing or insolvent partner later.

Example: A, B and C are equal partners doing business in State M. They agree to dissolve the partnership and appoint C with sole power to wind up the firm's affairs. Each partner has contributed $2,500 in capital, and each has loaned the firm $2,500. C sells all the assets of the firm for $10,000, with which he must pay partnership debts of $30,000. A moves into State N and refuses to make any contribution, and B is insolvent. C must first apply the $10,000 to the partnership debts. That leaves $20,000 of partnership debts unpaid. Each partner's share of this is $6,666.66. However, because B is insolvent and A refuses to contribute, C must pay the entire $20,000. C may then pursue A in State N and compel A to contribute toward the remaining firm debts. C should get judgment for $10,000 against A, not $6,666.66 (otherwise C would bear the entire risk of B's insolvency). If C recovers the $10,000 from A, then C has effectively paid $10,000 against the $20,000 firm debt. C then has a right against B for contribution of $3,333, because C only originally owed $6,666.66. If A pays the $10,000 to C, A also has a right against B for $3,333. UPA § 40(d) and (f).

4. **Agreement to vary the UPA's distribution rules:** The partnership agreement may provide for a different distribution of assets than that specified in UPA § 40.

Example: Four brothers orally agreed to form a partnership to operate a ranch. They also agreed orally that the last surviving brother would take all the assets of the partnership. A was the last surviving brother. He left all his assets to his niece. Other relatives claimed that the oral agreement to leave all assets to a surviving brother was invalid. They also argued that the last surviving brother had the duty to wind up the partnership before his death.

Held, though oral, the partnership agreement was valid. The partners could and did provide for the last surviving brother to receive all the partnership's assets. Therefore, A's niece was entitled to all the partnership assets. In the absence of an agreement to the contrary, the last surviving partner ordinarily has a duty to wind up and terminate a partnership. Here, the parties agreed to a continuation of the partnership business by the surviving brother. *Martinson v. Holso,* 424 N.W.2d 664 (S.D. 1988).

Note: Oral partnership agreements are not ordinarily barred by the Statute of Frauds, but an agreement to convey land to a partnership is not enforceable under the Statute of Frauds unless it falls within one of the exceptions. Bromberg & Ripstein, *Partnership* § 2.13(c), at 2:174 (1996).

5. **Payments when partner bankrupt:** The UPA provides that if a partner is bankrupt or insolvent, his individual assets are distributed first to his separate creditors, then to the partnership creditors, and finally to the other partners by way of contribution. UPA § 40(i). However, in federal bankruptcy proceedings, partnership

creditors are now on a par with individual unsecured creditors in making claims against a partner's personal assets. Federal bankruptcy law trumps the UPA with respect to federal bankruptcy proceedings.

6. **Distribution rules under RUPA § 807:** RUPA follows the same distribution rules as UPA § 40(b), except that creditors who are partners are technically on a par with outside creditors. However, since partners remain personally liable for unsatisfied outside debts, this change is merely formal and has little practical impact: it does not substantively change the status of partner-creditors vis-a-vis outside creditors. RUPA § 807, comment 2.

XI. UPA §§ 38, 39—EFFECT OF WRONGFUL DISSOLUTION, DISSOLUTION FOR FRAUD, AND DISSOLUTION FOR MISREPRESENTATION

A. **Wrongful dissolution (UPA § 38):** UPA § 38 is the section setting forth the rules controlling partners' rights to apply partnership assets to pay partnership debts. The section also deals with the rules which are applied when a partner causes wrongful dissolution of a partnership UPA § 38(2)(b), (c):

1. **Rights applied when dissolution contravenes the partnership agreement:** Those partners who have not caused the wrongful dissolution of the partnership have:

   • the right to apply partnership assets to pay partnership debts, and the right to apply any surplus to pay the net amount owing to each partner in cash; and

   • the right to damages against each partner who wrongfully caused the dissolution.

2. **Right to continue the business:** As an alternative to winding-up, if the partners who have not wrongfully caused the dissolution desire to continue the business in the same name, either by themselves or jointly with others, they may do so during the agreed term for the partnership, and they may continue to possess the partnership property to do so. However, they must pay any partner who has wrongfully caused the dissolution (or secure the payment with a court-approved bond) the value of his partnership interest at the dissolution, less damages for breaching the agreement. They must also indemnify him against present or future partnership liabilities.

3. **Rights of partner causing dissolution:** A partner who has caused the dissolution wrongfully has:

- if the business is ***not*** continued by the other partners, all the rights of the other partners to apply partnership assets to pay partnership debts and, also, the right to receive his share of any surplus in cash, less damages for his breach;

- if the business is continued, the right to have the value of his partnership interest ascertained, less any damages caused to his partners by the dissolution. The net amount will then be paid to him in cash (or secured by court-approved bond), and he will be released from all existing partnership liabilities. However, the value of the business' good-will is not considered in valuing the wrongful partner's interest.

B. **Effect of wrongful dissolution:** If any partner dissolves a partnership in breach of the partnership agreement, she is liable in damages to the innocent partners. The innocent partners do not have to continue the partnership business to mitigate the damages. They can demand immediate liquidation and recover all damages caused by the breach.

Example: A submitted the highest bid to buy some real property from the State Highway Commission. A, B and C formed a partnership to sell the property at a profit. B and C each transferred $18,956.77 to the partnership upon its formation. B decided that he no longer wanted to complete the purchase of the property. B sued A and C, seeking return of the payment he had made. A and C counterclaimed for breach of the partnership agreement. B claimed that A and C had suffered no substantial damage; they could have continued the partnership and purchased the property themselves.

Held, A and C were entitled to the full amount of the lost profits caused by B's wrongful breach of the partnership agreement. Under UPA § 38, innocent partners have an absolute right to compel partnership liquidation upon a dissolution caused by a partner's wrongful conduct. B's view would substantially limit the innocent partners' unconditional right to liquidate by forcing them to continue the partnership in order to mitigate the wrongdoer's damages. Such an interpretation is untenable. *Ohlendorf v. Feinstein,* 636 S.W.2d 687 (Mo. Ct. App. 1982).

1. **Right to continue the business:** When one partner has wrongfully caused the partnership dissolution, then the other partners may either wind up the partnership affairs or continue the business. If they continue the business, they must determine the value of the wrongdoer's interest in the partnership at the moment of dis-

solution and secure payment of that value to him, less the damages he has caused. UPA § 38(2)(b).

2. **Right of wrongdoer:** If the business is continued, those partners continuing the business must either pay the wrongdoer the value of his interest in cash, less damages for his breach, or secure payment to him through an appropriate court-approved bond. UPA § 38(2)(c).

3. **Right to bid at judicial sale:** The partner who wrongfully dissolves a partnership or wrongfully expels another partner ordinarily may bid at the judicial sale if the innocent partner demands liquidation.

   Example: A, B, and C formed a partnership. A and B each owned 42 1/2% of the business; C owned the remaining 15%. A and B sought to dissolve the partnership, claiming that C was derelict in his duties. A and B also sought the right to continue the partnership. C counterclaimed, seeking the right to wind up the partnership. The trial court found that C had not been derelict in his partnership duties and that he had been excluded from the partnership. The trial court also found that the exclusion was not in bad faith but was rather the product of the partners' inability to get along. The court ordered the partnership property to be sold. A and B purchased the property at the judicial sale. C appealed, claiming that A and B should not have been permitted to bid at the judicial sale.

   Held, A and B were properly allowed to bid at the judicial sale. First, there was no finding that A and B acted in bad faith or fraudulently in excluding C from the partnership. Moreover, C benefited from their bid. Their bid for the property was 15% higher than the next highest bid. If C was injured by the exclusion, he should have sought damages for breach of the partnership agreement under UPA § 38(2)(a)(II). *Prentiss v. Sheffel,* 513 P.2d 949 (Ariz. Ct. App. 1973).

4. **Rights where partnership is dissolved for fraud or misrepresentation (UPA § 39):** UPA § 39 deals with rescission of a partnership agreement for fraud or misrepresentation by one of the partners. It provides substantially that upon rescission, the rescinding party is entitled:

   • to a lien on, or a right to keep, the surplus in partnership property after paying outside creditors, in the amount the rescinding partner paid to buy a partnership interest, and for any capital or advances he contributed; and

- to stand, after all outside creditors have been paid, in the place of any partnership creditors to the extent of any partnership debts he may have paid to them; and

- to be indemnified by the partner guilty of the fraud or misrepresentation, against all of the partnership's debts and liabilities.

5. **Right of one fraudulently induced to become a partner to rescind the partnership agreement:** When one partner induces another to become a partner through fraud, the defrauded partner may ***rescind*** the partnership agreement.

    a. **Remedies:** After he rescinds the partnership agreement, a defrauded partner has several rights, including:

        i. **Lien:** a lien on any surplus partnership property after the firm debts are paid to the extent of any sum paid by him for the purchase of his interest in the partnership and for any capital or advances contributed by him;

        ii. **Preferred claim:** the right, after firm creditors are paid, to have the rest of the partnership property applied to the payment of his claims;

        iii. **Stand in place of creditor:** the right to recover the amount paid by him to any creditor of the partnership with respect to a partnership debt.

        iv. **Indemnification:** the right to be indemnified by the wrongdoer for any partnership liability.

            Example: B and C are partners. B fraudulently induces A to buy C's partnership interest for $1,000, to agree to continue the business, to pay $3,000 to capital, and to loan the firm $2,000. The B and C partnership owed T $4,000 and its property was worth $6,000. A has the following rights: first of all, he may rescind the partnership agreement. He must then apply the $6,000 in firm assets to pay the firm's $4,000 debt to T, leaving $2,000 remaining. Assuming A gets possession of this $2,000, as well as his $3,000 contribution and his $2,000 loan, he has a lien in the amount of $7,000 for repayment of the $1,000 he paid to C for his interest, his $3,000 contribution and his $2,000 loan. He can apply the $7,000 to the payment of his claims in the same way as a partnership creditor would. In addition, if B incurred partnership debts for which A is now personally liable, A can demand that B indemnify him against these debts. Further, A can sue B for any loss suffered by him beyond any of these amounts. A cannot, however, have both rescission, which places the parties in ***status quo ante,*** and an action in damages for deceit.

Note: The effect of UPA § 39 is to create a ***constructive trust*** in favor of the defrauded partner.

XII. LIABILITY OF PARTNERS CONTINUING THE PARTNERSHIP BUSINESS

A. Liability of persons continuing the business in certain cases (UPA § 41): UPA § 41 provides the following regarding liability of any partner who continues the business after the partnership dissolves:

- Under the following circumstances, creditors of the preexisting or dissolved partnership are also creditors of the continuing partnership: (a) when a new partner is admitted; ***or*** (b) when a partner retires and assigns (or a deceased partner's representative assigns) his rights in partnership property to two or more of the partners, or to one or more of the partners and one or more third persons; ***and*** (c) if the business is continued without liquidating the partnership affairs.

- Creditors of the dissolved partnership are also creditors of the continuing person or partnership, when all the partners but one retire and assign (or a deceased partner's representative assigns) their rights in partnership property to the remaining partner, who continues the business alone or with others, without liquidating partnership affairs.

- When any partner retires or dies, and the business is continued as in either of the above paragraphs, with the consent of the retired partners or of the representative of the deceased partner, but without any assignment of the right of the retired or deceased partner in partnership property, then the rights of the dissolved partnership's creditors and of the creditors of the person or partnership continuing the business shall be the same as if such assignment had been made by the retired or deceased partner.

- When all the partners or their representatives assign their rights in partnership property to one or more third persons who promise to pay the debts and who continue the dissolved partnership's business, creditors of the dissolved partnership are also creditors of the person or partnership continuing the business.

- When the remaining partners continue the business, either alone or with others and without liquidation of partnership affairs (as they are enabled to do under UPA § 38((2)(b), *supra*), after one of the partners has wrongfully caused a dissolution, creditors of the dissolved partnership are also creditors of the person or partnership continuing the business.

- When a partner is expelled and the remaining partners continue the business either alone or with others, without liquidating the partnership affairs, creditors of the dissolved partnership are also creditors of the person or partnership continuing the business.

- The liability of a third person who becomes a partner in the continuing partnership, under this section (§ 41), to the creditors of the dissolved partnership will be satisfied out of partnership property only.

- When a partnership business is continued under this section, the creditors of the dissolved partnership have a claim against the partnership or the person continuing the business which is prior to the claims of the separate creditors of the retiring or deceased partner (or the representative of a deceased partner), on account of the retired or deceased partner's interest in the dissolved partnership or on account of any consideration promised for such interest or for the partnership property rights of the retiring or deceased partner.

- Nothing in this section (§ 41) will be held to modify any right of creditors to set aside any assignment on the ground of fraud.

- The use of the partnership name by the person or partnership continuing the business, or the name of a deceased partner as part of the partnership name, will not of itself make the deceased partner's individual property liable for any debts contracted by such person or partnership.

B. Liability of partner who continues the business after dissolution: UPA § 41 protects the creditors of an existing partnership when the partnership dissolves after a change of partners but without liquidation. It makes creditors of the old partnership creditors of the partnership or person continuing the business. This section changes the common law by protecting existing partnership creditors.

Example: A, B and C are equal partners in the "A, B, C Co." C assigns all his rights, title and interest in the partnership to A and B, who continue the business under the firm name of "A & B Co." The new partnership does not agree to pay the former partnership creditors. M and N were creditors of the "A, B, C Co." X and Y are creditors of "A & B Co." Under UPA § 41(1) M and N are expressly made creditors of the new firm, "A & B Co.," and they have equal rights with the new creditors, X and Y. They will all share in the distribution of the new partnership's assets in the event it is dissolved by A and B. This does not in any way change the partners' personal liabilities.

1. **Continuing business by former partner:** When a partner dies or retires, and the business is continued by one or more partners or by a partner and a third person without liquidating the partnership, then the dissolved partnership's creditors are creditors of those continuing the business, whether or not the retiring or deceased partner (or his representative) has assigned her interest to those continuing. UPA § 41(3).

   Example: A and B are partners. A dies and B continues the business, crediting A's estate with profits and charging it with losses. The administrator of A's estate, C, approves of this practice, which continues for a number of years. T, a firm creditor, sues C as administrator of A's estate, seeking to charge it with liabilities incurred by the firm after A's death.

   Held, T may satisfy his claim from A's estate's interest in the partnership, but not from A's separate estate. When a business is continued after a partner's death with the consent of the deceased partner's representative, the legal effect is the same as if the deceased partner's interest had been assigned to the surviving partner. UPA § 41(3). The assignment subjects only the deceased partner's interest in partnership property (not his own separate property) to existing and future claims of partnership creditors. C had power to consent to B's retention of partnership assets in the continuation of the business without getting court authorization. C's consent is valid, but only A's interest in the partnership is subject to the firm's liabilities. *Blumer Brewing Corp. v. Mayer,* 269 N.W. 693 (Wis. 1936).

   a. **Effect of wrongful dissolution or of expelling partner:** If a partner wrongfully causes the partnership to dissolve, or if a partner is justifiably expelled from the firm, and the remaining partners continue the partnership business without liquidation, then the partnership creditors are creditors of the partnership or of those who continue the business. UPA §§ 41(5), 41(6).

2. **Liability of continuing person when all partners assign their interest:** When all partners assign their rights in the partnership property to a third person(s) who continues the dissolved partnership's business and agrees to pay its debts, then the creditors of the dissolved firm are also creditors of those who continue the business. UPA § 41(4).

   Example: A, B and C are partners who operate a retail store. The partners dissolve the partnership and convey all partnership property to D who agrees to pay all partnership debts and continue the business. M is a partnership creditor. After dissolution X, Y and Z become D's creditors. If D becomes insolvent, under UPA § 41(4), M shares equally or ratably with X, Y and Z in D's assets. M is a third party beneficiary of the contract between the partners and D.

3. **Liability of new partner joining existing partnership:** When a third person continues the business with other partners and the partnership creditors are made creditors of those continuing the business, the third person is ***not personally liable*** to old firm creditors, but creditors can satisfy their claims out of the partnership property. UPA § 41(7).

Example: A and B are partners operating a store. They take in C as a new partner without liquidation. When C joined A and B as a partner, the A and B partnership dissolved and a new firm was formed consisting of A, B and C. The new firm thereafter dissolves, leaving assets. M and N are partnership creditors of the original A and B firm. Under UPA § 41(7), the former A and B partnership property is still subject to A and B partnership debts, even though C now also has an interest in that partnership property. M and N may pursue the new firm's partnership property (including C's interest in it), A personally, and B personally, but not C personally.

XIII. RIGHTS OF RETIRING PARTNER OR ESTATE OF DECEASED PARTNER

A. **Rights of retiring partner or estate of deceased partner when the business is continued (UPA § 42):** UPA § 42 provides substantially that when:

(a) any partner retires or dies;

(b) the business is continued under § 41(1, 2, 3, 5, 6) or § 38(2)(b) (*supra*);

(c) there is no settlement of accounts as between the retired or deceased partner, or his estate, and the person or partnership continuing the business; and

(d) there is no agreement otherwise;

then the retired or deceased partner or his legal representative as against such persons or partnership

(a) may have the value of his interest at the date of dissolution ascertained; and

(b) shall receive as an ordinary creditor the value of his interest in the dissolved partnership with interest, or, at his or his legal representative's option, in lieu of interest, the profits attributable to the use of his right in the property of the dissolved partnership;

provided that the creditors of the dissolved partnership, as against the separate creditors, or the retired or deceased partner's representative, shall have priority on any claim arising under this section (§ 42), as provided by § 41(8), *supra*.

1. **Right to return on investment generally:** When a partnership is dissolved by a partner's death or retirement, and some of the partners continue the business without liquidation and settlement of accounts, then the retiring partner or deceased partner's representative has a right, but as an ordinary creditor, to the ***value of his interest*** at the time of the dissolution. In addition, he may choose either:

   - ***interest at the legal rate*** from the date of dissolution; or

   - ***the profits*** made by the use of his right to the property of the partnership from the time of dissolution. UPA § 42.

Example: A, B and C are equal partners. A dies and E is appointed his executor. Without any settlement of accounts, B and C continue the business. After a year E sues B and C for an accounting and a determination of how much E has coming from B and C. An investigation discloses that the value of A's interest in the partnership at the time of his death was $10,000. The legal rate of interest is 6% in that jurisdiction. The investigation discloses further that the B and C firm has made profits of $3,000 during the past year, one third of which was made from the use of A's share in the firm. E may recover $10,000 for A's share in the firm. E may also elect to receive either $1,000 for his share of the profits made from the use of A's share, or $600 for legal interest of 6% on A's share of $10,000. UPA § 42.

Note: In *Blut v. Katz*, 99 A.2d 785 (N.J. 1953), the court construed UPA §§ 42 and 41 (3) strictly. It held that a deceased partner's representative must ***consent*** to the continuation before he can elect to participate in profits. Because the deceased partner's representative had not consented to the continuation of the business, she was limited to the value of the deceased partner's share, including good will, plus interest from the date of dissolution. The court reasoned that without the consent to continue, the estate was not subject to the claims of new creditors of the business. Because the estate did not assume any additional risk, the right to share profits should be denied. The *Blut* decision has been criticized because it fails to effectuate the purpose of UPA § 42, which is to compensate retired partners or the estates of deceased partners, for the use of their capital in the partnership business. R&G, p. 366-67.

B. Election of retiring partner either to wind-up of the partnership or to its continuation: A retiring partner may elect a wind-up of the business or, if other partners want to continue the business, she may permit them to do so without her. If she elects a wind-up, she is entitled to her share of the final settlement valued as of the date of liquidation. If she elects to permit the partnership to continue without her, she is entitled to the value of her interest as of the date of dissolution, plus either interest on that value or the profits earned on the use of her share of the partnership property, from the date of dissolution.

Example: A and B operated a swimming pool installation business as partners. A decided to retire. B offered A $3,000 for A's partnership interest, but A refused this offer. Subsequently, A sued to recover the value of his partnership interest. The trial court found that there had been a wind-up. The trial court then determined the value of the assets as of the date of dissolution and divided the assets equally between the parties.

Held, the trial court erred in finding a wind-up without trying the issues. The appellate court remanded for a factual determination as to whether the retiring partner, A, had elected to wind-up the partnership or consented to a continuation. The trial court also erred in valuing the assets as of the date of dissolution. Even if A had elected a wind-up, he would have been entitled to the value of his interest at the date of liquidation. This would have enabled him to share in both profits and losses during the period between dissolution and liquidation (after other creditors had been paid). Under this election, the outgoing partner is not viewed as a creditor. However, if the trial court determined that A had elected not to wind-up, but to allow the partnership to continue, he was entitled to make a further election whether to earn profits or interest on the use of his share of the partnership property or interest on the value of that share during the period after dissolution. The outgoing partner does not have to make that election until after an accounting has been made of the earnings subsequent to dissolution. Under this option, the outgoing partner takes as a creditor and is not responsible for any debts of the partnership after dissolution (assuming the creditors have been given proper notice of dissolution). The court added that if the partner elected the option to continue, he would be entitled to be paid for his services after dissolution, if he contributed substantial labor and management services. *Lange v. Bartlett,* 360 N.W.2d 702 (Wis. Ct. App. 1984).

1. **Implied consent to continuation:** The withdrawing partner may be deemed to have consented impliedly to the continuation of the partnership, or he may be barred by the doctrine of laches or estoppel from denying that he consented, if he acquiesces in any of

the partnership's continuing acts or affairs. If he is deemed to consent, his interest will be valued as of the date of dissolution. In addition, he will be entitled to receive, at his election, interest on the value of his interest, or the profits earned by the remaining partners' in their use of his portion of the partnership assets, but he will not enjoy the benefit of any post-dissolution appreciation in assets.

Example: C convinced A and B to let him join them in a partnership to purchase and manage, develop and sell real estate. In exchange for a 1/3 interest in the partnership, C gave up his full-time law practice, worked full time for the partnership, and contributed $5,000. C thereafter withdrew from the partnership, and A and B accepted his withdrawal. Then C competed with A and B. For the next 2 1/2 years, offers and counteroffers were exchanged between A and B on the one hand and C on the other with respect to the value of C's interest. A and B continued to operate the business, including buying and selling property. C then sued A and B, contending he could compel them to liquidate the partnership and recover the value of his partnership interest as of the date of liquidation. A and B contended that C's interest should be valued as of the date of dissolution, plus interest on his share in the partnership, or the profits attributable to the use of that share. They also contended that C was not entitled to any share in the increase in value of property acquired before C's withdrawal.

Held, C had impliedly consented to continuation of the partnership. "Permitting [C] to compel liquidation after consenting to the continuance of a business for several years would work a manifest injustice on those partners whose time, energy, and funds were expended in that period on the assumption that at most C would insist on a valuation of his interests as of [the date C withdrew]." Thus, C's interest should be valued as of the date of dissolution. C could also share in the profits from sales of properties held at the time of dissolution, but C could not share in the post-dissolution appreciation in the value of the property, because C did not share in the risk if the property declined in value after the date of dissolution. The withdrawing partner is not viewed as having a continuing interest in the business; rather, he is compensated for the value of his share either in interest or in profits, because assets belonging to him are being employed in the business by the remaining partners. *Oliker v. Gershunoff,* 241 Cal. Rptr. 415 (Cal. Ct. App. 1987), *review denied* (Cal. 1988). See also *King v. Evans,* 791 S.W.2d 531 (Tex. Ct. App. 1990) (*error denied,* (1991), which held that a non-continuing partner may not share in the post-dissolution appreciation of assets.

C. Right to accounting, valuation, and distribution of interest:

1. **UPA § 43—Accrual of actions:** UPA § 43 provides substantially that, upon dissolution, any partner (or his legal representative) has a right to an account of his interest in the partnership, as against the winding up partner(s), the surviving partner(s) or the person or partnership continuing the business. The account is determined at the date of dissolution, unless there is an agreement to the contrary.

2. **Valuation of interest at fair market value or in accordance with buy-out agreement:** An outgoing partner's interest is valued at fair market value unless the partners have prescribed an alternative method of valuation in their partnership agreement.

   Example: A and B were the general partners in a limited partnership which owned and managed an apartment complex. B began using cocaine. His habit caused significant problems in the business. He began frightening tenants. He insisted irrationally upon converting the apartments into condominiums despite adverse tax consequences. He also insisted on raising the rents even though his earlier attempts to do so had caused massive vacancies. A sought judicial dissolution of the partnership and the right to carry on the partnership business. B then died. A amended the complaint, seeking the right to continue the business under the limited partnership agreement.

   Parties' contentions: B's estate contended that the initial complaint had dissolved the partnership, and that B was entitled to the fair market value as of the date of dissolution. A argued that the filing of a complaint seeking judicial dissolution had not dissolved the partnership, but that the partnership dissolved when B died, and the limited partnership agreement determined how the deceased partner's share should be valued (the value of the partner's capital account — i.e., his contribution plus his share of profits less losses).

   Held, the partnership did not dissolve upon the filing of the complaint; instead, it dissolved on B's death, and the partnership agreement determined how B's interest was to be valued. The complaint merely sought a judicial dissolution based upon B's wrongful acts. Although the acts, if proven, would have been sufficient to allow a court to grant judicial dissolution, dissolution did not occur because the partnership was dissolved by B's death before the court could act. The court said that, in the absence of a partnership agreement, a deceased partners' interest is valued at fair market value. However, because the parties had provided a different method of valuation, that method should be used even though B's estate would receive nothing for his partnership interest, which had a fair market value of over $76,000. *G & S Invs. v. Belman,* 700 P.2d 1358 (Ariz. Ct. App. 1984).

a. Book value used only if so provided in buy-out agreement: Compare the result in *Belman* with the result in *Mahan v. Mahan,* 489 P.2d 1197 (Ariz. 1971), in which the appellate court rejected the trial court's valuation of a partnership interest at book value. The appellate court said that in the absence of a buy-out agreement specifying the use of book value, the partnership assets should be liquidated, and the deceased or departing partner would receive the fair market value of his interest. If either party thinks that the price being paid for the assets is not a fair price, he can bid for them himself.

b. Good will: Good will is the value someone is willing to pay for a business in excess of the current fair market value of its net assets. Good will derives from a well-founded expectation that public patronage of a business will continue, and is often based on a history of earnings, longevity, managerial skills, new technological developments, and other factors to which a book value cannot be ascribed. Whether or not good will should be included when valuing a partner's interest depends entirely on the circumstances of the case.

i. Personal good will: The good will may be personal to the partners and not capable of being transferred, such as in a professional or personal service partnership.

Example: A and B are partners in the practice of law (or medicine, dentistry or architecture) in a small town. A decides to move to another community, but B continues to practice law in the same office. In the winding-up of their affairs, A insists that B pay him for his share of the partnership good will.

Held, A is not entitled to payment for good will. In all probability, A has clients who came to him because he was A and not because he was a partner of B. There would be no reasonable grounds to believe that those clients would continue to come to the office to see B after A's departure. In short, if B paid A for the good will, he would be unlikely to receive anything in return.

In *Stanton v. Comm'r,* 189 F.2d 297 (7th Cir. 1951), the court noted that "[a]bility, skill, experience, acquaintance, personal clientele, and other personal characteristics and qualification do not constitute good will."

ii. Partnership good will: When the good will belongs to the partnership as an entity, which is the usual situation, it is an asset which must be taken into account on dissolution.

Example: A and others are partners in a successful brokerage firm. A dies and the business is continued at its old location. The partnership pays A's executors for A's partnership interest, but does not pay anything for good will. Beneficiaries under A's will bring suit against A's executors to charge them with the value of partnership good will on the theory that they failed to collect it from the partnership. The defense is that the firm's good will was without value, and that previous incoming and outgoing partners never paid for or received any benefit for good will.

Held, there was no agreement not to pay good will; therefore, good will must be included in valuing A's interest. When good will exists as an incident of the business, it is presumptively an asset to be included in valuing a partner's interest, unless the partners have agreed otherwise. The fact finder may find a tacit or implied agreement that no good will is to be paid, but the trial court found no such agreement here. If good will is to be included in valuing a partnership interest, it must then be determined whether the good will has any value. The main element in determining whether good will has any value is ***continuity of place and of name.*** In this case, the partnership could continue at the same location under the same name. The new firm could notify customers that it had succeeded to the business, and although former partners could solicit the same customers for their own accounts, some customers would undoubtedly do business with the new firm. Thus, the business would benefit from good will, which is the expectancy of future business coming from "succession in place or name." *In re Brown,* 150 N.E. 581 (N.Y. 1926).

Note: In the *Brown* case the lower court improperly included profits from "odd lot" and "specialist" transactions in computing good will. This type of business comes from orders given to individual firm members on the floor of the stock exchange. Because the buyer of the business would gain no continuing loyalty from these branches of the business, they should not be included in computing good will.

3. **Order of distribution:** The court in *Mahan v. Mahan,* 489 P.2d 1197 (Ariz. 1971) (invoking fair market valuation rather than book value, in the absence of a contrary agreement) held that first, the

partnership assets had to be liquidated and the creditors repaid their claims. If the assets turned out to be insufficient, the partners had to share losses in the same proportion in which they shared profits. If there were assets left, the partners then were to be repaid their capital contributions. Capital contributions are whatever the partners initially contributed, modified by adjustments in capital accounts, provided the partners consented to modify the capital accounts. Finally, any profits would then be divided equally between the surviving partner and the estate of the deceased partner. (Note: that if partners had made any loans to the partnership, under UPA § 40 those would have been returned before the capital contributions of the partners.)

D. Right to damages from partner who caused the wrongful dissolution of the partnership: Each partner who did not cause the wrongful dissolution of the partnership has the right to damages against the partner who wrongfully caused the dissolution. UPA § 38.

CHAPTER 19

PARTNERSHIP BANKRUPTCY

ChapterScope

Because the Bankruptcy Reform Act of 1978 adopted the entity theory of partnership, partnerships are now subject to the Act when they become insolvent. In other words, partnerships can take advantage of the Bankruptcy Act and ask for reorganization under chapter 11, or they may be forced into involuntary bankruptcy by their creditors. However, a partnership cannot have its debts discharged in bankruptcy. Instead, the bankruptcy proceeding reaches out to include the assets of the individual partners to satisfy the partnership debts. Conflicts between state law and the Bankruptcy Act are resolved in favor of the Bankruptcy Act. This Chapter deals with these matters, as well as with the "jingle" rule and other matters relating to the impact of a bankruptcy filing on the partnership and on the individual partners.

I.   INTRODUCTION

A. Bankruptcy Act follows the entity theory: As we have seen, the RUPA differs from the UPA by adopting the *entity theory* of partnerships (*supra*, pp. 161, 162). Under this theory, partnerships are treated as entities rather than as an aggregate of separate individuals. The Bankruptcy Reform Act of 1978 ("Bankruptcy Act") also adopts the entity theory. R&G, pp. 375-83. Thus, partnerships become subject to the Bankruptcy Act when they are insolvent.

B. Definition of insolvency: Under the Bankruptcy Act, a partnership is insolvent if it "is generally not paying...debtor's debts as such debts become due, unless such debts are the subject of a bona fide dispute."

C. Partnership debts not discharged by bankruptcy: Unlike individuals, partnerships cannot discharge their obligations by filing a bankruptcy petition. The estate of the partnership in bankruptcy simply expands to include the partnership's right to obtain indemnification of its debts from the individual partners. The partners then become jointly and severally liable for the partnership obligations. An individual partner who is himself insolvent or who is made insolvent by the obligation to indemnify the partnership may file a bankruptcy petition in his own right. Eibl, *Strategies for Partners under the Bankruptcy Code when the Partnership is Insolvent*, 61 AM. BANKR. L.J. 37-42 (1987).

II. INTERPLAY BETWEEN THE UPA AND THE BANKRUPTCY ACT

The term "bankruptcy" in the UPA is defined by reference to the Bankruptcy Act. If there are conflicts between the UPA and the Bankruptcy Act provisions, the Bankruptcy Act takes precedence under the U.S. Constitution's Supremacy Clause.

A. **UPA references to the Bankruptcy Act:** The UPA refers to bankruptcy in a number of places. For example, UPA § 32 (*see* discussion, *supra*, p. 244) states that dissolution is caused by the bankruptcy of any partner or the partnership. This forces the courts to look to the Bankruptcy Act to determine whether a partnership is bankrupt within the meaning of the Bankruptcy Act.

1. **Majority view:** Any proceeding under chapter 11 of the Bankruptcy Act is a "bankruptcy." Most courts have agreed that a partnership reorganization under chapter 11 is a "bankruptcy" within the meaning of the UPA.

    Example: A and his wife B divorced. Rather than divide their assets, they transferred them to P & P Limited Partnership. A acted as the sole general partner. A and B were 50-50 partners. Subsequently, a court determined that A had breached his fiduciary duty to B. He awarded B damages; dissolved the partnership; and ordered A, as sole general partner, to wind up the partnership, pay creditors, and then pay 1/2 of the surplus to B. A filed a chapter 11 petition under the Bankruptcy Act for his personal estate. Thereafter, A filed a chapter 11 petition for the partnership. B argued that A could not file a partnership bankruptcy petition after filing an individual bankruptcy petition.

    Held, A cannot file a chapter 11 petition for his partnership after he has already received individual Bankruptcy Court protection. UPA § 35(3)(b) provides that a "partnership is in no case bound by any act of a partner after dissolution . . . [w]here the partner has become bankrupt . . . ." A's personal petition for a reorganization under chapter 11 of the Bankruptcy Act constituted a "bankruptcy" within the meaning of UPA § 35(3)(b). The purpose of this section is to avoid conflicts of interest between a partner's obligation to his creditors, after he has filed a personal chapter 11 bankruptcy petition, and his obligations to his partners.

    The court also held that the Bankruptcy Act did not preempt UPA § 35(3)(b). Rule 1004(a) of the Bankruptcy Act gives general partners the power to file voluntary petitions for a bankrupt partnership. A claimed that Rule 1004(a) preempted UPA § 35(3)(b) and therefore gave him the power to declare the partnership bankrupt. The court rejected that view, holding that there was no intent by Congress to preempt state law. Congress intended that "general partners" under Rule 1004(a) be defined by applying state law. *In re Phillips,* 966 F.2d 926 (5th Cir. 1992).

2. **Minority view:** At least one court has held that when a chapter 11 bankruptcy proceeding is initiated to reorganize a partnership, the partnership is ***not dissolved.*** *In re Safren,* 65 B.R. 566 (Bankr. C.D. Cal. 1986). This contrasts with a chapter 7 liquidation, which does dissolve the partnership. Under this view, post-chapter 11-petition transactions continue to bind the partnership.

Example: A and B were the general partners of Seaport Village. They filed a voluntary chapter 11 petition for partnership reorganization. Subsequently, both A and B individually became chapter 11 debtors. The partnership's chapter 11 proceeding was dismissed before confirmation of the reorganization plan; therefore, its debts remained due. The partnership lost its principal asset, a shopping center, through foreclosure. The only possible partnership asset remaining was its claim against the partners for payment of the partnership debts. After the chapter 11 filings, T, who found a tenant for Seaport Village and earned a $12,600 commission, filed a claim against A and B personally. A and B argued that T's claim was allowable only against the Seaport Village estate, not their individual estates. A and B also argued that they could not be bound because the partnership was already dissolved when T earned his commission.

Held, A and B's personal estates are liable for T's claim. A chapter 11 proceeding, unlike a chapter 7 proceeding, does not dissolve a partnership, whether the chapter 11 proceeding is filed on behalf of the partnership or an individual partner. Chapter 11 reorganization did not exist when the UPA was written; thus, the UPA framers did not contemplate that a mere bankruptcy reorganization would dissolve a partnership. A and B, as general partners, were personally liable for all partnership debts. If A and B had not become chapter 11 debtors themselves, they would have been personally liable for T's claim. Since they were in chapter 11, their estates were liable for T's claim. T is a general unsecured creditor against A and B's personal assets because partnership creditors are now on a par with each partner's individual creditors with respect to a partner's personal assets (see partial repeal of "jingle rule" below). *In re Safren,* supra.

a. **Bankruptcy Act preempts conflicting state law:** When the UPA and the Bankruptcy Act conflict, *the Bankruptcy Act prevails*.

3. **Conflicting definitions of partnership:** Under the UPA, a partnership can exist if the parties express their will that it shall exist. It can also exist by *estoppel* when one person *"holds out"* another as his partner; and there is a *change of position* by a third person who *reasonably relies* to his detriment on the *holding out*. (See *supra*, p. 210.) The Bankruptcy Act, however, requires the existence of an actual partnership; partnership by estoppel does not exist in bankruptcy law. R&G, p. 377.

4. **"Jingle" rule:** When both the partnership property and the assets of the separate partners are insufficient to pay creditors of the partnership, the partnership property is applied first to the payment of partnership debts, and the separate partners' assets are applied first to the payment of their respective individual debts. In this way, secured creditors of the partnership and of the individual partners are not deprived of their security. This is known as the *"dual priorities"* or *"jingle"* rule. UPA § 40(b).

   a. **Partially repealed by Bankruptcy Act:** The Bankruptcy Reform Act of 1978 partially repealed the jingle rule. Partnership creditors are now on a par with individual creditors in asserting claims against a partner's personal assets. This change was made in recognition of the fact that partnership creditors often rely on the assets of individual partners when extending credit to the partnership. Under the Act, partnership creditors continue to enjoy priority over the creditors of the individual partners with respect to claims against partnership property. Hynes, p. 383. This means that in those states adopting UPA § 40, there is a different standard between federal bankruptcy law and state laws governing state insolvency and receivership proceedings. Id.

   b. **Partially repealed by RUPA:** RUPA § 807 also partially *repeals the dual priority or jingle rule* of UPA §§ 40(h), (i). Under RUPA § 807, "partnership creditors share pro rata with partners' individual creditors in the assets of the partners' estates."

5. **Judgment liens against partnership property after filing of bankruptcy petition are invalid:** The filing of a bankruptcy petition stays the creation, enforcement or perfection of any liens against partnership property.

Example: Partnership acquired a house with partnership funds, but legal title was held in the name of two of the three partners. Partnership then filed for chapter 11 bankruptcy. Liens were filed against the house after the bankruptcy petition was filed, on account of debts incurred individually by the partners who held legal title. The partnership then asked the bankruptcy court to allow sale of the house free of any liens filed after the bankruptcy filing.

Held, the house could be sold free of liens filed after the bankruptcy filing. Since the property was purchased with partnership funds without evidence of a contrary intent, it became partnership property even though title was held in the names of two of the partners. Under bankruptcy law, the filing of a bankruptcy petition stays the creation and perfection of any new liens. Under state law, however, a good-faith creditor of an individual partner who is without notice of a partnership's equitable interest, may acquire a lien superior to those equitable interests. However, bankruptcy law supersedes any state law to the contrary. Therefore, the liens filed after the bankruptcy petition was filed are void. *In re Don/Mark Partnership,* 14 B.R. 830 (Bankr. D. Colo. 1981).

III. PROCEDURES IN BANKRUPTCY

A. Jury trial: In general, there is no right to a jury trial in bankruptcy proceedings. However, if a partner who has not joined in a bankruptcy petition, and against whom no petition has been filed, denies that she is a partner, she is entitled to a jury trial on that issue. *In re Lamb,* 29 B.R. 950 (Bankr. E.D. Tenn. 1983).

   a. Post-petition transfers: In general, if partners wish to pay personally partnership expenses incurred after the partnership files bankruptcy, but wish also to retain their right to be repaid their loans as a priority administrative claim, they must obtain court approval, give notice to creditors, and participate in a hearing for parties in interest.

   Example: A and B were general partners of a partnership in the business of buying and selling real estate. The partnership filed a petition in chapter 11 bankruptcy. To forestall foreclosure by a mortgagee of one of the partnership's properties, the partners personally loaned the partnership about $13,000 to pay the mortgage, as well as insurance and utilities. This enabled the partners to avoid foreclosure and sell the property for about $56,000. However, A and B did not get court approval to make these loans to the partnership, nor did they notify other creditors or conduct a hearing. A and B asserted that even though there was neither notice nor an opportunity for a hearing, their $13,000 claim should be entitled to priority status as an administrative expense, because it was made in the ordinary course of business. They asked the court to approve the loans retroactively.

Held, A and B's administrative claims were disallowed. Their loan was not in the ordinary course of the partnership business. Although sales by the partnership are part of the partnership business, real estate partnerships do not typically borrow funds from their general partners to pay their operating expenses. The court refused to approve the loans retroactively because exceptional circumstances did not exist. The court noted that if the partners' administrative claim were allowed, they would effectively be receiving double credit for the payments they had made. *In re Massetti,* 95 B.R. 360 (Bankr. E.D. Pa. 1989).

CHAPTER 20

LIMITED PARTNERSHIPS

ChapterScope

Limited partnerships were conceived of by businessmen, accountants and lawyers in an effort to create a business form which would combine the tax advantages of partnerships and the limited liability of shareholders in corporations. The limited partnership offers two kinds of participation: participation as a general partner and participation as a limited partner. The essential difference is that a general partner controls the business of the partnership but is liable for all partnership debts, while a limited partner exchanges freedom from liability, beyond his contribution, for a complete relinquishment of control over the business. Limited partnerships are governed by the Revised Uniform Limited Partnership Act (RULPA). In this chapter, we analyze the characteristics of a limited partnership. We also discuss its tax treatment and how it is formed and operates. We describe the liability and rights of the limited partner and of the general partner; the corporation as general partner; assignment of a partner's interest; and miscellaneous provisions of the RULPA. We also cover what happens when an investor erroneously believes he is a limited partner; what happens when a partner dies or becomes bankrupt; and other matters dealing with limited partnerships.

I. INTRODUCTION

A. ULPA and RULPA: The Uniform Limited Partnership Act (ULPA) was completed in 1916, and was for many years the basic law on limited partnerships. The ULPA is still the law in six states. In 1976, the National Conference of Commissioners on Uniform State Law issued a new Uniform Limited Partnership Act. This 1976 version was adopted by nearly all the states. In 1985, the 1976 act was extensively revised. This new 1985 act has already been adopted by 36 states, and several other states have adopted parts of the new act. Because the new 1985 act (the Revised Uniform Limited Partnership Act, or RULPA) reflects the present trends in the law, it is the focus of this chapter.

B. Purpose: The limited partnership is important because it permits a person to *participate in partnership profits without the risk of personal liability.*

C. Characteristics: A limited partnership is distinguishable from a general partnership in several respects. The basic characteristics of a limited partnership are:

   1. Statute: It is purely statutory in origin and it may be created only in accordance with the statutory formalities;

2. **Liability:** The liability of a *limited partner is limited to the amount of his capital contribution*; the liability of the **general partner** is the same as the liability of a partner in an ordinary (non-limited) partnership (i.e., essentially unlimited);

3. **Contribution:** A limited partner may contribute cash, property, or services, or a promise to contribute any of these later. The promise must be in writing signed by the limited partner making the contribution;

4. **Management:** A limited partner does not participate in the management or control of the partnership. If a limited partner *participates in the control* of the partnership, he may *lose his limited liability;* and

5. **Withdrawal:** Withdrawal of a limited partner does not result in a *dissolution* of the partnership.

II. ANALYSIS OF LIMITED PARTNERSHIP

A. **Limited partnership defined:** RULPA § 101(7) defines a limited partnership as "a partnership *formed by two or more persons* under the laws of this State and having *one or more general partners* and *one or more limited partners*."

1. **Types of partners; definitions:** Every limited partnership must have at least one general partner who will be liable for partnership obligations.

2. **Limited partner:** A limited partner is one who *contributes money, property or services, or a promise to contribute* any of these, and who runs the risk of losing his contribution, but *does not become personally liable* for partnership obligations. The limited partners *need not be named* in the limited partnership certificate.

3. **General partner:** The general partner is one who undertakes management and control of the partnership business. The *conduct of the business* becomes his sole responsibility. The general partner(s) assumes full personal liability for partnership obligations. General partners must be named in the limited partnership certificate.

B. **Purpose:** A principal purpose of the limited partnership form and of the RULPA is to permit the limited partner to contribute money, property, or services to the partnership without subjecting his individual assets to the business risks.

1. **Basic concepts:** Several fundamental principles guide courts in interpreting the RULPA:

a. Obtaining limited liability: The limited partner has limited liability unless he participates in controlling the partnership business.

b. Losing limited liability: The limited liability enjoyed by the limited partner is *lost* by his participation in controlling the partnership business, but only as to those creditors who transact business with the partnership *reasonably believing* that the limited partner is a general partner.

c. Joint role: A limited partner may also be a general partner. In this case, she is *liable in all respects as a general partner.*

III. TAX TREATMENT OF THE LIMITED PARTNERSHIP

A. **Desirability of partnership taxation:** Like partnerships, limited partnerships enjoy favorable income tax treatment. In partnership taxation, unlike taxation of a subchapter C corporation, there is *only one level* of taxation. The partnership itself does not pay income taxes; instead, the partners claim their pro rata shares of the partnership income on their individual returns. The partners are taxed on their share of partnership income at their respective *individual rates, not at corporate rates.* The income *keeps its character;* that is, capital gains remain capital gains, and ordinary income remains ordinary income.

1. **Claiming losses and deductions on individual returns:** with partnership tax status, the partners can claim the losses and deductions of the partnership on their individual tax returns. This is particularly useful in start-up ventures that often lose money in their early years. However, the Tax Reform Act of 1986 substantially limited the extent to which limited partners who took no active part in the partnership could use passive losses to offset their other income.

B. **"Check-the-Box" entity classification:** Under Treasury Regulations effective January 1, 1997, an unincorporated business entity with two or more members generally can elect whether to be taxed as a partnership or a corporation. Treas. Reg. § 301.7701 (1991) (as amended in 1997 by T.D. 8697). (Under RULPA § 101(7), a limited partnership must have at least two members.) In the same way, an unincorporated domestic business with one owner will be taxed as a sole proprietorship (which shares tax advantages similar to those of a partnership), and not as a corporation, unless corporate treatment is elected by the taxpayer.

C. **Publicly Traded Limited Partnership:** Limited partnerships can qualify for listing on a public stock exchange. Under § 7704 of the Internal Revenue Code, publicly traded partnerships are taxed as corporations.

1. **Exception for partnerships with passive income:** Section 7704 excepts partnerships with 90% or more of their gross income as "qualifying passive-type income." "Qualifying passive type income" includes interest, dividends, real property rents, gains from the sale of real property, income and gains from certain mining and natural resource activity, gain from the sale of capital assets or property held for the production of income and certain income and gain from commodities. (Qualifying income does not include interest from the conduct of a financial or insurance business.) The effect of this exception is that many oil, gas and real estate limited partnerships are exempted from this Act and will continue to enjoy partnership tax treatment. Partnerships in existence on December 17, 1987, were exempted until December 17, 1997.

IV. FORMATION AND BUSINESS OF A LIMITED PARTNERSHIP

A. **Certificate:** The requirements for the certificate of a limited partnership were relaxed considerably by the 1985 RULPA. RULPA § 201.

1. **Fewer items:** The following are the *only items* now required to be put in the certificate:

   - the *name* of the limited partnership;

   - the *address of the partnership office* and the *name and address of the agent* for service of process;

   - *the name* and the *business address* of each *general partner;*

   - the *latest date* upon which the limited partnership is to dissolve; and

   - *any other matters* the general partners determine to include.

2. **Filing:** The certificate is *filed with the Secretary of State* of the state in which the partnership is organized. The limited partnership is deemed formed at the time of filing or at a later date specified in the certificate, provided there has been substantial compliance with the provisions of section 201.

3. **Name:** The name of a limited partnership must contain the words *"limited partnership."* RULPA § 102.

B. Formation of a limited partnership: A limited partnership can be created only by *compliance with the statutory formalities;* it is a formal and public proceeding. This must be contrasted with a general partnership, which may be created informally.

1. **Composition:** Two or more persons may form a limited partnership, but there must be at least one general partner. There is no upper limit to the number of general or limited partners.

2. **Certificate:** The certificate of limited partnership must be *signed by the general partner(s) and filed* for record in the Secretary of State's office.

    a. **Compliance:** *Substantial compliance* with this filing requirement is enough to form a limited partnership. RULPA § 201(b).

    b. **Compare partnership agreement:** Although there must be a written limited partnership certificate to form a limited partnership, the agreement governing the relationship between the parties can be oral. *Mahon v. Harst,* 738 P.2d 1190 (Colo. Ct. App. 1987). The *Mahon* court held than an oral agreement in which the partners agreed that general partners could be removed by a 75% vote of the partners was enforceable.

3. **Capitalization:** *No minimum capitalization* is required. Contributions made or to be made by the limited partners need no longer be itemized in the certificate.

C. Nature of the business: The limited partnership certificate need no longer state the nature of the partnership business. A limited partnership may carry on *any business* which a general non-limited partnership may carry on, except as prohibited by statute. Some state statutes prohibit limited partnerships from engaging in banking or insurance.

D. Contribution of a limited partner: RULPA has expanded the definition of contributions permitted by a limited partner to include *services rendered* and *promises to contribute* money, property or services. RULPA § 101(2). Under the ULPA, contributions of services or promises were not permitted.

V. LIABILITY OF A LIMITED PARTNER

A. Four circumstances under which a limited partner is personally liable under RULPA: A limited partner has *no personal liability* unless:

(1) she is *also a general partner*;

(2) *she participates in the control of the business* (in which case she is liable only to creditors who have a reasonable basis to believe she is a general partner);

(3) she *knowingly permits her name to be used* in the limited partnership's name, unless (a) it is also the name of a general partner or the corporate name of a corporate general partner; or (b) the business of the limited partnership was carried on in that name before the admission of that limited partner (RULPA §§ 303, 102(2)); or

(4) there *has not been substantial compliance* with the statutory filing requirements.

1. "Control" by limited partner: The RULPA does not define the term *"control of the business"*. Nevertheless, it is the application of this term which renders a limited partner personally liable to creditors who rely on his activities.

    a. Issue of fact to be determined by jury: Whether the control exercised is sufficient to make a limited partner liable is heavily dependent on the facts of the case and is usually a jury question. *Gateway Potato Sales v. G.B. Investment Co.,* 822 P.2d 490 (Ariz. Ct. App. 1991); *Gast v. Petsinger,* 323 A.2d 371 (Pa. Super. Ct. 1974). In *Gast,* under ULPA, a genuine issue of material fact was generated as to whether limited partners were liable when several booklets described them as "Project Managers," and when they acted as independent consultants for the partnership on certain projects. There was a factual question whether their technical skills were such that their "advice" may have really constituted control over the general partner.

    Example: X is a limited partner, and also a shop foreman, in a limited partnership. He discusses major problems on numerous occasions with the general partner, who has exclusive control of the business.

      Held, X is not personally liable as a general partner. *Silvola v. Rowlett,* 272 P.2d 287 (Colo. 1954).

    b. Management, decision-making, and advising as control factors: Managing the partnership or being the ultimate decision-maker will constitute control. However, merely providing advice or counsel to the general partner will not necessarily be viewed as exercising control of the general partner. *Mt. Vernon Sav. & Loan Ass'n v. Partridge Assocs.*, 679 F. Supp. 522, 528 (D. Md. 1987).

Example 1. *Management and decision-making*: A and B were limited partners. A and B told the general partner which crops to plant. They also wrote checks on the partnership account. Finally, they required the general partner to resign as manager and appointed another manager. The partnership went into bankruptcy, and a creditor sued them on the theory that they had exercised control over the partnership.

Held, A and B took part in the control of the partnership and thus were liable as general partners. *Holzman v. De Escamilla*, 195 P.2d 833 (Cal. Dist. Ct. App. 1948) (decided under ULPA).

Example 2. *Giving advice*: A is a general partner and B is a limited partner in a limited partnership engaged in buying and selling securities. B has had many years of experience in this field, but A has had little experience. A makes all the decisions in conducting the business, but often calls on B at his home for advice. B's answer is invariably as follows: "I'm not telling you what to do, but if I were doing it I would do it this way," and explains the reason for his conclusion. Under these facts, A is making all the decisions in conducting the business, although he seeks advice as any prudent person would do. B insists that he is not telling A what to do. These facts standing alone indicate that B is not participating in the control of the business.

However, there may be other facts to consider, *e.g.*: the relationship of the parties (whether they are father and son or friends of long standing), whether A habitually relies on B's judgment without occasionally substituting his own judgment, whether or not A has just assumed control of the business after many years of control by B, whether A is subject to B's control in other relationships. These are all factors which the trier of fact must consider. If B actually did participate in running the business, then he is liable as a general partner at least with respect to creditors who have a reasonable basis to believe he is acting as a general partner. If he did not so participate, then he is not liable as a general partner to the firm's creditors.

2. **Activities allowed:** RULPA does, however, list certain activities, which may be carried on by a limited partner *without liability for*

participating in control. Here is this list of *"safe harbor"* activities, given in § 303(b):

- being a *contractor* for or an *agent* or *employee* of the limited partnership or of a general partner, or being an *officer, director,* or *shareholder* of a *general partner that is a corporation*;

- *consulting with and advising* a general partner about the limited partnership's business;

- *acting as surety* for the limited partnership or *guaranteeing* or *assuming* one or more of the limited partnership's obligations;

- taking any action required or permitted by law to bring or pursue a *derivative action* in the right of the limited partnership;

- requesting or attending a *meeting* of partners;

- proposing, approving, or disapproving, by voting or otherwise, one or more of the following matters:

    - *the dissolution and winding up* of the limited partnership;

    - the sale, exchange, lease, mortgage, pledge, or other *transfer of all or substantially all of the limited partnership's assets;*

    - *the incurrence of indebtedness* by the limited partnership other than in the ordinary course of its business;

    - a change in the *nature of the business;*

    - the *admission or removal* of a *general* partner;

    - the *admission or removal* of a *limited* partner;

    - a transaction involving an *actual or potential conflict of interest* between a general partner and the limited partnership or the limited partners;

    - *an amendment* to the partnership agreement or limited partnership certificate; or

    - matters *related to the business* of the limited partnership not otherwise enumerated in (RULPA) § 303(b) which the partnership agreement *states in writing* may be subject to the approval or disapproval of limited partners;

- *winding up* the limited partnership pursuant to RULPA § 803; or

- exercising any *right or power permitted to limited partners* under the RULPA and not specifically enumerated in § 303(b).

3. **Acting as surety for the limited partnership or guaranteeing or assuming an obligation of the partnership:** When a limited partner acts as a surety for the limited partnership or guarantees the partnership's obligations, she is not assuming control of the business so as to render her personally liable for other partnership debts. However, she may be liable for these debts if she actively persuades creditors to give credit to the partnership, and gives the appearance of exercising control of the partnership.

   Example: A was one of two limited partners in Ramsey Homebuilders. The sole general partner had a poor credit history and he could not borrow money or obtain credit to run the partnership business. A, who had a personal account with T, contacted T and secured an account in the partnership name. The partnership was then able to secure on credit the building materials that the partnership needed to survive. When the partnership failed to pay T, T sued A, claiming A's exercise of control rendered him liable. A argued that he was not liable under RULPA § 303(b)(3), stating that guaranteeing a partnership debt is not "control" sufficient to render a limited partner liable. A also argued he was not liable because he had not guaranteed the partnership debt in writing.

   Held, A was liable. A's activity in securing credit for the partnership constituted "control" sufficient to render A liable. T reasonably relied upon A's participation when he extended credit. Therefore, A exercised control over the business. The court rejected the Statute of Frauds defense because T had not sued A upon a suretyship agreement but rather upon the theory that A became a general partner when he participated in control of the business. *Pitman v. Flanagan Lumber Co. Inc.,* 567 So. 2d 1335 (Ala. 1990).

4. **Failure to comply with statutory formalities for forming a limited partnership:** If a limited partnership is not properly formed, limited partners may be exposed to personal liability for partnership debts. However, the limited partners can avoid personal liability if there is ***substantial compliance*** with the filing requirements. See *J.C. Wattenbarger & Sons v. Sanders,* 13 Cal. Rptr. 92 (Cal. Dist. Ct. App. 1961).

   a. **Contract claims:** Whether a limited partner is exposed to liability for contract claims depends partly on whether there was substantial compliance with statutory formalities for formation of the limited partnership.

      Example 1: On April 24, 1980, T sold a motel to Limited Partnership for cash and a note. All partners had signed a certificate of limited partnership on April 1, 1980, but it was not recorded in the county recorder's office until December 29, 1980. The limited partnership made payments on the note for two years. When the limited partnership defaulted on the note, T claimed that the limited partners were personally liable.

Held, the limited partners were not personally liable because the Nevada limited partnership statute permits limited partnerships to be formed upon substantial compliance with the filing requirements. The certificate was filed in the county recorder's office (as required by the Nevada statute) within a reasonable time after the limited partnership was formed. Moreover, T knew it was dealing with a limited partnership and it should not be allowed to circumvent the limited partnership and hold the individual limited partners liable. *Fabry Partnership v. Christensen,* 794 P.2d 719 (Nev. 1990).

Example 2: T furnished services worth almost $11,000 to Peaceful Bay Resort and Club. T did not know that the Club was actually a limited partnership. A certificate of limited partnership had been filed with the county recorder but no filing was made in the office of the secretary of state. In addition, the certificate did not show each partner's contributions or the share each was to receive as required under the ULPA. There was no indication on an assumed business name form, filed with the secretary of state, that the partners listed were limited partners. T sued the limited partners for failing to pay his $11,000. One limited partner did not formally renounce his interest in the business profits until 3 1/2 years after T filed a complaint against him. The other limited partners did not file any renunciations.

Held, the limited partners were liable as general partners because there was not substantial compliance with the statutory filing requirements. The court added that the limited partners could not avoid liability under ULPA § 11 (which permitted limited partners to avoid liability if they timely renounced their interest in the partnership income) because the renunciation was not timely. *Direct Mail Specialist, Inc.,* 673 F. Supp. 1540 (D. Mont. 1987).

Note: Unlike the ULPA under which the *Direct Mail* case was decided, RULPA does not require "prompt renunciation."

i. **Effect of failure to file:** One court has held that if no third party has been mislead, even failure to file with the secretary of state may not render a limited partner liable if there has been "substantial compliance in good faith with the statute." *In re Oakgrove Village, Ltd.,* 90 B.R. 246, 249-50 (Bankr. W.D. Tex. 1988). Compare *Grenada Bank v. Willey,* 705 F.2d

176 (6th Cir.), *cert. denied,* 464 U.S. 849 (1983). In the *Grenada* case, failure to record a limited partnership agreement made a limited partner liable on a judgment as if he were a general partner, even though there was no indication that the failure to record had affected the knowledge of third persons as to the partner's status as limited partner.

ii. Limited partner entering into contract before receipt of certificate of limited partnership: Limited partners who make contracts for the limited partnership before the secretary of state acknowledges a limited partnership certificate may be held personally liable as if they were general partners. *Deporter-Butterworth Tours, Inc. v. Tyrrell,* 503 N.E.2d 378 (Ill. App. Ct), *appeal denied,* 511 N.E.2d 427 (1987).

b. Tort claims: In the same way as in contract claims, limited partners may not be personally liability for the limited partnership's torts if there has been substantial compliance with the limited partnership statute and no third party reasonably believes the limited partners to be general partners.

Example: T was tortiously injured in Kentucky by a negligent act of Virginia Partners, a limited partnership. Virginia Partners had been certified as a limited partnership in Florida, its home state. However, its certification had lapsed the previous year. (Florida requires annual recertification.) Virginia Partners was not registered as a foreign limited partnership in the state of Kentucky. T claimed that the lapse in Florida certification and the failure to register as a foreign limited partnership in Kentucky rendered the limited partners personally liable for his claim.

Held, the limited partners were not personally liable. A Florida court had previously found that limited partners could not be held personally liable merely because of a certification lapse, because during the lapse the entity was a *de facto* limited partnership. The court also held that the partnership's failure to register as a foreign limited partnership in Kentucky did not render the limited partners liable. It found that the purpose behind the statute requiring registration was to encourage investment in limited partnerships with the promise of limited liability. These investments fuel the economy. In the instant case, **because no creditors were mislead and because the limited partners did not take part in running the business, the court refused to hold them personally liable.** However, the court added that failure to register as a foreign limited partnership could prevent the partnership from enforcing its contracts in Kentucky courts. *Virginia Partners, Ltd. v. Day,* 738 S.W.2d 837 (Ky. Ct. App. 1987).

B. Limited partner liable only if third person relies on her being a general partner: A limited partner who participates in partnership control is only liable to third persons who reasonably believe, based on her conduct, that she is really a general partner. RULPA § 303(a).

Example: X Corporation is the general partner of Limited Partnership. A and B are the sole stockholders of X Corporation. A and B, as X Corporation officers and directors, exercise day to day control over Limited Partnership. A and B are also individually limited partners of Limited Partnership, along with other limited partners. T sells appliances to Limited Partnership. When installments are not paid, T seeks to hold A and B personally liable (even though individually they are only limited partners) because they were officers of X Corporation and controlled its business. A and B contend that only X Corporation, a distinct corporate entity, is liable.

Held, A and B are not liable in their individual capacities. The reason to hold a limited partner liable as a general partner is to prevent third parties from concluding that a limited partner is a general partner and from relying on his general liability. T knew that the general partner was a corporation, and that A and B dealt with T in their corporate capacities, so P was not deceived. In these circumstances the corporate entity should be upheld; limited partners are not liable as general partners simply because they are active officers, directors or stockholders of a corporate general partner in a limited partnership. *Frigidaire Sales Corp. v. Union Properties, Inc.,* 562 P.2d 244 (Wash. 1977).

1. Exception is possible under former statutes: Under ULPA and an earlier version of RULPA, some courts imposed liability, even without reliance by third persons, on limited partners running the business. See *Delaney v. Fidelity Lease Ltd.,* 526 S.W.2d 543 (Tex. 1975). See also *Gateway Potato Sales v. G.B. Investment Co.,* 822 P.2d 490 (Ariz. Ct. App. 1991). In *Gateway,* the court interpreted the 1976 version of RULPA to mean that a limited partner could be personally liable if he exercised substantially the same control as a general partner, even though the third person had no knowledge of his participation and control.

VI. CORPORATION AS GENERAL PARTNER

A. Corporation as "person": A *corporation* can be a partner (either limited or general) in a limited partnership. RULPA §§ 101(7), 101(11).

B. Management of limited partnership by corporation:

1. **Actions under ULPA:** When a limited partnership is formed, a corporation may be the ***general partner*** and manage the partnership business. Under the ***old ULPA,*** some courts held limited partners personally liable when they served as agents or officers of the corporate general partner, because in that capacity they exercised individual control over the partnership. See *Delaney v. Fidelity Lease Ltd.,* 526 S.W.2d 543, 546 (Tex. 1975). Compare *Gonzalez v. Chalpin,* 565 N.E.2d 1253 (N.Y. 1990) Under *Gonzalez,* once a limited partner serves as a corporate general partner's agent and thereby exercises control over the partnership, the burden then shifts to him to show that he exercised control as an officer of the corporate general partner and not individually. A limited partner who failed to show that he had acted in his corporate capacity was held personally liable.

2. **Actions under RULPA:** Today, in most jurisdictions, the limited partners may manage their partnership through a corporate general partner and thus avoid personal liability so long as (1) they ***act only through the corporation*** and not in a direct, personal capacity; and (2) ***no fraud or manifest injustice*** is perpetrated upon third persons. Under RULPA § 303(b), a limited partner's actions as an officer or agent of a corporate general partner do not constitute control. A limited partner is only liable to third persons who believe, based on the limited partner's conduct, that he himself is really a general partner. RULPA § 303(a).

   Example: Defendant A was a limited partner of Limited Partnership. He was also one of three officers, directors and shareholders of X Corporation, Limited Partnership's corporate general partner. In that capacity, A exercised complete management and control in the negotiations with T for a sublease, without the advice or direction of the other officers and directors of X Corporation. T knew that A was one of the principals of the corporate general partner. T sued A, charging A was personally liable for wrongfully terminating their sublease. T claimed that A should not be able to avoid personal liability because he ran the limited partnership.

   Held, A was not personally liable. T was well aware that A was acting as an officer of the corporate general partner. Moreover, X Corporation was organized in good faith, its corporate formalities were observed and it was adequately capitalized. Therefore, the corporate veil would not be pierced to hold A personally liable. Furthermore, under RULPA § 303(b), acting as an officer of a corporate general partner does not constitute participation in the control of the partnership business. *Western Camps, Inc. v. Riverway Ranch Enters.,* 138 Cal. Rptr. 918 (Cal. Ct. App. 1977) (decided under the ULPA).

VII. ERRONEOUS BELIEF OF STATUS AS LIMITED PARTNER

A. **"Good faith" error:** A person who has contributed to a business erroneously but *in good faith,* believing that she has become a limited partner in a limited partnership, is *not* a general partner and is *not bound by the partnership's obligations,* if, on ascertaining the mistake, she:

- causes a limited partnership certificate or an amended certificate to be *executed and filed;* or

- *withdraws from future equity participation in the enterprise* by executing and filing in the Secretary of State's office a certificate declaring her withdrawal. RULPA § 304(a).

Example: In 1984, Briargate Homes Partnership was formed with A as one of its partners. A believed that she was a limited partner. In fact, the partnership operated as a general partnership from its inception. The partnership failed to pay certain debts owed to T. T sued A personally because the partnership had not been properly formed as a limited partnership. A defended on the ground that she had believed that she was investing in a limited partnership. The district court held her liable because it found that by 1986 she no longer believed in good faith that she was a limited partner, but that she failed to renounce her interest until about a year and a half later.

Held, the district court erred in failing to examine her good faith at the time of her contribution and in failing to determine whether there was any good faith reliance by the creditors upon A's being a general partner. The court stated that *good faith must be determined at the time a limited partner makes her contribution.* The district court had erroneously asked whether A had good faith in 1986, two years after her contribution. The court added that *"good faith" is an objective standard* that is to be determined by asking whether at the time she contributed to the enterprise she *reasonably believed* that she was a limited partner.

The court also held that the district court had erred in finding that A had not promptly withdrawn, without considering whether *creditors*

had relied on her being a general partner. The court added that A could only be held liable as a general partner for transactions prior to withdrawal, even if T relied on A's resources. *Briargate Condominium Ass'n v. Carpenter,* 976 F.2d 868 (4th Cir. 1992).

B. Purpose of RULPA § 304(a): This provision ***protects*** one who mistakenly believes that he is a limited partner, whether or not a limited partnership has been formed.

Example: A contributes $150,000 to become a limited partner in a partnership in which B and C are to be the general partners and managers of the business. The business is established, debts are incurred, and A receives his share of the profits. A believes that he is a limited partner. Then the business suffers reverses and A discovers that no certificate of limited partnership has ever been executed or filed for record. A immediately "renounces" his interest in the profits and all other compensation from the business. He does not return or offer to return the profits already distributed to him. T, a creditor, sues A, alleging that A is liable as a general partner.

Held, T may not recover. Failure to file the limited partnership certificate is in this instance a substantial failure precluding formation of a limited partnership. However, A contributed to "the capital of a business . . . erroneously believing that he has become a limited partner." Immediately upon discovering the mistake, A renounced his right to any further income from the business. A is not required to pay back what he has already received. A's reasonable belief at the time he invested, coupled with his immediate renunciation when he discovered there was no limited partnership, renders A not liable as though he were actually a limited partner, even though no limited partnership was formed. *Gilman Paint & Varnish Co. v. Legum,* 80 A.2d 906 (Md. 1951).

C. Liability only to creditors who at the time of the transaction believe in good faith that the limited partner is a general partner: A partner who invests in what he erroneously thinks is a limited partnership may be ***liable as a general partner to a third party,*** but only if the third party ***actually believed in good faith*** that the partner was a ***general partner at the time of transacting business*** with the partnership, ***and transacts business with it***:

- ***before that partner withdraws*** and a certificate is filed to show his withdrawal; or

- ***before a certificate is filed,*** showing that partner is not a general partner. RULPA § 304(b).

VIII. RIGHTS OF A LIMITED PARTNER

A. Generally: A limited partner has the same rights as a general partner in *most* respects. However, in one respect a limited partner's rights are significantly different from those of a general partner. A limited partner has *no right to participate in the control* of the business of the limited partnership. If she does participate, she may lose her status as a limited partner, and lose the benefits of limited liability that accrue with it. *See, supra,* p. 293.

B. Rights regarding books and records: A limited partner is entitled to have the firm's books kept at the principal place of business. A limited partner has the right to:

- *inspect and copy any of the partnership records* required to be maintained under RULPA § 105; and

- obtain from the general partners:

  - *true and full information* regarding the state of the business and the financial condition of the limited partnership;

  - promptly after they becomes available, *copies of the limited partnership's federal, state and local income tax returns* for each year; and

  - other information regarding the affairs of the limited partnership as is *just and reasonable*. RULPA § 305.

1. General partners may breach fiduciary duty by breaching RULPA § 305: A general partner who wilfully fails to furnish the limited partners with the financial information required under RULPA § 305 violates his fiduciary duty to the limited partners. *Mahon v. Harst*, 738 P.2d 1190 (Colo. Ct. App. 1987).

Example: General partners sold their interest in a limited partnership to limited partners. Their interest included part ownership in a building they had purchased for the limited partnership five years earlier. The contract provided that general partners "would provide partners with all information that may reasonably be requested." Limited partners never demanded information from the general partners concerning the presence of asbestos. General partners claimed they were not liable because they had no duty to disclose information in the absence of a request.

Held, general partners had a duty to reveal information they knew about the presence of asbestos even without request. The provision that general partners would provide information that might reasonably be requested could not alter general partners' statutory and common law duties of disclosure. Therefore, if general partners knew of the presence of asbestos and that limited partners did not know the same facts, they had a duty to disclose the facts. Although "partners are free to vary many aspects of their relationship . . . they are not free to destroy its fiduciary character." *Appletree Square I Ltd. Partnership v. Investmark, Inc.,* 494 N.W.2d 889 (Minn. Ct. App.), *review denied,* (Minn. 1993).

2. **Records required to be kept:** RULPA has expanded materially the scope of the records which must be kept. RULPA § 105, ***"Records to Be Kept,"*** provides substantially the following:

> Each limited partnership shall keep the following at its office within the state:
>
> - a current list of the full name and last known business address of each partner, separately listing the general partners alphabetically and the limited partners alphabetically;
>
> - a copy of the limited partnership certificate and all amending certificates, with executed copies of any powers of attorney authorizing the execution of any certificate;
>
> - copies of the limited partnership's federal, state and local income tax returns and reports, if any, for the three most recent years;
>
> - copies of any then effective written partnership agreements and of any of the limited partnership's financial statements for the three most recent years; and
>
> - unless contained in a written partnership agreement, a writing setting out:
>
>   - the amount of cash and a description and statement of the agreed value of the other property or services contributed by each partner and which each partner has agreed to contribute;
>
>   - the time when any additional contributions agreed to be made by each partner are to be made;
>
>   - any right of a partner to receive, or of a general partner to make, distributions to a partner which include a return of any part of the partner's contribution; and
>
>   - any events upon the happening of which the limited partnership is to be dissolved and its affairs wound up.

a. **Subject to inspection and copying:** The records are subject to inspection and copying at the reasonable request and expense of any partner during ordinary business hours.

C. Judicial dissolution: On application of a limited partner, a court may decree ***dissolution*** of the partnership when the partner shows that the partnership business can only be carried on at a loss, or that the business can no longer be carried on "***in conformity with the partnership agreement.***" RULPA § 802.

Example: A is a limited partner and B is a general partner in a real estate business in a rapidly growing community. A has contributed approximately $12,000 to the capital. Within a period of five years the partnership pays A over $37,000 in profits and dividends. Then the character of the community changes and the partnership starts losing money. The partnership agreement is to run for three more years. A asks B to agree to a dissolution and settling of the partnership affairs. B refuses. A petitions the court for a decree dissolving the partnership. A shows that in the future the partnership can be operated only at a loss, and that the business can no longer be operated for the mutual benefit of A and B. B's defense is that A has already received in dividends more than three times the amount of his original contribution; thus, A cannot lose money overall by continued partnership existence until the end of the term.

Held, the defense is not valid. The limited partner still has an interest in saving his investment in the partnership. When he has shown the business can be operated only at a loss and that it can no longer be conducted for the mutual benefit of both partners, then a decree of dissolution should issue. It is immaterial whether the dividends or profits in the past have been large or small. The court must be guided by the present status and future prospects of the business. *Wallace v. Sinclair,* 250 P.2d 154 (Cal. Dist. Ct. App. 1953). *See* also *Mahon v. Harst, supra.* In *Mahon,* the court held that judicial dissolution was proper because the general partner had exposed the partnership to potential liability by operating a nursing home without a license, and had also willfully failed to furnish the limited partners with financial information in violation of his obligation to do so.

D. Right to profits: Allocation of profits and losses, as well as distribution of cash and other assets, is controlled by the limited partnership agreement. If the agreement is silent, allocation is based on the value of contributions made, as shown in the partnership records. RULPA §§ 503, 504.

E. Fiduciary duty owed by general partner to limited partner: The general partner has a fiduciary duty to the limited partners to exercise utmost good faith, fairness and loyalty. Equitable relief may be granted if that duty is breached. *Boxer v. Husky Oil Co.,* 429 A.2d 995 (Del. Ch. 1981); RULPA § 403(b).

Example: Limited partnership owned undeveloped land. General partners requested rezoning of the undeveloped property, and the county tentatively approved the rezoning. General partners then hired an appraiser to value the undeveloped land, but did not tell the appraiser about the zoning change. Appraiser valued the property at $110,125. General partners offered to buy the property from the partnership at that price. A, a limited partner, objected, stating that following the zoning change, the property was worth between $300,000 and $400,000. General partners notified other limited partners of the objection. All limited partners except A eventually approved the sale. A sued the general partners for breach of fiduciary duty. General partners argued that they had not breached their fiduciary duty to the partnership, because the limited partnership articles gave them the power, without the consent of the limited partners, to purchase less than substantially all of the partnership's real property.

Held, the general partners breached their fiduciary duty. The limited partnership articles did not override their fiduciary duty to the partnership. They did not pay a fair price for the property and they concealed the rezoning from the appraiser, even after A objected. The general partners are liable for compensatory damages based on the difference between the price paid for the property and its fair market value. In addition, punitive damages can be awarded for breach of fiduciary duty if the parties' conduct is gross, wanton, malicious and oppressive or shows spite, ill will or reckless indifference to the interest of others. *Jerman v. O'Leary,* 701 P.2d 1205 (Ariz. Ct. App. 1985).

IX.   RIGHTS, POWERS AND LIABILITIES OF GENERAL PARTNER

A. Recital in certificate: The certificate of limited partnership must recite the name and business address of each general partner. RULPA § 201(a)(3). The original certificate must be signed by all general partners. RULPA § 204(a)(1).

B. Admission of new general partner: A new general partner may be admitted by agreement of the partners at any time. A new certificate amending the original certificate, reciting the name and address of the new general partner, must be filed within 30 days following the admission. The amendment must be signed by the new general partner and at least one of the existing general partners. RULPA §§ 202(b), 204(a)(2).

C. Duty to file amendment certificate: A general partner is under a *duty* to file an amendment to the certificate under certain other specified circumstances, including the withdrawal of a general partner and the continuation of the business after such withdrawal. RULPA §§ 202(b)(2), 202(b)(3).

D. Liability for false statement: A general partner is *liable in damages* to a third party who relies on a false statement in a filed certificate if the partner knew or should have known that the statement was false. RULPA § 207(1),(2).

E. Removal of general partner: A general partner may be *removed* by the other partners under the terms of the partnership agreement. Upon removal, he ceases to be a general partner. RULPA § 402(3). If the general partner refuses to accede to the partners' vote, the proper procedure to compel removal of a general partner is to seek to amend the certificate of limited partnership to reflect his removal. Again, *see Mahon v. Harst, supra.* In *Mahon,* the court held that mandamus was the wrong remedy because mandamus requires the exhaustion of remedies, and a limited partner may effect removal by amending the limited partnership certificate.

1. Removal of general partner by limited partners: The limited partners may remove the general partner and replace her with another partner. Although RULPA § 801(4) requires unanimous consent to continue the partnership when the *sole general partner* is removed, the partnership agreement may provide for continuation even without unanimous agreement.

Example: Seventy-four percent of the limited partners voted to remove and replace the sole general partner. The limited partnership agreement provided that the limited partners could remove the general partner for cause by a 66% vote; however, a subsequent limited partnership law permitted removal only by unanimous vote. The limited partners sued the general partner for fiduciary duty breaches and for violating the partnership agreement; the general partner alleged improper removal.

Held, because the partnership agreement provided for removal of the general partner by a 66% vote, and because Washington had a statute validating partnership agreements made before adoption of the limited partnership statute, the partners were free to alter the terms of RULPA § 801(4). Therefore, they could replace the general partner and continue the partnership even without the partners' unanimous approval. *Obert v. Environmental Research & Dev. Corp,* 771 P.2d 340 (Wash. 1989). *See* also *Curley v. Brignoli Curley & Roberts Assocs.,* 746 F. Supp. 1208, 1221 (S.D.N.Y. 1989, *aff'd and remanded,* 915 F.2d 81 (2d Cir. 1990), *cert. denied,* 499 U.S. 955 (1991). In *Curley,* the general partner's gross misconduct warranted the court in removing it as general partner. Under the partnership agreement, limited partners then were entitled to decide by vote whether to dissolve their limited partnership or to replace the general partner and continue the partnership.

Note: Another way to avoid the effect of RULPA § 801(4) is to appoint an additional general partner *before* the removal of a sole general partner. See *Lovell v. Hallelujah, Inc.,* 451 So. 2d 116, 121 (La. Ct. App.), *writ denied,* 458 So. 2d 484 (1984).

F. Bankruptcy of general partner: Unless otherwise provided in writing in the partnership agreement, a general partner is deemed removed if she *makes an assignment for the benefit of creditors or is declared bankrupt.* RULPA § 402(4).

G. Other events causing withdrawal of general partner: The *death* of a general partner, a *judicial adjudication* that the general partner is *incompetent*, or the *dissolution of a corporate general partner* are among other events which *terminate* the status of a general partner. RULPA§§ 402(6), (9).

H. No compensation of general partner: In the absence of a contrary agreement, a general partner has no right to compensation for managing the limited partnership. UPA § 18(f).

Note: The RULPA declares that the UPA governs in any case not provided for in the RULPA. RULPA § 1105.

I. General powers and liabilities of general partner: A general partner has the following rights and liabilities:

1. **Powers and restrictions are the same as partner in ordinary partnership:** Except as provided elsewhere in the RULPA or in the partnership agreement, a general partner has the same rights and powers and is subject to the same restrictions as a partner in an ordinary (non-limited) partnership. RULPA § 403(a).

2. **Same liability to creditors as partner in ordinary partnership:** A general partner of a limited partnership has the same liability to the creditors of the partnership as a partner in an ordinary (non-limited) partnership. RULPA § 403(b).

J. Contributions, sharing of profits and losses by general partner: A general partner may make *contributions and share in profits, losses and distributions.* RULPA § 404.

K. Right of general partner to be a limited partner: The general partner may also be a limited partner. When she is *both,* she has the rights and powers of both, and is subject to the liabilities and restrictions of both. RULPA § 404.

L. Effect of partnership agreement: Except as otherwise provided in the RULPA, the *partnership agreement controls the rights and liabilities of all parties* to the agreement, including voting rights, classes of partners and all other matters generally required for the conduct of the business.

X. ASSIGNMENT OF LIMITED PARTNER'S INTEREST

A. Right of assignment in general: The interest of a partner in a limited partnership is *personal property,* and may be *assigned* in whole or in part. Under RULPA, this right of assignment may be limited or modified in the partnership agreement. RULPA § 702.

B. Effect of assignment on partnership and partner status: The assignment of a partnership interest does not dissolve a limited partnership, although the assignor ceases to be a partner if he assigns his entire interest. The assignment does not entitle the assignee to become or act as a partner; it only entitles the assignee to receive the distribution to which the assignor was entitled, to the extent of the interest assigned. RULPA § 702.

C. Right of assignee to become limited partner: The assignee of a partnership interest, including the assignee from a general partner, may become a *limited partner if:*

- all other parties *consent;* or

- *the right of participation* is given to him by his assignor, but only if provided for in the partnership agreement. RULPA § 704(a).

D. Other rights of assignee-partner: An assignee who qualifies as a limited partner has the same rights and liabilities as specified in the partnership agreement and RULPA for other limited partners. She is *liable for the assignor's obligations to make contributions*. But she is not liable for the assignor's liabilities which were unknown to her at the time of assignment. RULPA § 704(b).

E. Liability of assignor-partner: Under RULPA § 704(c), the assignor-partner *continues to be liable,* even after the assignment, for:

- *False statements* of which he had knowledge in the filed partnership certificate, as provided for in RULPA § 207; and

- *Contributions he agreed to make,* unless provided otherwise in the partnership agreement. RULPA § 502.

XI. BUSINESS TRANSACTIONS OF A PARTNER IN A LIMITED PARTNERSHIP

A. Generally: A partner may **lend money** to and **transact other business** with the limited partnership, in the same way as any third party. This general right, may, however, be restricted in the partnership agreement itself. For these purposes, limited and general partners are treated equally. RULPA § 107.

B. Intent of RULPA § 107: This provision was intended to enable **both** limited and general partners who make unsecured loans to the partnership to **share repayments pro rata** with general creditors. However, this right may be limited under state insolvency laws or the Bankruptcy Act.

XII. RELATIONSHIP OF PARTNERSHIP AGREEMENT TO CERTIFICATE OF PARTNERSHIP

A. Information required in certificate: RULPA restored the importance of the partnership agreement by **limiting the information required** in the filed **certificate of partnership.** Under the ULPA, the filed certificate required listing the names and addresses of limited partners as well as most of the other essential provisions governing the partnership. Under RULPA, **only the most vital facts** required to give notice to creditors and the public, **need be stated in the certificate.** RULPA § 201, *supra,* p. 291. The facts required do not include the names and addresses of limited partners.

B. Importance of partnership agreement: In those states which follow the RULPA, one must now refer to the partnership agreement rather than the certificate to find the rights and liabilities of partners. The downgrading of the certificate was intended to eliminate the potential exposure of limited partners to creditors and others, and the **burden** to the partnership of supplying the information required, especially in the case of limited partnerships with many limited partners and in view of the need to file amendments whenever changes occur.

XIII. MISCELLANEOUS PROVISIONS OF RULPA

A. Office and agent for process: A limited partnership must maintain an office in the state of organization. It must also designate an agent within that state for service of process. The agent may be a state resident, a domestic corporation, or a foreign corporation authorized to do business in the state. RULPA § 104.

B. Foreign limited partnerships: The following RULPA provisions apply to *foreign* partnerships (i.e., those not organized within the state):

1. **Law governing:** The law governing the affairs, rights and liabilities of a foreign limited partnership is the law of the *state of organization*. RULPA § 901.

2. **Registration:** A foreign limited partnership must *register* with the Secretary of State of any state in which it plans to *transact business*. RULPA § 902.

3. **Failure to register:** If a foreign limited partnership *fails to register* in any new state, it may *not* file a *lawsuit* in that state. However, the failure does not *impair the validity of its contracts or acts* within the state or *prevent it from defending a suit in that state.* If it transacts business without registering, the Secretary of State is *automatically appointed* agent for the service of process. A partnership which *fails to register* may be restrained from doing business by a designated state official. A limited partner of a foreign limited partnership is not liable as a general partner in another state solely because the partnership transacted business in that state without registering there. RULPA §§ 907, 908.

C. Derivative actions: A limited partner may sue on behalf of the partnership by bringing a *"derivative"* suit that is similar to a shareholder's derivative suit on behalf of a corporation.

1. **Circumstances under which limited partner may sue for the partnership:** A limited partner may not ordinarily act for the limited partnership. However, he may sue for the partnership by bringing an action in the *"right"* of the partnership:

   - if the authorized general partner *refuses* to do so; or

   - if he is not likely to succeed in his efforts to *force* the general partner to act. RULPA § 1001.

   Example: Plaintiffs were five out of 350 limited partners in Limited Partnership 1. The general partners leased partnership property to another partnership, Partnership 2, of which they were also general partners. Plaintiffs claimed that Partnership 2 owed Limited Partnership 1 rent. The general partners argued that no such obligation was owed because, as general partners of Limited Partnership 1, they had released any liability by Partnership 2 to Partnership 1. Plaintiffs claimed that the release was invalid because the general partners had engaged in self-dealing. General partners also argued that plaintiffs, as limited partners could not bring a derivative action.

Held, limited partners have the right to bring a derivative action. Whether general partners engaged in self-dealing was an issue to be resolved on remand by the trial court. *Riviera Congress Assocs. v. Yassky,* 223 N.E.2d 876 (N.Y. 1966); *see* also *Klebanow v. New York Produce Exch.,* 344 F.2d 294, 297 (2d Cir. 1965).

2. **Expenses of derivative actions:** A limited partner who is wholly or partly successful in his action, or who recovers any money for the partnership, may apply to the court for her ***expenses,*** including ***attorney's fees.*** The remainder of any proceeds must be paid to the partnership.

XIV. GENERAL AND LIMITED PARTNERSHIPS DISTINGUISHED

A. **Statutes governing general and limited partnerships:** General and limited partnerships are generally governed by different statutes. In most states, general partnerships are governed by the UPA and limited partnerships by the RULPA. Note, again, that the RULPA states that whenever the RULPA is silent, the UPA will govern. RULPA § 1105. Some of the important differences between the UPA and the RULPA are reviewed below.

B. **Settling accounts:** The UPA and the RULPA have different rankings for creditors and partners in the settling of accounts after dissolution. The UPA ranks creditors *before* partners. See UPA § 40(a). The RULPA ranks partners (both general and limited) *equally* with creditors, in most instances. RULPA § 804.

C. **Dissolution:**

1. **UPA provisions:** Under the UPA, when a partner ceases to be associated with the general partnership, as in the case of his death, bankruptcy, incompetency or wrongful conduct, the business is ***dissolved.*** UPA §§ 29, 31, and 32. The partners can, however agree to continue the partnership upon any such event, or they can provide in the partnership agreement for continuation of the partnership notwithstanding the withdrawal, death or incompetency of a partner.

2. **Effect of RULPA:** Under RULPA, however, the same events— death, incompetency or bankruptcy (of a limited partner), etc. — do not cause dissolution. If the agreement permits, the business may be carried on and the general partners may continue to function. RULPA § 801(4).

D. Assignment of interest:

1. **Limited rights under UPA:** Under the UPA, a partner can assign her right to receive her share of the partnership business, but she cannot assign her right to manage it, unless the other partners agree unanimously or the other terms of the partnership agreement are met. There is some authority that the addition of a partner *dissolves the partnership*. *See* UPA § 29. However, Bromberg and Ripstein argue that UPA § 29 should not be so interpreted. Bromberg and Ripstein on Partnership § 7.07, at 7.71.

2. **RULPA contrasted:** Under the RULPA, the assignment of a partnership interest, whether by a general or a limited partner, does *not cause dissolution*. RULPA § 702, *supra*. The addition of new general partners also does not cause dissolution, unless the limited partnership agreement provides otherwise. If the agreement *does not provide for additional general partners,* all the partners may, by their written consent, agree to such addition. RULPA § 401.

CHAPTER 21

REGISTERED LIMITED LIABILITY PARTNERSHIPS (LLPs)

ChapterScope

The LLP is a recent innovation among business organizations. It offers the tax advantages of partnerships and some aspects of limited liability for the individual partner. However, it is relatively costly to organize and maintain and is not recognized in all states. Furthermore, there is more risk of personal liability for partners in contracts and in torts than for limited partners in a limited partnership or for members of a Limited Liability Company (LLC).

I. LIMITED LIABILITY PARNERSHIPS

A. LLPs as the newest form of partnership: The newest investment vehicle combining the tax status of a partnership with limited liability for the partners is a Registered Limited Liability Partnership (LLP). Beginning in 1995, 22 states and the District of Columbia had statutes allowing the formation of domestic LLPs, and similar legislation was pending in several states. In addition, several states have statutes that expressly or implicitly recognize foreign LLPs.

B. LLP formation: An LLP is very simple to form. The only requirement is that a certificate be filed with the Secretary of State. The LLP has an advantage over the LLC (Limited Liability Company) in that the LLP is run like a traditional partnership; therefore, there is no need to become familiar with LLC forms and terminology. LLCs are covered in Chapter 22.

C. LLP disadvantages: LLPs do have some drawbacks that may limit their use, however. These drawbacks include the cost to form and operate an LLP and the fact that LLPs do not limit individual liability as much as corporations and LLCs do.

1. Cost: LLPs are more expensive to form and to operate than LLCs. LLPs require the payment of initial and annual fees. In some states, such as Illinois, Texas and Delaware, the size of the fee varies with the number of partners. For example, in Illinois the annual fee is $100 per partner, up to a maximum of $5,000. Delaware and Texas additionally require that LLPs be insured for $1 million or $100,000, respectively, against any claims for which the partners are not liable.

2. Exposure to contract claim liability: Another major drawback of LLPs is that they do not provide the partners with feedom from liability in all transactions. Unlike ordinary limited partners in limited partnerships, LLP members can participate in managing the business without running the risk of being subject to personal liability. However, many LLP statutes do not shield partners from the claims of contract creditors; e.g., Del. Code Ann. tit. 6, § 1515(b).

a. **Partners may negotiate for non-liability:** Not all states agree with the Delaware approach. Under Ariz. Rev. Stat. Ann. tit. 29, § 1026 (1996), limited liability partners are not personally liable for obligations of an LLP, whether arising in contract, tort, or otherwise. In any event, an LLP can, of course, negotiate non-recourse or release arrangements with creditors, landlords, lenders or clients.

b. **Protection from tort claims made against other partners:** LLP limited partners do escape liability from certain tort claims made against their associates. An LLP partner is liable in tort only for her own conduct and for the conduct of those she supervises and controls. Partnership tort creditors can proceed against partnership assets as well as the assets of those partner(s) who are directly responsible for commission of the tort. *See, e.g.,* N.Y. Partnership Law § 26 (1997), which limits the liability of a partner in an LLP to his own negligent performance of his services, and to the negligent acts of of any person under his direct supervision while rendering professional services. As applied to law firms organized as LLPs, this would make a partner liable for his own negligence and the negligence of associates and other personnel under his supervision.

Example: A typical example is that of a partner in a Texas LLP. Tex. Rev. Civ. Stat. Ann. art. 6132b-3.08 (1997). A limited LLP partner is not liable for "debts or obligations of the partnership arising from errors, omissions, negligence, incompetence or malfeasance committed. . . in the course of the partnership business by another partner or a representative of the partnership," unless that person is working under his supervision and control; or the partner himself was directly involved in the misconduct; or the partner had notice or knowledge of the malfeasance by the other partner or employee and failed to take reasonable steps to prevent or cure it.

3. **Lack of recognition by other states:** An additional drawback for LLPs is that more states may refuse to recognize foreign LLPs than foreign LLCs, since currently almost all states have LLC statutes whereas only about half have LLP statutes.

D. Practical use of LLPs: Because of these disadvantages, LLPs will likely be used most frequently when LLC election is not possible. Many states, such as Texas, have not approved LLC status for lawyers, for example. For them, LLP status may be the next best thing.

CHAPTER 22

LIMITED LIABILITY COMPANIES (LLCs)

ChapterScope

Limited Liability Companies offer the tax treatment of partnerships and the limited personal liability of corporations. The requirements for forming an LLC are relatively simple and straight-forward, and LLCs are now recognized in most states. The LLC begins with the filing of its articles with the Secretary of State. An LLC may be managed by one or more of its members or by a manager who is not a member. It may be organized for almost any legitimate business purpose. Its members usually execute an operating agreement which defines the relationships among them, including such matters as management, voting, contributions, distributions, assignment, etc. Under limited circumstances, the courts will allow creditors of an LLC to reach the individual members, as in a corporation whose "veil" has been "pierced." LLCs are very flexible organizations and are finding increasing favor among entrepreneurs.

I. INTRODUCTION

A. **LLCs generally:** LLCs combine the best features of corporations, partnerships and limited liability partnerships. Generally, they allow investors to limit their liability to their investments, as in a corporation; and they allow flow-through taxation as does a partnership. In addition, unlike a limited partnership, they allow all investors to participate in the management of the business without risking personal liability. LLCs are a relatively recent creation. Wyoming adopted the first LLC statute in 1977.

B. **Comparison to partnerships:** LLCs have only a few drawbacks when compared with partnerships: the *filing fees are generally greater* than for partnerships, and attorneys and investors may *not* be as familiar with the process of organizing and operating LLCs as they are with partnerships.

C. **Definitions:**

The following terms are utilized in connection with LLCs:

- **Members:** investors in the LLC.

- **Managers:** those persons who are designated as managers of the LLC in the instrument under which it is formed.

- **Articles of organization:** analogous to articles of incorporations.

- **Operating agreements:** analogous to corporate bylaws. These agreements specify many operational details not included in the LLC's articles of organization.

II. MANAGEMENT OF LLCs

A. **Organizational structure:** The LLC's articles of organization can provide for management by either *one or more members* or by *one or more* managers. In most states, if the LLC is member-managed, each member has *one vote,* unless the articles of organization provide otherwise.

1. **Member-managed:** If the LLC is member-managed, the members can bind the LLC by acts that are within the scope of their authority. The same is true of managers in a manager-run LLC. The LLC governing documents (the articles of organization and the operating agreement) will show who has actual authority and the limits upon that authority. (Because the delegation of authority is governed by the principles of Agency, the student should refer to the discussion of an agent's power to bind a principal; *supra*, p. 47.)

III. FORMATION

A. **Forming an LLC:** Most LLC statutes require that there be *at least two members,* though a number of statutes now permit one-person LLC's. Depending on the state of organization, existence of the LLC begins when the articles of organization are filed, or when the Secretary of State accepts the articles of organization, or later (usually not more than 60 days), if so specified in the articles.

1. **How to form:** To form an LLC, an organizer must file articles of organization. Typical state statutes require that articles of organization contain the following:

   a. **Name:** The name of the LLC and the address of its principal place of business.

   b. **Purpose:** The purposes for which the LLC is organized. This may be generally stated, such as "the transaction of any or all lawful businesses for which an LLC may be organized under [the applicable act]."

   c. **Agent's name:** The name of its registered agent and the address of its registered office.

d. **Manager('s) name(s):** The name(s) and business address(es) of the initial manager or managers, if the LLC is to be managed by a manager or managers.

e. **Initial members:** The names and addresses of the initial members, if management of the LLC is to be retained, in whole or in part, by the members.

f. **Dissolution date:** The latest date upon which the LLC is to dissolve and other dissolution events, if any.

g. **Organizers:** The name and address of each organizer.

h. **Other provisions:** Any other provisions, consistent with law, for regulation of the internal affairs of the LLC, including any provisions that by law are required or permitted to be set out in the LLC's operating agreement. *See*, for example, Illinois: 805 ILCS 180/5-5 (1994).

2. **Language required in name:** The name of the LLC must contain the words "limited liability company" or "L.L.C." It must not contain any of the following words: "Corporation," "Corp.," "Incorporated," "Inc.," "Ltd.," "Co.," "Limited Partnership" or "L.P.," which are commonly used to designate a corporation or limited partnership. Additionally, the name must not violate any copyright, trademark, or common law or statute prohibiting unfair competition or unfair trade practice.

B. **Permitted LLC purposes:** LLCs can be formed to carry on any lawful business, although individual states may impose more specific restrictions. For example, several states, such as Oklahoma and Nevada, forbid LLCs to conduct business in banking or insurance. The broad purposes for which LLCs can be formed suggest that, unlike partnerships, they ***do not have to be organized for profit.***

C. **Requirement of registered agents, office, and records:** Each LLC must ***maintain continuously a registered agent and office*** in the state in which it is formed. LLC statutes typically require that at its registered office or principal place of business, each LLC ***must keep certain records, including:***

1. **Members' information:** the ***name and address of each member,*** with the date of initial membership, the amount of cash each contributed, a description and statement of value of other services and property contributed or committed;

2. **Articles of organization:** a copy of the ***articles of organization,*** including any amendments and any powers of attorney;

3. **Tax returns:** copies of tax returns for the three most recent years (federal, state and local);

4. **Written operating agreement:** copies of the current written operating agreement, including any amendments;

5. **Financial statements:** financial statements for the three most recent years;

6. **Contribution agreement:** a writing prepared or authorized by the managers (or by the members if there are no managers) which states:

   • times at which, or events upon which, additional contributions will be made;

   • any right of a member to receive distributions, including the return of any capital contribution; and

   • any power of a member to assign his membership to another party.

   A separate contribution agreement is unnecessary if its terms are already contained in the articles of organization or operating agreement.

D. **Operating agreements:** Although not required, *operating agreements are common to LLCs.* They are analogous to corporate bylaws and specify many details of operation not included in the LLC's articles of organization. Unless the articles provide otherwise, LLC members have the power to adopt or amend the operating agreement.

IV. LIABILITY

A. **Treated like corporate shareholders:** Members of LLCs are generally treated like corporate shareholders for liability purposes. As such, they are generally not separately liable for the company's debts or obligations.

   There are some *exceptions,* however, involving circumstances under which LLC members *can* be liable for the company's debts or obligations:

   1. **Liability for own misconduct.** LLC members and managers remain liable for their own tortious conduct, including malpractice.

   2. **Exception for capital contributions in case of bankruptcy:** LLC members are personally liable for the capital contributions they agreed to make in the operating agreement or in any other document between them and the LLC, and firm creditors can enforce

that liability in the event the LLC files for bankruptcy. *See* Ribstein, § 14.04.

3. **Exception for improper distributions:** In addition, members (or managers, in a manager-operated LLC) can be liable for any distributions that they authorize *in violation of either (a) the statute controlling the LLC, or (b) the articles of organization or operating agreement.* However, in most states, they will not be held liable if they relied, in good faith, upon the LLC's balance sheet and profit and loss statement, so long as these documents were (a) represented as correct by the person in charge of the records, or (b) certified by an independent public or certified public accountant as reflecting fairly the financial condition of the LLC. *See* the Illinois Prototype Limited Liability Company Act (1992).

4. **Piercing the LLC veil:** LLC members can be personally liable also under a theory similar to that of "piercing the corporate veil" (such as if they fail to observe the requisite formalities, or undercapitalize the venture). *Abu-Nassar v. Elders Futures, Inc.,* 1991 U.S. Dist. LEXIS 2794 (S.D.N.Y. Mar. 28, 1991).

   a. **Facts:** The Abu-Nassars were the principal officers and sole shareholders of Informative Investment Group, Ltd. ("Infovest"), a Lebanese LLC in the business of introducing potential customers to full-service brokers in exchange for a commission. Infovest became embroiled in a contract dispute with Elders, a full-service broker, with which Infovest had contracted to refer customers exclusively. Infovest sued Elders, seeking damages. Elders counterclaimed, claiming the Abu-Nassars were really the "alter ego" of Infovest and should be held personally liable for the debts of the company.

   b. **Failure to satisfy statutory requirements:** In denying Infovest's motion for summary judgment, the court first noted that LLC members may be liable for obligations even above their initial capital contributions *if the statutory requirements for an LLC are not satisfied.* Failure to observe formalities, coupled with *undercapitalization,* substantially increases the likelihood that LLC members will be held personally liable.

      i. **California statute:** Some state statutes explicitly prohibit "piercing the LLC veil" for certain actions. For example, the California LLC statute specifically provides that failure to hold member meetings or to observe company formalities will *not* cause LLC members to be personally liable.

   c. **Piercing the veil:** The New York court in *Abu-Nassar* found that the doctrine of "piercing the corporate veil," commonly used in corporate law, **applies equally** to LLCs. According to the court, the following factors must be considered in deciding whether to pierce the limited liability veil:

- **intermingling of personal and company funds** and siphoning of company funds by a member;

- **failure to observe company formalities** and to keep proper books and records;

- **failure to distribute funds to members** as agreed;

- **inadequate capitalization;**

- **insolvency;** and

- **perpetuation of fraud** by members in maintaining the LLC form.

The court also noted that this list is **not exhaustive,** and that "as a general rule alter ego liability [should] be imposed when doing so would achieve an **equitable result."** (Emphasis added).

B. Exposure to promoters' liability: Once the Secretary of State accepts the articles of organization, members are generally protected from liability for premature commencement of business. In many states, including Florida and Texas, engaging in the business before acceptance of the articles can expose members to promoters' liability, at least if they are actively involved in the business.

1. Delaware law: In accepting LLC articles of organization, the Delaware Secretary of State will not inquire whether the LLC has fully complied with the filing statute. Instead, the LLC is considered properly formed if there was "substantial compliance" with the act at the time the certificate of formation was filed.

V.   TAX TREATMENT OF THE LLC

A. Desirability of partnership taxation: A principal reason for forming an LLC rather than a corporation is to achieve partnership taxation. Partnership taxation means that, differently from a Subchapter C Corporation, **only one level** of taxation is applicable. Members are taxed on their share of LLC income at their **individual rates, not corporate rates.** The income keeps its character; that is, capital gains remain capital gains, and ordinary income remains ordinary income.

In addition, with partnership tax status, members can claim the losses and deductions of the LLC on their individual tax returns (subject to passive loss limitation rules). This is particularly useful in start-up ventures that often lose money in their early years.

B. "Check-the-Box" entity classification: Under Treasury Regulations effective January 1, 1997, an unincorporated business entity with two or more members generally can elect whether to be taxed as a partnership or a corporation. Treas. Reg. § 301.7701 (1991) (as amended in 1997 by T.D. 8697). In addition, the IRS will not tax a one member LLC as a corporation unless the owner elects that tax treatment. In the same way, an unincorporated domestic business with one owner will be taxed as a sole proprietorship (which shares tax advantages similar to partnership treatment), and not as a corporation, unless corporate treatment is elected.

C. Kintner Regulations: Until January 1, 1997, under the so-called Kintner Regulations, an LLC could get the advantages of partnership tax status *only* if it had at least *two of the following four partnership* features: *(a) unlimited liability, (b) lack of continuity of life, (c) restrictions on transferability of interests and (d) decentralized management.* Treas. Reg. § 301.7701-2(e)(1) (1991); Rev. Proc. 95-10, 1995-1 C.B. 501.

1. **Unlimited liability:** Usually, LLC members want *limited* liability; Under the Kintner formula, limited liability could not be achieved without classification as a corporation. Therefore, to be taxed as partnerships, most LLCs had to prevail on *at least two* of the three remaining Kintner elements.

2. **Continuity of life:** Corporations typically have "continuity of life" in a legal sense; they cannot be dissolved at will. Partnerships typically *can* be dissolved at will and *do not* have "continuity of life." (*See supra*, p. 234.) Since LLC members usually wanted the LLC to be classified as a *partnership* for tax purposes, they wanted to avoid being considered as having continuity of life. Generally, the LLC was considered *not* to have continuity of life if, under its operating agreement or by statute, it could be dissolved upon the death, insanity, bankruptcy, retirement, resignation or expulsion of any member.

3. **Free transferability of interest:** In a corporation, stockholder interests are freely transferable; stockholders are generally able to sell their shares to anyone. If an LLC provided that its interests could be freely transferred, it would be classified as a corporation. To achieve partnership status, it was forced to limit the transferability of partnership interests.

4. **Decentralized management:** Centralized management is a feature of corporations; the officers run the corporation under the management of the board of directors. Decentralized management is a feature of partnerships, with several or all the partners running the

business. An LLC was considered to have the decentralized organization required of a partnership if member-managers owned in the aggregate at least 20% of its total interests, or if the IRS determined that the members really controlled the LLC.

VI. FINANCES

A. Flexibility in distributions: LLCs can be ***very*** flexible in allowing division of capital, profits and distributions in any way the members specify in the operating agreement. If the agreement does not specify, the statute of the state of organization controls these divisions.

1. **State variations:** The default rules regarding allocation of profits and losses among LLC members vary greatly from state to state. In most states, such as Alabama, distributions, profits and losses are determined according to the value of members' ***initial contributions as adjusted*** by their subsequent contributions or withdrawals.

   In other states, like Colorado, distributions and allocations of profits and losses are made in proportion to the members' ***capital contributions without deductions*** for subsequent returns of capital.

   Still other states, such as Louisiana, provide that in the absence of an agreement to the contrary, each member shall receive equal distributions and be allocated an ***equal*** portion of profits and losses.

2. **Flexibility compared with corporations:** LLCs offer greater flexibility than corporations in several ways. For example, like partners in a partnership, LLC members can contribute ***any*** kind of service, cash or asset in exchange for their interest in the LLC. ***Unlike corporate shareholders*** in some states, LLC members can even agree to contribute ***future*** services. In addition, LLCs can issue interests to different persons at different times without concern about their giving equivalent or adequate consideration.

   LLCs also have more flexibility than corporations in their ability to make distributions. By using appropriate language in the LLC governing documents(s), the LLC can easily specify various rights of distribution or liquidation without having different classes of stock.

VII. ASSIGNMENT OF MEMBERSHIP INTERESTS

A. Right to assign interest: Each member's interest in the LLC is his ***personal property***. Without approval of any other members, any member can assign his right to receive the profits of the business. However, a member generally ***cannot assign*** his right to participate in the ***management*** of the business unless all the other LLC members approve. If members want to require simple majority approval for the transfer of management rights, they can do so in the articles of organization.

VIII. DISTRIBUTION AND RESIGNATION

A. **Right to receive distributions:** Generally, an LLC member may receive distributions

- upon the ***happening of events*** specified in the articles of organization or the operating agreement;

- ***as the managers specify*** (in a manager-run LLC); or

- ***as the members specify***, if there are no managers.

B. **Right to resign:** An LLC member can resign ***at any time.*** However, if she violates the articles of organization or operating agreement in doing so, she is liable for damages caused by the breach. The LLC then may offset the damage amount from the amount otherwise owed to the resigning LLC member. The resigning LLC member may also be liable for additional damages or for other state law remedies.

1. **Distributions upon resignation:** Upon resignation, a resigning member is entitled to receive as a distribution the amount specified in the articles of organization or operating agreement. If no amount was specified, the member is entitled to receive the fair value of her interest as of the date of resignation.

2. **Form of distribution:** Unless otherwise specified in the articles of organization or operating agreement, a resigning LLC member has no right to receive a distribution other than in cash. At the time a resigning member becomes entitled to receive a distribution, her status changes to that of a creditor of the LLC. She then has all the remedies otherwise available to a creditor.

ESSAY EXAM
QUESTIONS AND ANSWERS

The following are some sample essay exam questions dealing with various doctrines of Agency & Partnership. They will be useful for testing your knowledge and for practicing exam-taking. You should write out your answers fully in essay form and then check them against the sample answers. Note that while the sample answers demonstrate a good way to approach the questions, they are not the only good way.

Here are some suggestions for answering an essay exam question:

1. Remember that you are taking an essay examination. The complete essay examination answer must contain not only the "answer" to the question, but of greater importance, your **analysis,** the applicable **black letter law,** and an **explanation** of how you applied the black letter law to the facts and reasoned to the "answer."

2. Begin by **reading the question** thoroughly.

3. Next, **reread the question.** Read it as it is written; if you don't understand it, read it again until you do.

4. As you read, spot **key concepts, ideas and issues,** and the applicable **legal** principles and rules.

5. **Organize your thoughts** into an orderly, logical sequence.

6. **Analyze** the fact pattern and the key issues, terms, principles and concepts which you have spotted.

7. **Work out a game plan** for your answer, including the sequence of the things you are going to write about, the priority for each item, the space to be allocated to each and an allocation of your time for writing.

8. Make a brief **word-phrase outline** of your proposed answer.

9. Spend 25% of your time for each question on steps 1-8 **before you begin to write** the answer. An organized answer can be written quickly. If you are not organized when you begin your answer, you will waste time adding issues, crossing out parts of your answer, and writing too much about minor issues.

10. Begin writing with a short, clear, **decisive** sentence, answering the question precisely as it is asked. For example, if the question reads: "Rule on plaintiff's motion," your answer should begin: "Motion granted," or "Objection overruled." The balance of your answer should explain how you reasoned to that conclusion.

11. Write your answer in **clear, professional, lawyer-like English** using accurate **legal terminology** when appropriate. Remember: This is an essay examination in the English language, at the graduate level, in a learned profession.

12. Be certain to include **full sentences of black letter law** on each of the key issues. Failure to do this is the most frequent mistake made by students.

13. **Do not merely rehash the facts.** A complete answer requires analysis, black letter law and a description of how the black letter law applies to the specific facts in the question. Rehashing of the facts is not enough.

14. **Use short, complete, simple sentences.** Avoid long, wandering, convoluted sentences which deal with more than one issue.

15. **Reason to a lawyer-like conclusion.** If you have time and space, add a wrap-up concluding sentence to your answer.

16. **Reread your answer** to make certain that you have made no careless errors or omissions, and to ensure clarity and completeness of your answer.

17. **Use the full time allotted** for the question — no more and no less.

ESSAY QUESTIONS

QUESTION 1 (One hour 30 minutes)

Paul, a world renown karate fighter, was scheduled to compete in the karate world championships. Paul told his friend Al that his chief rival, Short-fuse, had a very quick temper. He told Al that if Short-fuse could be provoked into a fight, Short-fuse might be arrested and that that might eliminate him as a competitor in the championships. He told Al that if he could accomplish that, Paul would forever be in his debt.

Afraid to face Short-fuse on even terms, Al drove his car to Ace's house to purchase some brass knuckles. On route, Al negligently drove his car into Driver's car, injuring Driver.

Trainer, Paul's trainer and a friend of Ace, learned that Al was planning to nail Short-fuse with brass knuckles. Trainer did not tell Paul about the brass knuckles because he was afraid that Paul might get overconfident if he knew that his chief rival would almost certainly be knocked out of the competition.

After purchasing the brass knuckles, Al tracked down Short- fuse. Al began hurling insults at Short-fuse but without any effect. Realizing that insults would not work, Al sucker-punched Short-fuse, using his brass knuckles. Short-fuse was hospitalized and missed the competition. Paul competed and won the world championship. Paul then went to the ceremony, where he received his trophy for winning first place.

Al then told Paul what he had done and demanded compensation. Paul shouted: "Are you crazy!" Paul refused to pay him anything and threw him out of the room.

1. Is Paul liable to Driver for Al's negligence?

2. Is Paul liable to Short-fuse for Al's injuring him?

3. Does Al have a claim against Paul or does Paul have a claim against Al?

QUESTION 2 (One Hour)

Alice Associate worked as an associate for Paul Partner at Partner's law firm. Associate had a one year contract which provided that she could be fired before the end of the year only for good cause. Partner fired associate because his wife was suspicious that Partner and Associate were having an affair. (They were not.)

After she was fired, Associate hired Court Reporter to take a deposition (pre-trial statement under oath). During her employment at Partners' firm, Associate had hired Court Reporter to take depositions. Neither Partner nor Associate told Court Reporter that Associate had been fired by Partner and was now on her own. Associate also contacted clients on whose cases she had worked and gave them her new address and telephone number. She told them that they could choose to continue to use her as their new attorney or they could use someone else at Partner's firm.

1. Is Associate liable to Partner for what she has done?

2. Does Associate have a claim against Partner?

3. Does Court Reporter have a claim against the firm?

4. Does Court Reporter have a claim against Associate?

QUESTION 3 (2 hours)

A, B and C orally formed a partnership to buy and sell real property. The partnership bought property for clients from whom they received a commission. In 1994, the partnership also purchased Blackacre for the partnership with a view toward later resale. On two occasions they purchased property and obtained mortgages from First Bank.

On March 1, 1996, C secretly began contacting firm clients and discussed with them the possibility of their becoming clients of his at a new firm. A got wind of what C was up to and told him: "You are behaving outrageously and anybody who puts his own interests ahead of the partnership should leave." C then left the firm never to return, taking a couple of clients with him. A told B what happened. Thereafter, A ran the business himself with B's acquiescence. B became basically a silent partner. C knew that A was running the business but did nothing since he had already obtained a couple of the firm's clients and was willing to let sleeping dogs lie.

A then took on a new partner, D. A bought an additional piece of real estate and obtained a mortgage on the property from First Bank. First Bank did not know, at the time it granted the mortgage, that A and D were running the business by themselves with B as a silent partner. The property covered by First Bank's mortgage has declined in value.

Blackacre, which the partnership had originally purchased for its own account increased in value from $50,000 to $100,000 by March 1, 1996. By March 1, 1997, Blackacre was worth $500,000.

C's business faltered and he brought an action seeking to compel liquidation of the partnership. In particular, C sought his share of the increased value of the property held by the partnership for its own account. A and B counterclaimed against C. First Bank intervened and sued the partnership and A, B, C and D personally. The Bank would like to hold the partners personally liable if the partnership assets are insufficient to pay the mortgage. A would like to continue the partnership. In the alternative, he would like to be compensated for winding up the business.

Discuss the rights and liabilities of the parties.

ESSAY ANSWERS

ANSWER TO QUESTION 1

In determining whether Paul bears any responsibility for Al's conduct, the first question is whether Al is Paul's agent. In order to establish a principal-agent relationship, an agent must act on behalf of a principal and subject to the principal's control and the relationship must be consensual. Rest. (2d) § 1. In this case, Paul and Al agreed that Al would work on Paul's behalf. He was subject to Paul's direction and control. Paul told him that he wanted Short-fuse eliminated as a competitor and Al agreed to help. No consideration is required to establish an agency relationship.

1. Paul's liability for Al's negligent driving

In order for Paul to be vicariously liable for Al's negligence, Al must not only be Paul's agent but also his servant. The master-servant relationship requires that the master (employer) exercise or have the right to exercise detailed control over the physical movements of the servant (employee). Subject to the exceptions discussed below, an employer is not vicariously liable for the torts of his independent contractor. An independent contractor is "a person who contracts with another to do something for him but who is not controlled by the other nor subject to the other's right to control with respect to this physical conduct in the performance of the undertaking." Rest. (2d) § 2(3). It is questionable whether Al was Paul's servant. Paul did not control the details of what Al would do. *See* Rest. (2d) § 220 (2) (a)-(j). He did not know when or precisely how Al would provoke Short-fuse.

One of the factors cited by the Restatement of Agency in determining whether someone is a servant or an independent contractor is: who supplies the instrumentalities and tools for the job — the employer or the workman? Rest. (2d) § 220 (2) (e). Al drove his own car, and there was no arrangement for him to be compensated for driving the vehicle. *See Soderback v. Townsend*, 644 P.2d 640 (Or. Ct. App.), *petition for review denied*, 650 P.2d 927 (Or. 1982) (P hired A to negotiate gas and oil leases. A had been an independent broker for 26 years. P told A the vicinities in which he wanted A to acquire leases but did not give him specific travel routes. A's schedule was up to him. A was held not to be P's servant; therefore, P was not liable for A's negligence in causing an auto accident). In our case, it was not even clear that Al would actually go through with provoking Short-fuse. Under these circumstances, it seems doubtful that Paul could be liable for Al's negligence based on Al's being his servant.

However, even if Al is an independent contractor, Paul could be liable for his negligence if the case fits within one of the exceptions, such as conduct which is inherently dangerous or specifically authorized. This situation fits into neither. Al's driving to purchase brass knuckles was not specifically authorized. Paul only told Al to provoke Short-Fuse. Paul did not give Al specific instructions to drive to Ace's house to purchase brass knuckles.

Neither was driving to Ace's house inherently dangerous. Whether an act is inherently dangerous is determined by the likelihood of injury when the act is performed properly, *Hixon v. Sherwin-Williams Co.*, 671 F.2d 1005 (7th Cir. 1982) (laying of linoleum is not inherently dangerous when performed properly). Driving, like laying linoleum and unlike dynamite blasting, is not considered an inherently dangerous activity.

If Al is viewed as Paul's servant, Paul will be liable if Paul's conduct is within the scope of his employment. Rest. (2d) §228(1). If a servant goes off on a substantial *frolic* of his own, he may be viewed as outside the scope of employment. On the other hand, if the deviation from employment was only a minor *detour*, he may be viewed as being within the scope of employment. In this case it is likely to be a jury question as to whether Al was within the scope of employment. One factor would be how far Ace's house was from the route that Al would have to take to go to Short-fuse's house. If it was directly on the route or at least near to it, he might be viewed as having taken only a minor detour. On the other hand, if he was a great distance away, he might be viewed as having been on a frolic of his own. *See Prince v. Atchison, Topeka & Santa Fe Ry. Co.*, 395 N.E.2d 592 (Ill. App. Ct. 1979).

Another consideration in determining whether Al was acting within the scope of his employment is whether he was acting to serve his own purposes or Paul's when he went to get the brass knuckles. Under the dual purpose doctrine, if a servant is partly furthering his master's business and partly serving his own interests, he generally will be held to be acting within the scope of his employment. Al's act of driving to get Ace's brass knuckles could be viewed as partly serving his master's business because hurting Short-fuse would serve Paul's objective of getting Short-fuse out of the way. Even if Al were partly motivated by the need to protect himself, as long as he was partly serving his master's interest, he could be viewed as acting within the scope of his employment.

However, in this case, Paul would probably not be liable for Al's negligence because Al is not his servant and the act of driving is not inherently dangerous.

2. Paul's liability for Al's injuring Short-fuse

The next question is whether Paul is liable for the injuries which Al inflicted on Short-fuse. If Paul were considered an employee of Paul, Paul would probably be held liable on a *respondeat superior* basis. The conduct would be viewed as within the scope of employment. Even intentional torts can be within the scope of employment, depending on how serious they are and whether the master could reasonably anticipate them. In this case, given what Paul has told Al to do — provoke Short-fuse — fighting could reasonably be anticipated in the same way as with a tavern bouncer who uses excessive force to remove an unruly patron. *Novick v. Gouldsberry*, 173 F.2d 496 (9th Cir. 1949). *Cf. Mary M v. City of Los Angeles*, 814 P.2d 1341 (Cal. 1991) (the court found that a police officer who properly stopped an individual on suspicion of drunken diving, made her take a field sobriety test, drove her home and then raped her, was acting within the scope of his employment. The court found that the officer's initial actions were clearly within the scope of his employment). Under these circumstances, the use of brass knuckles by Al probably could be anticipated. Paul's best defense remains that Al was an independent contractor and not his servant.

However, Paul could still be liable even if Al was an independent contractor. A principal can be liable for the torts of his independent contractor if he specifically authorizes the activity. Rest. (2d) § 215. Paul could reasonably argue that he did not authorize Al to do what he did. He only intended that Al exchange words with Short-fuse. This is debatable. One could argue on Short-fuse's behalf that "provoke" is ambiguous and Al was impliedly authorized to do what he did. One could argue on Paul's behalf that when the conduct is an intentional tort, courts will not be quick to assume that the principal has authorized the activity. Short-fuse bears the burden of proving that Paul authorized Al's conduct. This is likely to be a jury question.

Finally, the question arises whether Paul ratified Al's conduct. Ratification is defined as a principal's affirmation of a purported agent's prior unauthorized act; ratification occurs when the act is treated as though it were originally authorized. Paul's act of accepting the trophy could be viewed as a manifestation of assent to Al's conduct. A principal cannot ratify only part of a transaction — accepting the good part and rejecting the bad. *Rakestraw v. Rodrigues*, 8 Cal. 3d 67, 500 P.2d 1401, 104 Cal. Rptr. 57 (1972). If Al's conduct is viewed as connected to Paul's winning the competition, Paul can not accept the benefits (the trophy) while rejecting the burdens (Al's conduct). On the other hand, Paul could argue that Al's conduct was not part of the same transaction as the competition. He could argue that he would have won regardless of whether Al punched Short-fuse. His argument would be that he earned the victory, and his acceptance of the trophy in no way constituted an affirmation of Al's conduct.

For ratification to be effective, the principal's action must be done with knowledge of the material facts of the agent's conduct. *Lewis v. Cable*, 107 F. Supp. 196 (W.D. Pa. 1952). As the purported agent, Al cannot be the source of imputed knowledge. One could argue that Trainer's knowledge should be imputed to Paul. However, an agent's knowledge is only imputed to his principal if the agent has a duty to reveal the information to his principal. Rest. (2d) § 272. In this case, Paul could argue that Trainer had a duty not to tell Paul for fear of upsetting him before the fight. This would not explain Trainer's not telling Paul after the fight. At that point, arguably a duty to disclose existed. If so, Paul may be viewed as having imputed knowledge of Al's conduct. As discussed above, the question would then be whether Paul's acceptance of the trophy constituted an affirmation of Al's conduct.

Alternatively, if Trainer's knowledge is imputed to Paul before Al punched Short-fuse, then, when Paul failed to clarify his instructions to Al, he either authorized Al to punch Short-fuse or is estopped to deny that he did so.

3. Whether Al has a claim against Paul or Paul against Al

A person who commits a tort against a third person is not relieved of liability to the third person merely because he is an agent or servant of someone else. Rest (2d) § 343. Therefore, Al is liable to Driver for his own negligence. An employer who is made vicariously liable for the torts of his servant has a claim against his servant for indemnification. Therefore, in the event that Paul were held vicariously liable for Al's negligent driving, he would have an indemnification claim against Al.

On the other hand, if Paul were held liable for Al's having punched Short-fuse, that liability would likely be based on his having impliedly authorized the conduct. Therefore, he would not be able to obtain indemnification from Al. Rest. (2d) § 401, comment d ("if the principal authorizes a tort, either advertently or inadvertently, he cannot recover for harm resulting to him from it.); Rest. (2d) § 415.

Al would not be able to get indemnification from Paul for having punched Short-fuse. In general, an agent can obtain indemnification for losses or damages resulting from carrying out the principal's instructions. However, where an agent commits a seriously wrongful act, public policy prevents him from obtaining indemnification. Rest (2d) § 438, comment a.

ANSWER TO QUESTION 2

Associate's liability to partner

Associate is liable to Partner for hiring Court Reporter. A principal has the power to fire an agent at any time, though he may be liable for breach of contract by doing so. Associate's actual authority to hire Court Reporter terminated when she was fired. An agent's apparent authority may continue after the termination of the agency relationship with respect to third parties who have previously dealt with the agent if no notice is given to those parties of the contract's termination. Therefore, Associate bound Partner by entering into a contract with Court Reporter, who had no notice. Since she lacked actual authority to enter into the contract, she breached a duty to Partner and would be obligated to *indemnify* Partner for the amount of Partner's liability to Court Reporter. Rest. (2d) § 401.

Although the issue is not free from doubt, Associate may not be liable to Partner for contacting former clients on whose cases she had worked. An employee may compete in business with her former employer after the employment is terminated, but may not use confidential information when doing so. Associate did not solicit former clients while she was at her old firm. *See, Adler, Barish, Daniels, Levin, & Creskoff v. Epstein*, 482 Pa. 416, 393 A.2d 1175 (1978), *cert. denied and appeal dismissed*, 442 U.S. 907 (1979). Moreover, she did not steal a written customer list. Nor did she contact clients on cases that she had not worked on. She could argue that clients had a right to decide whether to continue to use her as their attorney.

However, in those cases for which Associate was not the attorney primarily responsible, Partner would have a better argument that Associate breached her fiduciary duty to him. Some courts may find that Associate did breach her fiduciary duty because she exploited the confidential relationship that Partner had helped create for her at the firm.

Partner's liability to Associate

Partner would be liable in damages to Associate for breach of contract. Partner had the *power* but not the *right* to fire her without cause. Firing Associate because his wife believed that Associate was having an affair with him was not a valid cause. Since there was no valid cause, Partner is liable for breach of contract. Associate would be limited to the remedy of damages.

Court reporter's claim against Partner and associate

Court reporter has a claim against Partner. Partner hired Associate and gave her the actual and apparent authority to hire Court Reporter for her cases. She was a general agent since she had continuing authority to hire Court Reporter for a series of transactions. Rest. (2d) § 3. When Partner fired her, Associate's actual authority was terminated. However, as discussed above, since no notice was given to Court Reporter of the termination of Associate's authority, Associate continued to have apparent authority to deal with Court Reporter. *Courtney v. G. A. Linaker Co.*, 293 S.W. 723 (Ark. 1927).

Therefore, when Associate contacted court reporter, who reasonably believed that she was still working for Partner, Partner was bound by her contract. Although Partner might argue that his client, not he, should be liable to Court Reporter, custom dictates that attorneys are liable unless they specifically tell court reporters to look to the client and not to them for payment. *Ingram v. Lupo*, 726 S.W.2d 791 (Mo. Ct. App. 1987).

Associate is liable to Court Reporter for breach of warranty that she possessed the authority as Partner's agent to hire Reporter. *Husky Indus., Inc. v. Craig Indus., Inc.,* 618 S.W.2d 458 (Mo. Ct. App. 1981).

ANSWER TO QUESTION 3

The first issue is whether the partnership was legally formed, since there was only an oral agreement among A, B and C. A partnership is an association of two or more persons to carry on as co-owners of a business for profit. UPA § 6. A partnership arises by agreement among associates that it shall exist. The contract can be express or implied, oral or written. In our case there was an express oral agreement to form a partnership. This created a valid partnership. Partnerships can be formed orally. Under the majority rule, no writing is required even though the partnership was in the business of buying and selling real estate. A contract to buy real estate, of course, would have to be in writing to satisfy the Statute of Frauds.

The second issue is what event caused the dissolution of the partnership. UPA § 29 provides that the ***dissolution*** of a partnership is the change in the relation of the partnership caused by any partner's, ceasing to be associated in the carrying on of the business. On dissolution, a partnership does not immediately terminate, but continues until the winding up phase is completed. UPA § 30. UPA sets forth the causes of dissolution other than by formal court proceedings. C's act of secretly taking firm clients, by itself, probably would not constitute a dissolution of the partnership, since that is not one of the events for dissolution set forth in UPA § 31. However, it would clearly constitute a breach of C's fiduciary duty to the partnership. *See Town & Country House & Home Service v. Newberry*, 147 N.Y.S.2d 550, *aff'd* 147 N.E.2d 724 (1955).

Under UPA § 32, a court can decree a judicial dissolution when a partner has been guilty of such conduct as to prejudice the business or when a partner willfully breaches the partnership agreement or otherwise conducts himself in a manner that makes it impracticable to continue to conduct the business in partnership with him. However, in the absence of a judicial decree of dissolution under UPA § 32, C's act by itself did not constitute the express will of a partner to leave the partnership or any other ground for dissolution under UPA § 31.

In the instant case, since A and B did not seek a court dissolution after learning of C's conduct, the partnership was not dissolved at that point. (Note, there is some question as to whether C's conduct was sufficient to allow A and B to seek a judicial dissolution under UPA § 32, since the partnership was still profitable. A and B, however, could have argued that the serious nature of C's misconduct, the fact that it was done secretly, and the potential for wrecking the business all warranted a judicial dissolution under UPA § 32.)

A's statement to C that "you are behaving outrageously and anybody who puts his own interests over those of the partnership should leave," also probably did not constitute a dissolution. It probably should be viewed as a warning to C to behave properly. If A had actually ousted C from the partnership at that point without having sought a judicial dissolution under UPA § 32, it would be viewed as a dissolution by the express will of a partner when there was no definite term. Then, C would have been entitled to all the remedies of a partner, which would have included the right to insist on a liquidation at that point. *See Lange v. Bartlett*, 360 N.W.2d 702 (Wis. Ct. App. 1984). (If a partner is ousted in violation of a partnership agreement, he is entitled to damages for breach of the partnership agreement. UPA § 38 (2)(a)(I). In this case, since this was a partnership at will and not for a definite term, A would not be liable for breach of a partnership agreement by expelling C.)

C is also entitled to be paid for the value of his partnership interest, plus his pro-rata share of interest or profits earned by the partnership after his ouster. UPA §§ 38, 42. (Although UPA § 42 by its terms seems to be limited to situations where a partner dies or retires, case law has applied it to situations involving expulsions of a partner. *Wikestrom v. Davis*, 315 P.2d 597, 606 (Or. 1957); *Vangel v. Vangel*, 291 P.2d 25, 27 (Cal. 1955).) If C was ousted by A, and C did not object to continuation of the partnership, C would still have the right to be paid the full value of his interest. The value of C's interest would not be reduced for damages unless his conduct in leaving and taking firm business with him were viewed as a dissolution in contravention of the partnership agreement. (*See* discussion below.) If C were not guilty of wrongful conduct he would also be entitled to his share of the good will of the partnership. Good will means a well founded expectation that business and patronage will continue. In this case, that portion of the business connected with purchasing property for resale for clients would seem to have a good will component because clients would continue to seek out the firm in reliance on its reputation.

If C were ousted, he would also be entitled, at his option, to his pro-rata share of interest or profits earned by the partnership after his ouster. *Blut v. Katz*, 99 A.2d 785 (N.J. 1953). Once C lets A continue the partnership, regardless of who caused the dissolution, C would not be entitled to any share of the post-dissolution increase in the value of the partnership property. He would, however, be entitled to share in the increase in the value of the property which occurred up through the dissolution. *See Oliker v. Gershunoff*, 241 Cal. Rptr. 415 (Cal. Ct. App. 1987). *See also King v. Evans*, 791 S.W.2d 531 (Tex. 1990) (non-continuing partner not entitled to enjoy benefit of any post-dissolution appreciation of assets). If C had demanded that the partners wind up the business, he would have been entitled to the value of the business at the time of liquidation.)

However, it appears that the partnership may have been dissolved by C's leaving and not returning. UPA § 31 provides that dissolution can be caused at any time by the express will of any partner when there is no specific term of the partnership. In this case, the partnership is not for a specific term. Therefore, C's leaving may be viewed as his express will to terminate. C's conduct may be viewed as dissolution by the express will of a partner. *See Girard Bank v. Haley*, 332 A.2d 443 (Pa. 1975). The fact that D was added as a new partner further supports the view that the old partnership was dissolved and a new one formed. *Fairway Development Co. v. Title Ins. Co. of Minnesota*, 621 F. Supp. 120 (N.D. Ohio 1985). Thereafter, C's letting A and B run the partnership may be viewed as implied consent to a continuation under UPA § 42. *See*

Oliker v. Gershunoff. Then, under UPA § 42, C would be limited to his pro-rata share of interest or profits earned during the period after the dissolution plus the value of his interest at the time of dissolution.

UPA § 38 allows partners to recover damages from a partner who dissolves the partnership in breach of the partnership agreement. Although it is not clear, there is some authority holding that C's conduct in beaching his fiduciary duty and then leaving would give A and B the right to treat C's conduct as a wrongful dissolution under UPA § 38 (2)(b). *Page v. Page*, 359 P.2d 41 (Cal. 1961). If so, then they would be entitled to damages from C and could unanimously agree to continue the partnership without him. *See Infusaid Corp. v. Intermedics Infusaid, Inc.*, 739 F.2d 661 (1st Cir. 1984). However, they would be obligated either to pay C for the value of his interest as of the date of dissolution or secure payment by means of a bond. UPA § 38 (2) (b). If C breached his fiduciary duty, he would not be entitled to compensation for the value of the partnership's good will. Although A and B did not post a bond, laches or estoppel may preclude C from forcing them to liquidate. *See Oliker v. Gershunoff*. C may now be entitled to receive the value of his interest, or at least force A and B to post a bond to protect his interest and to require that they indemnify him against all present or future partnership liabilities. UPA § 38 (2) (b). And, at some point, C will be able to insist on payment in cash for the value of his interest at dissolution. *Oliker v. Gershunoff*. C will also be able to obtain interest on his share from the date of dissolution. Instead of interest, C may be able to elect to obtain profits attributable to the use of his portion of the partnership assets. UPA § 42. However, under *Blut v. Katz*, if C is viewed as not "consenting" to the continuation of the business, he will be denied the right to receive profits.

Under UPA § 37, unless otherwise agreed, the partners who have not wrongfully dissolved the partnership have the right to wind it up. A and B, but not C, would have the right to wind up the partnership if C's conduct wrongfully caused the dissolution. A could petition the court to be the sole person to wind it up based on the fact that neither B nor C was involved in the last phases of business. (D would not be able to wind up the former partnership since he was not a member of the partnership.)

Partners other than surviving partners cannot obtain compensation for winding up the partnership (UPA § 18(f)), though they may be able to obtain compensation for work in continuing the partnership, if they do so with the consent or acquiescence of the other partners. With regard to A's claim for compensation for his services, A could argue that his continuation of the partnership was with the acquiescence of B and C. His claim for compensation would be enhanced if his work resulted in profits. *See Lange v. Bartlett*, 360 N.W.2d 702 (Wis. Ct. App. 1984). However, if a court determines that A wrongfully ousted C or that A's continuation of the business was wrongful, he would be denied compensation for his services. C would not be entitled to compensation for winding up the affairs of the partnership, regardless of who caused the dissolution and whether or not the dissolution was wrongful. Only a surviving partner is entitled to compensation for winding up the affairs of the partnership; this problem does not involve the death of a partner. UPA § 18 (f). *See Resnick v. Kaplan*, 434 A.2d 582 (Md. Ct. Spec. App. 1981).

The dissolution of a partnership does not affect the existing liabilities of the partners. UPA § 36. Dissolution ends the partners's liability for new debts of the partnership, except for those incurred in the winding up process and except for those incurred by a partner or agent with apparent authority when there was inadequate notice to a creditor who relied on the appearance that the partnership was continuing. After the dissolution, B and C would be liable for claims that arose before it. However, they would not be liable for debts that were incurred after dissolution, provided proper notice was given to creditors. UPA § 36; *see Faricy v. J. S. Brown Mercantile Co.*, 288 P. 639 (Colo. 1930). In the instant case, First Bank was a creditor which had previously extended credit to the partnership. It had no notice of dissolution. Therefore, B and C would still be liable on the loan made to the partnership by First Bank after dissolution. UPA § 35(b)(I). Since A continued the business, C, as the partner who caused the dissolution, will be entitled to indemnity from A for any claim that First Bank makes against him.

New Partners are not personally liable for any partnership debts incurred before they become partners. But the assets they contribute to the partnership are subject to those liabilities. UPA §§ 17, 41(7). After the dissolution, D would not be personally liable for any claim that arose before he joined the firm (these claims could be satisfied only out of partnership property), but he would be liable for debts incurred after he joined. *see Wolff v. Madden*, 33 P. 975 (Wash. 1893). A, as a prior partner, would be liable for all debts that were incurred to the extent that the assets of the partnership were insufficient to cover them. In some states, creditors must exhaust the partnership assets before going after the partners personally. *See, e.g., Cunard Line Ltd. v. Abney*, 540 F. Supp. 657, 660 (S.D.N.Y. 1982). In those states where exhaustion of assets is not required, A would be entitled to indemnification from the partnership if there were assets left in the partnership. UPA § 18 (b). If there were insufficient assets left in the partnership, A could seek indemnity from B and D for their share of creditors' claims. UPA § 40 (d); *Eichberger v. Reid*, 728 S.W.2d 533 (Ky. 1987). Once again, D would only be liable for his share of these creditors' claims that arose after he joined the partnership.

UPA § 40 provides for distributing assets to satisfy liabilities of a dissolved partnership in the following order: (1) those owing to creditors other than partners; (2) those owing to partners other than for capital and profits; (3) those owing to partners in respect of capital; and (4) those owing to partners in respect of profits. First Bank, as a secured creditor, is entitled to be paid first. Even if First Bank had no security it was entitled to be paid before any of the partners was paid. Assuming his services were compensable (*see* discussion above), A would then be entitled to be paid for his services. Then, the partners would be paid for their capital. Finally, the partners would share in the profits of the partnership. UPA § 40.

TABLE OF CASES

TABLE OF REFERENCES TO THE
RESTATEMENT (2d) OF AGENCY

TABLE OF REFERENCES TO THE
UNIFORM PARTNERSHIP ACT (UPA)

TABLE OF REFERENCES TO THE
REVISED UNIFORM PARTNERSHIP ACT (RUPA)

TABLE OF REFERENCES TO THE REVISED UNIFORM LIMITED PARTNERSHIP ACT (RULPA)

SUBJECT MATTER INDEX

Products for 1997-98 Academic Year

emanuel®

Emanuel Law Outlines

Steve Emanuel's Outlines have been the most popular in the country for years. Twenty years of graduates swear by them. In the 1996–97 school year, law students bought an average of 3.0 Emanuels each – that's 130,000 Emanuels.

Civil Procedure ◆	$18.95
Constitutional Law	23.95
Contracts ◆	17.95
Corporations	18.95
Criminal Law ◆	14.95
Criminal Procedure	14.95
Evidence	17.95
Property ◆	17.95
Secured Transactions	14.95
Torts (General Ed.) ◆	17.95
Torts (Prosser Casebook Ed.)	17.95
Keyed to '94 Ed. Prosser, Wade & Schwartz	
Also, Steve Emanuel's First Year Q&A's (see below)	$18.95

The Professor Series

All titles in these series are written by leading law professors. Each follows the Emanuel style and format. Each has big, easy-to-read type; extensive citations and notes; and clear, crisp writing. Most have capsule summaries and sample exam Q & A's.

Agency & Partnership	$14.95
Bankruptcy	15.95
Environmental Law	15.95
Family Law	15.95
Federal Income Taxation	14.95
Intellectual Property	15.95
International Law	15.95
Labor Law	14.95
Neg. Instruments & Payment Systems	13.95
Products Liability	13.95
Professional Responsibility (*new title*)	15.95
Property (*new title*)	15.95
Torts	13.95
Wills & Trusts	15.95

◆ **Special Offer…First Year Set**
All outlines marked ◆ *plus* Steve Emanuel's First Year Q & A's *plus* Strategies & Tactics for First Year Law. Everything you need to make it through your first year.

Complete Set	*$97.50*

First Year Special Joint Offer…Get the Emanuel First Year Set and the *Law in a Flash* First Year Set together.

$192.50 if purchased separately	*$177.50*

Question & Answer Collections

Siegel's Essay & Multiple–Choice Q & A's

Each book contains 20 to 25 essay questions with model answers, plus 90 to 110 Multistate-style multiple-choice Q & A's. The objective is to acquaint the student with the techniques needed to handle law school exams successfully. Titles are:

Civil Procedure	Evidence
Constitutional Law	Professional Responsibility
Contracts	Real Property
Corporations	Torts
Criminal Law	Wills & Trusts
Criminal Procedure	

Each title	*$15.95*

The Finz Multistate Method

967 MBE (Multistate Bar Exam)–style multiple choice questions and answers for all six Multistate subjects, each with detailed answers – *Plus* a complete 200 question practice exam modeled on the MBE. Perfect for law school and **bar exam** review.

	$33.95

Steve Emanuel's First Year Q&A's

1,144 objective–style short-answer questions with detailed answers, in first year subjects. A single volume covers Contracts, Torts, Civil Procedure, Property, Criminal Law, and Criminal Procedure.

	$18.95

For any titles not available at your local bookstore, call us at 1-800-EMANUEL or order on-line at **http://www.emanuel.com**.
Visa, MasterCard, American Express, and Discover accepted.

Law In A Flash Flashcards

Flashcards

Civil Procedure 1 ◆	$16.95
Civil Procedure 2 ◆	16.95
Constitutional Law ▲	16.95
Contracts ◆▲	16.95
Corporations	16.95
Criminal Law ◆▲	16.95
Criminal Procedure ▲	16.95
Evidence ▲	16.95
Future Interests ▲	16.95
Professional Responsibility (953 cards)	32.95
Real Property ◆▲	16.95
Sales (UCC Art.2) ▲	16.95
Torts ◆▲	16.95
Wills & Trusts	16.95

Flashcard Sets

First Year Law Set — 95.00
(includes all sets marked ◆ *plus* the book
Strategies & Tactics for First Year Law.)

Multistate Bar Review Set — 165.00
(includes all sets marked ▲ *plus* the book
Strategies & Tactics for MBE)

Professional Responsibility Set — 45.00
(includes the *Professional Responsibility* flashcards
plus the book Strategies & Tactics for the MPRE)

Law In A Flash Software

(for Windows® 3.1 and Windows® 95 only)

Law In A Flash Interactive Software combines the best features of our flashcards with the power of the computer. Just some of the great features:

- Contains the complete text of the corresponding *Law In A Flash* printed flashcards
- Side-by-side comparison of your own answer to the card's preformulated answer
- Fully customizable, savable sessions – pick which topics to review and in what order
- Mark cards for further review or printing
- Score your answers, to help you spot those topics in which you need further review

Every *Law In A Flash* title and set is available as software.

Requirements: 386, 486, or Pentium-based computer running Windows® 3.1 or Windows® 95; 16 megabytes RAM; 3.5" high-density floppy drive; 3MB free space per title; Windows-supported mouse and printer (optional)

Individual titles	$19.95
Professional Responsibility (covers 953 cards)	34.95
First Year Law Set*	115.00
Multistate Bar Review Set*	195.00
Professional Responsibility/MPRE Set*	49.95

* These software sets contain the same titles as printed card sets *plus* the corresponding *Strategies & Tactics* books (see below).

Your bookstore sells flashcards and software together in a Combo pack, at a special discount price

---

Strategies & Tactics Series

Strategies & Tactics for the MBE

Packed with the most valuable advice you can find on how to successfully attack the MBE. Each MBE subject is covered, including Criminal Procedure (part of Criminal Law), Future Interests (part of Real Property), and Sales (part of Contracts). The book contains 350 actual past MBE questions broken down by subject, plus a full-length 200-question practice MBE. Each question has a ***fully-detailed answer*** which describes in detail not only why the correct answer is correct, but why each of the wrong answer choices is wrong.

☞ Covers all the new MBE specifications tested on and after July, 1997.

$34.95

Strategies & Tactics for the First Year Law Student

A complete guide to your first year of law school, from the first day of class to studying for exams. Packed with the inside information that will help you survive what most consider the worst year of law school and come out on top.

☞ Completely revised for 1997.

$12.95

Strategies & Tactics for the MPRE

Packed with exam tactics that help lead you to the right answers and expert advice on spotting and avoiding the traps set by the Bar Examiners. Contains actual questions from past MPRE's, with detailed answers.

$19.95

Prices effective through 7/31/98. Visit our website at **http://www.emanuel.com** for the latest product information.

 **emanuel** ®

We'd like to know . . . .
Professor Series on
Agency & Partnership (5th Ed.)

We value your opinions on our study aids. After all, we design them for *your* use, and if you think we could do something better, we want to know about it. Please take a moment to fill out this survey and feedback form and return it to us.

We'll enter you in our monthly drawing where 5 people will win the study aid of their choice! If you don't want to identify yourself, that's OK, but you'll be ineligible for the drawing.

Name: _____   **Address:** _____

City: _____   **State:** _____   **Zip:** _____   **E-mail:** _____

Law school attended: _____   **Graduation year:** _____

Please rate this product on a scale of 1 to 5:

General readability (style, format, etc.)................................*Poor*   ① ② ③ ④ ⑤   *Excellent*

Length of outline (number of pages)................................*Too short*   ① ② ③ ④ ⑤   *Too long*

Table of Contents..*Too detailed*   ① ② ③ ④ ⑤   *Not enough detail*

Essay questions and answers................................*Not useful*   ① ② ③ ④ ⑤   *Useful*

End-of-book aids (tables)................................*Not useful*   ① ② ③ ④ ⑤   *Useful*

Subject-matter index................................*Too detailed*   ① ② ③ ④ ⑤   *Not enough detail*

Outline's coverage of material presented in class ....*Incomplete*   ① ② ③ ④ ⑤   *Complete*

OVERALL RATING................................*Poor*   ① ② ③ ④ ⑤   ***Excellent***

Suggestions for improvement: _____

_____

_____

_____

☛ **What other study aids did you use in this course?** _____

_____

☛ **If you liked any features of these other study aids, describe them:** _____

_____

_____

☛ **What casebook(s) did you use in this course?** _____

☛ **For other subjects, what study aids other than Emanuel do you use, and what features do you like about them?** _____

_____

_____

☛ **Please list the items you would like us to add to our product line:**

Outline subjects: _____

Flashcard subjects: _____

Other products (e.g., software, multimedia, etc.): _____

☛ **If you win our drawing, what one study aid would you like?** _____

Send to: *Emanuel Law* **Survey**   OR   Fax to: *(914) 834-5186*
           1865 Palmer Avenue, Suite 202
           Larchmont, NY 10538

✂ Cut here ✂

Please
complete & return
the Survey Form
on the other side